Second Edition

Good
Writing!

Mary Meiser

University of Wisconsin—Eau Claire

Allyn and Bacon

Boston • London • Toronto • Sydney • Tokyo • Singapore

Vice President: Eben W. Ludlow
Series Editorial Assistant: Linda M. D'Angelo
Senior Marketing Manager: Lisa Kimball
Production Administrator: Susan Brown
Editorial-Production Service: Matrix Productions Inc.
Cover Administrator: Linda Knowles
Cover Designer: Suzanne Harbison
Composition Buyer: Linda Cox
Manufacturing Buyer: Suzanne Lareau

Copyright © 1998 and 1995 by Allyn & Bacon
A Viacom Company
160 Gould St.
Needham Heights, Mass. 02194
www.abacon.com

Library of Congress Cataloging-in-Publication Data

Meiser, Mary Jordan.
 Good writing! / Mary Meiser. — 2nd ed.
  p. cm.
 Includes bibliographical references (p.) and index.
 ISBN 0-205-27334-3
  1. English language—Rhetoric. 2. English language—Grammar.
 3. College readers. 4. Report writing. I. Title.
 PE1408.M454 1998
 808'.042—dc21   97-32641
                     CIP

Printed in the United States of America

10 9 8 7 6 5 4 3 2   02 01 00

Contents

Chapter 4   *Understanding the Writing Process*   88

Chapter 5   *Generating and Exploring Topics*   125

Chapter 6   *Writing from Personal Experience: Narration and Description*   164

Chapter 7   *Writing to Inform, Writing to Analyze*   198

Chapter 8   *Reading and Responding to Arguments*   244

Chapter 9   *Analyzing and Writing Arguments, Proposing Solutions   275*

Chapter 10   *Writing from Research*   *313*

PART TWO   A WRITER'S HANDBOOK   361

Chapter 11   Working with Sentences   363

PART THREE   EVALUATING WRITING   495

PART FOUR   STUDENT ESSAYS FOR REVISION AND EDITING PRACTICE   509

PART FIVE   KEEPING TRACK OF WRITING SKILLS AND PROBLEMS   525

Preface

From 30 years of working with students, I know well the disparity that arises in composition courses: students with academic potential but undeveloped writing skills. Thus, in this text I wish to acknowledge and celebrate students' intelligence and creativity, as well as to assure them that all they lack is experience with academic writing. From that basic assumption, I talk them through the processes of reading and writing in a systematic way, building skills in ways congruent with current research on language and writing. This text, then, is based on what we know about the processes of acquiring written language. Consequently, it asks for students' participation in every way.

Students work through the processes of generating, drafting, revising, and editing. Multiple drafts are assumed and essential for building skills and confidence. Revising is viewed from the perspective of content first: what to include, what to delete, what to change or move. Revising is then viewed from the perspective of sentences: completeness and clarity. Editing remains the final process of readying text for another's eyes: adherence to standards and conventions of written American English. This text is interactive in that students are asked to respond thoughtfully and analytically, first to themselves, then to peers and instructor. Students are also asked to work together. Not only does such collaboration and discussion assist learning, but also it makes learning more fun.

Similarly, students learn from reading and discussing other writers' work. This text thus uses many writing samples, mainly from other students, both in the rhetoric and the handbook. The writing tasks most often ask students to respond in full discourse. Most teachers know the discouragement associated with sentence-level work that fails to transfer to paragraphs or short essays. Composing is a messy business, and single sentences don't help students prepare for the many choices they must make in full discourse writing. Consequently, this text seeks to prepare them for the "messy business" of composing. Only the handbook section features sentence-level work, acknowledging that some students will need to focus on a specific skill for a short time. But for the most part, skills work is assumed to be a part of revising and editing within student drafts.

PART ONE   A RHETORIC AND READER

In Chapter 1, students are asked to consider the importance and role of writing, and most important, to understand themselves as writers in a community of writers. Group activities in this chapter help them to start that journey as a community, the first of many activities aimed at developing peer interaction and authentic response. Chapter 2 introduces students to the link between reading and writing processes. Readings from Sandra Cisneros, Kate Chopin, and traditional academic texts form a thematic base for activities and written response. Strategies for critical reading are explained and practiced, culminating in an exercise based on Deborah Tannen's work. In Chapter 3, students explore basic paragraph structure, including topic sentences, ways of organizing and developing a text, and the concepts of unity and coherence. Lively and interesting paragraphs, many from the popular press, are used both to illustrate the concepts and to draw active student response. Writing processes are explained in Chapter 4. Here, through light-hearted material and activities, students work through purpose, audience, and context and a writing task that requires complete immersion in each step of the writing process. To facilitate this process, students are provided with all the material needed for the writing task at hand.

With the introductory material completed, students next move into traditional academic work in Chapter 5. Systematically, they are asked to try out various strategies for generating and exploring academic topics. Activities are grouped around thematic readings, and in some cases, the readings themselves become the focus of response. Chapter 6, with its focus on narration and description, provides students with professional and student examples and then takes them through the process of developing an essay based on personal experience. Richard Wright, Sandra Cisneros, and Thomas Whitecloud provide views of life from the perspective of other cultures, and at the same time, show the universality of human experience. Student writers, ranging from 18 to 40-something, provide another poignant and thoughtful view of experience. With a base in narration established, students begin the academic tasks of analysis and exposition.

In Chapter 7, students explore and apply strategies for analysis, including traditional modes of development. Activities also take students through the concepts of support and organization in expository writing. Before developing their own expository essays, students evaluate peer essays. Moreover, a group analysis project illustrates how data can be used, or manipulated, in analysis and writing. Chapter 8 introduces students to argumentative writing. Student essays are the basis of reading and writing activities. Chapter 9 continues student experience with argumentative writing. Here students are introduced to common problems in reasoning. Because of its usefulness, the problem-solution essay is also featured in this chapter. After analysis of student papers, students are asked to develop their own position papers.

Chapter 10 recognizes the importance of research in the academic community; however, it does so in a nonthreatening way. Using appropriate methods of gathering and documenting data, students write a narrative based on research about their family names. Students use traditional library sources, human resources, and the Internet to gather information. All MLA information is provided in the chapter, making it easy for them to handle the various requirements. Various activities take them through the analysis and synthesis processes and citation forms, and student essays provide them with models and discussion. In addition to the library research project, students are introduced to field research. A project in oral language, involving observation and data collection in classes, eateries, and stores, provides students with ample data for analysis, synthesis, and written presentation. Again, students are introduced to a critical research method in a nonthreatening way, completing the chapter's intent.

PART TWO   A WRITER'S HANDBOOK

In the handbook, students will find variety. Some tasks are traditional, whereas others are contemporary. Similarly, some tasks use a provided text, and others require students to create their own text. Again, students are expected to interact with what they read, thoughtfully and analytically. The goal is understanding and application, ultimately the internalization of the rules and conventions of standard written American English. Special boxes call attention to problems commonly encountered by ESL writers.

The handbook first addresses problems with sentence boundaries (fragments, run-ons, comma splices), as well as other sentence problems such as misplaced modifiers and parallelism. It then moves systematically through coordination and subordination, including exercises in embedding. Because students should consider sentence revision before editing, two separate chapters address these processes. In sentence revision, students practice addition and deletion of text, including the punctuation needed in these syntactic processes. In the next chapter, general editing strategies are introduced. Here, usage (e.g., verb agreement, tense consistency, pronouns) is explained, and students work through exercises as needed. The final chapter deals with mechanics rules. In the spelling segment, students will find a few basic rules and lists of confusing word pairs and commonly misspelled words.

The handbook has a variety of exercise formats: sentence, paragraph, and short essay. Students are asked to observe and then formulate the rules as often as possible. Many of the exercises are drawn from student work or from interesting real-life news topics.

PART THREE   EVALUATING WRITING

This section of the text is generally not found in composition texts, despite its importance to novice writers. Inexperienced writers in particular seldom understand just how teachers and others judge whether or not a piece of writing is acceptable. In Evaluating Writing, they learn about criteria that can both guide the development of a text and serve as the measure of its success. Students are taken through the process of evaluating student responses to a specific writing task. Students first read excerpts from "To Kill a King," on which the writing task was based. They next examine the writing task and criteria for evaluation. Finally, they apply these criteria to student responses to "To Kill a King." After students have achieved some understanding of and comfort with the evaluation process, they are asked to apply evaluation criteria to other student pieces. This section should assist instructors as well. Through it, they can demonstrate that evaluation is neither as subjective nor as mystifying as it may appear. Instructors can then ask students to assist in developing criteria for evaluating their own drafts in narrative, expository, and argumentative writing.

PART FOUR   STUDENT ESSAYS FOR REVISION AND EDITING PRACTICE

Students need sustained experience in revising and editing texts if they are to achieve writing competency. Although these processes must be applied to their own texts, students nonetheless benefit from experience with texts other than their own. Such practice is nonthreatening and, as such, offers an opportunity for rigorous discussion and decision making. The essays also provide instructors with models for group or whole-class work.

Six paragraph-length and six full-length student essays provide full discourse practice in revision and editing. The full-length essays can be used in conjunction with personal-experience, expository, and argumentative writing tasks or separately.

PART FIVE   KEEPING TRACK OF WRITING SKILLS AND PROBLEMS

Students are introduced to the concept of logs in the handbook section. The logs provide a systematic way to analyze error patterns in everything from punctuation to spelling, from failure to develop essays to problems with controlling ideas. Separate logs for revision, editing, and spelling reinforce the idea that revision and editing are separate processes, that content should be revised before attention is placed on correction. The logs also provide an easily accessed record of progress or persistent problem areas. With this information, instructors can easily form groups needing additional instruction on specific skills, as well as groups ready for more advanced instruction. Once students understand the importance and "mechanics" of the process, the logs should become their responsibility.

ACKNOWLEDGMENTS

I wish to thank not only the students whose writing appears in this text but also those who unwittingly contributed to my learning as a teacher and, ultimately, as a writer.

I also wish to thank my reviewers. Their insightful comments informed every chapter and guided my judgments of what might best serve both students and teachers as a practical resource in composition: Grady Hillman, Austin Community College; Tina McGaughey, Austin Community College; Harry R. Phillips, Central Piedmont Community College; Karen Peterson Welch, University of Wisconsin—Eau Claire; and Leigh Westerfield, Manchester College.

And to Mark Heike, Bay Port High School, Green Bay, WI, a special thanks for sustained, helpful response as I revised this text.

A Rhetoric

and Reader

PART 1

CHAPTER 1

Becoming a Writer

WHY WE WRITE

Is Writing Old-fashioned?

With the wondrous telecommunications of the 1990s, it's not surprising that many people tend to think of voice rather than print when they want to communicate. In the time it takes to punch in 10 to 15 numbers, America and the world are accessible; families, friends, and businesses are linked—mere seconds away, 24 hours a day. For example, my son thinks nothing of calling home from such diverse places as the coastal highway between Los Angeles and San Diego or 31,000 feet over the Rocky Mountains. Being confined to a car or plane offers no barrier to communication these days; we can be wherever we want to be by punching in a series of numbers. Even when no one is physically present, we have easy access through answering machines and electronic mail. What's more, as we become part of a call-waiting triangle, even busy signals are no barrier to instant communication. Today, audio- and videotape, microchip, and satellite are a way of life. Consequently, print communication may appear to be as old-fashioned as a quill pen and inkwell.

But it isn't. The status and availability of the fax machine, for example, indicate that writing is still a major means of communication. And cards and letters retain their importance in both the world of personal relationships and the world of business. Further, our world revolves around written documents—everything from a job contract to a product guarantee, from marriage licenses to wills, from rules of conduct to laws governing our cities, states, and nations. Our most important documents, from the very beginning of settlement in America, have always been written. And even informally today, it's common to hear someone respond, "Put that in writing." We still expect important agreements to be written rather than oral. Analysis and evaluation nearly always require a written form, from the simple report cards of primary school to complex reports of the chief executive officer in a *Fortune* 500 company. Print communication is, and will continue to be, an important medium of communication.

Nonetheless, given the ease, efficiency, and sophistication of voice communications today, students understandably wonder just why they are required to take at least one composition course. Are colleges simply maintaining an old-fashioned course? Are teachers making too much of writing skills? Just why are students required to expend considerable time and effort in a composition course? Is it merely to satisfy a traditional college requirement? The response to these questions lies in the nature of writing itself. Writing is not just communication in the traditional school sense; it is, rather, an integral part of the thinking and learning process.

◆   Writing is a way of discovering what we mean, as well as what others are trying to tell us.

◆   Writing is a way of remembering and manipulating information, of preserving it for later reflection and better understanding.

◆   Writing is a way of thinking, of taking apart ideas and concepts, of examining relationships and meaning.

In brief, writing helps us make sense of ourselves, others, and our world. It is, simply put, a powerful tool, not just for college but for the world at large—a world that grows increasingly more complex, a world that depends on our ability to communicate well in both oral and written language.

How Does Writing Help Us?

Writing Helps Us Learn.   At times, you will write as a process of inquiry and discovery, not just from books but also from your own experiences and observations. We can run ideas and memories through our heads, but without writing them down, they quickly slip away. Further, without writing, we would have far less success in reflecting on their significance. Our memories are limited and subject to a very natural distortion. Writing, then, provides us with the means to capture experience and, ultimately, to learn from it. At other times, you will write to remember or to sort out class-related information. Writing notes, for example, is a common activity both in and out of college. Through notes, we sort out various kinds of information, provide timely information for others, and generally preserve information for later use. When we read, we use writing to outline, summarize, or annotate important areas. Most students learn quickly that writing while reading saves them from rereading, especially in preparing for exams. Although there are many reliable studies illustrating the power of writing in college, students seem to know almost instinctively that writing is a valuable tool.

Through writing, we are able to bring together ideas from many different sources—our reading, our discussions, and our personal experiences and observations. We can connect these ideas, clarify our understanding of them, and finally, relate them to new information or new ideas. Writing makes this process concrete—something we can see and manipulate—and therefore makes it easier. Writing also makes us active learners, virtually forcing us to interact with what we are reading or hearing, to interact with our brains and not just eyes or ears. Writing, then, is not just something to be used during times of examinations. It is, rather, a lifelong skill we can draw upon whenever we need or wish to learn.

Writing Helps Us Know Ourselves and Others Better.   Experienced writers often remark that through writing, they have come to know themselves, others, and the world around them in important ways. It might be that in the process of working out our ideas in print, we become more deliberate and thoughtful. Writing slows us down somewhat; in many cases, slowing down benefits our thinking processes. And quite often, we may not even know exactly what we feel or mean until we have written it out. The process of writing can help us in many ways: to understand our ideas and to explore them more systematically and thoroughly; to help us deal with conflicting ideas and emotions; and to help us solve both personal and professional problems. If we choose to save our writing, we have a wonderful record of how we felt about something or someone, and quite possibly, why we felt that way. Or we have a record of how we solved a problem or which alternatives we might yet pursue. Writing can be discovery, a special way of coming to know; through it, we have a powerful means of connecting self, others, and a world of ideas.

Writing Helps Us in the World of Work.   You might associate writing only with school tasks, and therefore you may think of it as something you'll leave behind when you complete your studies. However, we live in an information society, where the processes of gathering, analyzing, and dispersing information are essential. Much of what you learn in college relative to content knowledge will eventually become obsolete. Research has yielded new information in nearly every field of study and has forced us to discard both what we know and how we deal with that knowledge. A new and better mousetrap has evolved everywhere. But process skills such as oral and written language will become more and more valuable. The ability to sift through information, analyze it, and communicate your findings clearly and accurately will be invaluable to you and any employer.

BECOMING A WRITER

Learning to Talk, Learning to Write

When you learned to talk, you were in an ideal environment for gaining language skills quickly and effortlessly. You were immersed in oral language and encouraged to use it every waking hour. You had a genuine purpose for using it: to communicate with others, to be part of a family and community. Making errors was a normal and expected part of the learning process; everyone knew that with more exposure to language and more experience in using it, you'd be fine. And you were. The process of learning to talk was, in many ways, joyful and effortless. It was natural, unschooled, and continual between birth and starting school. When you entered school, you were already quite a sophisticated talker. Learning to write, however, is seldom as easy.

Although there are some parallels between learning to talk and learning to write, there are significant differences. Learning to write is not a natural, unschooled process. We are not surrounded by print every waking hour, nor are we continually urged to communicate through it. And our purposes for writing are less obvious and less clear than for talking. Our audience is remote, and thus we have to work harder at making ourselves understood, as well as in anticipating what our audience knows and needs to know. Further, writing appears to carry a certain vulnerability with it; our mistakes with spelling or grammar, for example, are visible, permanent in a way speech is not. Moreover, a tolerance for errors in writing, even from beginners, is far lower. People seem to forget that learning to write takes time, a great deal of time, and sustained experience—just as learning to talk did. Only recently have educators realized that providing beginning writers with an environment similar to that of beginning speakers would really make a difference for those writers. Consequently, teachers are working hard to ensure the writing classroom is a safe environment—one where mistakes are viewed as part of the learning process, where processes and strategies for writing are modeled, and where working with others is expected and valued.

Amazingly, most young children believe they can write. What's more, they like to. Free from restrictions of topics, rules, and time, children leave their mark everywhere. Those scribbles on walls, appliances, and every available surface represent authentic writing. Children believe adults can read their scribbles, and sometimes they are offended when adults ask for a translation. You may have been one of those children, writing before you started school, writing before it became complex and demanding in a school setting. Michael Rafferty, coming to college as a nontraditional student after military service, discovered that he was. The result was this essay for his composition course:

The Boxes

A question was posed to me recently, "when did you first start writing?" This question would have been hard for me to answer, if it had not been for a rather alarming discovery I made last week. I suppose the traditional response would have been, in kindergarten like everyone else. But thanks to my mother's pack rat tendencies, an archive of my early childhood grammatical expressions were unleashed to the world.

My mother and I were sitting around the old dining room table viewing some archaic family photo albums. There were two common phrases being aired that night, "oooh look at this," and "that's so cute." Of course each of these phrases were emanating from my mother. I suppose I could have enjoyed the session more if it was not for the minuscule dust particles irritating my eyes to the point of watering. Funny thing is, Mom thought the tears soaking my face were tears of joy or something.

After about an hour, I finally thought the session was coming to an end. That's when it happened. Out of the last photo album fell a pile of old Mother's Day cards drawn in crayon. Instantly I knew that this was truly my first viable link to the literary world. The earliest known date on the cards was Mother's Day 1970. At the conception of this card I would have been just about fours years of youth. Most people would think that a four year old human would not exactly be a trademark writer, but let me tell you I was. For each card I created ended in one specific way. "Write your name in the boxes" was printing at the tail of every card. This was followed by a sequence of mis-shaped box-like formations.

I was so overcome by this trademark technique, I called my grampa and gramma to verify my findings on the cards I had given to them. The grandparents did not hesitate to inform me that they also knew of this practice.

Since my early childhood, my writing has been in-frequent at best. To this day I can say I have written fewer than five letters to friends or family. It has been much easier to just pick up the phone, and much quicker. Primarly, over the last six years my writing has been restricted to filling out forms and paper-work.

Although writing is becoming an added pleasure to my life, I doubt it will ever be as original as "The Boxes."

Michael Rafferty

Writing Activity

Like Michael, you might have a writing memory tucked away. Wander around in your memory a bit. Many students find they have images of writing on a wall or sidewalk, of creating fantastic stories, or of making up a secret written code. Others find they suddenly see their drawings and stories displayed on the refrigerator. If wandering around in your memory doesn't produce an image of you as a child writer, check with family or friends. I recently found some notes from my son and daughter, for example, and I doubt they recall writing them. My son told me to stop covering him with a blanket, that he didn't want to end up a "pes of bernt bakon" (piece of burned bacon). My daughter told me that I "hert her fealings" after disciplining her; she also drew a picture of herself in tears, complete with sound effects written in invented spelling. Many caretakers have both a box of saved child writings and good memories of those early efforts.

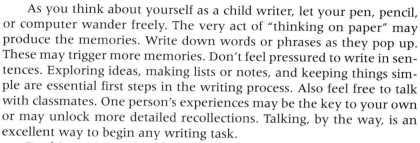

As you think about yourself as a child writer, let your pen, pencil, or computer wander freely. The very act of "thinking on paper" may produce the memories. Write down words or phrases as they pop up. These may trigger more memories. Don't feel pressured to write in sentences. Exploring ideas, making lists or notes, and keeping things simple are essential first steps in the writing process. Also feel free to talk with classmates. One person's experiences may be the key to your own or may unlock more detailed recollections. Talking, by the way, is an excellent way to begin any writing task.

Do this writing task in your journal. You may use these notes for a later assignment.

WRITING IN SCHOOL

If most young children consider themselves writers, why do so many adolescents and adults believe themselves to be "nonwriters"? The answer may lie somewhere in their experiences with writing in school. School writing is often linked to reporting what we know rather than to discovering new knowledge; school writing may also translate into criticism and grades. Therefore, writing was no longer the self-initiated, free, and flexible activity it had once been. And along with concerns about the limits of the assignment and the correctness of the product, came false notions of what writing is all about. These false notions are so common that both within and out of school, they have held many potential writers hostage. A few of the most widely heard are these:

✦ **Good writers are born, not made.**   Although some people may appear to be naturally gifted, they most likely have worked hard and long at their writing. It's true, of course, that some people are better writers than others, just as some people are better musicians or athletes. Along with sustained interest and motivation, there may be some natural talent. But without working to develop it, no writer, musician, or athlete would become "good." The naturalness arises from years of experience, from turning complex actions into routine actions.

✦ **Good writers get everything right the first time.**   No one, no matter how skilled or talented, gets everything right the first time. That just isn't the way writing works. Good writers expect to write several drafts. They know that revising and editing are essential parts of the writing process, allowing them the freedom to get down what they want to say before being concerned with the best way, or the correct way, to say it.

◆ **There's only one right way to go about writing.** Writing is a complex activity, and each of us brings different skills and experiences to the process. Consequently, each of us has to find the best way to go about writing. Although there are many strategies to help us, there is no single correct way to go about the process. If we take the time to try various strategies, we find that some work well. Similarly, if we pay attention to how, when, and where we work most efficiently, we develop habits that help us take on a writing task. The more we understand about ourselves as writers, the better. But there will never be a single, right way to go about the process. There are no formulas, no magic.

◆ **The written product is more important than the process.** Because students are used to being graded on the final product, they quite rightly consider that product important. And it is important: it is the cumulation of a great deal of thought and effort. However, the process of developing that product is just as important. Without a good writing process (prewriting, drafting, revising, and editing), a good product is very unlikely, if not impossible. The process is also critical to learning to write more effectively and easily. And sometimes, very good things happen in process, regardless of the quality of the final product. We might learn to handle some part of writing better, or to become more comfortable with it, even if the final product isn't as good as we would like it to be.

Writing Activity

Again, in your journal, walk around in your memory. This time try to recall some of your experiences with writing in school. Most students have rather sharp memories of a specific writing task that challenged, frustrated, or satisfied them. A specific teacher who encouraged their writing is also a common memory. Sometimes the memories are linked to the tools of writing: big, fat yellow pencils, rough gray paper with lines to guide the formation of letters, bright crayons or chalk, the magic of a computer. You might even recall some writing "rules" that baffled you. Don't be surprised if you have stored both good and not-so-good memories of writing in school. We all have them.

You might capture your memories in list or note form. You don't have to write in sentences unless you want to. Save these writings. You may use them later.

UNDERSTANDING WRITING

The Processes of Writing

Although it might appear to be a single process, writing is actually a series of processes: generating and exploring ideas (prewriting), drafting, revising, and editing. Each of these processes contributes to our ability to write a competent paragraph or essay. If we skip generating and exploring ideas, we run the risk of producing a very limited, and perhaps pretty dull, piece. If we fail to revise, we may end up with a disorganized or incoherent piece. We might also end up with too much material, thus boring our reader, or too little, thus confusing the reader. If we ignore the editing process, we may end up with errors in spelling, grammar, and punctuation. In brief, each process provides us with a focus and allows us to think about different aspects of developing our piece.

It would be a mistake, however, to think that these processes are linear and orderly; that is, that we proceed as though they were locked steps, start to finish. We can and do use any of the processes throughout our writing time. For example, while revising, a writer might discover the need for more material. At that point, he or she would go back to generating and exploring ideas. Or while generating and exploring ideas, a writer might turn to drafting, writing in paragraph form as a means of exploring an idea. Understanding the focus of and strategies for each of the writing processes is important. This knowledge helps us utilize each process fully, and at the same time, moves us through the entire process of developing a paragraph or essay.

The Writing Process: Understanding Terms

Traditionally, composition instruction focused almost exclusively on the written product rather than on the processes that led to that product. Today, we know that understanding and developing good processes are critical to becoming a skilled writer. Knowing the basic terms of the writing processes is the first step. Later, you will learn strategies that will help you take full advantage of each process.

Generating and Exploring Ideas

The process of generating and exploring ideas is also referred to as prewriting. During this process, writers use many strategies to discover and explore ideas for writing, including reading, writing, and talking.

You might be familiar with some specific strategies such as making lists, brainstorming, responding to specific questions, or mapping. You'll learn and practice these, and many other strategies, as you work through this textbook. What's important is that you find out which strategies work well for you.

Drafting

Drafting is the process of putting ideas on paper or computer screen. When writers draft, they move beyond words and phrases to sentences and paragraphs. Drafting is what most people refer to as writing, but drafting is more specific. It refers to developing and refining a written text; it also implies multiple drafts rather than one draft. Most people find a discovery draft, a really messy head-to-paper draft (or head-to-computer-disk draft), a necessity. A discovery draft frees writers from being orderly or neat; its very purpose is freedom to think, getting ideas out of the head in whatever form and order they come. In another draft, those ideas will be worked with; they will be put into some logical order, developed fully, and polished. And in yet another draft, sentences will be clarified and corrected. For some writing assignments, you will write only a first draft, a discovery piece. But for most, you'll work through several drafts. Think of multiple drafts as an opportunity to concentrate on different aspects of writing at different times.

Revising

Revising occurs when writers are satisfied with the content of the paragraph or essay, when they have a good sense that "this is what I want to say." Writers have to be quite certain that what they want to say and what they actually say match. Revision is the process that helps them achieve that certainty. During revision, writers reread the paragraph or essay, slowly and thoughtfully. They may decide to add material, delete material, or change the order of material. They then check on how ideas flow and how readers would get from one idea to the next without getting lost. Revision also occurs on the sentence level. Writers decide if sentences are clear and effective, and make changes in those that aren't. Finally, writers check on individual words, deciding if another would be more precise or effective. Revising is the writer's preparation for the reader, and it is a demanding task. Shifting the point of view from "I wrote this" to "How will someone read this?" requires considerable time and, often, a bit of help from peers or teacher. You'll learn revising strategies—specific ways of looking at your written text and making changes as needed—as you work through writing assignments. Work with peers will also provide you with experience in revising.

Editing

Editing is the one writing process that should stay in its place—last. When writers edit (editing is also known as proofreading), they are concerned with correctness. If writers worry about being correct too early in the writing process, they can literally stop themselves from writing. Or they can spend a great deal of time making a sentence correct, only to throw it out during revision. Many students, having been penalized heavily for incorrect spelling, grammar, or punctuation, are understandably concerned about being correct. They also know the final draft will be judged against the standards of written American English. As a result, they find it difficult to leave editing until the very end. Putting editing last, however, is important. Otherwise, writers may actually block the other writing processes and fail to gain the fluency they need. Editing is an important process, and learning to do it well is a critical writing skill. Because it is so critical, you may be asked to keep a personal editing log. In it, you will list the errors you typically make, as well as their corrections. A pattern will show up, and with that knowledge, along with explanations as needed, you'll be able to find and correct errors during editing.

STANDARD WRITTEN ENGLISH: THE LANGUAGE OF SCHOOL

The Dialect Nobody Speaks

None of us speaks the English of books, magazines, and newspapers. We have to learn that variety of English, called Standard Written English, because it is a dialect with its own rules and conventions. Writing, in other words, is not just speech written down. What is both expected and acceptable in our speech may be quite different from what is expected and acceptable in our writing. When we talk, for example, we can and do use incomplete and ungrammatical sentences:

A. "Looking good!"

B. "What next?"

C.   "He don't know that." (he doesn't)

D.   "I'm taller than him." (than he is)

E.   "Me and Jonah are friends." (Jonah and I)

These utterances are understandable. They work fine as communication. And for most people, they are acceptable. The exceptions would be "He don't" and "Me and Jonah," especially in school and business. "I'm taller than him" would probably be noticed only by English teachers. This nongrammatical form has become common and quite acceptable in most informal language settings. The key is knowing which language settings require Standard (school) English and having the versatility to use it when needed. It is not a matter of being understood, but rather, of fitting in. If you plan to work within a language community that uses Standard English, you need to know that dialect. It is, in brief, a matter of being practical. And being practical does not mean that you have abandoned or devalued your home dialect in any way. You have simply added to your versatility with English.

Each of us speaks a dialect that marks us as belonging to a certain ethnic group, gender, social class, and geographic region. No American dialect is superior to any other. Each is logical, grammatical, and systematic; each provides its speakers with a rich and effective means of communication. With the exception of speech related to age or profession, we retain our original dialect throughout our lives. Only when we change our role or status do we find it necessary to acquire another dialect. Thus people who enter academic, professional, or business situations may find they need to acquire the dialect labeled as standard. In fact, knowing and using the correct forms might be considered a survival skill.

Some students use two dialects daily, that of home and that of school, thus demonstrating an enviable versatility with English. In learning Standard Written English, these students gained another dialect and expanded their versatility further. Just as we use our spoken dialect to fit in with family, friends, and immediate community, we use Standard Written English to fit into academic, professional, and certain work environments. For this reason, time and effort invested in learning Standard Written English are worthwhile. Career goals are being well served.

A COMMUNITY OF WRITERS: KNOWING AND SHARING

When we gather with family and friends, we quite naturally exchange ideas, memories, feelings, and information. We also share tasks, build and strengthen ties, and become in many ways a small community within a larger one. In composition class, you will often share your ideas about many cultural and social issues; as you get to know one another better, you will probably share many memories and feelings as well. As you do so, you build ties and establish trust, and you become, in effect, a community of writers.

Group Activity

A Community of Knowing

To begin the process of community, read this tale from Southeast Asia and carry out the directions that follow it.

In former times, the Akha people had letters. One year, all the letters were swallowed by the water buffalo and imprinted on its skin. When the time came to make their yearly move, the people discovered the water buffalo's skin was too big and too heavy for them to move to their new location. The people were perplexed. They did not want to leave their letters, and they could not move the skin. They went to the Headman. He thought about the problems, "If we cannot move the water buffalo's skin, we must eat the water buffalo's skin. This way we keep the letters inside us forever." And so the water buffalo's skin was cut up into the number of people in the group. Each person swallowed a piece. Thus the letters were kept within the tribe forever.

From Nancy King, *Storymaking and Drama* (26)

1. **Write.**   On a small piece of paper, write a small bit of information that you would like to see remembered. Do not sign your name.

2. **Pass.**   Pass the papers to one person, who will mix them up and pass them back out.

3. **Share.**   Share with the group the bit of information you have just received.

4. **Reflect.**   What kinds of information are important? Is hearing the bits of information different from writing it in private? If so, in what ways? Was it easier for you to be candid when you didn't have to read your own paper?

5. **List.**   On the board or at your desk, write the bits of information that your group judged to be the most important. Why are they important? Is there a relationship among them? Can you categorize some of the bits into a single item?

6. Narrow and choose.   As a group, pick out one item that you agree is very important. What reasons led to choosing this item? Now brainstorm about it. What details or examples explain it?

Write: Keep notes about the information shared, particularly any piece of information that seemed important enough that most of the group agreed on it. As the discussion narrows the topic, again take notes—even if you disagree with some or all of the ideas. You may use these notes for a written paragraph later.

Group Activity

This I Keep . . .

Each of us has at least one possession that is special, for reasons that are as diverse as we are. In my case, it is a fourth-century Roman coin unearthed in Jaffa, Israel. History aside, why is it special? A friend associated it with me, adopted and with no family history, but drawn to the Mediterranean, and gave the coin to me. The coin not only brings back memories of our friendship but also memories of many trips to the Mediterranean. Moreover, it conjures up thoughts about who I am, where my family roots might be, and why I am so drawn to this area. Because of all these memories and questions, I have a rich storehouse of writing topics.

Most students have equally rich storehouses associated with a special possession—everything from the collar of a canine friend to a grandfather's immigration passport, from a baseball cap to an antique ring from a beloved grandmother, from a childhood toy to a ticket stub from a concert or a T-shirt in shreds. In the process of talking about such special possessions, they not only learn about one another but also find more memories tucked away in themselves—memories that often lead to wonderful writing.

For this activity, then, choose one possession (and if possible, bring it to class) and be prepared to talk informally about its significance. Listeners should ask questions and draw out more information from the speaker.

Write: As you prepare for this activity, spend some time thinking on paper about this possession: Why have you chosen it? What is its significance to you? What people, if any, are associated with it? What places, if any, are associated with it? Does it have specific memories? When you are sharing this information orally, note any questions that listeners ask and your response to them. Save your written notes for a possible written paragraph later.

— Group Activity

Tell Me About . . .

Each person will select a topic from the suggestions below and begin talking about it to his or her partner. While one person is talking, the other should do the following:

✦ **Focus attention on the person who is talking.**   The focus is lost, for example, if the listener starts talking about his or her own ideas.

✦ **Ask good questions about the topic.**   Draw out the speaker's ideas; help the speaker elaborate on the topic.

✦ **Listen without judging.**   The topics are personal ones, and if the listener makes judgmental comments, the speaker will understandably hold back or stop.

Topics

How you helped someone once

Something good that has happened to you as a result of a choice you made

Something that you are proud of, that you worked hard to accomplish

Something good you have done that few people know about

A difficult choice you have made

Something you did that took courage to do

Some important decision that you made alone

Something difficult that you have learned

Something you have done that you would do differently now

A choice you made that didn't work out as you had hoped

A change you would make in yourself

A choice you made that turned out very well

Something that was difficult to leave behind you

The most significant change in your life in the past six months

The most important thing you learned in the past six months

A change you would like to make in yourself

A long-held belief that was shattered

An act of prejudice (ethnicity, gender, disability) that you experienced or witnessed

A time when you gave in to peer pressure

A time when you rebelled against authority or deliberately broke a home, school, or community rule

A change of opinion about someone (e.g., held in high esteem)

Write: Although this is an informal conversation, it is focused on a single idea and may form the basis for a written paragraph. As you prepare for the conversation, do some thinking on paper—notes only. As a listener, keep notes on the conversation and give them to your partner. Later, compare the two sets of notes and combine ideas that strike you as the heart of the experience you spoke about. Save your notes for a possible writing assignment.

A COMMUNITY OF WRITERS: WORKING TOGETHER

Whether you work with a single person or a small group, working with others is an essential skill in improving your writing. It is also an essential skill for many jobs these days, where employers rely on workers to consult with one another and combine their efforts to achieve a goal, whether it be a report or a presentation. Your participation in small-group work is thus another practical aspect of preparing for a career.

Because small groups allow more students to participate in discussions and other class work with increased frequency and depth, many writing teachers use both groups and pairs on a regular basis. Within these structures, students often feel free to say what they really think, ask questions that perhaps they wouldn't in a large group, and generally explore their ideas more thoroughly. Although many students are somewhat nervous about sharing their ideas and written work in groups, they soon find that their group becomes an enjoyable and helpful resource for their writing—a safe place for exploration and constructive criticism. In writing class, partners and small groups provide help all the way through the writing process, from the early stages of generating and exploring ideas through the final editing of the written product.

Although the help classmates provide is perhaps the most important reason teachers like writing groups, there is another reason. Groups discourage the false notion that there is a single "right" answer to a writing problem—and that a teacher has it. Writing is a complex problem, with many paths and processes that are "right" for an individual writer. With the multiple perspectives of a group, a writer has a better chance of discovering and using those many paths and processes to solve his or her problem. Differences in personality, culture, social background, and gender are the heart and strength of the group; we are able to get outside of our singular point of view and gain a multiplicity of views that clarify and strengthen our own view.

Group Work During Generating and Exploring Topics

As we begin a writing project, our group can help us create knowledge: generating ideas, getting at our memories, taking a certain point of view, expanding or changing the direction of our topic, to name just a few. This initial process is largely oral, with limited notes taken just as a memory aid. During this group work, all members should contribute through asking questions or making comments about one another's topic, with ground rules of respect and helpfulness. No question or comment should be perceived as "dumb" or simplistic. In the early part of this process, the whole idea is exploration, so everyone's contribution should be considered potentially useful.

Only two kinds of commentary are potentially useless or harmful: the "feel good" and the "me first." When group members agree with one another too quickly and too easily, they are probably taking a shortcut to a safe and superficial exploration of a topic. Everyone may "feel good" about each other, but it is doubtful that a thorough, many-sided discussion has taken place. People who respect one another can and do disagree or take very different points of view. In exploring a writing topic, such diversity is helpful. Just as the "feel good" approach is unhelpful, the "me first" is not only unhelpful but also destructive to the group. Students who believe theirs is the only perspective, who fail to take others seriously or consider other points of view, are not functioning within the group at all. What's more, they can be pretty annoying.

To avoid either extreme, you need to be a good listener. That means putting yourself in the other person's shoes during a discussion. You don't have to agree or accept everyone's ideas, but you should listen well nonetheless. Listening well means more than just hearing the words. The tone, body language, and eyes are all cues to what is being said. So maintaining good eye contact with the speaker, nodding or smiling to show you are listening, and taking notes are all good group responses.

Group Work During Revising

Once we have produced a written draft, we return to our group for specific help: we test our ideas and request feedback, both oral and written. We get help with what we have said and how well we have said it. Here once again, the group's ability to be both respectful and honest is the key to how much help one gets. The writer receives no help if everyone simply follows the "feel good" approach. No early draft is very good, so saying that it is, is not only dishonest but also unhelpful to the writer. The whole idea of the group is response: what works, what doesn't work, what might work and why. Revision means to "see again," and with the group's eyes on the draft, that process should become easier. Some students fear giving honest commentary, thinking they will damage group relationships. They won't. Constructive criticism is an essential part of writing. And if you start out with what works in the piece, things you particularly like or feel are well-done, and then move on to things that aren't working, the process will work fine.

Group Work During Editing

Still later, we return to the group for "new eyes" to help us weed out errors in grammar or mechanics. Because we are so close to what we have written, understanding in our heads what we want to say, we can easily read over and through material that causes problems for a reader. The group, then, becomes that outside reader and helps us make the essential transition from writer to reader. However, it would be a mistake to think the group will correct errors; their task is to point them out, and if needed, explain the problem. Correcting them is the job of the writer. Editing is perhaps the least stressful group work in that the errors are just that, errors, and not an evaluation of the writer's ideas or presentation. Understandably, some students are afraid that their drafts have so many errors in grammar, mechanics, or spelling that their group or partner will think they are incapable of getting things right. In reality, everyone makes these kinds of errors, and as the writing class progresses, everyone will make fewer of them. Getting others' help in the process is a smart and efficient thing to do.

Writing Activity

Your teacher may ask you to return to the notes made earlier in this chapter, where you explored your memories, thoughts, and opinions on topics close to your experience. It might be your personal writing history or your most treasured possession, a shattered belief or a mo-

ment of courage. Whatever it happens to be, focus on only one thing for your paragraph. For example:

A dog collar sounds like a funny thing to love—but I do. [why?]

I thought good friends never lied. [what happened?]

I knew my brother was in trouble, but I didn't know what to do about it. [how decide?]

Preparing to Write

In talking with classmates, you have actually been preparing to write. In fact, talking is one of the earliest ways in which we explore our topics—not just in classrooms but everywhere we spend time. However, talking is a natural activity; writing is not. We have to structure our writing into complete sentences and well-developed paragraphs that logically lead our reader from point to point. Understanding how we structure our thoughts in writing is thus a critical basis for writing well. To gain this understanding, we need to turn to reading, to see the connections between reading and writing. We also need to explore strategies for becoming a better reader. In doing so, we gain skills essential to becoming a better writer.

CHAPTER 2

Becoming a Critical Reader

When we write, we also draw upon our reading skills, especially when we're revising or editing. Revising and editing depend upon our ability to read carefully—to step out of the role of writer and become a reader. Thus, although this is a text about writing, it is also a text about reading. You will be asked to read carefully and thoughtfully, to observe, to analyze, and, finally, to evaluate written texts.

RESPONDING TO WHAT WE READ

As individual readers, we approach a written text with a personal frame of reference. All of us are influenced by our past experiences, as well as by our present situations. Each person's age, gender, and ethnicity affect how that person responds to a piece of writing. Even if several people share similar backgrounds, each will nonetheless bring an individual response to what is read. We weave our own images, sensations, and emotions into what we read; we blend emotional and logical responses. We bring ourselves to those marks on a page, interact with them, and take something away. Someone in an unhappy relationship, for example, will bring sad experiences and emotions to a reading that explores relationships. Someone who has experienced or observed racial discrimination will bring those images and feelings to a reading dealing with race relationships. This response is what makes reading so powerful, and good writing so important.

As you respond to readings, as well as to class discussions about those readings, you will gain insight into topics and issues, as well as into yourself. These insights are a critical part of writing well. The reading strategies that follow will provide you with systematic ways of bringing your responses to the surface, of using them to think about what you want to say and why. You will probably like some strategies better than others, and that's fine, but give each of them a fair trial. The more strategies you have, the more options you have—which is just what you want as a reader and writer.

RESPONDING THROUGH WRITING

A Reading Journal

To learn more about responding to writing, you will keep a reading journal. You will be asked to write various types of entries in your reading journal. At times, you will explore your knowledge or beliefs about a topic before and after you read. At other times, you may find yourself summarizing the main ideas, arguing with them, asking questions, or connecting with your own experiences in some way. In your journal, you will be writing to explore ideas—another writer's, your own, a classmate's, a friend's—and to make connections. Later you may be asked to communicate those ideas and your responses to them more formally. The journal, however, is simply a place to explore—freely and honestly. Don't worry about complete sentences, grammar, spelling, or punctuation. What's important here are your ideas, understandable only to you.

Responding as You Read.   As you read, respond to words, phrases, passages—anything that interests you, confuses you, intrigues you, angers you. One way to make this process more orderly is to divide your journal page into two halves. On the left-hand side, write down words or sentences that evoked a response as you read. When you've completed the reading, respond more fully on the right-hand side of the journal.

Responding After You Read.   Sometimes you'll be asked to share your ideas with classmates, focusing on questions raised by that piece of reading, or perhaps to develop your own questions about what you read.

A HOUSE OF MY OWN

Sandra Cisneros

Sandra Cisneros, a noted Hispanic writer, is best known for The House on Mango Street.

Not a flat. Not an apartment in back. Not a man's house. Not a daddy's. A house all my own. With my porch and my pillow, my pretty purple petunias. My books and my stories. My two shoes waiting beside the bed. Nobody to shake a stick at. Nobody's garbage to pick up after.

Only a house quiet as snow, a space for myself to go, clean as paper before the poem.

In your journal:

What questions does Sandra Cisneros raise for you?

Do you think males and females might have different responses?

What two things would you have in a house of your own?

BEAUTIFUL AND CRUEL

Sandra Cisneros

I am an ugly daughter. I am the one nobody comes for. Nenny says she won't wait her whole life for a husband to come and get her, that Minerva's sister left her mother's house by having a baby, but she doesn't want to go that way either. She wants things all her own, to pick and choose. Nenny has pretty eyes and it's easy to talk that way if you are pretty.

My mother says when I get older my dusty hair will settle and my blouse will learn to stay clean, but I have decided not to grow up tame like the others who lay their necks on the threshold waiting for the ball and chain.

In the movies there is always one with red lips who is beautiful and cruel. She is the one who drives the men crazy and laughs them all away. Her power is her own. She will not give it away.

I have begun my own quiet war. Simple. Sure. I am one who leaves the table like a man, without putting back the chair or picking up the plate.

In your journal:

What are your most immediate responses to Cisneros's ideas? Why?

Before you read "The Story of an Hour" by Kate Chopin (1851–1904), examine for a moment, in your journal, your own knowledge and feelings about marriage. Do you, for example, believe that a marriage vow is sacred, that marriage is for life, regardless of individual happiness or fulfillment? Do you consider love to be complex? Or is it fairly straightforward—you either love or do not love someone? Do you believe the death of a spouse or partner is always a tragedy?

In order to form some point of identification with Chopin's story, respond to the following:

My definition of marriage is _____

I got this definition through _____

As you read Chopin's story, keep your reading journal beside you. Jot down words, phrases, and passages that evoke strong images or responses in you; write questions you might have concerning things you wonder about or don't understand.

THE STORY OF AN HOUR

Kate Chopin

Knowing that Mrs. Mallard was afflicted with heart trouble, great care was taken to break to her as gently as possible the news of her husband's death.

It was her sister Josephine who told her, in broken sentences; veiled hints that revealed in half concealing. Her husband's friend Richards was there, too, near her. It was he who had been in the newspaper office when intelligence of the railroad disaster was received, with Brently Mallard's name leading the list of "killed." He had only taken the time to assure himself of its truth by a second telegram, and had hastened to forestall any less careful, less tender friend in bearing the sad message.

She did not hear the story as many women have read the same, with a paralyzed inability to accept its significance. She wept at once, with sudden, wild abandonment, in her sister's arms. When the storm of grief had spent itself she went away to her room alone. She would have no one follow her.

There stood, facing the open window, a comfortable, roomy armchair. Into this she sank, pressed down by a physical exhaustion that haunted her body and seemed to reach into her soul.

She could see in the open square before her house the tops of trees that were all aquiver with new spring life. The delicious breath of rain was in the air. In the street below a peddler was crying his wares. The notes of a distant song which some one was singing reached her faintly, and countless sparrows were twittering in the eves.

There were patches of blue sky showing here and there through the clouds that had met and piled one above the other in the west facing her window.

She sat with her head thrown back upon the cushion of the chair, quite motionless, except when a sob came up into her throat and shook her, as a child who has cried itself to sleep continues to sob in its dreams.

She was young, with a fair, calm face, whose lines bespoke repression and even a certain strength. But now there was a dull stare in her eyes, whose gaze was fixed away off yonder on one of those patches of blue sky. It was not a glance of reflection, but rather indicated a suspension of intelligent thought.

There was something coming to her and she was waiting for it, fearfully. What was it? She did not know; it was too subtle and elusive to name. But she felt it, creeping out of the sky, reaching toward her through the sounds, the scents, the color that filled the air.

Now her bosom rose and fell tumultuously. She was beginning to recognize this thing that was approaching to possess her, and she was striving to beat it back with her will—as powerless as her two white slender hands would have been.

When she abandoned herself a little whispered word escaped her slightly parted lips. She said it over and over under her breath: "free, free, free!" The vacant stare and look of terror that had followed it went from her eyes. They stayed keen and bright. Her pulse beat fast, and the coursing blood warmed and relaxed every inch of her body.

She did not stop to ask if it were or were not a monstrous joy that held her. A clear and exalted perception enabled her to dismiss the suggestion as trivial.

She knew that she would weep again when she saw the kind, tender hands folded in death; the face that had never looked save with love upon her, fixed and gray and dead. But she saw beyond that bitter moment a long procession of years to come that would belong to her absolutely. And she opened and spread her arms out to them in welcome.

There would be no one to live for her during those coming years; she would live for herself. There would be no powerful will bending hers in that blind persistence with which men and women believe they have a right to impose a private will upon a fellow-creature. A kind intention or a cruel intention made the act no less a crime as she looked upon it in that brief moment of illumination.

And yet she had loved him—sometimes. Often she had not. What did it matter? What could love, the unsolved mystery, count for in face of this possession of self-assertion, which she suddenly recognized as the strongest impulse of her being!

"Free! Body and soul free!" she kept whispering.

Josephine was kneeling before the closed door with her lips to the keyhole, imploring for admission. "Louise, open this door! I beg; open the door—will you make yourself ill. What are you doing, Louise? For heaven's sake open the door."

"Go away. I am not making myself ill." No; she was drinking a very elixir of life through that open window.

Her fancy was running riot along those days ahead of her. Spring days, and summer days, and all sorts of days that would be her own. She breathed a quick prayer that life might be long. It was only yesterday that she had thought with a shudder that life might be long.

She arose at length and opened the door to her sister's importunities. There was a feverish triumph in her eyes, and she carried herself unwittingly like a goddess of Victory. She clasped her sister's waist, and together they descended the stairs. Richards stood waiting for them at the bottom.

Someone was opening the front door with a latchkey. It was Brently Mallard who entered, a little travel-stained, composedly carrying his gripsack and umbrella. He had been far from the scene of the accident, and did not even know there had been one. He stood amazed at Josephine's piercing cry; at Richards' quick motion to screen him from the view of his wife.

But Richards was too late.

When the doctors came they said she had died of heart disease—of the joy that kills.

In your reading journal, respond to the following questions:

▬ Thinking About Content ▬▬▬▬▬▬▬▬▬▬▬▬▬▬▬

1. Early in the story, Mrs. Mallard is described as weeping with wild abandonment, a "storm of grief." This is a strong, very poetic image. Do you change your image or notion of Mrs. Mallard's "storm of grief" as the story progresses? Explain.

2. The final line of the story: "When the doctors came they said she had died of heart disease—of the joy that kills." What is meant by "the joy that kills"? Do you believe the doctors were correct? How do you know?

3. In your own words, characterize Mrs. Mallard's marriage and life. What in the story leads you to these conclusions?

▬ Thinking About Writing ▬▬▬▬▬▬▬▬▬▬▬▬▬▬▬

1. Reread paragraphs 5 and 6. Chopin is creating a mood that is somewhat unusual for a story about death and loss. What details make us think more about life than about death?

2. Who tells this story? Would the story be different if it had been written in the first person (*I*)? Rewrite the opening paragraphs, about the first 25 lines, in the first person. Then, consider the difference

between first and third person "telling." Which version do you like better? Why?

3. List some of the images that provide us with the sense of life and freedom that Mrs. Mallard was experiencing. How does Chopin connect with our senses?

__Personal Connections_____

1. Reread Mrs. Mallard's first response to news of her husband's death, paragraphs 3 and 7. Have you ever responded this way to some personal tragedy or bad news? Do you think males and females respond differently? Explain.

_____

_____

_____

2. Do you think personal freedom is stressed too much in American culture? Not enough?

_____

_____

_____

3. Imagine Kate Chopin sitting across from you, having a cup of coffee in the student center. What would you say to her? What would you want to know from her?

_____

_____

_____

__Making Connections_____

Writing a hundred years ago, Kate Chopin offered us a view of women in her society. Sandra Cisneros, a contemporary writer, offers us another. Despite a century between them, are there similarities?

___Group Activity___

Discuss the following questions thoroughly. If you disagree with someone, ask questions to learn more about this person's viewpoint. If people disagree with you, try to clarify your views through more specific details, examples, and reasons. You may want to keep some notes from this discussion: What surprised you? Amused you? Puzzled you? Disturbed you? Did you think about some very different points of view because of your classmates?

1. Do males and females respond differently to important events, show joy and sadness in significantly different ways? Does culture play a role in such response? Provide examples.

2. Do males and females have significantly different ideas about marriage? About degrees of freedom within marriage? Do different cultures have different ideas about marriage? Why would it be important for a culture to develop its own notion of courtship and marriage? Are cross-cultural relationships doomed from the start? Are attitudes about cross-cultural relationships changing in the 1990s?

3. How do young people build ideas about love and marriage? Are these ideas always valid?

4. Do humans need relationships? Does living alone result in an unfulfilled life? Is being alone the same as being lonely?

5. Are relationships complicated in the 1990s?

AN ESSENTIAL SKILL: SUMMARIZING

You have been responding to ideas stimulated by Kate Chopin's story. But it is also important to ask about the accuracy of your reading: Can you pick out the main idea or events and key support details? A popular college writing assignment will ask you to both recount what you read and respond to it; you will be asked to write a summary or synopsis. Doing so even without being asked is an important reading and writing skill. It will help you condense many pages of reading into less than a page. Let's try it with "The Story of an Hour."

✦ List only the main events in the order in which they happened.

✦ List only as many supporting details as you need to explain the main events.

✦ Keep your opinions out of the summary.

◆ Use quotation marks if you use any of the original text for your summary.

◆ Be sure the summary is only about one-fourth the length of the original text.

The key to a summary is accuracy and brevity. When you ask someone about a movie, for example, you want a one-minute response that tells you who was in it and what happened—not every detail. You may want that person's evaluation as well, but you need a summary first. In an academic summary, you will reserve your opinions for later—and give them only if asked for your response to material in the summary.

Writing summaries will be an important part not only of your academic work but also of your professional life. Regardless of whether it is a small hometown business or a *Fortune* 500 company, the business world uses summaries for everything from marketing reports to proposals for change. The medical field constantly uses summaries to maintain records, provide procedural knowledge, and update busy professionals. Educators often rely on summaries of professional research and must themselves summarize student progress, problems, and their own curricular goals and plans. It is difficult to think of an area where summaries are not used to provide information in a form that is both brief and accurate, whether it be in person or print. With the overwhelming response to e-mail, and earlier, to the fax, your ability to write concise messages will be a skill used and appreciated for years to come.

As a literary piece, "The Story of an Hour" represents one type of reading task common to school settings. The following excerpt, taken from a college sociology textbook, represents another. Although its authors also discuss love and marriage, their purpose is very different from Chopin's. In your reading journal, respond to the following questions before you read:

1. Do you know anyone who married solely for economic reasons? For reasons of gaining social status? Given the "hype" of love in modern America, do you think anyone would admit to marrying for any reason but love?

2. What are your views on marrying for reasons other than love? How has your culture influenced your thinking? Your family?

Keeping a journal for textbook reading is a good study habit. On the left-hand side, jot down words, phrases—anything from the text that strikes you. Note any ideas that are confusing, difficult, and so on. When you complete your reading, review what you've just recorded. Then, on the right-hand side, respond more fully to those notes.

THE LOVE REVOLUTION AND THE RISE OF FEMINISM

Randall Collins and Scott Coltrane

THE LOVE REVOLUTION

The basic principle of the modern love revolution was to connect love with marriage. Love existed in previous societies, to be sure. But it simply was not expected to be the reason for marrying someone. In tribal societies, kinship rules that specified, for instance, that one should marry one's cousin on the father's side but not on the mother's side obviously excluded love as a motive for marriage. Similarly, where marriage was a matter of family politics or economics, the sentiments of the individual counted for very little. By the mid-twentieth century, though, marrying for love became *the* dominant ideal, so much so that one is embarrassed to admit marrying for any other reason. This change, which came about gradually in the 1700s and 1800s, may be referred to as the *love revolution*. [p. 126]

ECONOMIC AND POLITICAL RESTRICTIONS ON LOVE

. . . Marriages were just too important economically for other considerations to enter in very much. The man who wanted to be a property owner running his own farm or small business had to be married and he chose a wife who could help him with the work, oversee the servants and apprentices, and, if possible, bring in some money or property to get started. The woman had even less choice in the matter. She needed a husband in order to have an economic establishment in which she could share; if she wanted any kind of career or social status, she would have to do it by helping her husband's trade. . . .

The fact that people did not live long contributed to a somewhat mercenary attitude toward marriage. Since men were generally older than their wives (though not necessarily by much), many women were left widowed. If a widow inherited a substantial business or farm and her children were still too young to run it, she would very likely remarry in order to have a man to help work the enterprise. On the other hand, the life expectancy of women was shorter than that of men, mainly because many women died in childbirth. When this happened, a widower married again as fast as he could, since a wife was needed, not for sentimental reasons, but in order to have someone help run the household business. [pp. 129–130]

. . . [In the 1700s] Marriages became more a private affair between the couples themselves, less of a political or business arrangement. . . . As business moved out of the home, the work of wives (at least in the middle class) became less crucial economically. As the private domestic sphere emerged, women found themselves confined within it [the house and family]. . . .

> For although men now needed little from marriage besides sex and domestic help, women still found themselves economically dependent upon a husband. To ensure their own economic well-being it was important to attach men to themselves personally, and with a strong and lifetime tie if possible. This is what the new love ideal did. . . . [It] made [love] the emotional insurance that kept a woman and her loyal bread-winner tied together "until death do us part." [pp. 136–137]

In your journal, respond to the following questions:

__Thinking About Content_____

1. How does this factual look at love and marriage as it emerged in the nineteenth century compare with Kate Chopin's fictional look at marriage during the same time period?

2. What is meant by political or economic marriages? Do either or both of them exist today? How do you know?

3. If society has changed its views on sex, love, and marriage throughout the course of world history, what are the implications for the future generations? What do you think sociologists will be writing fifty years from now? A hundred years from now? What in this reading led you to these conclusions?

__Thinking About Writing_____

1. This type of writing, very common in academic settings, is expository writing. How would you characterize it?

2. Kate Chopin's story is an example of fictional narration. How is it different from exposition? What differences did you notice in your reading of each type of writing?

__Personal Connections_____

1. Do you think "until death do us part" is considered important in a modern love relationship? Is this phrase still part of marriage vows?

2. Based on the information in the above reading, do you believe that marriage was more or less complex before the twentieth century? Do you think marriage in the twenty-first century will be complex?

The following passage also deals with love. Since it is expository—informational writing rather than literary—what might you expect?

A SHORT HISTORY OF LOVE

Lawrence Stone

Historians and anthropologists are in general agreement that romantic love—the usually brief but intensely felt and all-consuming attraction toward another person—is culturally conditioned. Love has a history. . . . It is common only in certain societies at certain times, or even in certain social groups within those societies, usually the elite, which have the leisure to cultivate such feelings. Scholars are, however, less certain whether romantic love is merely culturally induced psychological overlay on top of the biological drive for sex, or whether it has biological roots that operate quite independently from the libido. Would anyone in fact "fall in love" if they had not read about it or heard it talked about?

Before you can begin to summarize the information presented here or to compare it with ideas in "The Love Revolution and the Rise of Feminism," you have to make sure you understand some key terms: anthropologist, conditioned, elite, induced, and libido.

✦ Define new terms.

✦ Write a summary of "A Short History of Love."

Now return to "The Love Revolution and the Rise of Feminism."

✦ Define new terms.

✦ Write a summary.

Because you will read many texts, as well as hear many lectures, on the very same topic, summarizing is an essential skill. It allows you to handle a great deal of information, retain what you need, and go on to the next reading and lecture. It allows you to compare information from different sources in a most efficient manner. Without summary, preparing for exams or gathering information for a writing task is virtually impossible.

▬ Group Activity ▬

With your partner or group:

✦ Compare your summaries from "The Love Revolution and the Rise of Feminism" and "A Short History of Love."

✦ What information is similar?

✦ What information is different?

✦ How does information from these two sources help you understand the concept of love a little better?

Writing Activity

Turn back to your reading journal responses. Review your notes, paying attention to questions where you had quite a bit to say or strong personal ideas. Mark these areas with an asterisk (*). Your ideas on one of these questions will form the basis of a brief writing task. Choose one question, write it on a clean sheet of paper, then list the various ideas you have already explored in response to it. What do these ideas suggest? Do you have a main idea, a single point of view, in these notes? If so, it may serve as the basis of a brief piece of writing. Now respond once more to the ideas on the page. What other thoughts come readily to mind? Write them down in whatever form suits you. Again review what you have and formulate a main idea for a paragraph.

Writing Activity

Write a paragraph based on one of the questions following "A House of My Own," "Beautiful and Cruel," "The Story of an Hour," or "The Love Revolution and the Rise of Feminism." Use the question as the base for your response, forming a single sentence (a topic sentence) that will guide you in developing your paragraph. Here are some student examples:

"Until death do us part" has not anywhere the meaning it had, because our society generally doesn't care about ethics, morals, the long term, or religious practices like it once did.

Matt

Culture plays a role in the ways that males and females respond to significant events.

Mark

Sexual freedom has definitely weakened the marriages of the 1990s.

Laura

As you consider your focus for this paragraph, review your notes again. Then ask "Why?" as a means of addressing the topic and thinking about ways to support your main idea. Have you already answered "Why?" in your notes? Continue to jot down ideas as they occur to you, in any order. Then review the list and decide if you want to include all the ideas. In a single paragraph, you need to be very focused. Perhaps one reason or one example is all you need. This student focused on one television show to make his point:

The Image of Relationships

In the age of soap operas, Al Bundy, and frequent divorces, young people are building ideas about love and marriage that can scar a child's image of it forever. The daytime soaps romanticize affairs, sex outside of wedlock and glamorous people whose love for someone changes every time there's an advertisement. This is not a good impression on a young person trying to start a relationship they can enjoy. For a couple trying to take the final step of marriage, <u>Married with Children</u> shows life after marriage doesn't exist. It's plagued with constant quarreling between spouses and their children. It portrays marriage as torture or punishment for making a relationship permanent. People may laugh at the couple's arguments, but soon the image is subconsciously with them. Today's skyrocketing divorce rate only enforces the sitcoms' message. Society must do something to offset these negative and unrealistic images of relationships.

Joe Cronick

Supporting Your Ideas

When you think about "why?", reasons may come readily to mind. But you need to support those reasons. Otherwise, you're asking someone to just accept your word for it, "because I say so." In academic writing, you need to present your reader with facts, observations, or experiences that provide a basis for your reasons. Facts are statements that can be proven to be accurate and true. For example, if you were to say something to the effect that more marriages end in divorce today than 10 years ago, you should be able to present statistics to prove it. Someone else could then look up these statistics and verify that your statement is accurate. Observations and experiences provide details of some event that you yourself either saw or experienced. In using experience to support your main idea, you let the reader see and hear what you saw or heard. Or you may use someone else's experience, something you heard directly from that person or through television, radio, or film. And if you are clear about its origin, you can even present an imaginary experience, something you only thought about.

You will learn many ways of supporting your ideas in later chapters. For now, use observations or experiences that provide specific and relevant support for your main idea.

ACTIVATING READING STRATEGIES

In working through your personal responses to what you have read, as well as in keeping a reading journal to hold on to your thoughts, you have gained an important skill. We need to think about what we read, actively think about it. But we also need to delve more deeply into the written text, especially those that are far from our personal experience or previous knowledge. To help us, we can use specific reading strategies.

Although you have been a reader for many years, becoming a reader of academic texts poses a challenge for most students—at least until they develop good reading strategies. Just as there is nothing magical about developing good writing strategies, becoming a good reader is similarly a nonmagical process of understanding and applying strategies.

ACTIVATING STRATEGIES WE ALREADY HAVE

To understand a written text, we need to think about what we already know about the subject. From this background, however limited, we have something on which to hang new ideas found in the text. In other words, we connect new ideas with old knowledge. We actually engage in this process often; we just don't think about it. Moreover, we have strategies already present that help us in reading a new text. When we add our motivation to learn into the mix, the process is activated— and we are on our way. A good example of this process can be found in my most recent new "text": football.

Reading a New Text: Confessions of a Football Junkie

A few years ago, I started watching professional football. At first, it was a half-hearted, "well, it's on, so . . . " situation. Then, my Green

Bay roots took over, and I started to watch with my heart, not just my eyes. Nonetheless, I wasn't able to "read" this football text very well. I could enjoy or flinch at the obvious, but I lacked the knowledge to watch with my head as well as my eyes. How did I eventually bring heart, eyes, and head together? Through strategies that we all use in everyday life: close observation, questions, predictions, confirmations, analysis, and interpretation.

Observation was my first and easiest strategy, and I started with the most obvious, the very best individual players. For example, knowing that Packer quarterback Brett Favre often had butterflies in the first five minutes, I was no longer surprised or distressed when he threw his first passes into the upper deck. Observation had taught me that he would settle down, and what's more, how many ways he posed a threat to the opposing team. The more I observed, the more I began to understand the talent and quirks of certain players, why coaches called the kinds of plays they did, and what they expected from certain players. Later, I began to test my hunches, predicting and confirming action both by individuals and the team as a unit. More games passed, and through continued close observation, I understood the football "text" better, and my enjoyment of the game deepened. It was no longer just a bunch of guys with no necks earning a ton of money for a Sunday afternoon's work.

Before long, I could read my football "text" by comparing new elements with what I already knew. I gained more knowledge by asking questions, making some guesses, and listening to commentators and players. By the time my hometown team went to the Super Bowl, I had become a more skilled reader of the football "text" in general and the Green Bay Packers in particular. I not only understood what I saw those Sunday afternoons, but I was able to analyze, interpret, and evaluate it to a certain degree. I had progressed from a sometime, half-hearted watcher to a critical observer, skilled enough to silently argue with and be annoyed by the expert panels on every major network.

What strategies did I use to read my football "text"? I observed, closely, and began to link old information with new, a process I also used with football terms. The word *blitz,* for example, first made some sense when I realized it might be related to *blitzkrieg,* "lightening war." I also questioned: If that is a penalty, why isn't it always called?—and started to understand deception and dumb luck. I predicted: What would happen if they tried to run the ball on that side? When they actually did, I confirmed my hunch that no one, but no one, runs over a 700-pound mass of granite wearing numbers 92 and 93. As I asked myself questions, I found answers, if not through observation then through listening or reading. With time and growing confidence, I could evaluate players' expertise, coaching calls, and the commentary of others, only because I already had some real-world strategies, and I applied them. Reading a written text requires the very same strategies:

◆   Thinking about what we already know

◆   Connecting what we know with what we are learning

◆   Observing closely and thinking about what we see

◆   Defining new terms

◆   Questioning

◆   Predicting

◆   Analyzing

◆   Evaluating

Each semester, you will read many texts, and in order to be a skilled and efficient reader, you will need specific strategies—strategies just like those that helped me with my new text, pro football. Although you already possess and use many of these strategies in your daily life, applying them to an academic text requires a bit of practice. The following reading activities will provide that practice.

DEVELOPING GOOD READING STRATEGIES

Previewing What We Read

One of the first strategies involves thinking about the first few lines or first paragraph of the text. Here we get our first impressions of what this piece is all about—as well as our first response to it. What do we expect to learn? Why? What do we already know about this topic? And how do we feel about it?

◆   Read the following passage from Langston Hughes' autobiography. Ask yourself what you already know, as well as what you think you are going to learn if you read beyond this first paragraph.

SALVATION

I was saved from sin when I was going on thirteen. But not really saved. It happened like this. There was a big revival at my Auntie Reed's church. Every night for a week there had been much preaching, singing, praying and shouting, and some very hardened sinners had been brought to Christ, and the membership of the church had grown by leaps and bounds. Then just before the revival ended, they held a special service meeting for children, "to bring the young lambs to the fold." My aunt spoke of it for days ahead. That night I was escorted to the front row and placed on the mourners' bench with all the other young sinners, who had not yet been brought to Jesus.

1. What knowledge popped into your head when you read Hughes's description of the revival? Have you attended or viewed services similar to these?

2. What would you expect to learn after you read "I was saved. . . . But not really saved."? Do you expect a sense of disillusionment?

3. Have you ever experienced situations where there was pressure by family members to adopt certain values or beliefs? Can you relate to Hughes?

4. What would you expect Hughes to tell you in the rest of "Salvation"? Why?

This is an important reading strategy: to read a passage, stop, and ask yourself what you already know, how you know it, and what you think you will learn when you finish the rest of the section.

✦ Now read the introduction to a newspaper article by Anna Quindlen.

EVAN'S TWO MOMS

Evan has two moms. This is no big thing. Evan has always had two moms—in his school file, on his emergency forms, with his friends. "Ooooh, Evan, you're lucky," they sometimes say. "You have two moms." It sounds like a sitcom, but until last week it was emotional truth without legal bulwark. That was when a judge in New York approved the adoption of the six-year-old boy by his biological mother's lesbian partner. Evan, Evan's Mom, Evan's other mom. A kid, a psychologist, a pediatrician. A family.

1. What is your first reaction? Why? What do you bring to this reading? What are your notions of "family"? How do you respond to the word *lesbian*?

2. Anna Quindlen is a nationally syndicated columnist who explores political and social issues. Knowing this, what do you anticipate the rest of her piece might say?

✦   Reading a biographical note of the author is another strategy for previewing what you will read. Professional writers have areas of expertise and special interest; knowing this background, you can form some early ideas about what the piece will explore.

Let's try this strategy out on a passage by Randy Shilts. He has written a book entitled *Unbecoming: Gays and Lesbians in the U.S. Military,* for which he interviewed more than 1,000 gay military men and women. In this book, Shilts traces the history of homosexuals in the military from the 1950s through the Persian Gulf War.

WHAT'S FAIR IN LOVE AND WAR

On the first night of the Scud missile attacks on American troops in the Persian Gulf, an army specialist fourth class with the 27th Field Artillery found himself cramped in a foxhole with three other men. Like many young enlisted men, the specialist (who asked that his name not be used) had previously confided to the other men, his friends, that he was gay. During the night in the foxhole, they huddled together in their suffocating suits meant to protect them from chemical and biological agents. They could not see one another, but to reassure themselves that they were still alive, each man kept one hand on the other. Nobody seemed to mind that one reassuring hand belonged to a homosexual, the soldier recalls—there were more important things to think about.

1. How does it help you to know something about the author's work?
2. Now ask what you already know about the context of this passage: the Persian Gulf War and Desert Storm; the issue of homosexuals in the military.
3. What terms are new? *Scud missile* is one term that should be defined, because the nature of the attack is important to the passage.
4. What questions can you ask after reading this brief introduction?
5. What predictions can you make about the rest of the reading selection?
6. What background do you personally bring to this subject? Do you have strong feelings that affect your reading? Do you have biases that need to be acknowledged?

Knowing that Shilts has written an entire book on this subject, and interviewed military personnel to do so, should help you evaluate the credibility—can you trust what he says? You may have watched some of the Gulf War on television, or you may know people who served in that war or are presently in the military. You may have watched television programs or read about recent court cases involving homosexuals in the military. In any case, you know that homosexuality is an issue in many areas of American life. What questions arise even with this brief passage? Perhaps the first asks if we will learn more about gays in the military in general, in war situations, or just in this most recent conflict in the Gulf. Can we predict where Shilts is going with his article? Will he argue for or against gays in the military, or will he just present information and let us judge for ourselves? Finally, we need to be honest about our own feelings on the topic. In college settings, we are introduced to many subjects, many views—some of which may evoke negative feelings. That's no problem as long as we recognize that we bring these feelings to the reading and can set them aside for the time being—long enough to read as objectively as possible.

◆   We also need to question connections, and if necessary, use a dictionary or other resource to help us get the immediate links the author is forging. Read this passage from Emily Prager's "Major Barbie" and make a note of people or things that you need to know in order to understand where the author might be going.

MAJOR BARBIE

I read an astounding obituary in the *New York Times* not too long ago. It concerned the death of one Jack Ryan. A former husband of Zsa Zsa Gabor, it said, Mr. Ryan had been an inventor and designer during his lifetime. A man of eclectic creativity, he designed Sparrow and Hawk missiles when he worked for the Raytheon Company, and, the notice said when he consulted for Mattel he designed Barbie. If Barbie was designed by a man, suddenly a lot of things made sense to me, things I wondered about for years.

1. Who is Zsa Zsa Gabor? What might she have to do with Barbie, the most famous doll in America?
2. What are Sparrow and Hawk missiles? How high-tech are they?

Now we need to turn to some of our other previewing strategies: defining terms, asking questions, and making some predictions about what will be coming up.

3. What does the term *eclectic* mean? Why is it important here?
4. Why would a high-tech military designer be involved with a toy company?
5. What brought Jack Ryan from military missiles to Barbie?
6. What do you already know about Barbie dolls?

Emily Prager, a former contributing editor to *National Lampoon*, also writes a political and social satire column for *Penthouse*.

7. How does this information about the author help us? What might we reasonably expect when we read the rest of this piece? Should we expect a serious or humorous piece? Should we expect a bit of satire?

◆ Titles are another critical part of previewing our reading. Read the following passage written by Carol Kaesuk Yoon, without its title, and decide what this piece is all about.

In northern Costa Rica on a warm, moonless night, two men stare into the glow of a black light reflecting off a sheet that flutters in the breeze. Attracted by the light, hundreds of brightly colored moths, beetles, and katydids descend from the darkness. A few dangle brightly from the surrounding tree branches, lit up like sparkling Christmas tree ornaments. The men grab excitedly at this one or that, turning the tiny beast over in their hands. The insects are the gold these prospectors have come in search of, the treasure they believe may be the best hope for protecting the world's dwindling diversity of species.

1. The descriptive opening reads like a novel. What do you think will follow?
2. What does the analogy of the gold mine suggest? Why would anyone be that excited about a bunch of insects? Is it merely a conservation movement, saving certain species from extinction?

Now consider the title chosen by Kaesuk Yoon, a freelance science writer for major American magazines and newspapers: "Drugs from Bugs."

3. How does this title change and guide your expectation of the article?

A good title is an important reading clue; it gives us, at the very least, the topic, and at the very best, insight into the topic.

Reading Strategy: Previewing the Text

You have been systematically previewing the text:

◆ What does the title suggest?
◆ What does information about the author suggest?
◆ What do I already know or think about the topic?

✦   Do I bring experience or prior knowledge to the topic?

✦   Do I have strong feelings or biases about the topic?

✦   Based on this initial information, what do I expect to learn?

✦   Do I need to define terms?

Whether we read a football game, a sheet of music, or an academic text, we make meaning by following a procedure. We think about what we already know. We try to figure out what we have in front of us before we get into "the thick of it." The next strategies help us when we are "in the thick of it."

Reading Critically

Thus far, we have talked about previewing the text, getting a sense of what it is about. With a longer piece of academic writing, we would also skim the text—read quickly through the introduction and first page or so, asking what the author is promising to tell us. Is this what I expected to learn? Are there words I need to define? The next step, going back to the beginning and reading slowly, involves a series of strategies that help us respond to what we read. In other words, we talk back to the text. In doing so, we become an active reader—with our brain, not just our eyes. Being an active reader helps us concentrate on the text: analyze it, interpret it, and eventually evaluate it. These processes are the heart of academic reading and writing.

As noted earlier, writing is one of the most important means we have of understanding what we read. Thus, keeping a reading journal is a great strategy. However, some students prefer to write in the margins or on Post-It notes, both of which are good strategies. Other students like to use a highlighter pen to mark out key sentences or phrases. Whichever strategy you use, remember that brevity is the goal. You want key ideas and your responses to them.

Reading Strategy: Highlighting and Notes

With a pen or highlighter, mark out information that answers these questions:

✦   What is the main idea?

✦   What evidence supports the main idea?

With a pen, react to the ideas you are encountering:

✦   What you agree with

✦   What you disagree with

◆ Any exceptions to what the author has said

◆ What the author is implying

◆ What would be the result if . . .

◆ Any personal associations with what is said

◆ Any connections to other readings or lectures

In a nutshell: What's going on here and what do I think about it?

Trying Out Strategies

Try out the previewing and critical reading strategies in the excerpt that follows. When you complete them, we will add the final strategies of reviewing and evaluating a text.

Deborah Tannen is a linguistics professor whose expertise in male/female conversational styles has made her a best-selling author. *You Just Don't Understand: Women and Men in Conversation* and *That's Not What I Meant: How Conversational Style Makes or Breaks Relationships* are among her most popular works. The following passage was adapted from *You Just Don't Understand* for the *New York Times.*

LINGUISTIC BATTLE OF THE SEXES

In the April [1990] issue of *American Psychologist,* Stanford University's Eleanor Maccoby reports the results of her own and others' research showing that children's development is the most influenced by the social structure of peer interactions. Boys and girls tend to play with children of their own gender, and their sex-separate groups have different organizational structures and interactive norms.

I believe these systematic differences in childhood socialization make talk between women and men like cross-cultural communication, heir to all the attraction and pitfalls of that enticing but difficult enterprise. My research on men's and women's conversations uncovered patterns similar to those described for children's groups.

For women, as for girls, intimacy is the fabric of relationships, and talk is the thread from which it is woven. Little girls create and maintain friendships by exchanging secrets; similarly, women regard conversation as the cornerstone of friendship. So a woman expects her husband to be a new and improved version of a best friend. What is important is not the individual subjects that are discussed but the sense of closeness, of a life shared, that emerges when people tell their thoughts, feelings, and impressions.

Bonds between boys can be as intense as girls', but they are based less on talking, more on doing things together. Since they don't assume talk is the cement that binds a relationship, men don't know what kind of talk women want, and they don't miss it when it isn't there.

Boys' groups are larger, more inclusive, and more hierarchical, so boys must struggle to avoid the subordinate position in the group. This may play a role in women's complaints that men don't listen to them. Some men really don't like to listen, because being the listener makes them feel one down, like a child listening to adults or an employee to a boss.

Reading Strategy: Reviewing the Text

Reviewing what we read is an important check on our understanding of the text. It might seem silly to you at first, going back over text that you believe you have carefully read in the first place. However, responding and reviewing will save valuable time later, when you face exams or need notes for a written project. Reviewing means that you identify and explain in your own words the main ideas; it means you can interpret what you have read. When you review, you are well beyond just understanding the words and ideas; you are building your own ideas about this topic.

✦ In your own words, state the main idea in the Tannen piece.

✦ What connections can you make with these ideas? How will you be able to recall them later?

Reading Strategy: Evaluating the Text

The final reading strategy is similarly important; we need to evaluate what we have read. We started to evaluate when we first questioned the author's credibility: Does he or she have the background and expertise to write about this subject? Now we need to evaluate how well the author has written about the subject and whether the ideas expressed have merit. When you are sure that you do understand the text, that you have an accurate reading, you are ready to evaluate. Often, students feel as though they are not qualified to judge professional writers—but they are. Don't be afraid to evaluate what you have read.

Again with the Tannen piece, respond to the following:

✦ Has Tannen written in a clear and convincing manner?

✦ Can we believe what Tannen says or suggests?

✦ Are the ideas worth exploring?

✦ What support does she offer for her ideas?

- ✦   If research is involved, can we trust it?
- ✦   Is everything in the article relevant?
- ✦   Does anything seem out of place or jarring, like it just doesn't fit?
- ✦   Does Tannen hold our interest?

With college textbooks, you can be reasonably sure that the author has credibility and that the ideas are in the mainstream of the academic discipline. However, you will often read shorter pieces where you must evaluate their worth, especially when you plan to use them as the basis of a written assignment. Similarly, if you use the Internet for research, you must evaluate the source. Anyone can put anything on the Net, and failure to search out the credibility of the author could result in material that is not only flawed but completely off base.

You might have noticed already that the reading strategies can be turned around and used as writing strategies. Many of the same questions that you ask of an author are questions that you need to ask yourself in the revision process. They are also the same questions you will use in peer response. Teachers will tell you that their best writers are also their best readers. The two processes are mirror images, and the more skilled you are as a reader, the more skilled you will be as a writer.

Exploring Structure: From Paragraph to Essay

Although we never seem to run out of ideas when we are talking, or have many problems putting those ideas into an order that our listeners can follow, writing down our ideas can be a problem—and not just because writing requires complete sentences and correctness in grammar, mechanics, and spelling. Writing requires far more structuring of our ideas. We must "package" them in complete sentences, fully developed and logically sequenced, and thus ready for a distant "listener" unable to request clarification. When our ideas are expressed in sentences, we again "package" them, this time in a larger unit, the paragraph. In the paragraph, we provide one more structural element, the topic sentence, to guide our readers through the paragraph. No matter how brief or lengthy the writing, the paragraph provides the basic structure for our ideas.

A BASIC STRUCTURE: THE PARAGRAPH

A paragraph may be loosely defined as a group of sentences about a single topic. The average paragraph has 100 to 150 words. However, it may be slightly longer in formal writing and considerably shorter in other places, such as newspapers and magazines. Generally, we adjust paragraph length to help our readers. If we have a great deal to say about a single topic, we will do it in several short paragraphs rather than one lengthy one. Doing so will keep our readers alert and ease eyestrain. Sometimes, a single paragraph is in itself a short essay, requiring no further development of the topic. At other times, a single paragraph is one of several in an essay or report, each paragraph contributing to the development of the essay's topic.

Unfortunately, there are no rules or guidelines requiring that a paragraph be a certain length or that an essay contain a certain number of paragraphs. As one teacher I know puts it when asked about paragraphs: "Have some." That's good advice. We need paragraphs to force our readers to pause for a moment, to regain their attention as we continue our discussion of the topic. But you as writer must decide where those paragraph breaks will come. Most experienced writers respond intuitively to the need for more or fewer paragraphs, guided by their own knowledge of the topic, their readers' needs, and their purpose in writing. There are, however, basic guidelines for constructing a good paragraph:

✦ Formulating a clear topic sentence

✦ Developing relevant and adequate support through details, examples, or reasons

✦ Staying on the topic

✦ Organizing information sequentially or logically

✦ Connecting sentences logically

A good paragraph, beyond its structural components, also includes good thinking about the topic. No matter how well constructed, a paragraph that lacks real engagement with the topic won't be considered a "good" paragraph. Therefore, the writer's interest in and analysis of the topic is at the core of a solid paragraph. In choosing topics, then, you need to be honest about the reasons behind the choice—and go with your heart, as well as your head. Readers know when we are merely fulfilling a task, as well as when we are enmeshed in a wonderful exploration of something we care about.

Structurally, the topic sentence is the key to writing good paragraphs. It announces what the paragraph is all about; then, we "fill in the blanks" with support for that topic sentence. It's important to note that not all paragraphs have a stated topic sentence. There are several reasons for this: some types of writing, such as personal experience, rarely need them; highly experienced or professional writers may not need them to stay on topic; some paragraphs are mere extensions of the single topic being developed, so a new paragraph only makes the reader pause and refocus. In academic writing, however, most paragraphs have a topic sentence. What's more, most teachers like and expect topic sentences in essays or exams. Students who write clear topic sentences signal a clear understanding of the topic, as well as suggest that good organization will follow. We will look at topic sentences carefully a little later. First, we need to be a good reader of paragraphs, something you have already begun to do with reading strategies.

Examining the Paragraph

One way in which we develop a good sense of paragraph structure is through examining well-written paragraphs. As you read the paragraphs that follow, note how professional writers follow through on the promise made in the topic sentence.

✦ Jane Goodall—first observations

Jane Goodall settled in Tanzania, East Africa, to investigate the behavior of chimpanzees in their native habitat. Her research has fascinated and informed not only scientists but also a worldwide audience of "ordinary people," most of whom saw a bit of themselves in the chimps' behaviors. The following paragraphs are from her book *In the Shadow of Man.*

PARAGRAPH 1

While many details of their [the chimps] social behavior were hidden from me by the foliage, I did get occasional fascinating glimpses. I saw one female, newly arrived in a group, hurry up to a big male and hold her hand toward him. Almost regally, he reached out, clasped her hand in his, drew it toward him, and kissed it with his lips. I saw two adult males embrace each other in greeting. I saw two youngsters having wild games through the treetops, chasing around after each other or jumping again and again, one after the other, from a branch to a springy bough below. I watched small infants dangling happily by themselves for minutes on end, patting their toes with one hand, rotating gently from side to side. Once two tiny infants pulled on opposite ends of a twig in a gentle tug-of-war. Often, during the heat of midday or after a long spell of feeding, I saw two or more adults grooming each other, carefully looking through the hair of their companions.

✦ What is the main idea of this paragraph?
✦ What sentence guides the main idea?
✦ How does Goodall develop the main idea?

PARAGRAPH 2

At that time of the year the chimps usually went to bed late, making their nests when it was too dark to see properly through binoculars, but sometimes they nested earlier and I could watch them from the Peak. I found that every individual, except for infants who slept with their mothers, made his own nest each night. Generally this took about three minutes: the chimp chose a firm foundation such as an upright fork or crotch, or two horizontal branches. Then he reached out and bent over smaller branches onto this foundation, keeping each one in place with his feet. Finally, he tucked in the small leafy twigs growing around the rim of his nest and lay down.

✦   What is the main idea of this paragraph?
✦   What sentence guides the main idea?
✦   How does Goodall develop the main idea?

Developing Topic Sentences

The sentences guiding the main idea of the paragraph are topic sentences. Within these two paragraphs, we can see that Goodall uses clear topic sentences to guide her paragraph. She develops only one idea in each paragraph. And she develops each paragraph with a different method. In the first paragraph, she uses examples and in the second, she uses an orderly, chronological process. This is not unusual. Sometimes we use examples, sometimes we use detail arranged in chronological or spatial order, sometimes we use reasons, and sometimes we use more than one of these methods at once. We do this in everyday conversations. When someone asks, "What do you mean?" the response is likely to be an example. When someone asks, "Why?" the response is likely to be a reason. We use examples, as Goodall did, when we describe the world and the people and things in it; we use examples when we want to illustrate a point; and we use examples when we analyze an idea, event, or problem. We use detail in chronological order when we want to provide the reader with a step-by-step process or show how something unfolded over time. We use spatial detail when we describe how something or someone looked, picking a point to begin our description and filling in the picture in an orderly fashion. We use reasons most often when we argue a point or evaluate something or someone.

Although we don't have to think very hard to come up with supporting details in conversations, while writing we usually spend more time and thought on choosing just the right ones, mainly because we won't get a second chance. When we talk, we continually add, change, and modify according to the needs of our listener. In writing, we have to anticipate the needs of a distant reader. It's one of the reasons why writing is demanding and time-consuming. It is also the reason we need clearly stated topic sentences to remind us that we have promised to discuss a single point, and thus, that we have to stick to it.

In academic writing, the topic sentence expresses the main idea of the entire paragraph; it makes the point. The topic sentence is helpful in that it prepares us for what the paragraph is all about. As readers, we gear up for a specific discussion on a single point; we look for details, examples, or reasons to support that single point. The topic sentence (1) announces the topic, (2) focuses attention on it, and (3) limits the topic.

✦   Read Goodall's topic sentence once more:

> While many details of their social behavior were hidden from me by the foliage, I did get occasional fascinating glimpses.

She has announced, focused, and limited her topic. We expect to read something of the chimps' social behavior, but we also know we are getting only glimpses of it—not a complete or detailed list.

In the second paragraph, she notes:

> I found that every individual, except for infants who slept with their mothers, made his own nest each night.

Again, she has announced and limited her topic to the chimps' nest-making each night. She then goes on to describe that process—and only that process—in a single paragraph.

✦   The following passage from a sociology textbook illustrates another way in which a topic is announced and limited; it also shows us another way of developing the topic sentence.

NORMS

Judson Landis

All societies have rules that specify what people should do in specific situations. Sociologists call these shared behavioral standards **norms**. Norms describe the accepted or required behavior for a person in a particular situation. For example, when a person gets into a car, that person unconsciously begins to behave according to a whole set of norms relating to driving procedure. In America, the driver knows that he or she should drive on the right side of the road, pass on the left, signal before turning, and so on. The norms vary from place to place, but they always exist. These shared standards for behavior allow us to predict what other people will do. Without even thinking about it or knowing the individual, I know how the driver of a car approaching me will behave. The system of norms allows us to predict what other people will do in specific situations and to pattern our behavior accordingly.

✦ How has this author announced, focused, and limited the topic?

✦ How has the author developed the paragraph?

✦ What was the author's purpose in writing this paragraph?

Sociologists and psychologists aside, few people use the term *norms*. So the author used a good strategy to develop the meaning for us—using something familiar to explain something new and somewhat abstract.

This author has defined "something" for us, norms. Every paragraph you write will be about "something": it may describe something or someone, question something, explain something, analyze something, argue something. "Something" is usually identified in the topic sentence, and often, it will express your attitude or reaction to the topic. Here are some examples:

John Lennon was one of the most influential musicians of modern times.

Natural disasters bring out the best in Americans.

Television violence has negative effects on young viewers.

Each of these sentences has a key word or phrase that tells the reader what to expect in the paragraph. For example, what is meant by "influential"? The reader would expect details, examples, and reasons that show Lennon was indeed influential. A paragraph about natural disasters bringing out the best in Americans could describe the acts of care and kindness, of bravery even, found during hurricanes and floods. A paragraph supporting the idea that television violence has negative effects would first of all have to provide examples of television violence and then illustrate the negative effects.

The topic sentence serves as a reminder: this paragraph is about something. Every sentence in that paragraph then serves to develop the idea, the something. Not every paragraph will or must have an explicit topic sentence, but every paragraph nonetheless is organized around a single something. Very experienced writers sometimes omit the topic sentence, but they never violate the idea of developing a single paragraph around a single something. However, student writers usually state their topic sentence. Because it helps unify their ideas within the paragraph, a stated topic sentence helps them stay on track.

For example, if you decide to write about natural disasters bringing out the best in Americans, you would be choosing specific acts of kindness or bravery related to natural disasters, such as hurricanes or floods. If you then thought about some acts of kindness or bravery related to an apartment fire, you would have to set them aside. Your topic sentence specifically noted natural disasters, not acts of human destruction. You could, of course, come up with a new topic sentence that included man-made destruction. More likely, however, you would stick with a more focused, limited topic sentence, and then eliminate any idea that doesn't relate to it.

Developing the Idea

One strategy for developing a paragraph evolves from the idea that each sentence derives directly from the sentence before it; it responds to that sentence in some way. Considered this way, the paragraph is a series of sentences that carry both the reader's expectations and the writer's response. For example:

Bart Simpson is every teacher's worst nightmare.

The reader expects to learn why Bart is a "worst nightmare." The next sentence thus might define "worst nightmare." It could be something to the effect that Bart is mouthy, unproductive, and defiant in school. From there the reader would expect several examples of Bart in action. The writer could describe Bart's language in the classroom, his efforts to avoid homework or class activities, and finally the language and acts of defiance against authority. Anyone who was a regular watcher of *The Simpsons* could easily supply details and examples on this single topic.

Ways Topic Sentences Evolve

Topic sentences can evolve in two ways: (1) We might think of a general idea—like Bart Simpson being a teacher's nightmare—and then fill in all the details and examples that fill out that general idea. (2) We might have the details and examples first and work toward the general idea that becomes our topic sentence. We might have been making notes about *The Simpsons,* listing all the things Bart does to drive teachers crazy, and then come up with a sentence that provides the main idea: "Bart is a teacher's worst nightmare." Any method that you use or that just occurs is fine, as long as you check that the topic sentence really matches your details and examples.

Placing the Topic Sentence

Although typically placed as the first sentence of a paragraph, topic sentences may come as the last sentence or somewhere in the middle. In this way, writers vary their writing style.

At the Beginning. If you put the topic sentence first, you provide readers with a clear statement of intent for your paragraph. Whenever you write to inform or explain something, the topic sentence as first sentence is best. You want your reader to grasp your main idea quickly. School essays and exams, business reports, and on-the-job writing often require a clearly stated topic as the first sentence. For example:

> *Bart Simpson is every teacher's worst nightmare.* Bart not only defies and mocks authority at every opportunity, he also finds ways to make teachers look totally incompetent. In a recent episode, he twisted the teacher's lesson into nonsense by asking impossible questions and challenging every reasonable attempt at answers. By the time the class ended, the teacher was babbling into her mirror and Bart was happily plotting his next move.

At the End. If you develop a paragraph using inductive reasoning (where you have gathered specific examples or evidence from which you draw a conclusion—the Sherlock Holmes approach), the topic sentence will quite naturally be at the end of the paragraph. For example:

> Setting fire to the wastebasket was a monthly occurrence. Once the smoke reached the teacher's desk, the classroom emptied out quickly and permanently. Another scheme to gain freedom involved classroom fish tanks and mysterious leakage over the teacher's grade book and lesson plans. Yet another introduced some small rodents into storage crates being used for daily writing assignments. *Bart Simpson's plans to disrupt school seemed endless.*

Trying Out Topic Sentences

A good topic sentence provides a blueprint of the paragraph: it announces our topic, focuses the reader's attention, and limits our discussion to a single point. Usually, there is a key word or phrase that directs development.

Topic Sentence: Air travel has become a nightmare.

The focus is air travel, not bus, car, train, or hitchhiking. The reader's attention goes to "nightmare"—and the writer has promised evidence to support that description. If you are a frequent flyer, you can probably fill in some of that evidence: examples from personal experience. You might also have factual evidence (something that can be checked, verified as true) from business or government reports.

✦ From personal experience: five flights delayed due to mechanical problems; 28 hours, rather 2 hours, enroute due to weather; sleeping on airport floor; no airport restaurants open between 10 P.M. and 6 A.M.; baggage lost; denied boarding on one airline because another had the luggage; rude or inattentive flight attendants; unruly children; check-in lines with up to an hour's wait; inconsiderate travelers, dropping luggage from overhead bin and climbing over others every five minutes

✦ From reports: customer complaints for all major airlines are up 25 percent in the last year; complaints for two major airlines are up 75 percent in the last year; airlines reduced passenger seat size, resulting in more discomfort

While thinking about the topic, you might have recalled some positive things as well: on-time records are generally better; some of the food is more innovative, offering healthy choices. However, the focus is "nightmare," so any positive example or detail must be left out. With the word *nightmare,* the writer's attitude toward the topic is also expressed, another essential in guiding the reader.

Group Activity

Pick out the key word or words in the following topic sentences. Then, brainstorm a list of examples, reasons, or details that would develop the topic sentence.

1. Being in love is very time-consuming.
2. Television commercials insult our intelligence.
3. Not all fast food is bad food.
4. Not all professional athletes are poor role models.
5. Buying a used car is stressful.
6. Dieting can be dangerous.

7. Some television shows are harmful for young children.
8. Teens who work after school develop good skills.

Focusing the Topic Sentence

For a single paragraph, we need a focused topic sentence; that is, we don't want to promise too much. Notice the difference in these pairs:

Students who work constantly battle time.
Students who work have less time for friendships.
Students benefit from exercise.
Students who exercise regularly are more alert.
Exercise is beneficial.
Exercise improves the cardiovascular system.
Air travel is a nightmare.
Air travel during the Christmas holiday is a nightmare.

The first sentence in each pair might guide development of an entire essay, whereas the second sentence focuses and limits the discussion.

▬ Group Activity ▬▬▬▬▬▬▬▬▬▬▬▬▬▬▬▬▬▬

Narrow the focus of each sentence.

1. Going home can be stressful.
2. Athletes are overpaid.
3. The new technology is frustrating.
4. Cheating is commonplace.
5. The government wastes money.
6. Movies are pretty stupid.

Types of Topic Sentences

Although we have general requirements for a good topic sentence, we also have more specific requirements depending upon the purpose of our paragraph. If we are writing to present a problem, for example, our first requirement is to identify that problem; if we are writing to describe something, our first requirement is to provide an overall impression. Notice how the topic sentence changes with a different purpose:

Purpose	Topic Sentence	Example
Narration	Guide through who, what, where, when	Walking into the classroom, I panicked.
Description	Give overall impression	The classroom was chaotic.
Compare/Contrast	Show similarities/ differences	Mr. Jones and Ms. Smith differed in their approach to classroom discipline.
Cause/Effect	Identify cause or effect	Dieting may have serious consequences for teenagers.
Process	Show "how to" or how something works/occurs	A child's language skills develop quickly at age 3.
Present Problem	Identify problem	Managing money is difficult for most first-year students.
Propose Solution	Identify problem and solution	Maintaining a budget log is one way to manage money.
Argument	State your position	Students should not have to pay extra fees for school events.

▬ Group Activity ▬

Examine the topic sentence, determine the key word or phrase that the author promises to develop, and decide what you believe would logically follow. What would the writer have to do to follow through with the topic sentence? Wherever possible, suggest examples, details, or reasons that would fulfill the promise of the topic sentence.

1. Female firefighter, diapering dads; adults are slowly escaping the confines of traditional sex roles. But when it comes to kids' toys, gender stereotypes still exist.
2. If that Snickers bar you're eating seems a bit less sweet this time of the year, you might be experiencing a newly discovered symptom of seasonal affective disorder (SAD), the so-called winter depression that strikes as many as 15 million people during these months. It turns out that SAD dampens not only your mood but also your taste buds.

3. If you find yourself tossing and turning night after night, the problem could be your diet.

4. Thinking of wearing black to that pickup football or hockey game you play on weekends? Think again. While donning dark duds may score you fashion points, outfitting your team in black may also make it more likely you'll suffer the wrath of the ref.

5. Unused gym memberships, running shoes whose treads grip nothing but the closet floor. Who hasn't abandoned a noble vow to exercise at one time or another? Though you may think your disinterest in shaping up is a matter of sloth, sometimes even the best-laid workout plans are doomed to fail simply because the exercise we've chosen clashes with our personality.

6. As one of the few expressions of creativity and personality allowed to men, a tie has a lot of responsibility.

7. Man's best friend may also be his best source of social support. Better, even, than a spouse. We all know that turning to friends and family can buffer the psychological effects of stress. But the ideal source of social support, according to Karen Allen, Ph.D., may be a pet dog.

8. According to researchers, everyone gossips, and we begin almost as soon as we learn to speak. But kids' gossip is decidedly different from adults'.

9. With just a tap of your finger, imagine unlocking your house, withdrawing money from your bank account, or even shopping. It may seem like a futurist fantasy, but electronic fingerprint identification can no longer be relegated to the realm of science fiction.

10. Undernutrition triggers an array of health problems in children, many of which can become chronic.

11. For my mother, life in America was not what the promoters had told her father it would be. She grew up very poor.

12. If you thought your child's bookshelves were finally free of openly (and not so openly) discriminatory materials, you'd better check again.

13. But the mark on basketball of today's players can be measured by more than money or visibility. It is a question of style. For there is a clear difference between "black" and "white" styles of play.

14. A good example of manufacturers using descriptive names to psychologically promote their products is underarm deodorants.

15. Though we no longer run for food and survival, the importance of this activity is still evident in the sports we most enjoy watching.

Organizational Patterns of Paragraphs

The topic sentence guides the purpose of our paragraph and helps us select appropriate information. However, after our initial draft, a "zero" or discovery draft that gets information out of our heads and on paper, we have to think about a logical order for that information. Knowing that there are specific organizational patterns helps us with the process. The following patterns are common in English prose:

✦   Order of importance

As the title implies, we arrange information from least important to most important, bringing the reader to the most critical point last—mainly because we usually recall best what we read last.

✦   General to specific

We start with an overall description or general statement and move on to smaller and more specific details that explain the general statement.

✦   Specific to general

We begin with specific details or examples and end with a general statement that describes or summarizes those details and examples.

✦   Spatial order

We draw the reader's eye through space, as though he or she were physically there. We want a systematic description, like clockwise or head to toe.

✦   Chronological order

We present information in a time sequence, usually first to last.

✦   Simple to complex

We move from the least-complicated ideas, the most easily grasped or familiar, to the most complex, the most difficult to understand or furthest from our own experience.

✦   Topic with illustration

We state the topic and then give an illustration of some type (e.g., an example, a fact or statistic, or expert opinion), explaining the significance as we go.

Activity

As you read through the following paragraphs, decide which organizational pattern the writer has chosen and why. Where do you think the writer is headed in the rest of the piece?

A.

Indians were eating popcorn long before Europeans arrived in the New World, according to the Popcorn Institute. Columbus found the natives in the West Indies selling popcorn decorations such as corsages. Cortez got his first sight of popcorn in 1519 when he invaded Mexico and came into contact with the Aztecs. Popcorn was an important food for the Aztec Indians, who also used it to decorate ceremonial headdresses and ornamental statues of their gods.

Karen Herzog, "Munching Moments"

B.

We modern Americans are the tell-all type. No longer bound by the prudish mores of our ancestors, or even by the manners of our parents' generation, we talk and talk and talk about the most intimate details of our lives. We go on Sally and Ricki and Oprah and confess. We write autobiographies that make readers blush and publishers wealthy. And even when the policy is "don't ask, don't tell," we do. We spill our secrets like so many lost, dirty pennies.

Shari Roan, "Discretion May Be Good Thing for Our Tell-All Society"

C.

Most black Americans are not poor. Most black teenagers are not crack addicts. Most black mothers are not on welfare. Indeed, in sheer numbers, more white Americans are poor and on welfare than are black. Yet one would never deduce that by watching television or reading American newspapers and magazines.

Patricia Rayborn, "A Case of Severe Bias"

D.

There is a long-standing myth in our society that the great friendships are between men. Forged through shared experience, male friendship is portrayed as the most unselfish, if not the highest, form of human relationship. The more traditionally masculine the shared experience from which it springs, the stronger and more profound the friendship is supposed to be. Going to war, weathering crises together at school or work, playing on the same athletic team, are some of the classic experiences out of which friendships between men are believed to grow.

Marc Feigen Fasteau, *The Male Machine*

E.

But the techniques of molecular genetics, which can reconstruct time and the biological descent of animals alive today tell a different shaggy dog story. Wayne and his colleagues studied the regular clock-like evolution of genetic material contained in the cell's energy-producing complexes called mitochondria, which are inherited through maternal ancestors. Mitochondrial DNA changes at a relatively constant rate, and the number of changes increases with time. To determine how long ago dogs emerged, the researchers looked at the DNA sequences from a control region to the mitochondrial genome that has a very high mutation rate—the same molecular clock used by other scientists to trace the descent of human beings to early African ancestors.

Robert Lee Hotz, "Pooch Pals: Man's Tie to Dog is Ancient"

F.

If you're a single woman under 35, you have a pretty good chance of finding a sweetheart to spend Valentine's Day with. Sorry, guys. There's a bit of single-man glut. Census Bureau figures suggest that for every 100 unmarried women under 35, there are about 118 men of that age group.

Jennifer Batog, "Love by the Numbers"

G.

Half a block down from the record store was a market that opened out onto the street. Crates of lemons and oranges and banana squash were shoved together along the sidewalk; the squashes were cut open, and the webbed clusters of their yellow seeds spilled out onto the wood and concrete. . . . Above the market was a row of small apartments. Some of the windows were cracked and held in place with masking tape that crisscrossed the glass. Others were smooth. And still others decorated with lace curtains, tied carefully back. The window above the place were Lillian had parked her car had orchids on the sill and a cactus with bright red flowers.

Mike Rose, *Lives on the Boundary*

DEVELOPING THE PARAGRAPH

The topic sentence sets the stage for the rest of the information in the paragraph, leading the reader into the heart of what a writer says. A general pattern of organization provides an overall direction, but there is a bit more to development and organization, and more specific strategies to help us. The following paragraphs illustrate various strategies for "filling in" information—and making paragraphs more interesting.

▬ Group Activity

Read each paragraph below carefully; pick out the topic sentence or main idea of the paragraph. In some examples, the topic sentence is not stated explicitly, but the main idea is clear. When possible, note the general pattern of organization. Tell how each writer uses the specific development strategy to guide the reader into the topic—as well as gain the reader's interest in that topic.

Strategies for Development

✦   Illustrating the point through description

The sign announced that we could get our passport photos *and* our children's first communion pictures here—quickly. Next to it, above another storefront, hand-lettering invited us to visit—*visitenos*—for this was a wholesaler open to the public: *precios de mayoreo al publico*. A little shop selling *articulos religiosas*—pictures, medals, and statues of Jesus and the Blessed Virgin Mary—was next to a dark, dark bar with a blond speaking Spanish on a Budweiser poster, and that bar was cheek-by-jowl to a *zapateria* with unclaimed, dusty shoes in the window below a promotional sign that read, in English, "invisible half-soling." It was all part of a walking tour of Brooklyn Avenue with Lillian, a compatriot in the Teaching Corps, who translated the Spanish along the busy East Los Angeles street. . . .

Mike Rose, *Lives on the Boundary*

✦   Developing the point with anecdote

I'll never forget the day I was supposed to meet him. We had only spoken on the phone. But we got along so well, we couldn't wait to meet face-to-face. I took the bus from my high school to his for our blind date. While I nervously waited for him outside the school, one of his buddies came along, looked me over, and remarked that I was going to be a problem, because his friend didn't like dating anybody darker than himself.

Charisse Jones, "Light Skin versus Dark"

✦   Developing the point with personal experience

I was twelve, and in my first year of junior high school in San Francisco, when I discovered dark brown was not supposed to be beautiful. At that age, boys suddenly became important, and so did your looks.

Charisse Jones, "Light Skin versus Dark"

✦   Using analogy to make the point

The face is familiar, but my goodness, check out the style: lime green jumper, trashy purple beads, red lace fingerless gloves. She's hot. She now. She an eighties kinda gal—Minnie Mouse, who has undergone a startling fashion make-over, from plain Jane to downtown fun machine. A rodent Madonna.

"Who Said Minnie Was Mousie?"

For people with dyslexia, reading can be like watching a game of musical chairs, as words and letters change places unexpectedly.

Psychology Today

RAT-A-TAT-TAT. RAT-A-TAT-TAT. RAT-A-TAT-TAT. If scientists could eavesdrop on the brain of a human embryo 10, maybe 12 weeks after conception, they would hear an astonishing racket. Inside the womb, long before light first strikes the retina of the eye or the earliest dreamy images flicker through the cortex, nerve cells in the developing brain crackle with purposeful activity. Like teenagers with telephones, cells in one neighborhood of the brain are calling friends in another, and these cells are calling their friends, and they keep calling one another over and over again, "almost," says neurobiologist Carla Schatz of the University of California, Berkeley, "as if they were autodialing."

J. Madeleine Nash, "Fertile Minds"

✦   Using historical process

Although most of us enjoy and engage in it, gossip is a slippery subject with a sullied reputation. The idea of gossip originated with the Old

English word "godsipp," meaning "a person related to one in God," or a godparent. Until about the 1800's, "gossip" denoted a man who drank with friends and the fellowship they shared, or a woman who was a family friend and helped during childbirth.

Psychology Today

✦ Defining

Today, gossip is a national growth industry and the dictionary defines it simply as "chatty talk; the reporting of sensational or intimate information." Despite its banal definition, gossip is often perceived as a dangerous weapon, one that can ruin reputations, poison relationships, and halt careers. . . . But social scientists who have researched the subject insist that gossip is more closely related to its seventeenth-century meaning. In the vast majority of cases, they contend, it's beneficial. Gossip serves important social and psychological functions; it's a unifying force that communicates a group's moral code. It's the social glue that holds us all together.

Psychology Today

Geek n. (1) a performer of grotesque or depraved acts in a carnival. (2) any person considered to be different from others in a negative or bizarre way. Geeky, geekier, geekiest, adj.

"The richest man in the world is a geek," says Robert Stephens. He's talking about Bill Gates, founder of Microsoft Corp. As far as Stephens is concerned, it's something to emulate—being rich, that is. At 26, Stephens is very enthusiastic about making money. He radiates with entrepreneurial ambition. And as far as being a geek, Stephens likes the word so much that he's named his year-old computer-support service the Geek Squad. Customers think it's a hoot when scruffy-looking computer experts—Stephens calls them his "special agents"—turn up at 3M or Paisley Park wearing a shirt imprinted with the Geek Squad logo, ready to fix a crashed hard drive, revive a dead laptop, or solve a complex software problem.

David Hawley, "Revenge of the Nerds"

✦ By comparing/contrasting

According to researchers, everyone gossips, we begin almost as soon as we learn to speak. But kids' gossip is decidedly different from adults': it's more innocent and often more cruel.

By college, gender differences in gabbing are even more striking.

Psychology Today

✦   Using facts and statistics

The prevalence of malnutrition in children is staggering. Globally, nearly 195 million children younger than five years are undernourished. Malnutrition is most obvious in the developing countries, where the condition often takes severe forms: images of emaciated bodies in famine-struck or war-torn regions are tragically familiar. Yet milder forms are more common, especially in developed nations. Indeed, in 1992 an estimated 12 million American children consumed diets that were significantly below the recommended allowances of nutrients established by the National Academy of Sciences.

Scientific American

As the AIDS epidemic begins its second decade, it's time to face some unpleasant realities: AIDS is the No. 1 health problem for men in the United States; it is the leading cause of death of men aged 33–45; it has killed more American men than were lost in the Vietnam War.

Michael S. Kimmel and Martin P. Levine, "AIDS: A Real Man's Disease," *Los Angeles Times*

✦   Using expert opinion

Tennis great Arthur Ashe once noted that a successful player needs quick hands, quick feet, and a quick brain. But while coaches enthusiastically teach the first two, they've pretty much ignored mental quickness. Their rationale: If you're not born with it, you'll never develop it. Not so, insists esteemed sports psychologist Robert Singer, Ph.D. In a study at the University of Florida—sacred to sports buffs as the birthplace of Gatorade—Singer and his colleagues showed that even novices can train their brains to react more quickly.

Psychology Today

✦   Using example

The key, says Singer, is to look for the right cues. Take hockey. As an opposing player prepares to shoot, amateur goalies tend to watch the puck. Seems logical enough, but professional goaltenders focus mostly on the shooter's *stick.* That tells them the puck's probable speed and destination even before the shot is complete. Then there's tennis. When a player who's serving tosses the ball a bit behind him, it's a clue the serve may have lots of spin. A forward serve, though, will probably be flat.

Psychology Today

For Christine Pfeifer, it all began in the bathtub. As a child, every night she would take a bath with her feet over the drain and every night her parents would argue. Then, one evening, she happened to bathe facing the opposite direction. To her amazement, peace prevailed in the household. "After that, I always wanted to take a bath with my feet to the back," she recalls more than three decades later. And though the parental cease-fire didn't hold, Christine's compulsion to bathe backward did. Christine, like so many of us, is superstitious. The dictionary defines superstition as "an irrational belief that something unrelated to the event influences its outcome." But most of us think of it as the kooky thing we do to ensure success or ward off disaster.

Lauren Picker, "With a Little Bit of Luck"

▬ Group Activity ▬▬▬▬▬▬▬▬▬▬▬▬▬▬▬▬▬▬▬▬▬▬▬▬▬▬▬▬▬

With your writing partner or group, identify the topic sentence. Then brainstorm several specific strategies that would develop that topic sentence. These paragraphs are deliberately brief to allow you greater freedom in your thinking.

But man's need for dark spectacle hasn't gone away, and a new generation of entrepreneurs has found a way to allow people to experience the vicarious thrill of the dark, the sleazy, and the tawdry—all without leaving the safety of their homes. The gateway to this dark world is daytime talk shows.

Charles Oliver, "Freak Parade"

McDonald's is bad for your kids. I do not mean the flat patties and the white-flour buns; I refer to the jobs teen-agers undertake, mass-producing these choice items. As many as two-thirds of America's high school juniors and seniors now hold down part-time jobs, according to studies. Many of these are in fast-food chains, of which McDonald's is the pioneer, trend-setter, and symbol. At first, such jobs may seem right out of the Founding Fathers' educational manual for how to bring up self-reliant, work-ethic-driven, productive youngsters. But . . .

Amitai Etzioni, "Working at McDonald's"

People often refer to being "hooked on TV." Does this, too, fall into the lighthearted category of cookie eating and other pleasures that people pursue with unusual intensity, or is there a kind of television viewing that falls into the more serious category of destructive addiction?

Marie Winn, "TV Addiction"

Writing Activity

To practice developing a paragraph with a clear purpose and specific pattern of development and organization, follow the directions below.

1. Most teens admire celebrities (athletes, musicians, movie stars), even if adults don't always share their enthusiasm. Decide on a good or poor celebrity role model for teenagers, and use examples to support your choice.

2. Choose a current phrase or word that would be unknown to your grandmother (and fit to define for her). Explain this word. *Hint:* examples, comparisons, and telling how "it" works are all ways to define and explain.

3. Choose an item that didn't exist in 1955 (for example: CD, Walkman, video games, breadmaking machine, inflatable athletic shoes, cell phone, personal computer). Write a brief letter to someone living then (like a grandparent) and explain the 1990s item in terms of its physical appearance and function.

UNITY AND COHERENCE

Our paragraphs need two other elements to be well written: unity and coherence. Unity refers to everything in a single paragraph staying on a single topic; coherence means that the sentences flow from one to the next in a logical way, with transitions that make it easy for a reader to follow the idea.

Unity

When a paragraph is unified, each sentence relates to the topic sentence or main idea of that paragraph. No stray thought or idea introduced by the writer is there to derail the reader. For example: If a writer were discussing the exorbitant salaries some pro athletes make, and all of a sudden added a sentence about the cost of going to a baseball game, even though one could see that there is some relationship between high salaries and high ticket prices, the paragraph would nonetheless lack unity. Its topic was the salaries—not potential effects of those salaries. Staying on one topic, and one topic only, provides unity.

Notice how these writers stay on topic:

Change is in the sugar-dusted air where little candy hearts have rolled off the same machines every Valentine's Day for generations. This year, messages like "E-mail Me" and "Page Me" have joined standbys like

"Be Mine" on the pastel-colored hearts, while "Hot Stuff" has gone the way of "Groovy" and other outdated catch phrases. The new lines among the 125 phrases stamped on the hearts in red dye also include "Excuse Me" and "Hello." Some of the banished phrases: "Buzz Off," "Stop," "Try Me," "Bad Boy" and "Say Yes."

Richard Lorant, Associated Press

◆ What's the topic of this paragraph?
◆ What word or words keep reminding us of the topic?

How does your body do that? And for heavens sake—why? Take blushes, for example. They're genetic, a legacy from mom or dad. During stress, the mouth gets warm and dry, triggering a "blush" message to the brain. To prevent an embarrassing glow—when you are about to tell a whopper, for example—suck an ice cube. The drop in temperature stops the action. Blushes are just one of the 400 "feelings" or quirky ways your body uses to talk to you, says Dr. Alan P. Xenakis.

Karen S. Peterson, *USA Today*

◆ What is the topic?
◆ How are we reminded of the topic?

Lovers often claim that they feel as though they are being swept away. They are not mistaken; they are literally flooded by chemicals, research suggests. A meeting of eyes, a touch of hands or a whiff of scent sets off a flood that starts in the brain and races along the nerves and through the blood. The results are familiar: flushed skin, sweaty palms, heavy breathing. If love looks suspiciously like stress, the reason is simple: the chemical pathways are identical.

Anastasia Toufexis, "The Right Chemistry"

◆ What is the topic?
◆ How does the writer stay on topic?

Coherence

Staying on the topic is one requirement—but making connections is another. We have to be able to follow the writer's path from one idea to the next. In writing, this path is known as coherence. Although we may not consciously think of coherence when we are reading, especially when the writer has done a good job of providing it, we are jarred when we find it lacking. Sentences that have no words or phrases connecting them to one another are not merely annoying; they may lead to an incomprehensible paragraph. Our brains like order, and in writing, one important way we achieve order is through a variety of strategies that connect our ideas from sentence to sentence and paragraph to paragraph.

Ways to Achieve Coherence

✦   Repetition

We use synonyms and pronouns, and we even repeat the same words to help keep the reader on track.

As you read these two paragraphs, notice how the writer links her ideas:

> **Happily never married? The words** just don't seem to belong together. **They're** an oxymoron, like military music or honest politician. **Never-married women** are supposed to be **needy neurotics** who are frantically hunting down a spouse, **lonely depressives** who hole up with a clutch of cats, or, a more recent image, **icy workaholics** who trade the cozy warmth of husband and home for glitzy high-power careers. No matter how you **look** at **them, they're** unloved, unwanted, unhealthy.
>
> **Take a closer look.** After years of being dismissed and ignored, **the never married** are coming into the spotlight. And much to everyone's surprise, psychologists are discovering that **"happily never married"** rings true as fine crystal.
>
> Anastasia Toufexis, "When the Ring Doesn't Fit . . . "

✦   Bridges

We can move from one sentence to the next by creating a bridge for related ideas:

No matter how you **look** at them, they are unloved, unwanted, and unhealthy. Take a **closer look.**

Toufexis carefully links the final idea of one paragraph with the first idea in the next with the word *look*. She also gives the reader a sense of where she is going by stating "Take a closer look." We are prepared for ideas that contrast the assumption that never-married people are unhappy.

✦   Transition Words

One of the most common ways we link sentences and paragraphs is through transition words. Our readers need words or phrases that help them connect what we just said with what we are now saying. Knowing that a new idea is a contrast or an addition to what comes next, for example, helps us organize our thoughts as readers. For example: Nike makes excellent shoes; **however,** the shoes are overpriced. The transition word alerts us that a contrast is coming. Because transition words are so direct, they are critical in making clear connections in our writing.

As you read the following paragraphs, pay close attention to words and phrases that help you connect the ideas from sentence to sentence.

A BRIEF HISTORY OF DRINKING

In colonial America, drinking was much more prevalent that it is today. Men, women, and children all drank, **and** it was considered acceptable for all to do so. This practice may not seem consistent with our present-day image of the Puritans, **but nevertheless** the Puritans did not object to drinking. **Rather** they considered alcohol one of God's gifts. **Indeed, in those years** alcohol was often safer than unpurified water or milk, **so** the Puritans had a legitimate reason to condone the consumption of alcoholic beverages. What was not acceptable to them was drunkenness. They believed that alcohol, like all things, be used in moderation. **Therefore**, the Puritans established severe prohibitions against drunkenness **but** not against drinking.

Linda Brannon and Jess Feist, "Using Alcohol and Drugs"

WHAT MAKES IT 'POP'?

Ever wonder what makes popcorn pop? Water plays an important role according to the Popcorn Institute. Water is stored in a small circle of soft starch inside each kernel. **As** the water is heated, **so** is the trapped water. Heated water quickly becomes steam, **as** the water molecules expand. The pressure inside the kernel causes the outer hard shell, called the hull, to collapse. **When** the hull collapses, the water expands even further **and** the kernel explodes. **When** the kernel explodes, the soft starch leaps out. The entire kernel turns inside out, **and** the corn has popped. Some Indian tribes had **another** explanation. They believed a tiny demon lived inside each kernel, **and** that the demon's anger caused the popcorn to pop **when** the kernel was subjected to heat.

Karen Herzog, *Milwaukee Journal Sentinel*

Some Common Transition Words

The following are often used for specific connections between one sentence or one paragraph and the next.

- ✦ To mark time: later, now, recently, meanwhile, then, as, when, soon, after, before, first, second, next, the day before

- ✦ To mark direction: on the right/left, behind, in front of, to the side, underneath, close by, far away, opposite, above, below, near

- ✦ To emphasize: obviously, understandably, clearly, certainly, to be sure, indeed, truly

- ✦ To summarize: in brief, in other words, in sum, on the whole

- ✦ To add: and, also, too, moreover, furthermore, in addition, further, in the second place, next, besides, again, as well

- ✦ To contrast: on the other hand, in contrast, however, nevertheless, but, yet, conversely, or, unlike, instead, but, on the contrary

- ✦ To compare: likewise, similarly, in like manner

- ✦ To show result: therefore, then, as a result, because of, due to, accordingly, thus, consequently, so

- ✦ To concede: on the other hand, even so, in spite of, despite, even though, at least, with that in mind

- ✦ To show purpose: for this purpose, therefore, for this reason, because, with this objective, to this end

- ✦ To show condition: although, if, unless, as soon as, though

- ✦ To qualify, limit: in most cases, some, sometimes, mainly, with some exceptions, for the most part, with few exceptions, by and large

- ✦ To give examples: for example, in this case, to illustrate, for instance

---

More Than Just a Word or Phrase

To help our readers make sense of what we write, we often use a combination of ways to provide coherence. As you read the following passage about a major mistake by a major athletic shoe company, note how the writer has led you through the ideas.

REEBOK DOESN'T KNOW WHAT POSSESSED IT . . .

So you're a bunch of highly paid creative types brainstorming a **name** for a new athletic shoe. Michael Jordan? Taken. Chuck Taylor. Taken. **Here's** an idea: **Name** a women's running shoe **Incubus**, after a **mythical demon** that has sex with **women in their sleep**. **Reebok** did. **Now it's** doing some major backpedaling.

[Reebok spokesman] Dave **Fogelson** said in-house marketers came up with **the name** in 1995. **He** said the legal department even researched **the name** to make sure no one else had patented it. **He** didn't know whether anyone bothered to look it up in a **dictionary**. "I cannot imagine any responsible individual knowing what this name means and deciding that it's appropriate," **Fogelson** said. The **dictionary defines "incubus"** as an **evil spirit** that was thought in medieval times to descend upon **women in their sleep** and have sex with them. A **second definition** of the word is simply "nightmare."

It is **not the first time** a major company has goofed over a name. Toyota named a car model after Cressida, a woman in Greek mythology mainly known for being unfaithful to her warrior husband, Troilus, during the Trojan War. **Other missed meanings** occur because of language differences. The classic example is the Chevrolet Nova. *"No va"* is Spanish for "It doesn't go."

Associated Press

◆　How many different coherence strategies did this author use?

◆　How did the author maintain unity?

SPECIAL PARAGRAPHS: BEGINNINGS AND ENDINGS

As you move from writing one paragraph to multiple paragraph essays, you will need to consider your first and final paragraphs as somewhat special: the first and last thoughts to connect and linger with your reader.

Introductory Paragraphs: Engaging Openings

Readers usually make quick judgments about whether or not they want to keep reading—mainly due to how the writer has pulled them into the piece through the introductory paragraph. For that reason, paying attention to a high-interest start is worth the trouble.

Note the strategies these professional writers use:

✦   Ask a Question

FLUFF 'N' STUFF

Hey! What happened to that red string in Band-Aid wrappers? How many different kinds of animals are there in a box of animal crackers? Why are Hostess Cup Cakes now packaged in a plastic tray instead of on the time-honored cardboard base? And why do Hostess Twinkies still come on cardboard? Why isn't anyone else asking these questions?

To fill the void, to discover these and other essential corporate truths, I turned to the unsung heroes of the American economic machine: the customer service people at the other end of the 800-number phone lines. There I found both enlightenment and entertainment: these underpaid, underappreciated, toll-free toilers know almost everything.

Paul Lukas, "Fluff 'n' Stuff"

DANGLING MODIFIERS

Question: What does the typical teenage mall rat of today have in common with the great noblemen of Renaissance Europe? Answer: Not much, except for the belief that earrings look just as cool on a guy as on a girl. Distraught parents may be loath to admit it, but their son's earring has a far longer and more distinguished fashion pedigree than that pair of chinos he won't wear.

Civilization

✦   Quotation

LOVE (SONGS) AMONG THE RUINS

"Love don't make things nice. It ruins everything. It breaks your heart. It makes things a mess. We aren't here to make things perfect. The snowflakes are perfect. The stars are perfect. Not us. Not us. We are here to ruin ourselves and to break our hearts and love the wrong people and die." Despite Hallmark Cards' and pop radio's efforts to convince us otherwise, that philosophy, as issued by Nicolas Cage to Cher in *Moonstruck,* is pretty much the way things are down here on terra firma.

Jim Walsh, *St. Paul Pioneer Press*

◆ Name Recognition

CROSS-DRESSING FOR SUCCESS

Dennis Rodman [pro basketball player], it turns out, wasn't the first public figure to see benefits in cross-dressing. Long before Rodman scored a PR coup by squeezing into a wedding dress, Hatchepsut, female king of Egypt, indulged in a little gender bending to the great benefit of her career.

Civilization

◆ Using Statistics

ROOTLESSNESS

Americans are a rootless people. Each year one in six of us changes residences; one in four of us changes jobs. We see nothing troubling in these statistics. For most of us, they merely reflect the restless energy that made America great. A nation of immigrants, unsurprisingly, celebrates those willing to pick up stakes and move on: the frontiersman, the cowboy, the entrepreneur, the corporate raider.

David Morris, "Rootlessness"

KIDS MUST STOP BANKING ON SPORTS

Let's start with the topic. According to a Northeastern University study published this week in a national news magazine, 66 percent of African-American youths between 13 and 18 believe they can earn a living playing professional sports. That's two out of every three. That's more than twice the percentage of white kids who believe the same thing. Is it true?

Gary Washburn, *St. Paul Pioneer Press*

◆ Description

FOR MY INDIAN DAUGHTER

My little girl is singing herself to sleep upstairs, her voice mingling with the sounds of the birds outside in the old maple tree. She is two, and I am nearly 50, and I am very taken with her. She came along late in my life, unexpected and unbidden, a startling gift.

Lewis P. Johnson, "For My Indian Daughter"

✦ Language Devices

JELL-O TURNS 100

It shimmers, It bobbles. It wriggles so unpredictably that it seems guided by its own personal laws of physics. But once you accept the mystery qualities of this odder-than-odd substance, one indisputable fact remains: Jell-O is America's most beloved dessert.

David Lyman, *Wisconsin State Journal*

TOY STORY

Female firefighters, diapering dads: adults are slowly escaping the confines of traditional sex roles. But when it comes to kids' toys, gender stereotypes still rule.

Psychology Today

✦ A Revealing Anecdote

WHEN SIBLINGS ARE UNLIKE PEAS IN A POD

Mark Twain was a bit of a hell-raiser as a boy, always getting into scrapes that frustrated and exasperated his long-suffering mother. His younger brother, Henry, was the opposite, a sweet, docile child who did everything that was expected of him. In *The Adventures of Tom Sawyer,* Twain made delightful use of this difference between siblings, portraying Tom as even more of a hellion than he had been, and casting Tom's half-brother Sid as the kind of righteous goody two-shoes that every spirited child loves to hate. The 19th century humorist and author was focusing on a phenomenon that continues to baffle psychologists today: why siblings, who share 50 percent of their parents' genes and are raised in the same family, sometimes grow up to be so different.

Alison Bass, "When Siblings Are Unlike Peas in a Pod"

✦ An Unusual Piece of Information or Revelation

HOW DO YOU LIKE THE N.B.A. NOW, KOBE BRYANT?

He was named after a pampered Japanese cow that is not allowed to range freely, is fed beer and soybeans to make it fat and is massaged with sake [a liquor] daily by human hands to break down its muscle and distribute its fat. This makes the cow's meat so exquisitely tender that when it is slaughtered at an early age, a steak from that cow costs more than $100 a pound.

> Kobe (pronounced KO-bee) Bryant is 6 foot 6 and weighs 200 pounds. He is a handsome, sinewy youth with a shaved head, impish features and a charming smile—accompanied by a delicate flutter of his eyelashes. He has a deferential slouch and skin the color of caramel. In June, Bryant, playing guard for the Los Angeles Lakers, became one of only six players to be drafted into the NBA from high school without at least a year's stop at college. At 18, he is worth more than $4 million, which makes him, pound for pound, more valuable than the cow his parents named him after.
>
> Pat Jordan, *New York Times Magazine*

Avoid These Openings

Just as good introductory paragraphs pull us in, others send us away in search of a different essay or article. Here are some openings to avoid:

- ✦ **The Platitude.**   An essay that begins with "The human life cycle inspires awe" or "We can only wonder at the survival skills of ancient peoples" or "Music is important to our lives" is an essay that probably won't excite or inspire readers—despite most readers agreeing with the writer.

- ✦ **The Unwanted, Unnecessary Fact.**   An essay on John F. Kennedy and the Bay of Pigs should not start out with "John F. Kennedy, who served as President of the United States . . . ". The reader already knows that.

- ✦ **The Boring Definition.**   An essay on an educational trend known as "back to the basics" needs more than "Back to the basics is an educational trend that favors drill." Although the statement is true, it certainly wouldn't hook anyone into more reading.

- ✦ **The Apology.**   An essay that begins "Darwin's theory of evolution is more complex than people think, but I will try to explain it" does not gain the reader's confidence!

- ✦ **The Excuse.**   A tactic that may seem clever to the writer may backfire and annoy both reader and instructor, probably fatally. "Although I began this essay (or research) mere hours ago, I believe I have found . . . " Whether it is honest or sheer manipulation, this opening will doom the essay.

Beyond the "Hook" in Introductory Paragraphs

You have been exploring opening paragraphs from the perspective of "hooking" the reader, creating interest that draws a reader in. But introductory paragraphs must do more than simply create interest; they must provide a clear idea of what the piece is all about. You will work with this requirement in later chapters when you work with expository and argumentative writing, but briefly, here are the other elements of good introductions:

✦ **A controlling idea or thesis statement.**   A controlling idea might be considered a "giant topic sentence." Where the topic sentence guides a single paragraph, the controlling idea guides the entire piece. For example:

The human brain, according to an emerging new body of scientific research, **comes in two different varieties, maybe as different as the accompanying physique.**

Nicholas Wade, "How Men and Women Think"

In the essay, Wade considers whether biological differences between men and women really exist, and if they do, could they cause behavioral differences. His controlling idea, then, sets the stage for this exploration of male/female brains.

Pamela Weintraub also explores this question, but she makes an assertion—a thesis statement:

Are the brains of men and women different? If so, do men and women differ in abilities, talents, and deficiencies? A scientific answer to these questions could affect society and culture, and variously shock, intrigue, delight, depress, and reassure people of both sexes. Now an answer is coming into sight: **Yes, male and female brains do differ.**

Discover

We most often use a thesis statement when we wish to argue a point. Weintraub, interestingly, writing 13 years earlier, states a position. Wade, by contrast, explores a possibility.

David L. Evans, a college admissions officer, writes about the lack of black males in his college's applicant pool. Notice his thesis statement:

What is happening to these young men? Who or what is influencing them? **I submit that the absence of male role models and slanted television images of black males have something to do with it.**

"The Wrong Examples"

Evans is very clear in his assertion that gender differences in college enrollment is linked to two major factors. His essay, then, would make the case.

◆   **A brief blueprint.**   As readers, we generally want to know what's ahead. The opening paragraph (or in a longer piece, paragraphs) provides us with a blueprint.

Anatasia Toufexis not only has an engaging opening but also provides a controlling idea that is a blueprint to "The Right Chemistry."

O.K., let's cut out all this nonsense about romantic love. Let's bring some scientific precision to the party. Let's put love under a microscope.

When rigorous people with PhDs after their names do that, what they see is not some silly, senseless thing. No, their probe reveals that **love rests firmly on the foundations of evolution, biology, and chemistry.** What seems on the surface to be irrational, intoxicated behavior is in fact part of nature's master strategy—a vital force that has helped humans survive, thrive, and multiply through thousands of years. Says Michael Mills, a psychology professor at Loyola Marymount University in Los Angeles: "Love is our ancestors whispering in our ears."

Time

We are prepared for Toufexis's discussion of love as the product of human evolution, human biology, and human chemical processes. With her lively style, we also get a sense that the discussion is going to be fun.

◆   **Context.**   Introductory paragraphs also provide us with a social, cultural, or political context for what will follow. We don't write in a vacuum; people, places, events, and ideas stimulate us to write about them. But we have to share that background with our readers, that is, bring them into the essay with a good sense of where we are or how we got there, or why something compels us to write. We may also have to provide background information that sets the stage for what we will say.

Kerry Leigh Ellison provides such a context in "Satan in the Library: Are Children in Danger?"

Last Halloween, in New Castle, Pennsylvania, school librarian Nancy Prentice faced accusations of practicing satanism after she read the folk ballad "Tam Lin" to a group of fifth graders. A few months later, library aide Debbie Denzer of Kalispell, Montana, lost her job for lending her own books on the history of witchcraft to two seventh grade girls. The single largest category of book challenges last year consisted of religious objections, primarily the mention of witchcraft, satanism, and the occult. Are our children in danger from books on satanism, Halloween, magic, and New Age religions?

School Library Journal

Concluding Paragraphs

In addition to starting well, we need to finish well. Most readers carry away the final thoughts, not the entire piece. The concluding paragraph is important to that process. Many of the strategies for developing a good introductory paragraph also work well in the final paragraph. But it is particularly important that readers not only latch onto the main point of the essay once more but also extend their thinking beyond that single essay. Further, we want to provide our reader with a satisfying closure, a feeling of "Gee, I'm glad I read this."

Notice how these authors end their essays, leaving us with a single important idea and compelling us to extend our thinking about that idea. Although you do not have the essay itself, examine these conclusions for the main idea the author wants his or her readers to remember, as well as for the extension of that idea, the larger implication.

DOES ONE SCENT FIT ALL?

So are sexually ambiguous scents here to stay? Probably for a while. But then, we'll undoubtedly come to our senses and want to smell unique.

Christine C. Summer, *Psychology Today*

✦ What was the subject of Summer's essay?

✦ What is her point? Her attitude? How do you know?

THE BLACK AND WHITE TRUTH ABOUT BASKETBALL

And what makes basketball the most intriguing of sports is how these styles do not necessarily clash; how the punishing intensity of "white" players and the dazzling moves of the "blacks" can fit together, a fusion of cultures that seems more and more difficult in the world beyond the out-of-bounds line.

Jeff Greenfield, *Esquire*

✦ What had Greenfield explored in his essay?

✦ How does he move from basketball to a much larger social issue in this paragraph?

THE MEANING OF A WORD

So there must have been dozens of times that *nigger* was spoken in front of me before I reached the third grade. But I didn't "hear" it until it was said by a small pair of lips that had already learned it could be a way to humiliate me. That was the word I went home and asked my mother about. And since she knew that I had to grow up in America, she took me in her lap and explained.

Gloria Naylor, "The Meaning of a Word" [Editor's title]

- ◆ What is Naylor's topic?
- ◆ How does she, like Greenfield, extend the reader's thinking on this topic?

Avoid These Attitudes

- ◆ **The Wimp.**   Never apologize for what you have just written. If you can't stand behind what you have said, better not to say it. An apology will leave readers wondering why you bothered to write the piece.

- ◆ **The Braggart.**   Never brag about what you have presented, (i.e., the knowledge that you have accumulated and presented). Your reader, will be annoyed. And an annoyed reader is likely to tear apart what you have said and find fault even when there is no reason to.

Avoid These Conclusions

- ◆ **The Image in the Mirror.**   Don't simply repeat what you said in the opening paragraph or repeat the main point of every body paragraph. This type of conclusion is boring, mechanical, and unnecessary.

- ◆ **The Dust Bin.**   Don't gather every bit of information you couldn't use in the essay and throw it into the final paragraph, as though it's just too good to leave in the dust, too good to sweep away and discard. Your final paragraph should not contain new information or bits and pieces that didn't fit in anywhere else.

- ◆ **The Bold Claim.**   Don't leap beyond the information and evidence presented; don't make a bold claim that is only marginally true or not supported by the essay.

◆   **The Fade.**   Don't end with a "tired out/out of time" or a "gee, there's a lot more out there that I could have said" paragraph. Be confident in what you have presented, and conclude with a strong, upbeat (and interesting) conclusion.

◆   **The End.**   Do you recall as a little kid writing "The End" as your only conclusion to every piece of writing? Most of us did that, and most teachers and parents smiled as they read it. As an adult, however, you can't simply stop, put a neon "The End" in place, and expect readers to accept it. Avoid abrupt conclusions, ones that leave the reader thinking "hey, what happened here?"

Effective Conclusions

Effective conclusions

◆   bring ideas together without repeating them.

◆   offer insight into the topic or issue.

◆   make a point.

◆   make us think.

◆   let us know if action is warranted.

◆   give a sense of satisfaction.

Tying Initial and Final Paragraphs Together

When you write an essay of several paragraphs, bringing your reader "full circle" is important. That is, we want the beginning and end to tie together—without repeating exactly what we said in our opening or simply repeating our main idea for the essay. Each of the pairs below represents the first and final paragraph of an essay. As you read, pay close attention to the various ways in which these writers take us "full circle." Also notice the strategies that pull us in or bring closure.

THE RIGHT CHEMISTRY

O.K., let's cut out all this nonsense about romantic love. Let's bring some scientific precision to the party. Let's put love under the microscope.

. . .

O.K., that's the scientific point of view. Satisfied? Probably not. To most people—with or without PhDs—love will always be more than the sum of its natural parts. It's a comingling of body and soul, reality and imagination, poetry and phenylethylamine. In our deepest hearts, most of us harbor the hope that love will never fully yield up its secrets, that it will always elude our grasp.

Anastasia Toufexis, *Time*

✦ List the grammatical similarities in words or sentences that tie both paragraphs together.

✦ How does Toufexis get our interest in the first paragraph?

✦ How are we left with some important thoughts about love?

"MOMMY, WHAT DOES NIGGER MEAN?"

I remember the first time I heard the word nigger. In my third-grade class, our math tests were being passed down the rows, and as I handed the papers to a little boy in back of me, I remarked that once again he had received a much lower mark than I did. He snatched his test from me and spit out that word. . . .

. . .

So there must have been dozens of times that the word "nigger" was spoken in front of me before I reached the third grade. But I didn't "hear" it until it was said by a small pair of lips that had already learned it could be a way to humiliate me. That was the word I went home and asked my mother about. And since she knew I had to grow up in America, she took me in her lap and explained.

Gloria Naylor, *New York Times*

✦ List specific words that link the two paragraphs together.

✦ What strategy is Naylor using to bring us into her essay's topic?

✦ How does her final paragraph lead us into the larger social issue?

ZIPPED LIPS

Earlier this month a fellow named Sam Young was fired from his grocery-store job for wearing a Green Bay Packers T-shirt. All right, this was Dallas, and it was a little insensitive to flaunt the enemy team's logo on the weekend of the N.F.C. championship game, but Young was making the common assumption that if you stay away from obscenity, libel, or perhaps in this case, the subject of groceries, it is a free country, isn't it? Only problem was he had not read the First Amendment carefully enough: It says *government* cannot abridge freedom of expression. Private employers can, on a whim, and they do so every day.

. . .

When employers have rights and employees don't, democracy itself is at risk. It isn't easy to spend the day in a state of servile subjugation and then emerge, at five P.M., as Mr. or Ms. Citizen-Activist. Unfreedom undermines the critical spirit, and suck-ups make lousy citizens.

Barbara Ehrenreich, *Time*

✦   What is the specific link between these two paragraphs?

✦   What strategy has Ehrenreich used to get us interested in the topic?

✦   What strategy has she used to give us a sense of closure?

LOVING YOUR ENEMY

The last time I saw my father, he had his eyes closed and his hands across his chest. He was in the middle of a dank room with frayed wall-to-wall carpeting and a dim overhead light. My father was stretched out inside a large four-ply cardboard box, a white sheet folded to the center of his chest. He had been dead less than 48 hours and in three hours would be cremated.

. . .

I stood in the center of the room, alone with my father, my back and chest wet with sweat. Five more hesitant steps and I was staring once again at his silent features. I bit my lower lip and fought back the tears. I held the side of the cardboard box and shook my head.

"You bastard," I said to my father. "You dirty bastard."

Then I sank to my knees and cried over the body of the one man I loved more than any other.

Lorenzo Caraterra, *New York Times Magazine*

✦   List specific words or phrases that tie the paragraphs together.

✦   How has Caraterra captured our attention in both paragraphs?

LET KIDS BE KIDS, ADULTS BE ADULTS

It's time to go back to gas chandeliers and believing the world is flat. Things are getting too crazy around here. We need to return to stepping into horse plops instead of diesel spills or reading Poe by candlelight instead of watching cheap horror flicks on TV. . . .

. . .

Someone needs to advocate to allow children to just be. Be muddy, silly, loud and annoying. Be masters of make-believe and baby talk. Be innocent and unaware. Be immature. And if we have to fall off the edge of the Earth to do it, I say we set sail immediately.

Terry Norton, *St. Paul Pioneer Press*

✦   List the specific historical reference that links the two paragraphs.

✦   How has Norton used repetition in the final paragraph to create memorable lines?

Titles: An Invitation to Read

Although the title may be the very last line you write for your essay, it is the very first line anyone reads. As such, it is immensely important. You want to project a sense of "this is an interesting topic" or "I know something pretty interesting—come and find out what it is." The title is also the first clue to your essay's content—helping readers get into the subject, and even know your attitude toward that subject, immediately.

Activity: Evaluate the following titles for (1) interest, (2) preview of essay content, (3) attitude, and (4) tone. See if you can figure out the topic before checking the key.

1. The Hole Story

2. Baby Fat or Baby Fate?

3. Take Two Schnauzers and Call Me in the Morning

4. A Brief History of the Male Bimbo

5. Rare Lair

6. Lowdown on Rubdowns

7. Skin Deep

8. Get a Rug, Julius

9. Wired for Profit

10. The Brain Gain

11. Dr. Tinkertoy

12. Chomp Champ
13. The Butterfly Solution
14. The Tarzan Syndrome
15. The Curse of QWERTY

And the topics are . . .

1. Body piercing
2. Fat as genetic
3. Dogs as pets are better than medicine
4. A historical look at males who fit the classic female "bimbo" label
5. Profile of pet store specializing in snakes
6. Classification and explanation of massage
7. Tattoos
8. Male baldness, with allusion to Julius Caesar
9. Profile of student business making fake I.D.s
10. Multiple intelligences, not just IQ
11. Profile of scientist working with DNA
12. Strength of T. Rex's bite
13. Suggestion that scientists look at natural solutions to technological problems
14. Concept of self-awareness setting humans apart from apes
15. Bad design of typewriter (and computer) keyboard letter placement.

A title should provide "truth in advertising." Readers may resent "My Life Behind Bars" turning out to be a summer working at the local tavern. Similarly, they would probably be offended if a serious topic, such as AIDS, had a frivolous or flippant title like "Being a Piece of the Quilt." A title like "The AIDS Quilt: Squares of Memory, Squares of Love," however, would convey the subject, the tone, and the attitude of the writer. With a light-hearted subject, however, a light-hearted title is not only appropriate, but desirable.

Finding Titles

One of the most obvious places to find the title is right in your essay. A strong or interesting phrase or dominant theme or idea may serve as a good title. You might also find a quotation either directly related to your subject or in some way illustrative of your main idea. Or playing with language—rhyme, for example—might give you just the right title. A proverb or common saying is another source.

Activity: Review the titles accompanying the paragraphs in this chapter. Choose those that you believe are most and least interesting, most and least helpful to the reader; in small group, see how your choices (and rationale for choosing) match up.

FROM PARAGRAPH TO ESSAY

Sometimes you will write a single paragraph, and all by itself, it forms a complete essay: you have expressed what you wanted to, but briefly. That often happens with essay examinations, where making the point quickly and accurately results in a single-paragraph response. However, more often in school writing, you will be asked to develop and explore your ideas in a longer piece. All that has been said about writing single paragraphs applies to writing a piece with two or more paragraphs:

✦ Develop a good topic sentence for each paragraph.

✦ Provide good development/support for topic sentence.

✦ Have a good organizational plan and follow it.

✦ Ensure unity and coherence.

One major change, however, involves developing a good controlling idea or thesis statement for the entire essay. The topic sentence of each paragraph then fills out the controlling idea or thesis. We will talk more about developing a good controlling idea or thesis statement for the entire essay in Chapter 5. For now, we'll just look at the overall pattern of a multiparagraph essay.

The overall plan for an essay is essentially a blueprint, a visual outline that tells us what to cover and in what order. Using a blueprint for a single-paragraph essay is similarly important; the blueprint will help ensure that the point we want to make is supported with sufficient and relevant examples, details, or reasons. A visual outline also forces us to think about the best order for this information: most important first or last? which example first? chronologically accurate? The time spent in planning is some of the most important time we give to a writing task.

However, in order to ensure that we move from our plan to a good paragraph or essay, we have to pay attention to the writing processes themselves. There's no question that we have to come up with a good written product—it is, after all, what we are evaluated on—but that product will only be as good as the processes that generated it.

Introductory Paragraph

Controlling Idea: Students who work more than 20 hours a week often find themselves in academic trouble.

Body Paragraph 1
Topic Sentence: Time at work means time away from general study.
Support: Fewer hours of reading just to keep up with lectures. No time to meet with study groups or informal work with peers.

Body Paragraph 2
Topic Sentence: Work hours interfere with research and library time.
Support: Research requires sustained time, not scattered hours. Library hours and professional staff are limited.

Body Paragraph 3
Topic Sentence: Time for exam preparation or paper-writing is limited.
Support: Exams generally turn up at the same time in several courses. Writing papers requires time for multiple drafts.

Body Paragraph 4
Topic Sentence: Dividing time between work and school usually results in a lack of sleep, lack of energy and concentration, and stress.
Support: Start missing classes. Inattentive when in class. Overwhelmed by assignments and exams.

Closing Paragraph

CHAPTER 4

Understanding the Writing Process

We have been looking at how writing is structured—those basic elements of paragraph and essay design. However, even a well-crafted paragraph and essay won't be appreciated if we don't have interesting things to say in them. Generating and developing interesting things to say involves a series of processes, and within them, various strategies to help you work efficiently. There's no argument that writing is hard work, but we make that work easier when we have both an understanding of all the processes involved and specific strategies that work for us. The writing processes—generating, drafting, revising, and editing—are basic to every piece of academic writing, large or small. And each has its own set of strategies to make the task more manageable. We will explore them in this chapter, but first we will look at the heart of a writing task: why we write, to whom we write, and what context or situation frames our writing. When you determine your purpose, audience, and context, you will have a framework in which to place your ideas. Thus, these three basic considerations will be our starting point.

UNDERSTANDING PURPOSE, AUDIENCE, AND CONTEXT

If someone asked why you are writing, your first response might be something to this effect: "Because I have to." With school tasks, we often feel that way! However, a second response to that question would probably indicate a specific need to communicate something to someone. In brief, you'd have a purpose, an audience, and a context for writing. These would help you decide what to include, as well as what your tone and language would be like. For example, a note telling a friend to meet you or one telling a roommate to clean up the kitchen would probably illustrate different tones and language choices. Similarly, a note telling your boss why you were late for work would illustrate yet another tone. In the workplace, a report on the effectiveness of a certain machine has different requirements than a report outlining customer dissatisfaction with a product. When we write, then, we consider purpose, audience, and context:

Purpose   Why we write; what we want to accomplish in this piece of writing.

Audience   To or for whom we write; our readers.

Context   The situation or place in which our writing will be understood; academic, work, cultural, political, social, and so on.

But regardless of why and for whom we write, we have to ask and answer a basic set of questions:

✦   What do I want to accomplish in this piece?

✦   What will readers expect from me?

✦   What will readers already know? Need to know?

✦   How will I develop my ideas?

✦   How will I organize my ideas?

✦   How much information is enough?

✦   How much information is excessive?

✦   What information is my best information?

✦   Do I need outside resources?

✦   What language is most appropriate?

✦   What tone is most appropriate?

✦   How will readers get a sense of me, the writer?

These are practical questions. The answers to them reflect some of the choices we make as we work through the writing process. Our purpose may make some choices for us. For example, if a job application requires a cover letter, I would know that I must explain clearly and briefly both why I want this job and why I should be considered for it. I would also know I have to use formal language and a standard business letter format, as well as Standard Written English spelling, usage, and mechanics. However, I would still have other questions to answer: How much information about me is enough, and how should I organize it? Every time we write, we make decisions that guide the development of that piece of writing. And every piece of writing shares questions of purpose, audience, and context—even within a common form such as newswriting.

ANALYZING THE NEWS

As you examine the news pieces that follow, determine the purpose of each. Also consider the audience: (1) What assumptions can you make about the audience? (2) Does it make any difference if the reader's social or cultural background differs from the writer's? (3) What do readers expect and why? Finally, consider the questions that each writer had to ask and answer; how successful was each news writer?

Two Mexican Adventures

CONGRATULATIONS!!!

You have been selected to receive one of the following exciting holidays of your choice:

A Mexican Vacation that includes 2 round trip Airfare and Hotel accommodations for 2
(Not Including Meals)

Your Choice of Mazalan, Puerto Vuarta, Cancun
(Suggested Retail Value $1,100.00)

YOU MUST CALL WITHIN 72 HOURS to claim your holiday.

Call toll free
1-800-232-0000
Monday–Friday 9:00 A.M.–9:00 P.M. Eastern Standard Time

Rules: No Purchase Necessary. Must be at least 18 years old. Some restrictions apply.

A.   What is the stated purpose of this "good luck" piece of writing? Are there other purposes involved? How do you know? What is the writer counting on from the reader?

_____

_____

_____

B.   As a reader, how do you feel about a company that is offering you a trip to a place whose name it cannot spell correctly (Mazalan = Mazatlán? Puerto Vuarta = Puerto Vallarta? Is this a case where

Standard Written English (or Spanish) makes a significant difference in effect and confidence?

_____

_____

_____

C. What information is given? Lacking?

_____

_____

_____

D. Does this piece of writing accomplish its purpose?

_____

_____

_____

Mexico also figures in the next example. However, the context changes radically, and our view of "Mexico" shifts to a critical descriptive word. How many of us would recognize a Mexican redhead parrot? Or would it be enough to simply know "parrot"?

—— REWARD ——

On August 13 a Mexican Redhead Parrot was stolen from Tropic Waters Pet Center. $200.00 Reward for information leading to a conviction.

Please call:
839-4706 Steve
OR
832-0174

TROPIC WATERS PET CENTER

A. What is the writer's purpose?

_____

_____

_____

B. Did the writer provide enough information in this piece? What questions do you as a reader have? Do you really need them answered or are you just curious?

_____

_____

_____

The British Act and Speak Out

Next determine how these two pieces of British "news" provide insights into purpose, audience, and context.

SARAH GIVES HUSBAND ROYAL ROASTING

London—A paint bucket, a pair of shears, and a grudge against her prospective ex-husband have made a celebrity of Lady Sarah Graham-Moon.

Lady Sarah, who is divorcing Sir Peter Graham-Moon after 25 years of marriage, says she has dumped paint over her husband's BMW and trimmed four inches off the left sleeves of 32 of his suits in the past few weeks.

She also confessed to anyone who inquired that she had distributed 70 prime bottles from his wine cellar around the village of East Garston, about 60 miles west of London.

Sir Peter has said nothing, and the police said no complaints had been lodged.

A. Although the general purpose of newswriting is to inform, what do you think the writer of this piece intended?

_____

_____

_____

B. Did you enjoy this piece? Why? Did the specific pieces of information the writer chose to include provide a certain effect? What if the writer had included only the incident about dumping paint? Would the effect be the same?

_____

_____

_____

Now consider this excerpt from a letter from the vice chairman of the Cambridge Women's Luncheon Club:

> Our first lunch will be on Wednesday 10th October, at the University Arms, when Dr. Colin Lattimore, a very eminent and knowledgeable Speaker will tell us about the History of the Longcase Clock.
>
> After much heartsearching we have decided to revert to a three course sit-down lunch with a more varied menu of higher quality. The buffet did not prove to be popular with everyone, and in the interests of peace and harmony, the Hotel has agreed that the entire lunch will be silver served.
>
> Do please make sure that one of the officers is informed of absence at least 48 hours before the lunch, otherwise a place will be laid for you and a meal provided. Empty seats are so daunting to a speaker.
>
> I hope you will enjoy our new programme and that the luncheons will provide you with the opportunity to make some new friends and maybe startle your family with your newfound knowledge.

A. How do you envision the audience for this letter? When you write a letter, do you have a mental picture of your audience? How does knowing your audience help the writing process?

_____

_____

_____

B. What is the letter's obvious purpose? Could there be a more hidden purpose or agenda? What makes you think so? Have you ever received a letter in which you did as much reading between the lines as reading of actual lines?

_____

_____

_____

C. How does the language match the audience and purpose? In letters you may have written or received, has the language been appropriate to the purpose and audience, namely you? How does the tone of this letter strike you? What does tone have to do with purpose and audience?

_____

_____

_____

D. Although they are generally understood by speakers of both languages, American and British English are not identical. What differences do you notice in the letter? What do they suggest to you as a speaker of American English? Can writing represent or suggest our cultural upbringing? Does tone sometimes relate to the culture of the writer?

_____

_____

_____

Dear Ann Landers

Now examine the following letter written to advice columnist Ann Landers. Before you read it, quickly run through what you already know about purpose: Why do people write to a distant advice columnist? What kind of response might they expect? What do you know about Ann Landers? Can you anticipate the type of response she might give? Does she have any advantages when she writes a response? For example, can she draw on experts or research to help her?

Dear Ann Landers:

Are people becoming more insensitive, more vicious, crueler and maybe crazier as time goes by? I wonder where mankind is heading when I read about the hideous things that are happening all around us. For example:

A lawyer in Maryland pleaded guilty to breaking into the home of a friend's estranged wife to look for documents that had to do with the couple's divorce. He encountered the family kitten running loose in the kitchen, became annoyed by the "nuisance underfoot," picked up the kitten and tossed it into the microwave. He then "accidentally" turned the oven on. Of course the poor little thing died instantly.

When the woman discovered the kitten she was horrified. The man was prosecuted for this heinous act and pleaded guilty. His defense was that he had been drinking and "wasn't thinking straight." The penalty— are you ready for this?—probation!

What is this world coming to when a person can break into a home, nuke the family pet and not be punished? Again I ask, are people becoming crueler, more vicious and crazier?

—Richmond, VA

• • •

Before you read Ann Landers' response, think about how you would respond. Do you have all the information you need in order to make an appropriate response? What would you want to learn before responding? How would you get the information you need? What would be your purpose in responding to Richmond? What do you know about her or him from the letter?

_____

_____

_____

_____

Dear Rich:

Check the Bible and you will find that the cruel, vicious and crazy have been among us for a long time. Because of the advances in communication, however, we not only hear about atrocities the moment they happen but get instant replay in our living rooms on TV. Now back to that poor cat. My friends at the *Baltimore Sun* informed me that the lawyer was sentenced to one year in prison, which was then suspended, given 18 months probation, required to receive alcohol counseling and do 40 hours of community service and fined $1000 plus court costs. He also faces disbarment proceedings.

...

Meet the Bride and Groom

We've been looking at these diverse pieces of writing with an eye and ear for their purpose, audience, and context. In other words, we want to know why a piece was written, for whom it was written, and the situation that helps us make sense of this type of writing. We have also looked at specific language and tone in some of the pieces. How is language the product of both purpose and audience? What do writers reveal about themselves in their choice of language? Examine the two wedding announcement pieces with that question in mind. Do we learn as much about the writer as about the bride and groom?

WEDDING 1

"VALLEY" SPEAK BRINGS THEM TOGETHER

Eeeww, like, totally awesome. Faye Cregger met Victor Velasquez by accepting a double dare to walk up to him and talk to him in "valley" speak, which spoofs the way some California teen-age girls speak.

Like, ya'know. Faye wasn't expecting too much of a response. "To my surprise, he spoke back in valley talk," she said. "Weeks after meeting him, I found out that he had just learned to valley talk two days before we met."

In addition to their shared linguistic skills, the couple said they make a good pair because they're both short, "which makes us very compatible. At least it helps when kissing."

Victor proposed in 1990 on his birthday, Nov. 28, while they were out for dinner.

They were married Feb. 15 in St. Patrick's Catholic Church, Doylestown. They had a Mexican/American wedding with a few Mexican traditions.

WEDDING 2

Laura Bartell and Stanley Harr were married on Feb. 29 in the First Unitarian Society Meeting House, Madison, The Rev. Max Gaebler and Judge Angela Bartell, the bride's sister-in-law, officiated.

The bride is a partner in the international law firm of Shearman & Sterling, working in its Manhattan office. The daughter of Joyce Bartell and the late Gerald Bartell, she is an honors graduate of Stanford University and of Harvard University Law School, where she was on the *Law Review*.

The bridegroom taught music in the Madison Public Schools for 25 years, principally at West High School. He graduated from North Central College in Naperville, Ill., where his late father was dean of the theological seminary. He also has a master's degree in music education from UW-Madison.

A. Although the purpose, audience, and context are determined by the fact that both these pieces are public wedding announcements, how has each writer provided a thoroughly individual announcement? What is the effect of each on you as a reader?

_____

_____

_____

B. Does your personal preference of writing style affect how you responded to each piece? Does your background influence how you respond?

_____

_____

_____

Making a Match

Again, note how purpose and audience influence choice of language in these pieces of writing. Does gender or age appear to make any difference in the type of information provided? Do you think geography has any influence on the information?

FROM A SOUTHERN CALIFORNIA NEWSPAPER

Able bodied 33, tall and good looking and fit physically and mentally. Seeks in shape lady for exercising, bicycling, the beach, summer fun and romance.

Attractive, intelligent, philosopher college student, mystic, misfit, introvert, 25 in North County. Seeking similar/interested lady, 18–25, to spend time with.

East County urban cowboy looking for urban cowgirl 40–48, country western dancing. Live East County. Fishing, camping, like classic vehicles. Blue eyes, 5'10", 175 lbs. white (shy).

Here's the good stuff. I'm handsome, tall (6'1"), fit (180 lbs), strawberry blond (and not losing it), green eyes (two), self-employed and secure (no debt). Christian, can cook. Interests include art, antiques, football and lots of golf. Now for the other stuff: I smoke and drink and use profanity on occasion. I'm a perfectionist but not perfect. I work too much, and care too much. I'm notorious for running away to Mexico on short notice, If you are a very attractive, Intelligent woman (28–33) that is happy with yourself, share similar interests and realities and have no children, you probably don't exist! But if you do, I would enjoy meeting you!

Vegetarian goddess, seeking confident 6'+ Pices-Cancer-Capricorn (higher consciousness). I'm vivacious, sensual, shapely, holistic, metaspiritual, intense, deep, playful, young, happy, Intelligent, multifaceted. Let's fly!

FROM A COLLEGE ALUMNI MAGAZINE

NYC lady, 60-ish, youthful, vibrant. Enjoys adventures, travels, city/country pleasures. Searching for harmony with healthy, intelligent, witty man with zest.

LA arts professional, attractive 50s. Serene, loving. Seeks single male, integrity, achievement.

Widower. Early 60s. Interests include Boston Symphony, Harvard football, tennis, theatre, travel. Democratic politics. Seeking nonsmoking woman with similar interests.

Journalist/artist, 60s, male, NYC. Children grown, politics left, music classical. 5'8", high energy, successful, happy. Seeks lovable, intellectual, active woman to share the rest of our lives.

FROM A MIDWEST METROPOLITAN NEWSPAPER

Intelligent, young, handsome, successful European 6'2", 190, seeks commitment-oriented woman, to 28, prefer blonde, red, light brown hair, blue eyes, sturdy full build, household-oriented with strong desire for having children. Exceptional opportunity for sincere, serious woman. No cigarette smokers.

I am a single white professional female, age 28. Do you enjoy long walks through the suburbs, shopping at Target [a discount store] on Sunday afternoons, fine dining at the Embers [low-cost restaurant not known for its decor or chef], and discussing cars? Do you find the music of Barry Manilow inspiring? If so, please do not reply.

A.   How does the language of these ads convey a sense of personality?

_____

_____

_____

B.   Would you be tempted to respond to any of them? Why or why not?

_____

_____

_____

People often make fun of matchmaking ads. But as a piece of writing, they are as legitimate and important to their writers as any other piece of writing. What's more, the ads demand careful attention to language. Every word counts heavily in the message and impression it creates. Other considerations such as the effect of humor or satire also enter into this type of writing. Similarly, the degree of formality or informality says something about the writer.

As you look back on these news articles,

✦ Which would you give high marks for engaging you as a reader?

_____

_____

✦ Which depended heavily upon a cultural context for reader acceptance and understanding?

_____

_____

✦ Which had definite "rules and regulations" (spoken or un-spoken) for including specific information?

_____

_____

Be sure to have specific reasons and examples to support and illustrate your response.

ANALYZING THE NEWS: HOW OUR PURPOSE FOR WRITING EMERGES

When we write, we have a specific purpose for doing so. We may not always think of it consciously, especially in everyday writing, but it is there nonetheless. These purposes vary, everything from describing a cell under a microscope to narrating the week's events in a letter to a friend, from defining a principle of psychology to arguing for better day care or a smoke-free environment. Understanding the purpose of our writing helps us make other decisions. For example, if our purpose is to describe a cell, we would organize information differently than if we wished to argue for better day care. Sometimes your purpose for writing will be clear immediately; at other times, you have to explore topics. The following activity will show you how exploring topics can lead to purpose.

TRYING OUT THE PROCESS

Group Activity

Follow along as one member of the group reads Article 1 aloud. Think about the different writing topics the article suggests. When you have a list of topics, discuss them.

A. Why would you be writing this particular essay? Would your primary purpose be to inform or explain? To argue for or against a point of view or an action? To describe something or someone? To narrate an incident? Although you might include description, for example, in a piece that is argumentative, your primary purpose would be argument. Consider, then, your true purpose for writing the piece.

_____

_____

_____

B. When you have determined purpose, consider the audience. To whom would you direct this writing? What do you know about this audience? Are they likely to agree or disagree with you? What kind of language and tone would be most appropriate for this audience?

_____

_____

_____

As you consider topics suggested by the following article about Bulgarian diplomats visiting the United States, think about purpose. Keep a record of the topics, no matter how far out or unlikely they may appear at first. Some of our best writing topics surface when we allow our minds to travel freely. Then follow the general directions already provided.

ARTICLE 1

DIPLOMATS MISTAKEN FOR GYPSIES

St. Anthony, Minn. (AP)—A delegation of Bulgarian diplomats who were ordered out of a grocery store after the manager mistook them for Gypsies plans to file a human-rights complaint over the incident.

Dana Penoff, a U.S. State Department interpreter escorting the group, said Sunday that she would talk to state government officials Monday about filing the complaint.

The diplomats and journalists visiting the Twin Cities as part of a U.S. Information Agency tour were forced to leave the Apache New Market Friday, she said.

"They just wanted to see what a neighborhood shopping center was like," Penoff said Saturday. "Almost immediately after we walked in, we heard this announcement that there was a suspicious group, that every shopper should be alert. It turned out that every one of us was being followed and watched," she said. Penoff said she tried to tell store owner-manager Vern Berggren that the Bulgarians were guests of the United States. He said, "Put everything down and leave. We don't want your kind of people in this store," she said.

Berggren said he was concerned after hearing reports that bands of roving thieves struck stores in Minnesota and Wisconsin on March 24. Law enforcement officials used the term *Gypsies* when comparing notes about the shoplifting incidents last weekend.

When you read this article, stereotyping and discrimination may have been high on your list of possible writing topics. Or you might have discussed shoplifting, real or imagined. Americans' response to foreigners, guests, or immigrants may have generated some topics as well. In any event, you should have a list of topics, along with the specific purpose that would guide your development of an essay on each topic.

If the general topic were stereotyping, for example, you might have come up with more refined topics such as these:

✦ Why people stereotype others
✦ How stereotypes harm various racial or ethnic groups
✦ School programs addressing stereotyping
✦ Athletic logos that stereotype

Each of these topics has writing to explain or inform as its purpose. The emphasis would be on the subject matter, stereotyping. By restating the topic, however, we could shift our purpose to one of argument, where the emphasis would be on convincing our readers that we have a valid and logical point. For example:

✦ Schools should stop using stereotypic logos, such as those depicting Native Americans.

✦ Professional sports team should stop using Native American logos (e.g., Washington Redskins, Cleveland Indians).

✦ Schools have to do a better job with multicultural education.

You have many options when you explore topics and determine your purpose for writing. Although some academic assignments are given to you, many others allow you to choose. Trying out topics and thinking about purpose, especially with classmates or friends, is a good start to the writing process.

Now continue your work with topics and purpose with articles on a stressed-out Florida student and tuna for cats—or humans?

ARTICLE 2

STUDENT BARRICADES HIMSELF IN OFFICE

Tallahassee, Fla. (AP)—A Florida State University student who barricaded himself in a state Capitol office early today demanded marijuana, liquor and doughnuts, authorities said.

The man, who had a two-way radio, told police he was armed, but authorities do not believe he took any hostages, said Leon County Undersheriff Larry Campbell.

No one was injured, and no shots had been fired. As a precaution, police diverted traffic around the building and kept out state workers.

The Legislature is not in session, but several hundred full-time staff members were scheduled for work. David Coburn, chief of staff for House Speaker T. K. Wetherell, said they were sent home with instructions to call in later.

"There are some jumpy people out there. These kind of incidents make you wonder about your security," he said.

A dozen members of a police SWAT team and six hostage negotiators entered the building at 9:30 A.M. to try to get the man to surrender, said sheriff's spokesman Dick Simpson.

Simpson identified the man as a student at the state university in Tallahassee but did not release his name.

ARTICLE 3

TUNA TURNS OUT TO BE CAT FOOD

Newark, N.J. (AP)—Federal agents have seized 38,640 cans of cat food that had been labeled tuna for human consumption.

The 6½ ounce cans, confiscated Monday from a Teterboro warehouse, were labeled Ocean King Chunk Light Tuna in Water but instead contained decomposed tuna fit only for sale as pet food, the Food and Drug Administration said.

Some of the cans were sold, the FDA said. The agency said all canned foods are sterilized during processing, so it isn't dangerous. "But who wants to eat decomposed cat food?" asked Lillian Aveta, an FDA compliance monitor.

M. Chu, president of Ocean King in New York City, did not immediately return calls Monday. The cans belonged originally to a lot of 25 million to 50 million cans produced in 1985 at a cannery in St. Andrews, Canada, the FDA said. The Canadian government closed the cannery because of unsanitary conditions.

The tuna was supposed to be labeled 7th Heaven cat food in the United States. "But at some point, some cans were relabeled as tuna," Aveta said. "We don't know yet how many, or when or by whom."

The investigation was prompted in July by complaints in Minnesota, including one from Darlene La Musga of St. Paul, who opened the can and took a bite.

"I went to pull off the label, and I saw there was another label underneath," she said. "It said . . . 7th Heaven cat food. It gagged me, and I threw up in the waste basket."

ARTICLE 4

SUPPLIER: CHUNK MEAT REALLY WAS TUNA

La Crosse—The supplier of IGA brand tuna that was recalled after some consumers found a cat food label under the outer label says the cans contained tuna meant for humans, not cats. . . .

Some customers called it a shock to find the pet food label under the outer wrapper. Vicki Rundquist of Deer Park said she was recycling cans earlier this week when she discovered the double labels and suddenly felt ill to her stomach.

Darlene La Musga said she opened a can of tuna Wednesday in her mother's kitchen in St. Paul, took a bite and prepared to make tuna salad. "I went to pull off the label, and I saw there was another label underneath," she said. "It said Tuna Treat and it also said 7th Heaven cat food. It gagged me, and I threw up in the waste basket."

Writing is both demanding and time-consuming; therefore, knowing the "why" and "for whom" is basic to writing well. If we don't, the entire process is short-circuited, and frustration is sure to set in. But sometimes, we have only a vague idea of why we want to write and what we want to say, just the niggle in the back of the head. Even when we have an initial sense of purpose, we may not be much further along than general purpose. For example: We might want to come to terms with something that happened, give advice to someone, enlist someone's support, or analyze a confusing situation; we might want to tell an important story, promote a policy, present one side of an issue, or clarify a difficult idea. But these are simply initial impulses; to arrive at a clear purpose for our writing, we need to understand how writers journey through the writing process. The first step in the writing process itself helps us clarify and explore both "why" and "what." Generating, also called prewriting or inventing, is that first step.

WORKING THROUGH THE PROCESSES OF WRITING

Generating

Every time you explored ideas, either alone or with your classmates, you were readying yourself for potential writing tasks. Reading and responding, talking to others, and making notes for yourself are all good strategies for generating ideas for writing. There are many other strategies, which we'll explore in Chapter 5, but for now we'll stick with some general ideas about getting started and staying with the process.

You probably associate generating or discovering ideas with the start of a writing task. However, we also find ourselves generating ideas while we draft. Sometimes, it's only in the act of writing that we discover that we need more or different material. At that point, we have to return to strategies that help us generate ideas. One of those strategies, strange as it may seem, is getting away from writing.

All through the writing process, we face times when we need to get away from the writing task. It's very normal to feel worn down and out of ideas, and to wish for the entire draft to go up in flames. Writing, even when it's going well, is hard work. Inexperienced writers sometimes feel guilty for doing just what they need to do—take a break. We can never really shut down the brain, so even if you think you're not working on your writing assignment, you probably are. It's somewhere in your brain, even if you are not consciously aware of it. Professional writers refer to this process as incubation. The ideas are there, growing and changing until the moment when they are born consciously.

You will try out many generating strategies in the weeks ahead. Once you discover which of them work best for you, you can apply them both when you start an assignment and when you get stuck. Seeing words appear on the paper is tangible evidence that you're working on the assignment. Some people do the strategies in their heads; it's the way they always work. Others can't function that way at all. Some writers need more "people" assistance than others, finding that talking through the writing task or certain segments of a draft is a tremendous help. What's important about generating is knowing what helps you.

Drafting

Discovery Drafts.   Drafting is the process of developing the written text. Most people think of drafting as the writing itself—not revising or editing but developing the content that will later be revised and edited. When we start to write in paragraph form, we usually think of it as drafting. Once we have a workable draft, we go on to the process of revising it. A special form of drafting is the discovery draft, which is a generating strategy for many writers. It's a good way to get many ideas down quickly, simply letting ideas evolve without concern for how they match or whether they are even usable. Discovery drafts often appear messy and are generally unintelligible to everyone but the writer. However, because some writers do a form of drafting in their heads, they turn up with a fairly organized discovery draft. This student's discovery draft turned out to be a rich resource for a personal-experience essay:

What a jerk! I just came from the blue-gold room [student union] for a coffee and a smoke where I heard this guy ranting to a friend. The subject was Native American rights and I couldn't believe my ears. Apparently this man is some big activist, probably employed to look out for native americans rights. His endless condemnation of the "white, upper-middle-class drug culture" and its responsibility for drug and alcohol abuse among Native Am.s was typical of the fanatic without a cause. That isn't what bothered me. It was the way he talked about a list of indian leaders that didn't approve of his philosophy in every aspect. This firey, radical, irrational, condemnation of his ENE-MIES belied his true pathetic nature. I tried first to

> listen objectively to what he was saying, then I tried assuming that all the things he said are true. Anyway you slice it, this guy was power hungry, afraid of other leaders, a back-stabber, interested only in his own views, not interested in general debate . . .

When you examine this discovery draft, you find that Roy was really letting off steam on paper. It's not focused. There are many ideas in it, and Roy would have to pick one to center his essay on. He's written a narrative account of an incident that had just happened to him, just as though he were talking to us about it. But if we were talking, we'd be asking Roy questions about this incident and pushing him to describe the scene and the object of his anger more clearly and fully.

Group Activity

Write down statements or ideas from Roy's discovery draft that you believe would be good ones as the focus of an essay. Then discuss each idea in terms of the type of essay it might lead to. For it to be a personal-experience essay, a narrative, it would have to focus on Roy. How could Roy use what he has described to say something significant about himself, about his own experience, his view of self and world? What could lead to an expository essay, one that informs or explains, where the emphasis is on the subject being discussed, not the writer? What could lead to an argumentative essay, where the emphasis is on the reader, on efforts to bring the reader around to acknowledging or accepting the writer's point of view? List each potential topic and the possible purpose of the essay, and then discuss what would be needed to support the idea. Refer back to the draft for ideas. Prepare your group's work for full-class discussion.

First Drafts.   The first draft of an essay is usually the most difficult. However, sometimes people make it more difficult by worrying about grammar, sentences, punctuation, and spelling—in other words, worrying about Standard Written English. Writing Standard American English is important, if only because it is the written dialect of school and business. But we attend to it in a final draft and not before. When we are in the process of getting things down on paper, we don't need to be concerned about getting things down correctly. Although worrying about correctness is understandable and normal, especially among inexperienced writers, it can get in the way. If we're thinking, "Is this correct?", we're not thinking, "What else can I say?"

In our first drafts, we need to attend to the content, to what we want to say. When we are satisfied with the content, we can turn to revising and editing. Multiple drafts are the way in which we work our essay into an understandable, correct, and interesting paper. Sometimes, you will write only a first draft. But most of the time, academic writing requires several drafts.

Writing Activity	To try out the writing processes, you'll take on a light-hearted task with you at its center. Though not a serious academic topic, it nonetheless requires you to work through the basic strategies you would use in any writing task. And, since you are the topic, you will be able to work rather quickly to develop a draft. You'll start with a discovery draft. Keep in mind that this draft may be a real mess, understandable only to you. And save every scrap of this initial exploration; you may want to return to these ideas later in the process.

Horoscope: Hogwash or Heaven?

Almost every newspaper carries a horoscope column, and most people can either take it or leave it, laugh or believe it—but a lot of people read it, regardless. Similarly, most people eagerly break open the Chinese fortune cookie arriving with their check. Why? Is it because we are drawn to descriptions of ourselves and our lives, however untrue? Or that we would like to believe that fate does play a role in what happens to us? That we aren't really responsible for our words and actions? Or like most Chinese fortune cookies tell us, that good things are ahead? Whatever the reason, let's explore a few messages.

✦ Aries (March 21–April 19)
Your enthusiasm makes a difference and helps you zero in on your desires.

✦ Taurus (April 20–May 20)
Take a backseat until you figure out which way to go.

✦ Gemini (May 21–June 20)
You'll want to handle a personal matter differently once you realize what the issues are.

✦ Cancer (June 21–July 22)
Take the lead, but listen to a partner's feedback.

✦ Leo (July 23–August 22)
Reach out for someone who is at a distance.

✦ Virgo (August 23–September 22)
   One-to-one relating is important for you in the long run. Be more nurturing.

✦ Libra (September 23–October 22)
   Agree with someone who makes a big difference in your life. Stop imposing rules.

✦ Scorpio (October 23–November 21)
   Make work your highest priority. Handle frustration or anger more appropriately.

✦ Sagittarius (November 22–December 21)
   Your sense of adventure peaks, and it seems there's no stopping you.

✦ Capricorn (December 22–January 10)
   Emotional and financial security will make your life work.

✦ Aquarius (January 20–February 18)
   You are shaking foundations a bit hard. Others are having strong reactions.

✦ Pisces (February 19–March 20)
   You know which way to go. Now do it.

As you read your "advice for the day," did you have any sense of it being on target? Or was it so far off that you laughed? Either way, you could respond in writing to the day's advice, warning, or good news. For example, I'm a Capricorn: "Financial security will make your life work." Well, of course, it would! Who wouldn't find life a bit easier with financial security? But to write about it, I would have to supply examples, reasons, and details so that a reader would know exactly why I agree. I could list all kinds of things that would bring increased financial security—like no house mortgage, no car payments. Or I could have some fun with it and suggest that winning a lottery and laying down $500,000 for a seaside cottage in La Jolla, California, would *really* make my "life work." The horoscope is so general that finding material to support it is no problem.

Writing Activity

Using either the horoscope provided here or one in a daily newspaper, weekly television guide, or a monthly magazine, respond. List all the reasons, examples, or details that would show the horoscope is utter nonsense or hits the mark pretty well. Don't edit out anything—give your thoughts free range here.

Perhaps even more intriguing to many people are the descriptions of their character that come with the zodiac. This intrigue certainly doesn't mean that anyone believes them, but rather it reflects our interest, once again, in ourselves. Let's see what happens if I turn to the general characteristics of a Capricorn:

Positive: reliable, determined, ambitious, sense of humor, disciplined
Negative: rigid, pessimistic, conventional, mean

Not exactly, a great group of descriptors—but accurate enough in the positive. To write a single paragraph, I would have to choose just one descriptor and then provide concrete examples and details to "prove" that I match it. For example, I am totally reliable. When people ask me to do a task, I complete it; when I have to meet someone, I am always on time. When students ask for a recommendation, I write and mail it long before the deadline. I could find lots of real-world examples to show a reader that I do fit that description. Because you know yourself, you can conjure up information like this quite readily. And this information can form the basis of a single paragraph or short essay.

Students Tackle the Zodiac

Notice how these students handled their zodiac characteristics.

Pisces

Pisces is a fishy subject, and I feel I am a true Pisces, right down to my favorite color, blue. Showing you the traits will be like showing you my life story. In the beginning, there is a very emotional boy. He is the one who sat in the third row and cried through half of the movie after Bambi's mother was killed. Later, like all true Pisces, I grew into a sensitive and sympathetic man. . . .

A Pisces is said to have a magnetic and charming personality; I don't know about the magnetic, but each year in high school I was voted "most charming."

Being a Pisces is not all good. We don't take criticism well, and it is very hard for me to blow off a comment like, "You don't know what you are talking about." It will stick with me for days, weeks, and possibly months.

Leo

A myth that has haunted Leos for years is that we are very hard to get along with. On the contrary, Leos are very romantic, and I am definitely a romantic. When I am in love, no expense is spared. One of my best moves is to surprise a girl with a dozen roses or dinner at a great restaurant.

Leos need to be the best at whatever they do. This characteristic fits me perfectly. I'm one of those people who has to work for everything he gets. I'm not a natural at very many things, but through hard work, I can usually improve myself. For example, when I was on the freshman football team, I hardly played. I was too slow and too weak for my position as a running back. Over the summer, I dedicated myself to improving; I lifted weights three times a week and ran every day. The hard work paid off when try-outs for the sophomore team were held and I earned a starting position.

Sagittarius

An eerie feeling swept over me as I read the Sagittarian passage. It was as if someone were describing my inner most thoughts, some of which I myself was unaware of. Sagittarius is both a fire sign and a travel sign. Typical characteristics range from rebellion and impatience to being Julia Child's worst nightmare in the kitchen.

Sagittarians have a spirit of adventure that intrigues them with foreign places. We'd prefer to experience what life and the world have to offer than get our knowledge or thrills secondhand. When a female Sagittarian does travel, she likes to go first class. This desire forced me into a small financial problem over Christmas break, when a friend and I vacationed in South Padre, Texas. My parents had to wire me money when my extravagant taste outgrew my billfold.

The Best and the Worst of Us

The following descriptions will provide you with plenty of raw material from which to draw a characteristic and explain why it fits or doesn't fit you. You will need specific examples or details to support your description. Find your birth date in the previous horoscope sample; then, check out your best and worst features from the list below.

◆ Aries
Positive: adventurous, highly energetic, loves freedom, courageous, direct
Negative: selfish, impatient, quick-tempered

◆ Taurus
Positive: practical, reliable, patient, trustworthy, warm-hearted
Negative: possessive, lazy, stubborn, obsessed with routines

◆ Gemini
Positive: intellectual, witty, adaptable, lively, talkative
Negative: restless, cunning, two-faced, inconsistent, superficial, gossip

◆ Cancer
Positive: kind, sensitive, powerful imagination, cautious, thrifty
Negative: over-emotional, touchy, moody, snappy temper

◆ Leo
Positive: generous, creative, enthusiastic, good organizer, dramatic
Negative: power-mad, conceited, intolerant

◆ Virgo
Positive: modest, tidy, analytical, discriminating, hard worker
Negative: fussy, a worrier, hypercritical

◆ Libra
Positive: charming, easy-going nature, romantic, diplomatic, idealistic
Negative: frivolous, indecisive, flirtatious, resentful

◆ Scorpio
Positive: powerful emotions, purposeful, imaginative, persistent
Negative: jealous, resentful, stubborn, suspicious, secretive

◆ Sagittarius
Positive: optimistic, open-minded, sincere, dependable, adaptable
Negative: restless, prone to exaggeration, boisterous, capricious

◆ Capricorn
Positive: reliable, ambitious, patient, disciplined, good sense of humor
Negative: rigid, pessimistic, miserly, "wet blanket"

✦   Aquarius
   Positive: friendly, independent, loyal, inventive
   Negative: unpredictable, rebellious, tactless, fixed in opinions
✦   Pisces
   Positive: sensitive, adaptable, compassionate, intuitive, emotional
   Negative: careless, secretive, easily confused, impractical

Writing Activity	Choose a characteristic that either describes you perfectly or is totally unlike you. Respond with examples, details, reasons why. As before, don't edit out anything, and save every scrap of material.

Partner and Group Strategies for Generating Ideas

There are several ways that your classmates can help with generating ideas for your writing topic:

✦   You can come in with notes and talk about what you have thus far. Your partner or group will ask questions, make suggestions, and help plan the next draft.

✦   You and your classmates can start the entire process together, before you have any notes. In this case, you will have only a general idea of the topic, or perhaps none at all. Talking, with one person taking notes on the ideas surfacing during discussion, will help you narrow the possibilities and focus on a single topic or idea as the starting point.

DRAFTING

Developing a Discovery Draft

Writing Activity	A. Now it's time to write a discovery draft. Review your notes from the first two writing activities, and choose the material for your draft. Think about this material for a few moments, and then just start writing—everything and anything that comes to mind. Discovery drafts are messy and need only make some sense to the writer.
	B. When you have completed the discovery draft, review it. If you have handwritten your draft, use a different colored ink for the next step.

With this new color, circle anything you wish to save in this draft. Then, review what you have circled and place numbers on each circle to indicate a potential order for using this material. You may change your mind later, delete some material, add some material, or rearrange what you have, but for right now, the numbers will serve as a general indicator for order.

C. Evaluate your audience and purpose. Who is your audience? What would you expect your audience to already know? Have you assumed too much background knowledge? Are you using any special terms or vocabulary associated with a specific place, group of people, hobby, activity, and so on? What is the purpose of your writing? What are you trying to do in this piece of writing? State your purpose in a single sentence.

D. List what you believe you need to do to shape the discovery draft into a good draft, concentrating on what you want to say and the order in which you want to say it. At this point, ignore problems with sentences, grammar, punctuation, and spelling. All you need to do here is make a list, like the kind you make when you have 10 things to do on a very busy school or work day.

Writing with a Word Processor.   More and more students are finding word processing a wonderful tool for drafting, revising, and editing. Although the "brain work" is just as demanding, the physical ease of word processing has changed the way in which many writers approach these tasks. Multiple drafts are an essential part of most academic writing, but having each draft evolve from the previous one on disk or hard drive makes the "multiple" part much easier. Drafting involves lots of ideas, sometimes jumbled and half-formed, and with word processing, most of us feel a bit less apprehensive about the initial drafting "mess." We can try out many ideas, adding and dropping them easily, changing and moving them just as easily. What used to take a great deal of physical energy and time now takes far less, freeing up energy for thinking about our ideas.

Adding, deleting, and moving text have been simplified through key commands or that friendly mouse. Revising that previously required rewriting on paper now can be done on a screen, with fresh copies available within minutes. Editing too has become much easier. Computer programs offer spelling checkers, and some even signal the writer when an incorrect spelling occurs; other programs check everything from sentence length to grammatical forms. In brief, word processing will help ease the journey from generating to drafting, from revising to editing.

When you write with a word processor, you will still need to print out hard copies. The screen has limited vision; we have to scroll back and forth to revisit what we have written. Since revision is literally "re-seeing," we need the entire document or large parts of it to make decisions about what stays, goes, or moves. Because we can later change our minds about what stays or goes, we need backup copies available throughout the writing time. It is always a good idea to make backup copies on disk or hard drive too. Computers are, after all, machines—subject to glitches—and ensuring that nothing erases your hard work is worth the few moments it takes to back up your writing.

Word processing skills are a lifelong investment. The various electronic communication skills essential in the world of work today will only increase as we move into the twenty-first century. Your ability to use them with comfort and expertise will be a professional asset throughout your lifework.

Writing Activity

From Discovery Draft to Draft 1

Review your comments (and any from a classmate) on the discovery draft. Then take the plunge into the next draft. This draft will be your first solid draft. Don't worry about sentence structure, grammar, punctuation, and spelling at this point. Concentrate only on developing what you want to say. If you get stuck during this drafting process, try one or more of the following strategies:

WIRMI: What I Really Mean is . . .   When you are bogged down trying to get an idea out of your head and onto paper, or when you are struggling with getting the sentence to say what you want it to, switch from writing to talking to yourself. Say to yourself, "What I really mean is _____ ." You should then have something tangible to work with.

Notes Only.   Another strategy is to stop writing in sentence form and write only in phrases—short notes for yourself. Your brain can handle only so many tasks at once. Cutting back to phrases will lighten the load.

Visual Notes.   Working with an idea visually, not just in the head, is another useful strategy. Notation techniques are usually very helpful: write alternative phrasing, words, and the like one under another so you can emphasize or see the various options more clearly; put boxes around words or ideas so as to focus your concentration on them; draw lines or arrows from one idea or word to another. You will consider relationships more carefully if you see your thinking "in the lines."

Make Do.   Try "making do." Even though you know that what you put down is not the full idea or the right word or the way you want the sentence to read—put it down. Tell yourself that it's okay for now. You may not be satisfied, but you have let yourself move on. When you come back to the unfinished part, you will be able to see it with fresh eyes.

Take a Break.   When you're stuck, spinning wheels for an hour and getting more and more frustrated, take a break. If you have been sitting at a desk for an extended period of time, with nothing going right or nothing going at all, it's time to do something else. The ideas will run around in your head, regardless, and when you return to write, chances are you will return refreshed and ready with some ideas of what to do next. Letting ideas incubate is a good practice in any case. After you generate ideas, allowing some time for them to sit in the head is not wasting time. Similarly, while drafting, thinking about the next un-solved problem in your draft is often more productive when you are not sitting at a desk or computer. Some of your best thinking may oc-cur when you are walking to class, driving to work, relaxing in the stu-dent union, or making a sandwich.

Revising

Revising an essay requires a new set of eyes. When we draft, we try to get our ideas down on paper, concentrating on what we want to say, the content. When we revise, we take another look at that content, this time concentrating on how we might improve it. Sometimes, we add material; other times, we delete it. Or we might change the organiza-tion of our material. In revising, we also take another look at our sen-tences, hoping to make them clearer or more "alive," more interesting. And finally, we examine individual words and phrases, usually asking ourselves if we can make them more precise or vivid.

Revising Draft 1.   Whether or not you use a word processor, you will probably be reviewing your draft on paper. Without a hard copy of your draft, you may not be able to make decisions about what you have said and what you still need to say. Although revising can be a very indi-vidual process, with each of us going at it slightly differently, you nonetheless want to be systematic. In other words, you should have a process that you can turn to, regardless of the type of writing task as-signed. It's hard to read your own essay and see what it needs. Because you know in your head what you are saying, you can read over parts that need work without noticing the problems. For this reason, you need to have a writing conference with yourself. Double-space your draft and leave ample margins. You need room to make notes and changes.

Marking the Text.   Before addressing questions for revision, you need to have some tangible tools for revision. Keep in mind that revision is messy. Your draft will be slashed, circled, cut apart, and marked up in various ways. Here are some marks and methods to help you with this important process:

Carets	Carets (^) show where you want to insert a new word or phrase. Carets work best when you are adding a very small amount of information.
Arrows	Arrows (→) allow you to connect information, whether present in the draft or added, to the place where you want to insert it.
Asterisks	Asterisks (*) are good for marking the place where you want to insert big chunks of new information, something too large for a caret or arrow to accommodate. You may want to make a note next to the asterisk to identify the material you'll add.
Spider legs	Narrow strips of paper called spider legs are another method of adding information. You write new material on the spider leg and staple or clip the strip to your draft at the appropriate place. Keeping the strips narrow helps us avoid being too wordy.
Cut and paste	You can add, delete, or move part of your essay by cutting and pasting. Workable sections from an earlier draft can be retrieved and reattached to subsequent drafts. Scissors and staples or tape are your instruments here. If you are working with a word processor, a few commands will do the job. However, you should keep hard copies of everything. We never know when we may need to go back to an earlier draft and retrieve or revive a section of text. We can also inadvertently hit the wrong key and lose parts we wanted to save.
Circle in color	As noted earlier, circling in colored ink is a technique for reorganizing material. Using a fine-point colored pen, circle in one color all references to one topic; in

another color, circle all references to another topic; and so on. On the next draft, combine all of the sections marked with a single color.

Circling   Circling is also a way to indicate the parts of your draft that you'll keep. This technique is especially useful if you hate crossing things out—and most of us do. After the time we spend generating and drafting a text, every word seems golden and necessary. Nonetheless, revision means deciding what stays and what goes.

Having a Writing Conference with Yourself

You've generated information, written a discovery draft, and written another draft that is ready for revision. Although revision is very hard work, it can also be satisfying. With systematic questions and procedures, you will make progress that you can actually see. And that's a good feeling.

Asking Questions About the Heart of the Essay.

1. Don't ask what's wrong with the draft. Rather, ask yourself where you want to head with it. A revision is not a matter of getting out the bad sentences, incorrect grammar, or spelling errors. It is a new "seeing" of the entire draft, its focus, content, and organization. Sometimes a draft will be pretty good but still need work to shape it into a better, far more interesting paper. Write down where you want to go with the draft: What strikes you as important to develop or refine? Keep in mind your purpose for this essay.

2. Ask yourself where the most important part of the draft is, the part that is most interesting, most exciting, most energetic—the heart of the essay. Identify it and mark it.

3. Ask yourself whether anyone would say, "So what?" after reading this essay. If the answer is yes, you haven't made clear why your experience is significant, why you chose to write this particular essay, or why anyone should care about what you have shared. Write down your response to the "So what?" question.

Asking Questions About the Development of the Essay.   No matter how interesting your topic may be, too little or too much information will spoil the essay. Your reader may give up because there are too many blanks to fill in or too many details to plow through. Evalu-

ate how well you have developed the essay by asking and answering the following questions:

1. Do I have enough information? Have I shown (not told) by using examples and illustrations? Have I told my thoughts and feelings at points where my reader will wonder about them? Have I described the scene, event, and people with enough detail so my reader can see them? Would dialogue help?

2. Is there any part that will confuse my reader? Have I explained each part well enough so that my reader will know what I mean, will not be thinking, "What's going on here?"

3. Have I assumed too much? Does my reader have the background or knowledge needed to understand this situation or event?

4. Do I have too much information? What parts really aren't needed— don't add anything important to my narrative?

5. What is this essay really about? Are there parts that are about something else? Can I delete them?

6. Do I have more than one story here? Which story is the one I want to tell?

7. Have I made this a dawn-to-dusk narrative, a 24-hour piece detailing everything, rather than focusing on the important part?

8. Have I added too many details and too much dialogue, made the piece very "fussy and busy"?

Use marking strategies to help you sort out what stays and what goes. Remember two basic questions: What am I trying to say in this piece of writing? Is there a point to this narrative? If you learn that you need more or better material, return to generating strategies.

Asking Questions About Organization and Unity.   How easily your reader moves from point A to point B, from idea to idea, incident to incident, or detail to detail depends upon your organization of material. We can organize an essay in many different ways. Our purpose helps us decide which organization is best. In narratives, we most often move chronologically (time order) and spatially (movement from place to place, descriptively). In brief, we are asking, "How did I get from here to there?" A second question involves unity, whether everything in the essay actually belongs there, whether we have gotten "off the track" somehow. We have to ask if each part of the essay is related to its main idea, if each part contributes to development of the main idea.

1. How have I established a meaningful organization for my essay? Am I relating a single event (or person) within a certain time and

space? Am I relating more than one event within a certain time and space?

2. How does each paragraph move the narration forward? Is each paragraph contributing to my main idea? Does each paragraph stick to one point or idea? To find out, try this process:

   a. Number each paragraph in the left-hand margin.

   b. Read each paragraph. In a word or phrase only, write down its main point or idea. What is this paragraph actually saying? If you find out that the paragraph has more than one point, and that you really can't reduce it to a few words, your narrative is off track.

   c. Now scan the paragraphs again. This time ask what each does for the essay as a whole. Why is that paragraph there? To ensure that you write down what the paragraph *does* rather than what it says, use this sentence to guide you: "This paragraph is here because it _____ ." If you can't fill in the blank, you know that the paragraph needs attention.

3. How does each paragraph connect to or build upon the previous paragraph? Would more explicit connections (transition words) help readers to understand the flow of ideas better?

4. If you are still a bit shaky about organization and unity, make a scratch outline, nothing fancy but good enough to show you the main points, their order, and what support you have for them. You should be able to see rather quickly where you have too much, too little, or repetition.

Checking on Coherence.   Coherence means that your reader can move easily from sentence to sentence and paragraph to paragraph. In the previous questions on organization, you were also checking on coherence to a certain degree—making sure that each paragraph related to the one before and after it. When an essay is coherent, the reader understands the relationship between what you have just said and what you are saying now. When an essay is incoherent, the reader becomes confused and, ultimately, irritated. When you are satisfied that the essay's content and organization are okay, check for coherence.

1. Are there enough transition words (e.g., *however, also, for example, because, although, additionally, furthermore, as a result*, etc.) to show relationships among sentences?

2. Are key words repeated in some appropriate way (e.g., synonyms)? Be sensible about coherence: your essay is coherent if your readers know where they have been and where they are going as they read.

You may not need many transitions in this particular essay, and sprinkling them throughout the piece may only clutter it up. More is not always better.

Checking Beginnings and Endings.   Your opening paragraph can make or break the essay; a reader may immediately decide whether or not to continue. Consequently, you want your "lead" to be effective, to draw the reader in.

1. Ask if your opening paragraph, your lead, brings your reader right into the narrative, into the main idea or action.
2. Ask yourself where the narrative actually begins. Can you cut the first paragraph? The first two? The entire first page? That suggestion may seem extreme, but sometimes we "beat around the bush" a lot when we first get started on a piece of writing. Just getting started can be difficult, and rambling in the first paragraph or so is not unusual. However, you have to be rather brutal with yourself in assessing the worth of those opening paragraphs.

Your concluding paragraph is also critical. The reader will carry away a sense of the entire essay from your conclusion, so you want it to be a strong one, complete and memorable.

1. Ask if your conclusion just drops off, leaving the reader to wonder, "What's happening here?"
2. Ask if your conclusion rambles on, repeating and aimless.
3. Ask yourself how you want a reader to feel at the end of the narrative. Does the conclusion do it?
4. Ask yourself what you want a reader to know at the end of the narrative. Does the conclusion do it?

Considering the Title.   Although your title may be unformed at this point, consider it another important element to be checked upon completion of the essay. When you have finished revising and editing, you'll need to add a title. Consider these questions: Does the title fit this essay, provide a glimpse of what it's all about? Does the title "grab" the reader, draw him or her into the essay?

Checking for Voice.   When we speak, we carry an individual voice: tone, pacing, emphasis, rhythm, vocabulary. In effective writing, the reader gets this sense of the author; it is one of the distinguishing marks of an essay. Sometimes students think that academic writing is characterized by its lack of voice, by a dry, nondescript, very vacant author. It may be that years of reading textbooks have left that impression. But in truth, good academic writing carries a sense of the writer. If you reread the student writers in this chapter, you will find their voices to be both individual and important to the overall effect and success of the narrative. Although writing is *not* speech written down, it nonetheless conveys our individual voices through the way in which we use words and sentences.

Writing Activity	When you have completed the writing conference with yourself, write your next draft. Some of your classmates will read this draft, evaluating its development, organization, unity, and coherence. For right now, don't worry about punctuation, grammar, and spelling.

▄ Group Activity

In your group, take turns reading and responding to one another's drafts. Bring enough copies for your group, but hold onto them until you have completed reading your draft to the group.

A.   **Read to the group.**   Read slowly and clearly, adding no comments about your draft. Read the essay in its entirety. Comments and questions will come when you have completed the reading.

B.   **Listen to a peer.**   First, put your own draft aside and try to forget about it for a few minutes, which is understandably hard to do. Concentrate on the reader's ideas:

What part is most interesting to you? Why?

What was the most important point?

What would you like to know more about?

C.   **Discuss each reading.**   After each reading of a draft, discuss it orally, focusing on the content.

D.   **Read the draft silently and individually.**   Fill in the top of the peer response sheet (author's name, reader's name, date, and title of draft). Then respond briefly to the following questions. If you believe the essay was fine with regard to any question, say so rather than leave it blank. On the draft itself, note problems with items 2, 3, and 4.

   1. What's at the heart of the essay, the "So what?" factor? If you are unsure, say so.

   2. Where did you feel you needed more information, better details, examples, and so on?

3. Where did you feel you were getting too much information, getting bogged down, and the like?

4. Did you lose track of the "story" at any place, feel confused, or wonder how things fit together?

5. Did you have a sense of the writer's voice?

6. What did you like best? Why?

7. What specific suggestions do you have for improving the essay?

Writing Activity

Review the comments and questions arising from your small-group review. Allow yourself some time to absorb both the suggestions and your response to them. Incubating, allowing the ideas to sit on the brain for a short time, is just as effective in revising as it is in generating. Then, revise your draft once more. When you are satisfied that you have included what you want to say, in the order in which you want to say it, and that a reader would not suffer any jolts in following your narrative from start to finish, you're ready to look at the next level of revising: sentences.

EDITING

The final step in the writing process is editing. This step has to do with correctness, and as such, it is the final step. There is no point in editing before you have completed your draft. When you are satisfied with the content, you are ready to check that your final draft will meet reader expectations of Standard Written English.

✦ Sentences

Is each sentence complete and marked by a capital letter and appropriate end mark?

Is each sentence clear, easily understood by a reader?

Are sentences joined with a connector (and, but, or) separated with a comma before the connector?

✦ Punctuation

Are items in a series separated by commas? (dogs, cats, and canaries)

Are dates separated by commas? (March 3, 1980, is my birthday.)

Are places separated? (I was born in San Diego, California, on March 3.)

Are apostrophes marking ownership? (My mother's idea of a joke . . .)

Are apostrophes indicating a contracted word? (can't, won't)

Are song titles enclosed in quotation marks? ("Forever")

Are titles of movies, television shows, books, and magazines underlined or italicized? (The Lost World, Seinfeld, Jurassic Park, *Sports Illustrated*)

✦ Usage

Do subjects and verbs agree? (The *box* of photos *is* lost.)

Do nouns and pronouns agree? (*Paul and Leo* lost *their* notes.)

Are pronouns used correctly? (Cal and *I* left at once. *Those* prices were high.)

✦ Spelling

Are common sound-alike words correct? (there, they're, their; to, too)

Are easily confused words used correctly? (affect, effect)

Are easily confused letters in the right place? (receive)

✦ Capitalization

Are names of specific people (including titles) capitalized? (Dad, Aunt Lydia, Dr. Searle, Mr. Tweke, Coach Evans)

Are places and products capitalized? (Chicago, The Hard Rock Café, Memorial High School, Coca-Cola, Nike)

Are titles of songs, books, movies, and television shows capitalized?

Partner or Group Strategies for Editing

A. Bring a typed copy of the draft. The author reads one paragraph at a time while the partner or group makes a check mark in the margin when noting an error. When you complete reading one draft, talk about it. Then repeat the process with each group member. Check the handbook if you are uncertain about a rule.

B. Check the draft for only one area at a time. First, read for complete sentences, ignoring punctuation unrelated to sentence completeness. Then read for all punctuation. Next, read for usage, and so on. Although this strategy takes a bit longer, it is a thorough way to edit a draft.

CHAPTER 5

Generating and Exploring Topics

You already know one powerful way in which we generate and explore ideas for writing—through responding to what we have read. There will be times, however, when you'll be asked to come up with your own academic topic. When that happens, you need to problem solve: generate your topic, explore it, and emerge with a workable idea. No matter what topic we choose, we all face a common set of questions once we begin to work on that problem:

✦   How do I get started?

✦   How can I keep my ideas going?

✦   How do I make sense out of all the ideas?

✦   Once I've decided on an idea, what then?

✦   What if I get stuck in the middle of my draft?

Although there are no formulas or single solutions for writing problems, we do have specific strategies to help us. Some work better than others, mainly because we have different styles of working and learning. To find out which are best for you, give each a fair tryout. You may find that some work well as study strategies or exam preparation too.

GATHERING IDEAS

Good writing starts with good ideas. But how do we get them? It is not, as some students believe, just a matter of sitting down at a desk and thinking hard. Rather, we need an active search for good ideas and specific strategies to help us get started. One of the first places we should search is our own interests:

First Questions

- ✦ What do I like to do in my spare time?
- ✦ What special talents or interests do I have?
- ✦ What issues, ideas, places, or things have caught my interest recently?
- ✦ What do I think about _____ ?
- ✦ How does _____ interest me?
- ✦ Why does _____ interest me?
- ✦ What idea or issue would I like to explore? Why?
- ✦ What do I already know about _____ , and what do I want to find out?

This last question is a good one for academic topics. If you list, note form only, what you already know about a topic of interest, you can move on to listing what you would like to find out. This strategy often yields potential topics and helps focus our attention on the best of those topics.

Tuning In

The world of electronics is a good resource. Leading issues, as well as human interest stories, are everyday fare on radio, television, and the Internet.

- ✦ Which topics are turning up everywhere?
- ✦ Why should I care about any of these topics?
- ✦ Which topics are suitable for academic writing?
- ✦ Which topics have been talked "to death"?
- ✦ Which topics hold my attention? Why?
- ✦ Which topics would I like to learn more about? Why?
- ✦ Which topics get my thoughts spinning? Why?

The World of Print

Although many students think "book" and "research" when they visit a public or school library, they should think a bit further. The library has information on just about everything—and much of it is not in traditional book form. As a result, the library is a great place to get ideas for writing, and not just for researched pieces.

The local, regional, and national newspapers provide more than just daily news; they also have feature articles on a wide variety of people, places, things, and ideas. The editorial page, letters to the editors, and other opinion pieces similarly offer a range of ideas, a diverse collection of opinions on diverse subjects. You don't have to be from New York City, Washington, D.C., or Los Angeles to find the *New York Times,* the *Washington Post,* or the *Los Angeles Times* very useful and interesting resources.

Browsing the magazine section of a public library may also bring you face-to-face with special interests and new topics, things you may never have considered before. It seems there is a magazine for every hobby from gardening to collecting antiques, for every interest from cars to computer technology, psychology to architecture, fine arts to athletics, and for every need from child care to purchasing a new couch or playing the stock market. Let the colorful covers draw you in, then check the table of contents for possible topics of interest.

The World of Talk

Because it is so obvious, we sometimes forget about talk: it is all around us, it is filled with topics, and it is easily accessed. In your classes, what issues come up both as part of structured discussion and as the small talk among peers? Out of class, what topics are on everyone's lips? Which ones interest you? Why? When you talk to family members, what family or community topics are on their minds? How do you respond? Where do your opinions and feelings lie?

Tapping into Personal Experience

Even with academic topics, we sometimes need to use our own experience as a starting point or as an example. Besides asking questions similar to those you explored in Chapter 1 (e.g., What difficult decision did you make alone? What act of courage or cowardice have you witnessed?), you can ask questions that open one of our most valuable storehouses of experiences: our five senses.

✦ **Sight.**   What powerful visual images remain of a person, place, or event? When you close your eyes and concentrate on an image, which colors dominate?

✦ **Sound.**   What sounds do you associate with a place or an event? How many different sounds are there? Can you collect them into a single dominant sound?

◆ **Touch.**   What textures emerge as you think about this place or thing? Smooth or rough? Soft or hard? Fabric or wood?

◆ **Taste.**   What taste sensations remain: bitter, sweet, salty, or tart? Familiar flavors such as chocolate, vanilla, cinnamon? Ethnic flavors?

◆ **Smell.**   What smells do you associate with a place? Antisceptic? Baking bread? Musty? Spices? Floral?

You may be surprised at the flow of memory that one or more senses unlocks. For example, when a travel agency asked me to write a piece for their newsletter, the purpose being to interest others in Italy, the key to every memory lay in my senses, often all of them reacting at once. As I sorted through the senses, I also sorted through the memories and could isolate the most important for my writing. An illustration: At the annual Florentine feast day *Calcio Storico* (a Renaissance game combining soccer, rugby, and Greco-Roman wrestling), I was bombarded by sight and touch (sixteenth-century costumes, men on horseback, women on ancient balconies, white oxen with garlands of flowers in their horns, sweat glistening on the bodies of the players), sound (drums, a haunting chant during the game), smell (oxen and horses, athletic sweat). By themselves, these sense impressions were just that, impressions. But when I pushed my thinking a bit further, I realized what this kaleidoscope meant to me: schoolgirl fantasies of life in another historical time—with all of the beauty but none the hardship or cruelty of those times. If I had been writing an academic essay rather than a travel piece, I would have focused on that realization. But my starting point was the senses.

Idea Mapping

Another "sense" strategy involves combining images with words. If you check out the margins of notebooks, desk tops, or notepads lying around the house, you are likely to find doodles. Although we often dismiss them as silly scribbling, doodles are far more than that. Our brain works with two halves: on the left, we find logic, language, analysis; on the right, we find creativity, associations, spatial relationships. When both halves are stimulated, we may respond with both images and words—doodles. Because we don't consciously think when we doodle, the result may contain some clues to ideas or issues that are important to us.

Similarly, real-world symbols suggest our thinking about people, places, issues, or events—and may well stimulate some thinking that leads to writing. When we see a row of XOXOs, our thoughts turn to affection, hugs and kisses; when we see $$, those thoughts shift to money. The symbol, a visual image, represents personal as well as public shortcuts to sometimes complex emotions and experiences.

Traditional Strategies for Academic Writing

When we write, we often use more than one strategy to generate and explore ideas, attitudes, and issues—and not just when we begin a writing project. Although we associate these strategies with finding a topic, we need also remember that they are useful all the way through the writing process. It is not unusual to reach a point in revision where we realize we need more or different material; at that point, we need to return to strategies that work especially well for us. You'll work through these in this chapter:

Freewriting	Mapping
Looping	Directed reading
Listing	Cubing
Reporters' questions	Charts and outlines
Personal questions	

FREEWRITING

Freewriting might be considered "babbling on paper," a steady stream of thoughts on paper—thoughts that are often unrelated, disjointed, and incomplete. However, the very process of letting loose, of not censoring or editing out ideas, is valuable for writing. Too often, we stop ourselves, thinking, "Oh, this is stupid," or, "I don't know what I mean," rather than letting the words pour out. Since there is no discussion and no feedback on freewriting, there is no need to worry about how bizarre it might appear.

If you can freewrite at a computer, all the better. The physical ease of typing often helps stimulate ideas and allows for a more sustained writing period. It's important to write for at least five minutes nonstop. If you can't think of anything to say, simply say that: I can't think of anything. You'll find you can't shut down your brain, and pretty soon you'll find all kinds of words flowing again. Freewriting is a good strategy when you have no idea at all of what you want to write about.

LOOPING

Looping builds from freewriting. It's a strategy that helps us find a focus or a main idea for an essay.

1. At the top of a clean piece of paper, write a possible topic.

2. Now freewrite for at least five minutes on that topic. If you suddenly go "blank," write that you are "blank," and continue until something else pops up.

3. Stop and read what you have. Underline the most important part—it could be a word, a phrase, or a sentence.

4. Take that important idea and write a complete sentence about it. This sentence represents your best idea out of the first loop.

5. Take a short break.

Take a clean sheet of paper. Take your best idea from the first loop and write it at the top. Now repeat the looping process. Again find your best idea and write it out as a complete sentence. After a short break, repeat this process. For most people, three loops provide enough focus, allowing formulation of a good general statement for writing. If they don't, try another strategy.

LISTING

Listing is just what it sounds like: writing down words or phrases with no concern for order. Quantity is what counts here. Later, you will go back and sort out what's there; you'll see related ideas and can then begin to do some sorting and grouping. This strategy is used with a topic—putting down everything that comes to mind—and it is as useful when you are in the middle of an essay as when you are trying to get started on one. If you suddenly go blank in the middle of an essay, listing is a good way to get yourself back to writing.

Reading and Writing Activity

Before you read the following news articles on college students and cheating to get good grades, list your ideas about grades. Then as you read the three articles, highlight or underline the main points.

BIG LIES HAVE SMALL BEGINNINGS

Erma Bombeck

Michael Moore, a 24-year-old junior at Rutgers State University, thinks he is breaking new ground with his paperback, "Cheating 101: The Benefits and Fundamentals of Earning the Easy A."

His dream of elevating cheating to an art form offers such techniques as wearing a Walkman, using the stick-shift method (which indicates multiple choice directions) and being paged by a beeper during a test and getting answers from friends on an outside phone.

You call that creative? I knew people in college who cheated 30 years ago. They wrote answers on breath mints and ate the evidence, recorded answers on the ends of their fingernails and then bit them off. A few put notes on the soles of their shoes, and several rummaged through wastebaskets in the mimeograph room looking for master sheets.

But there is one glaring difference. The cheaters weren't the norm 30 years ago. They were the scum who were dishonest and brought shame and embarrassment to a university. Without integrity, they missed what education was all about. They were neither admired nor accepted, nor the stuff of which books were written.

According to Moore: "It's understood between students that cheating is a reality. You take it for granted that they have [cheated] in the past and will in the future." I want to be disgusted with Michael Moore, but he has to wait his turn. First I have to show my real contempt for politicians who lie and captains of industry who are consumed with greed, for plumbers who overcharge and lawyers dedicated to exploitation, for law enforcement officers who take advantage of people's trust and writers who accept Pulitzer Prizes for stories they invented.

They are the ones who paved the way for Michael Moore's book. Before any of us is too complacent about putting the blame on those mentioned above, look into your own lives. What kind of message are you sending to your children?

You can't break into a car, but it's OK to fish without a license.

You can't steal a bicycle, but its all right to filch a few office supplies.

Don't lie to your mother, but you can tell the person at the box office you're big for 11.

The fall from integrity doesn't happen when you stub your toe over a large lie in your path. It's stumbling along a rough road mined with one decision after another of what is right and what is wrong. The important thing to remember is that a lot of books have been and will continue to be written on "cheating." Most of the authors, however, are serving time.

CHEATING MAY BE ON THE UPSWING AT UW–MADISON

Joe Schoenmann

She gets an A in cheating. She's so good that even when she got caught, the University of Wisconsin–Madison junior lied well enough to get out of it. "I could have done it without cheating, but I get nervous and I'm a very academic person and I really want to do well," she said, speaking on condition of anonymity.

It's not something she's very proud of—cheating in class to get A's—but the pressure to get grades is stiff, she said.

"And here, you can be anonymous in cheating because: So what? How many academic misconduct cases are there? Lots. And if you're caught, you can deny it. You can just say no."

During the 1988–89 school year, UW officials tracked 51 cases of cheating: 15 in the fall, 33 in spring and 3 in summer. The number rose to 71 cases in 1990–91, 27 in the fall and 44 in the spring. No cases were reported in the summer. This year, 28 cases were reported last fall. Most cases result in grade reductions (40 in 1988–89), followed by reprimands (13), expulsion (5), or additional work (2). Rarely do students appeal decisions (4 in 1988–89).

Peggy Miezio, assistant dean of students, keeps track of the numbers and usually deals personally with students who get caught. Over the years, she's found little change in the reasons students choose to cheat. "It's usually, 'It was stupid, I panicked, I wasn't prepared,' " Miezio said. But she's not sure if more students are cheating or more are getting caught.

Numbers might be up, she suggested, because of a UW code change four years ago that makes it easier for faculty to penalize those who violate academic conduct rules. That isn't exactly scaring the students. That won't happen, Miezio notes, until students feel more of an attachment to the institution. "Students don't see their own personal connection to the university. They'll say: Why does it matter? I'm just a number."

That's just what Rutgers University student Michael Moore says in his book, "Cheating 101." "Education is impersonal, and when we have professors that have other pressures on them—the publish or perish mentality—education becomes secondary," said Moore from his Hopewell, N.J., home. "Students pick up on these," he said. "They realize the professor really isn't interested in teaching, and they say to themselves, 'Why should I be interested in learning?' and they find shortcuts and take them."

Moore's book, an irreverent look at faculties and university systems, details methods of cheating. It caused a mild uproar when printed last fall. "I got good reactions from students and people with senses of humor and bad reactions from uptight administrators," he said.

REVIEW OF "CHEATING 101" (EXCERPTS)

Anthony Flint

Moore makes no excuses about the profits he reaps from the book, and acknowledges that he set out to make money. But he also considers "Cheating 101" to be a commentary on the shortcomings of higher education: ill-prepared professors more concerned with research, dreary required courses and the lack of training for real-world applications.

Rutgers officials, while praising Moore's entrepreneurial skills, have sharply criticized "Cheating 101" as a blatant violation of academic ethics.

But Moore denies that he's engaging in anything unethical. "I don't think people that are buying the book have never cheated before. They already know a lot of the methods. I'm not making a cheater out of anybody," he said, adding that he advises students not to cheat in their major or in nonrequired courses in which they really want to learn the material.

To see how your views compare with those of Bombeck and Moore, make a chart.

Bombeck's Views	My Views
A. _____	_____
B. _____	_____
C. _____	_____

Moore's Views	My Views
A. _____	_____
B. _____	_____
C. _____	_____

Even if you share some of Moore's views, do you have to draw the same conclusions as he does?

＿Group Activity ＿＿＿＿＿＿＿＿＿＿＿＿＿＿＿＿＿＿＿

Bring your chart to small-group discussion. Do most of you have similar views? Why or why not? If you were to write an essay on this topic, what position would you take, and how would you support it? Reach a consensus and bring a position statement, along with relevant support, to full-class discussion. Consensus, by the way, means that you can agree on the topic—but not that everyone agrees with the same degree of enthusiasm. Being able to reach a consensus is an important skill, not only in school but also in the workplace, the community, and one's home.

USING REPORTERS' QUESTIONS

Asking questions of a topic is another way of exploring it in a systematic way. From asking initial questions, you can move to asking more questions or formulating statements from the question.

Now read these two news articles on cheating, and use reporters' questions to sort out the information presented:

STUDY SHOWS HIGH SCHOOL, COLLEGE STUDENTS CHEAT, LIE

Marina Del Ray, Calif. (CPS)—College and high school students admitted to cheating, lying and stealing in a two-year national study on ethics, according to a report released this month.

The study, undertaken by the California-based Josephson Institute of Ethics, involved interviewing 8,965 young people nationwide and focused on ethics.

"There is a hole in the moral ozone and it is probably getting bigger," said Michael J. Josephson, president of the institute.

The report, he said, is indicative that the present 15-to-30-year-old generation is more likely to engage in dishonest and irresponsible behavior than other generations. Among the findings from the survey:

✦ Sixteen percent of college students and 33 percent of high school students admitted to shoplifting.

✦ Twenty-one percent of college students said they would falsify a report if necessary to keep a job.

✦ Sixty-one percent of high school students and 32 percent of college students admitted they cheated on an exam in the past year.

STRESSING SAT BRINGS CRIMINAL RESULTS

Lisa Baumann

When 19-year-old Lawrence Adler of Potomac, Md., paid his friend $200 to take the Scholastic Aptitude Test for him a year ago, he relieved himself of the anxiety and fear that can come with taking the test.

Adler probably experienced anxiety and fear at the highest level last month after a judge sentenced him to six months in jail for saying under oath that he took the SAT.

Adler not only paid off David Farmer, a freshman at the University of Virginia; he then lied to cover it up.

The case is believed to be the first criminal prosecution to stem from cheating on the SAT.

Criminal prosecution stemming from cheating on the SAT? Absurd.

Many students are required to take this test to apply to colleges. It's just another form of pressure put on teenagers. Don't they have enough to show from their years in school without the extra pressure?

Anyone who has taken a big test can relate. Students wait in a classroom, seated every other one in small desks. The atmosphere is tense and quiet, with students knowing that this test helps determine their future.

One test should not have such an effect on the life path.

FairTest, the National Center for Fair and Open Testing, has found the SAT to show inaccurate results based on biased context and format. Although the questions passed a sensitivity process, researcher Phyllis Rosser found that 40 questions on the SAT had extreme bias in favor of one gender or the other; 34 questions favored boys.

Should we prosecute the creators of the SAT because they claim it is unbiased and accurate?

We should take a step back and ask what these kinds of tests really prove. They show who is good at test-taking under pressure.

Test developers and users should throw out the SAT altogether. Then teens could concentrate on becoming well-rounded people.

Then Adler could concentrate on his studies, instead of paying someone else to do it for him.

At the top of a sheet of paper, write *cheating* and then write as many questions as you can addressing that topic:

Who?	Who cheats?	What kind of people cheat?
Why?		
How?		
Where?		
What?		

You can also pair questions?

How/Why?

Where/Why?

Who/Why?

What/Why?

QUESTIONS TO EXPLORE ONE'S VIEWS

Read Robert Samuelson's essay on young adults, their parents, school, and academic achievement. Highlight or underline Samuelson's major points. Note how he supports his ideas. How convincing is he? Why? When you finish the essay, respond through looping. At the conclusion of three loops, review what you have written and respond to the questions at the end of the essay.

TEEN-AGERS IN DREAMLAND

Robert J. Samuelson

Meet Carlos. He's a senior at American High School in Fremont, California. He's also a central character in a recent public television documentary on U.S. education. Carlos is a big fellow with a crew cut and a friendly manner. We see him driving his pickup truck, strolling with a girlfriend and playing in a football game. "I don't want to graduate," he says at one point. "It's fun. I like it."

If you want to worry about our economic future, worry about Carlos and all those like him. It is the problem of adolescence in America. Our teen-agers are living in a dreamland. It's a curious and disorienting mixture of adult freedoms and childlike expectations. Hey, why work? Average high school students do less than an hour of daily homework. Naturally, they're not acquiring the skills they will need for their well-being and the nation's.

Don't mistake me: I'm not blaming today's teen-agers. They are simply the latest heirs of an adolescent subculture—we have all been part of it—that's been evolving for decades. American children are becoming more and more independent at an earlier and earlier age. By 17, two-fifths of Americans have their own car or truck. About 60 percent have their own telephones and television. Adult authority wanes, and teen-age power rises. It's precisely this development that has crippled our schools.

The difference, Coleman concluded, lies with parents. "Parents [of public school students] do not exercise as much authority over their high-school-aged students as they once did," he recently told a conference at the Manhattan Institute. Since the 1960s, public schools have become less demanding—in discipline, required course work and homework—because they can't enforce stiffer demands. By contrast, parents of parochial school students impose more control. "The schools therefore [are] able to operate under a different set of ground rules," Coleman said.

There are obviously many good public schools and hard-working students. But the basic trends are well-established and have been altered only slightly by recent "reforms." Change comes slowly because stricter academic standards collide with adolescent reality. In the TV documentary, Tony—a pal of Carlos—is asked why he doesn't take tougher math courses to prepare him as a computer technician, which is what he wants to be. "It's my senior year," he says, "and I think I'm going to relax."

Adolescent autonomy continues to increase. "Teens have changed so dramatically in the past decade that more advertisers . . . are targeting 'adults' as 15-plus or 13-plus rather than the typical 18-plus," notes Teenage Research Unlimited, a market research firm. It estimates that the average 16-to-17-year-old has nearly $60 a week in spending money from jobs and allowances. By junior year, more than 40 percent of high school students have jobs.

These demanding school-time jobs are held predominantly by middle-class students. Popular wisdom asserts that early work promotes responsibility, but the actual effect may be harmful. In a powerful book (*When Teenagers Work*), psychologists Ellen Greenberger of the University of California (Irvine) and Laurence Steinberg of Temple University show that jobs hurt academic performance and do not provide needed family income. Rather, they simply establish teen-agers as independent consumers better able to satisfy their own wants. Jobs often encourage drug use.

Our style of adolescence reflects prosperity and our values. We can afford it. In the 19th century, children worked to ensure family survival; the same is true today in many developing countries. Our culture stresses freedom, individuality and choice. Everyone has "rights." Authority is to be questioned. Self-expression is encouraged. These attitudes take root early. My 4-year-old daughter recently announced her philosophy of life: "I should be able to do anything I want to do."

Parental guilt also plays a role. The American premise is that the young ought to be able to enjoy their youth. Schools should not spoil it, as if an hour and a half of daily homework (well above the average) would mean misery for teen-agers. Finally more divorce and more fami-lies with two wage-earners mean that teen-agers are increasingly left to themselves. They often assume some family responsibilities—shopping or caring for younger children. Many teen-agers feel harried and con-fused, but the conflicts among all these roles (student, worker, child and adult) are overwhelming.

Americans, young and old, delude themselves about the results of these changes. A recent study of 13-year-olds in six countries placed Americans last in mathematics and Koreans first. But when students were asked whether they were "good at mathematics," 68 percent of the Americans said yes (the highest) compared with only 23 percent of the Koreans (the lowest).

This was no quirk. Psychologist Harold Stevenson of the University of Michigan, who has studied American and Asian students for years, finds the same relationship. Americans score lower in achievement, but, along with their parents, are more satisfied with their performance. "If children believe they are already doing well—and their parents agree with them—what is the purpose of studying harder?" he writes.

Good question. No one should be surprised the U.S. businesses complain about workers with poor skills, or that a high school diploma no longer guarantees a well-paying job. More school spending or new educational "theories" won't magically give students knowledge or skills. It takes work. Our style of adolescence is something of a national curse. Americans are growing up faster, but they may not be growing up better.

Respond to Samuelson's ideas *after* you've completed a looping ex-ercise. Review what you've written and apply these questions:

1. What am I saying? Is this a reflection of something I really believe or merely a mood right now?

2. Am I consistent? Do I always feel this way? Does what I have ex-pressed here match my opinions? If not, how different? Why might I have expressed different views or opinions?

3. What's shaped my opinion or feeling on this topic? What experi-ences or observations have led me to my current opinion?

4. Where does this opinion, feeling, or belief lead? What does it sug-gest about me? About the world I live in? What, if anything, am I trying to say about my personal vision of the world?

If you were going to write an essay on this topic, how would these questions have helped you?

MAPPING

Mapping, sometimes called clustering, is one of the most visual strategies we have for exploring a writing topic. We store a great deal of information in the brain, often forgetting we have it until something calls it into consciousness. So if we can call up one piece of information or memory, we may be tapping into a wealth of information. Because it is graphic and concrete, mapping can help the brain make the connections. For this reason, mapping is an excellent study technique as well.

Start the process by writing the subject or general topic in the center of a clean piece of paper. Draw a circle around it. Then, write down every word or phrase that pops into your head as you look at the subject. When you have a number of words or phrases, circle them, review them, and join related ones by lines, as shown in the example.

Because the map shows the relationship among ideas, you can quickly see which area holds the most potential for development. The map also suggests major points for such development. For example, the general area of *pressure* to cheat suggests five major reasons: maintaining athletic eligibility, raising a grade point to ensure admission into graduate school or a strong application for a top job, maintaining or applying for a scholarship, and family expectations or continued financial support. These offer plenty of material for writing an essay.

Now review your map and choose one area that interests you or that you believe might be best for further exploration and development. Make a scratch outline indicating what your purpose and major points would be.

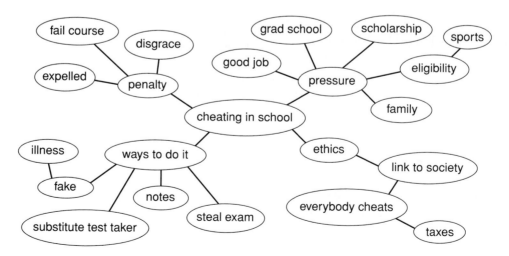

READING TO EXPLORE OUR IDEAS

Each of us approaches a written text with a personal frame of reference. We are influenced by our past experiences as well as by our current situation. We are also influenced by our gender, ethnicity, and age. Even people with similar backgrounds and ages will nonetheless interpret what they read somewhat differently. Something happens when we read: a weaving of personal sensations, images, and responses— some logical and some purely emotional. Therefore, you need to trust your responses. The meaning of that written text is not in the teacher. Nor is the meaning totally in those marks on a page or solely in you. It evolves from the dynamic interaction between you and what you read.

You can use this interaction consciously. It will help you better understand both what you read and your response to it. At the same time, this process can help you to develop topics for writing. Using Diane Ravitch's essay, you'll systematically explore the ideas and your immediate response to them through the following activities:

Summarize the Main Idea

Before you read the entire article, read the first and final paragraphs. Then, skim the entire article, looking only for main ideas, underlining or highlighting them as you come across them. Ask yourself, How did Ravitch get from her major point in the introduction to her conclusion? Now read slowly and carefully. When you complete the reading, write down Ravitch's main idea.

Argue with the Author

In the margins, note when you agree or disagree with the points being made, the ideas being presented. Also note why you agree or disagree. Imagine the author sitting across the table from you. What would you say to her? What would you want to know?

BACK TO THE BASICS: TEST SCORES DON'T LIE

Diane Ravitch

When I was in public high school in Texas in the 1950s, one of the last things a girl wanted was a reputation as a good student. Girls who got good grades were "brains," and brains were socially handicapped. Most girls strived to cultivate the June Allyson image: a follower, not a leader; cute and not too smart; or at least not so smart that the guys felt threatened. Apparently—despite the women's movement and the presence of significant numbers of successful women as role models—it is still considered inappropriate in most schools and colleges for girls to seem "smart." As a female student at Hunter High School in New York City recently explained: "I make straight A's, but I never talk about it. . . . It's cool to do really badly. If you are interested in school and show it, you're a nerd." In elite institutions where students are chosen for their academic ability, girls are more willing to challenge the boys academically than they are in nonselective schools and colleges. But with the demise of most single-sex girls' schools and colleges, there are now even fewer institutions where girls can be leaders and achievers without feeling like freaks. The popular culture—through television, movies, magazines, and video—incessantly drums in the message to young women that it is better to be popular, sexy, and "cool" than to be intelligent, accomplished, and outspoken: Madonna has replaced June Allyson.

In 1986 researchers Signithia Fordham and John U. Ogbu found a similar antiacademic ethos among both male and female students in an all-black high school in Washington, D.C. They noted that able students faced strong peer pressure not to succeed in school. If they did well in their studies, they might be accused of "acting white." Fordham and Ogbu observed that "peer group pressures against academic striving take many forms, including labeling (e.g., 'brainiac' for students who receive good grades in their courses), exclusion from peer activities or ostracism, and physical assault."

These attitudes, whether expressed by boys or girls, blacks or whites, discourage academic achievement. If boys or girls who study are derided as "goobs" and "dweebs"—two of the many pejorative terms for good students catalogued in a recent *New York Times* survey of teenage slang—then most boys and girls are going to avoid studying. Permissive parents and permissive educators don't help the situation by leaving adolescents adrift in a culture shaped largely by mass media. A national mathematics assessment released in 1988 revealed that American teenagers know the basics taught in elementary school, but their academic performance trails off as they get older and peer pressures begin to take effect. Only half of all 17-year-olds "reached a level of proficiency associated with material taught in junior high school mathematics."

Unfortunately, outside the cultural bubble inhabited by Madonnas and dweebs lies a real world, and in that world poor academic achievement is not without consequences. Last March, a comparison of students in 17 nations reported that our fifth-graders ranked eighth out of the 17; our ninth-graders ranked 16 out of 17 (beating out Hong Kong only); and our 12th-graders ranked last in biology, third from the last in chemistry, and fourth from the last in physics. Just a few weeks ago another international test of mathematics and science was released by the Educational Testing Service, with the same dismal results. Compared to 13-year-old students in Ireland, South Korea, Spain, the United Kingdom, and four provinces in Canada, our students scored last in mathematics and well below the mean [average] In science.

There is a growing real world correspondence between our declining test results and our declining economic prowess. Those countries that promote hard work and self-discipline in school have surged ahead, eroding the technological edge that we once enjoyed. According to the *New York Times,* Japan's annual share of American patents grew over the past 15 years from 4 percent to 19 percent, while our own share dropped from 73 percent to 54 percent. Experts point to the lack of a well-educated labor force as one of the prime causes of our diminishing economic position. Government policy is partially responsible, as are inadequate levels of savings and investment. But we have wounded ourselves, socially and economically, by failing to nurture scientists, engineers, inventors, and, in fact, a general citizenry who can read, write, compute, and adeptly use technology. In the 17-nation science study, the bottom quarter in the ninth grade of U.S. schools is described as "scientifically illiterate."

So what are we doing about it? Among the nations that regularly lead the world in international competitions, like Korea and Japan, there is a strong core curriculum that begins in elementary school. U.S. educators should be demanding that all future teachers get a solid liberal education, one that includes math, science, history, literature, and foreign language; and some educators are. Educators and concerned citizens should also be insisting that all children learn science and mathematics and history and literature and a foreign language in every grade from elementary school onward; but few educators are, because they either don't believe in doing so or know there aren't enough qualified teachers to offer such a rich curriculum.

What we shouldn't be doing is denying that a problem exists, or jettisoning objective measures that reveal our educational shortcomings. . . . [Ravitch argues that rather than use the SAT as a college admission test, schools should measure what students have actually studied in science, history, literature, mathematics, and foreign language—an achievement test which, she believes, would force high schools to teach subjects that matter.]

But no matter what kind of test is used, we will continue to have serious cultural problems undermining educational achievement: the negative attitudes of parents who urge their sons to strive and achieve but not their daughters; and the negative attitude of educators who accept the destructive peer culture, not acknowledging their responsibility to establish a climate in which academic achievement, hard work, and brain power are honored. . . . We will continue to lose ground and squander our educational resources until teenagers and their parents come to recognize that academic achievement requires the same motivation and active involvement as achievement in sports or music.

Question Yourself

What wasn't clear to you? Think in terms of asking the author what she means. Fill in the blank:

I don't understand _____ .

I wasn't ready for _____ .

I was surprised when I read _____ .

Connect with Your Experience

What did you think of as you read? What other issues came to mind? Do your observations and experience lead you to agree with Ravitch or oppose her?

Establish the Point of View

To whom do you believe Ravitch is writing? What seems to be her attitude toward students? Toward parents? Toward teachers? Toward society in general? How do you know?

Keeping Your Reading Journal at Hand

Earlier, we talked about maintaining a reading journal as a way of understanding what you read and generating possible writing topics. The questions and statements in the preceding activities are merely an expansion of that idea. If you apply them consistently, they will lead you to the issues and to your ideas about those issues.

Group Activity

As you discuss the following questions, be sure to allow each person enough time to express his or her views. Take notes on anything you find interesting or might want to explore further. Ask questions when you don't understand someone's views.

1. What does Ravitch mean when she writes about the *destructive peer culture?* What evidence does she provide to back up her use of *destructive?* Do you agree with her view?

2. Who or what does Ravitch blame for what she believes is a terrible situation in American education? Does your personal experience or observation lead you to agree or disagree with her point of view?

3. According to Ravitch, everyone in America should be concerned about the state of public education. What case does she make for this point? How do you think she would respond to people who have no children in school and say, "Why should I care what goes on there?"

4. "So what are we going to do about it [the problem]?" asks Ravitch. What does she suggest as possible solutions? Evaluate her solutions: What are they? What would each require and from whom? Is each solution workable? Would it be supported by parents? Educators? Taxpayers?

5. Compare Robert Samuelson's ideas with those of Ravitch. Both writers address American teenagers, schools, and problems with attitudes. Both are exploring a serious issue. If they make the same point, do they use the same examples or reasons to support it? Do you find one writer more convincing than the other? If so, why?

Writing Activity

Ravitch argues that "the popular culture—through television, movies, magazines, and video—incessantly drums in the message to young women that it is better to be popular, sexy, and 'cool' than to be intelligent, accomplished, and outspoken." Samuelson argues that "Americans are growing up faster, but they may not be growing up better."

Choose one of these statements as your topic. Then use at least two different strategies to generate and explore your ideas on that topic.

Save your work; you may use it for a later writing assignment.

CUBING

Cubing, named for the six-sided perspective of a cube, is a powerful strategy and especially well suited for academic writing. Through it, we can systematically examine a subject from multiple points of view: six angles, six different perspectives. Like freewriting and looping, cubing depends upon sticking with it for three to five minutes of writing on each angle.

1. **Description:** What something looks like; its general characteristics, physical qualities; facts and figures that help us see it; defining features.

2. **Comparison:** How something is similar to or different from something else.

3. **Association:** What memories something stirs in us; personal connections; thoughts, examples, experiences.

4. **Analysis:** What something's made of, the parts; reasons why something happens; controversies, investigations, supporting evidence.

5. **Application:** How something's used, what it can do; what problem is solved or created.

6. **Argumentation:** Opinions, conclusions, recommendations for or against; criticism.

Using an idea from Samuelson's essay, that today's high school students lack self-discipline and serious work habits, we can see how cubing works.

1. **Description:** What characterizes today's high school students? lazy? who says so? evidence of? bored? how know? what's the racial mix of students? does that make any difference? family structures of students? important? urban kids, suburban kids, rural kids—all the same? bright? turned off? why? defiant? talented? caring? self-centered?

2. **Comparison:** Males/females; Caucasian, African American, Hispanic American, Asian American, Native American; achievement in science/math vs. humanities; U.S.A. vs. Japan or Germany; students in 1950s vs. students in 1990s.

3. **Association:** Not working in math, working hard in social studies, hating physics; giving Sara a tough time because she did all the assigned work; nobody really caring about what I had to say; dumb questions in textbooks; English teacher = robot; even when interested, didn't want to look like it.

4. **Analysis:**   Causes for lack of school work—assignments seem dumb and boring, unrelated to life; family not care if kids do them or not; working too many hours outside of school; sports more important; never had to work around home or have any responsibility; have too many home responsibilities, no energy left; disruptive family; teachers not demanding quality work.

5. **Application:**   Problems created by lack of self-discipline—never get sense of satisfaction of doing a job well; habit that stays around in adult life; can get into serious trouble; when decide want to work, get a particular job, etc., not be able to prove can do it.

6. **Argumentation:**   Revolution in curriculum—make pertinent for 21st century and kids will tune in and work harder; many kids have serious family problems that affect school and work habits—get at the family problems first; get rid of so much TV watching; create better homework assignments and structure classwork for active participation.

> Which perspective or angle do you like best? If you were going to write an essay on this general topic, which perspective might you use and why?

Writing Activity

Pick a topic, perhaps one you've been exploring already, and try the cubing exercise. You should spend about 30 minutes on it. When you have finished with the exercise, choose one of your cubing perspectives. Formulate a statement that could be the basis for an essay. How would you support this statement? Now choose a different perspective and formulate a statement. How would your essay be different? Has your purpose for writing changed?

USING TRADITIONAL PATTERNS OF DEVELOPMENT AND ORGANIZATION

Thinking about purpose, aligned with a traditional pattern of development and organization, can be a good starting point to generate or explore a topic. Additionally, considering purpose provides us with a way into developing a controlling idea for an essay.

Pattern	Purpose
Narration	To tell about, a story
Description	To present a picture, to detail
Exemplification	To give specific examples
Classification	To group and explain related things
Process Analysis	To explain how to do something or how it happens
Comparison/Contrast	To point out similarities or differences
Cause and Effect	To provide reasons for, consequences of
Definition	To explain what a term or concept means
Argumentation	To present a point of view, seek acceptance of it
Proposal/Solution	To present a reasonable solution to a problem

Developing a Controlling Idea for an Essay

You've been exploring the topic of student cheating. Now you'll try out two different topics, ones with added complexity: American families and the American homeless. Consider this complexity as you try out ideas and learn how to develop a good controlling idea for your essays.

Just as a topic sentence guides the development and content of a paragraph, a controlling idea guides the development of an entire essay. In academic writing, the controlling idea is usually stated rather than implied; an explicit statement is generally found within the first paragraphs. It tells us what the essay is about, what major point the writer will develop. It may also tell us the writer's opinion or judgment on the subject, as in this example:

Due to more economic freedom for women, marital relationships today are significantly different from those of a generation ago.

What would you expect the writer to develop? What information is promised to the reader? Chances are you would expect to know just what "economic freedom" means. Then you would expect to learn how this freedom has brought about a change, and just what that change entails. You would need the contrast between women of your mother's generation and your own. The writer is promising you an illustration of "significantly different." Here's another example:

> Domestic relationships today are more stressful than those of my parents' generation.

Again, what would you expect to learn? First, you would expect the writer to define or limit what is meant by domestic relationships. Some relationships might carry more stress than normal, simply because they are more nontraditional. Second, you would expect to learn what the writer considers to be stressful. And you'd expect to see the comparison between two generations laid out clearly for you to evaluate. The writer is making an assertion, that relationships today are more stressful. As a reader, you have every right to expect that the writer can "prove it," or at the very least, convince you that the point is valid.

There are various ways in which a writer states a controlling idea, each carrying a promise to the reader. If the general topic were American families, the following offer possibilities:

Descriptive   American families today look different from those of a generation ago (would describe the various configurations of single-parent families, lesbian and gay families, cross-cultural families).

Explanatory   Childless couples searching for adoptable white infants have found eastern Europe a new resource (would explore this new baby market, perhaps provide readers with information on how to proceed).

Analytical   Statistics show that the American family continues to shrink, and polls state that economics is the major factor (would analyze the economic reasons for a reduction in family size).

Evaluative   Until families provide more stability, many children will fail to develop their learning potential (clearly the writer's opinion, a judgment that will need support).

Sometimes these categories overlap. With a controlling idea such as "serial marriages are commonplace today," our writing would be both descriptive and explanatory. Our readers would expect to learn just what serial marriages are and how and why they came to exist. We might also analyze the situation. However, there is no hint of evaluation, of judgment, present. If we stated that "serial marriages are destructive" or "serial marriages make good sense," we have changed to an evaluative controlling idea. However, we would need to be descriptive as well, to explain just what we mean by the term "serial marriage."

It's important to state a clear controlling idea. Your reader wants to understand your purpose for writing the essay "up front."

Using Strategies to Develop Controlling Ideas

People have a tendency to respond quickly to some issues, perhaps out of a strong emotional feeling about them. However, quick responses are often superficial, reducing a complex issue to a simple one. Using a generating strategy will help you avoid this situation.

Topic: the homeless in America

Because this topic is a fairly complex one, cubing might be a good way to generate more ideas for exploration and writing.

Description.   What things look like, characteristics, definitions.

Who are the homeless? Where are they living? What is a shelter? What is the life of a homeless person? Homeless men—characteristics; homeless women—characteristics; ethnicity of homeless; new homeless—blue-collar worker of the 1980s and 90s; children of the new homeless.

Comparison.   How is something or someone like or different from . . . ?

Homeless in America vs. homeless in _____ ; male vs. female homeless; difference between a home and a shelter; are all shelters the same? Do different states have different rules and regulations regarding the homeless; are all private agencies alike?

Association.   Personal connections; memories, experiences.

Homeless in Boston and Cambridge, sleeping on bench on Brattle Street; homeless in Berkeley, sleeping on lawn across from dorm; police; women with grocery carts laden with junk, belongings; sleeping in subways, doorways; mentally unstable, singing and talking to self, personal uneasiness.

Analysis.   Reasons, controversies, investigations.

Why an increase in homeless; why more families homeless; why more women homeless; economics, tearing down affordable housing, letting people out of institutions, lack of affordable mental health care, lack of jobs, lack of job training, losing jobs, drugs, alcoholism, family abuse; who's educating the children of the new homeless?

Application.   Problem solving, social implications, economic implications, what can be done?

State and federal assistance; new definition of equality; health care; renovation of inner city, expansion of low-cost housing; job training; new vision of jobs for the 90s.

Argumentation.   Opinions, recommendations, criticism, conclusions.

Renovate inner city, affordable housing; national health care; job training; change economic policies that created recession; better rehabilitation; tougher laws on drug and alcohol abuse; tougher laws on family abuse (wife beating); stop forcing people into shelters—issue of personal freedom; literacy/education.

Cubing provided many ideas that could be worked into a controlling idea:

✦ Female homeless represent a new and growing problem for American cities.

✦ Economic policies of the 1980s are responsible for the increase in homelessness.

✦ A new definition of homeless in America, blue-collar workers.

✦ Renovate the inner city.

✦ Redefine jobs and job training for the 1990s and beyond.

✦ Develop a national health care plan.

✦ Children of the homeless, lost to illiteracy, ill health, maintaining the cycle of poverty and hopelessness.

✦ Redistribute some foreign aid into American cities.

We can try out a couple of these ideas and see what might develop as controlling ideas and major points:

Controlling idea: The female homeless represent a new and growing problem for American cities.

Who are they?

Why an increase?

✦ Family abuse and desertion

✦ Welfare cutbacks

◆   Letting mentally ill out of institutions

◆   Cutbacks in social welfare programs

◆   Eliminating cheap housing

Controlling idea: The economic policies of the 1980s are responsible for the increase in homelessness in America.

What were these policies?

How did they contribute to homelessness?

◆   Loss of jobs

◆   Loss of affordable housing

◆   Values, attitudes of Reagan and Bush administrations

◆   Failure of Congress/political partisanship

◆   Widening gap between wealth and poverty

◆   Cutbacks on social welfare programs

◆   Recession

▬ Group Activity ▬▬▬▬▬▬▬▬▬▬▬▬▬▬▬▬▬▬▬▬▬

Statistics from the U.S. Department of Housing and Urban Development say that more than 25 percent of the homeless are children and that 40 percent of the homeless are families (*USA Today,* March 18, 1992, p. 1A). Using "children of the homeless" as your topic, develop at least two controlling ideas. Follow the model that has been presented, asking questions and listing potential material for development of major points.

INFORMAL OUTLINING AND ORGANIZING

Scratch Outline

When people hear the word "outline," they often get a mental picture of a complicated system involving different types of numbers and alphabet letters—a very formal presentation of major points and subpoints. That kind of outline is a useful reading guide, helping us see at a glance what the text is all about. For writing, however, a very brief, informal outline is more useful. It's not necessary to use any numbers or letters, only some indentations or titles to indicate the difference between the major point and its support points. For example:

Controlling idea: The female homeless represent a new and growing problem in America.

Who are the female homeless?

✦ Age, race, unemployed, uneducated

Why on street now?

✦ Leaving abusive homes
✦ Lack of social programs to assist
✦ Lack of inexpensive housing
✦ Letting mentally ill out of hospitals
✦ Cutback on welfare benefits

Why should anyone care?

From this initial outline, we can do more refined planning and make changes that are needed. An outline good enough to guide our writing, a plan, is all that is needed. We don't want something so refined, so complete that we are reluctant to make changes. *An outline good enough to help us and not too good to throw away is best.*

Comparative Outline

Informal organizational plans can also help us determine our controlling idea.

Topic: The new homeless in America, a result of economic policies of the 1980s

Economic Policies of 1970s	Economic Policies of 1980s
_____	_____
_____	_____
_____	_____
_____	_____

Alike: _____

_____

Different: _____

_____

What conclusions can I draw?

_____

_____

_____

What point do I want to make?

_____

_____

_____

Possible controlling ideas?

_____

_____

_____

Cause and Effect Relationships

A controlling idea can be a cause and its effects, as in this example:

Topic   Children of the homeless

Cause   Family on the street

Effects   At risk—educationally
medically
emotionally
physically

Or there might be a causal chain, one cause or effect leading to the next step:

cause→effect→cause→effect→

recession→job lost→home lost→family on street/homeless

Children at risk—educationally
medically
emotionally
physically

What conclusions can I draw?

_____

_____

_____

What point do I want to make?

_____

_____

_____

Possible controlling ideas?

_____

_____

_____

Comparison and Contrast Chart

Yet another graphic way of looking at a topic can help us see the similarities and differences quickly:

TOPIC: CHILDREN AT RISK		
	1970s	**1990s**
Similar	Immigrant children Migrant workers' children Below poverty line	
Different		Gangs and gunfire Crack babies AIDS babies Working-class children Breakup of family Lack of immunization

What conclusions can I draw?

_____

_____

_____

What point do I want to make?

_____

_____

_____

Do I want to go further, investigate reasons for similarities or differences?

_____

_____

_____

Controlling idea: An increase in violence has put city children at risk in the 1990s.

Why? In what ways?

_____

_____

_____

What would be my purpose in writing?

_____

_____

_____

New controlling idea: Children are born at risk in the 1990s.

Now what is my purpose?

_____

_____

_____

New controlling idea: The breakdown of the American family in the past 20 years has left more children at risk.

What would be my purpose in writing?

_____

_____

_____

Opinion Chart

A chart such as the one on the next page can help us lay out ideas for a position paper or some sort of argumentative essay, a common writing assignment in college classes.

My Opinion: _____

_____

Headings: _____   _____   _____

Why: **Reason/Evidence**   **Reason/Evidence**   **Reason/Evidence**

_____   _____   _____

_____   _____   _____

Details/Examples   **Details/Examples**   **Details/Examples**

_____   _____   _____

_____   _____   _____

My Conclusion: _____

_____

After you read Allan Bloom's thoughts on college students in the following excerpt from *The Closing of the American Mind,* study the two responses worked out in chart form.

SELF-CENTEREDNESS

Allan Bloom

Students these days are, in general, nice. I choose the word carefully. They are not particularly moral or noble. Such niceness is a facet of democratic character when times are good. Neither war nor tyranny nor want has hardened them or made demands on them. The wounds and rivalries caused by class distinctions have disappeared along with any strong sense of class (as it once existed in universities in America and as it still does, poisonously, in England). Students are free of most constraints, and their families make sacrifices for them without asking for much in the way of obedience or response. Religion and national origin have almost no noticeable effect on their social life or their career prospects. Although few really believe in "the system," they do not have any burning sentiment that injustice is being done to them. The drugs and sex once thought to be forbidden are available in the quantities required for sensible use. A few radical feminists still feel the old-time religion, but most of the women are comfortably assured that not much stands in the way of their careers. . . . Students these days are pleasant, friendly, and if not great-souled, at least not particularly mean-spirited. Their primary occupation is themselves, understood in the narrowest sense. . . .

There is, indeed, a certain listlessness about them, an absence of a broad view of the future. . . .

But the great majority of students, although they as much as anyone want to think well of themselves, are aware that they are busy with their own careers and their relationships.

Response 1.

My Opinion: *Most women are not "comfortably assured" that there are no*

barriers in the way of their careers.

Headings: *Business*   *Medicine*   *Education*

Why:	**Reason/Evidence**	**Reason/Evidence**	**Reason/Evidence**
	Few top women in	*Women medical*	*Few women*
	top management	*students/M.D.s*	*administrators*
	jobs	*harassed*	
		Discouraged in	*Few rank as*
		surgery specialty	*professors*

Details/Examples	**Details/Examples**	**Details/Examples**
Fortune 500 Co.	*Stanford U.*	*1 of 10 in*
	harassment incident	*local university*
Local businesses	*Local clinics*	*1 of 8 in high school*
		Only 4% prof. female

My Conclusion: *Although women have made some career gains, they still don't have the same access as men. Women students can't assume entry into the career they want.*

Response 2.

My Opinion: *Students are not free of most constraints.*

Headings: *Economic*   *Sexual*   *Family*

Why:

Reason/Evidence	**Reason/Evidence**	**Reason/Evidence**
Lack of money	*Awareness of*	*Responsibility*
	disease	*for others*

Details/Examples	**Details/Examples**	**Details/Examples**
Piling up student	*Fear of AIDS*	*Nontraditional*
loans	*Other sexually*	*students*
Working 1 or 2 jobs	*transmitted diseases*	*Single parent*
Recession/inflation		
Parents not able to		
support student		

My Conclusion: *Professor Bloom might have found students at the U. Chicago in the late 1980s to be free of constraints, but that's not the situation of students today.*

Writing Activity	Using information from Joan Beck's essay "Why America's Students Are Falling Behind" or Susan Chira's "Some Challenge Notion That U.S. Schools Are Failing," prepare an opinion chart. Use your own ideas, observations, experience, and discussion notes, as well as what is presented in the article. You may take either side of the issue, but in either case, be reasonable and logical in your choice of evidence.

WHY AMERICA'S STUDENTS ARE FALLING BEHIND

Joan Beck

It's worrisome enough that the Japanese can build better cars and more TV sets than Americans. But that they are producing smarter students should be of far greater concern. Why are Japanese—and Chinese—children doing better academically than American youngsters?

There is no doubt American elementary students lag seriously behind comparable Asian children. Long-term, cross-cultural studies, taking into account socioeconomic status, language differences and cultural factors confirm the disparities.

The reason is not because Asian children are innately more intelligent than their American counterparts, says a new book, *The Learning Gap*. It's because of crucial differences in how Asian schools are run, the amount of time Asian and American youngsters spend on academics and the attitudes toward school and achievement youngsters absorb from their parents and their culture.

The book suggests several changes in American schooling, some of them surprising, some of them in conflict with prevailing wisdom. Harold W. Stevenson and James W. Stigler, who wrote *The Learning Gap*, did much of the extensive, long-term research that documents the problem. Both are professors of psychology, Stevenson at the University of Michigan and Stigler at the University of California, Los Angeles.

The studies on which this book is based involve large, representative samplings of same-age children in Minneapolis, suburban Chicago, Sendai (Japan), Taipei (Taiwan), and Beijing (China). The tests were painstakingly constructed to be culturally fair and comparable.

Asian children not only spend much more time in school—longer schools days, half-day classes on Saturday, less vacation time—but they do more homework, even during vacations. Asian families make the home more conducive to studying than do American families. No matter how cramped the home or how poor the parents, most Asian children have their own study space and desk.

Asian parents believe—and their children are expected to understand—that academic learning is their primary responsibility. They spend less time in play and organized sports than American youngsters and do fewer household chores because their parents don't want to interfere with studying.

American parents and teachers are likely to assume that innate abilities play a major role in how well children do in school. But Chinese and Japanese parents think achievement is directly related to hard work and effort. The difference has far-reaching consequences in how children behave, how schools are set up and how school and home interact.

American children who see their success or failure directly related to innate factors have little reason to work hard, the book notes. Asian youngsters who are taught the hours they invest in school work will pay off in achievement and that low marks indicate insufficient effort, try harder at their studies.

American parents are more likely than Asian parents to be satisfied with their children's academic performance and to think they are doing well, when international comparisons show that they are not. So they underestimate what their youngsters are capable of doing and the children see no reason to work harder.

The problem may get worse, with the growing emphasis on teaching children to have self-esteem and to feel good about themselves, regardless of their achievements. Such attitudes rob youngsters of motivation and limit what they accomplish, Stevenson and Sigler suggest.

Many American parents fear that raising expectations for their children will create harmful stress. But Stevenson and Stigler say there is no evidence to support such fear. "Meeting reasonable challenges enhances self-confidence and self-esteem," they point out. "Lack of challenge accomplishes little. Americans accept this precept in athletic achievement—surely the same principles apply to academic achievement."

More money alone won't solve this country's education problems, say Stevenson and Stigler. The United States already spends more money per student than almost every other nation in the world, including Japan, Taiwan, China—and a larger percentage of its gross national product.

Based on observations of successful schools in Asia, Stevenson and Stigler urge teachers be given smaller course loads and more time for preparation. They see no problem with increasing class sizes. And they urge more whole-class instruction rather than in-class grouping or tracking by ability.

American children often feel isolated and lonely because they do so much school work independently, even in the classroom, the researchers say. That may be a major reason they are less enthusiastic about school than their Asian counterparts, they suggest.

The book also advocates more challenging and interesting textbooks, more recess breaks during the day so children can work off energy and socialize, more opportunities for professional development for teachers, more interaction between home and school and a national educational policy to clarify the mission of the schools.

"The belief in the importance of hard work is not alien to Americans," the book points out. The problem is we have become reluctant to teach our children its value. As a result we—and they—are losing out competitively in far more important areas than cars and TVs.

RENEGADE RESEARCHERS OFFER REBUTTAL: U.S. SCHOOLS ARE BETTER THAN MANY SAY

Susan Chira

Forget all the bad news about American schools. There is no crisis in American education, say a number of renegade researchers whose ideas have touched off a bitter debate with broad implications for education policy in an election year.

By falsely claiming all American schools are failing, these critics charge, the Bush administration and others divert attention and money from the real crisis: poor inner-city and rural schools.

The debate itself reveals how little Americans know about their schools' performance and how far away the country is from defining just how good its schools should be.

The defenders of American education wave a batch of surprising statistics: test scores and drop-out rates have held steady for at least 15 years, the percentage of top-scoring students is roughly the same as it was 15 years ago, and comparisons that show American students trailing those in nearly every other country are distorted by faulty methodology.

"Most schools in America are better than they were in 1981," said Harold Hodgkinson, director of the Center for Demographic Policy, a research organization in Washington. "I'm interested in a focus on the worst kids in the worst schools. Given the fact that everyone agrees that the bottom third of our kids are awful [sic], they get very little spent on them."

But the purveyors of bad news are regrouping, charging the renegades with complacency, and fighting them statistic by statistic. Even if schools over all are not much worse than they were 15 years ago, they say, they are nowhere near good enough and they still trail America's competitors.

"The critics are wrong in saying the schools are just as good as they ever were," said Diane Ravitch, an assistant secretary of education. "That is deeply damaging; it inspires complacency and a false sense of self-esteem. To say we do as well today as we did 20 years ago—our kids are not going to be competing with their parents but with children being educated in other countries." . . .

[Defenders of American education] believe that whatever declines do exist have occurred because schools now, unlike those of a generation or two ago, are trying to educate everybody—more immigrants, more minorities, most students who once would have dropped out and gotten good jobs on the assembly line. And they say international comparisons are flawed because American students as a whole are being compared to other countries' elite. . . .

Moreover, children are scoring at about the same level on the most reliable standardized test—the federally financed National Assessment of Educational Progress, widely known among educators as the nation's report card.

Reading scores are about the same as they were 20 years ago. Math scores have held steady since 1973. Science scores are somewhat lower than they were in 1969, but scores of 9- and 17-year olds have improved steadily during the 1980s. Both these tests and SAT tests show that scores for minority students have also risen. . . . Average scores on tests required to attend business schools also rose. The percentage of students scoring above 600 points (out of 800) on the SAT math and verbal scores fell until 1975 but has held steady since.

Yet for virtually every statistic the researchers produce, critics of American schools offer a rebuttal. Scores on the "nation's report card" tests may have stayed about the same for 20 years, but they are stuck at low levels, according to the National Center for Education Statistics, part of the Department of Education. . . . While American schools still produce some brilliant students, Ravitch argues that even at the top there is reason to fear. The percentage of students who scored above 600 on the verbal SAT may have stabilized since 1975, she says, but go back only three years, to 1972, and the numbers show a drop of 35% in the last 20 years.

Many scholars argue that the researchers are right to say that schools have not gone downhill, but are drawing the wrong conclusions. "It's true, but it's irrelevant," says Marc Tucker, president of the National Center on Education and Economy, a Rochester, N.Y., research center. "Doing as well or slightly better than we used to do is doing appallingly badly relative to the rest of the world."

Group Activity

Compare your opinion charts. Determine a single controlling idea (in this case, one that states an opinion). Pool all ideas that would support your controlling idea, and choose the best supporting material for it. Then, create an informal outline, just as though you were going to write the essay.

Writing Activity

Review all the writing topics you've explored in this chapter. Choose one topic to develop into a brief essay.

CHAPTER 6

Writing from Personal Experience: Narration and Description

Most often, we begin writing as a way of sharing our experience. From the first crayon mark on the wall to a school essay, we draw upon our personal world—events, people, thoughts and dreams, hopes and dashed hopes. Personal-experience writing is powerful because it arises from our very core. Writing about personal experience can also be very satisfying, providing an exploration that might be left unsaid or quite limited in the give-and-take of conversation. Through writing, then, we can explore ourselves and our world in important ways. Narration is one of the most basic and most important of these.

NARRATION

When you read Kate Chopin's piece, you were reading a narrative. Although narratives don't usually state their main idea explicitly, we nonetheless could form a very good idea of Chopin's main idea. We also grasped its significance; what Chopin told us mattered. Telling a story that matters is at the heart of narration. We want to care about the people and events, and we want what happens to reflect our human experience, such as growing up or dealing with relationships. Narratives are a powerful means of connecting us not only with others, but also with ourselves.

Characteristics of Narration

Narration is one of the most common forms of writing we encounter, often starting as early as age one or two through picture books.

Oral narratives, in many cultures, take the place of written forms; they contain the same elements as the written form, and capture listeners through the same techniques. Narratives tell a story, most often presenting a series of incidents, recording a slice of life through time. That time may be five minutes or five years. Generally, narratives are linear; that is, they take us from point A to point B; first this happened, then this happened. Within this structure, the writer can emphasize an incident, paint a verbal picture, and highlight feelings. However, some narratives start at the end and then return to the real beginning through flashbacks. We often see this technique in movies or television programs, where we know the outcome and then follow the story line to learn how people and events reached that outcome. It can be a very effective strategy for keeping the reader's attention.

Although it seems easy enough to get from point A to point B to point C, there are potential problems. If the writer jumps ahead too quickly, not preparing us for the outcome, we'll probably become confused. Or if the writer leaves out important details, we will become equally confused and, most likely, irritated. If the writer gets sidetracked, wandering off the story line, we will get bored and put aside the narrative. We may also get bored if the writer doesn't use enough specific detail, enough examples, to draw us into the story. Good narratives depend upon selecting words that provide the reader with a concrete sense of person, place, events. The connection between writer and reader lies in our senses—touch, taste, hearing, sight, and smell—and the ability to evoke both physical and emotional images and associations.

Characteristics of Description

Our senses are the key to description. Recreating or evoking images of sight, sound, touch, and smell allow the reader to take part in the narrative. Words that bring color, size, shape, texture, and sound to the text will bring the reader to the setting and mood, to the people and events, both physically and emotionally. Therefore, close attention to words that name, compare, and detail is mandatory for writing effective description.

It's important to note, however, that description has to have a point to it. When we talk, we don't just describe someone or something for no reason at all; we understand that our listener will share in our experience only if he or she has more explicit and vivid detail. Similarly, when we write, we describe because it is the best way to draw the reader into our experience; we paint images, whole pictures, whatever will bring the reader closer to sharing.

When we narrate, we

- ✦ tell a good story.
- ✦ choose incidents or people with real significance for us.
- ✦ paint a verbal picture of people, places, and events.
- ✦ use specific detail and examples.
- ✦ maintain an orderly story line.

When we describe, we

- ✦ use our senses: sight, sound, touch, smell.
- ✦ use words that bring color, shape, size, texture, and sound.
- ✦ use words that name, compare, and detail.
- ✦ use words that show action or emotion.
- ✦ paint a verbal picture, physically and emotionally.

Effective narratives, those that leave us with a sense of "I'm really glad I read this," have captured us through the writer's attention to specific detail, as well as through the careful ordering of that detail. Spatial description may play a large role in narratives. The writer has to consider the ways in which our eyes move over an object, person, or scene. We usually start at a set point and return to that point, taking in everything en route. Sometimes, we focus on a single detail first, a dominating detail that draws us to it before we shift our gaze to other things. Descriptions may be realistic, such as those in dictionaries and encyclopedias—or police reports, for that matter—but they may also be nonrealistic, painting a picture not as it would appear with a camera but with an artist's brush. This type of description, not intended as scientific accuracy, provides us with a picture nonetheless, often a mood or atmosphere essential to the narrative. In Richard Wright's narrative, we see both.

Before you read this excerpt, explore your ideas on discipline in your reading journal.

- ✦ Do you believe parents have an obligation to discipline their children? In what ways?

- ✦ Do disciplinary practices get passed from generation to generation, a child repeating the same type of discipline as was practiced with him or her?

- ✦ Do children have rights? Have you had any experience with an adult as lawgiver? If yes, can you recall your feelings, responses, and so on?

As you read, keep your double-entry journal open. On the lefthand side, write down words, phrases, or sentences that evoke strong responses in you; ask questions or argue.

THE KITTEN

Richard Wright

Richard Wright was among the most gifted writers of the 1940s and 1950s, one of the voices exploring themes of racial inequality and injustice. Born in Mississippi, he moved from one urban center to another, and finally, to Paris, where he died in 1960. "The Kitten" is taken from Black Boy, *his autobiography.*

In Memphis we lived in a one-story brick tenement. The stone buildings and the concrete pavements looked bleak and hostile to me. The absence of green, growing things made the city seem dead. Living space for the four of us—my mother, my brother, my father, and me—was a kitchen and a bedroom. In the front and rear were paved areas in which my brother and I could play, but for days I was afraid to go into the strange city streets alone.

It was in this tenement that the personality of my father first came fully into the orbit of my concern. He worked as a night porter in a Beale Street drugstore and he became important and forbidding to me only when I learned that I could not make noise when he was asleep in the daytime. He was the lawgiver in our family and I never laughed in his presence. I used to lurch timidly in the kitchen doorway and watch his huge body sitting slumped at the table. I stared at him with awe as he gulped his beer from a tin bucket, as he ate long and heavily, sighed, belched, closed his eyes to nod on a stuffed belly. He was quite fat and his bloated stomach always lapped over his belt. He was always a stranger to me, always somehow alien and remote.

One morning my brother and I, while playing in the rear of our flat, found a stray kitten that set up a loud, persistent meowing. We fed it some scraps of food and gave it water, but it still meowed. My father, clad in his underwear, stumbled sleepily to the back door and demanded that we keep quiet. We told him that it was the kitten that was making the noise and he ordered us to drive it away. We tried to make the kitten leave, but it would not budge. My father took a hand.

"Scat!" he shouted.

The scrawny kitten lingered, brushing itself against our legs, and meowing plaintively.

"Kill that damn thing!" my father exploded. "Do anything, but get it away from here!"

He went inside, grumbling. I resented his shouting and it irked me that I could never make him feel my resentment. How could I hit back at him? Oh, yes. . . . He had said to kill the kitten and I would kill it! I knew that he had really not meant for me to kill the kitten, but my deep hate of him urged me toward a literal acceptance of his word.

"He said for us to kill the kitten," I told my brother.

"He didn't mean it," my brother said.

"He did, and I'm going to kill 'im."

"Then he will howl," my brother said.

"He can't howl if he's dead," I said.

"He didn't really say kill 'im," my brother protested.

"He did!" I said. "And you heard him!"

My brother ran away in fright. I found a piece of rope, made a noose, slipped it about the kitten's neck, pulled it over a nail, then jerked the animal clear off the ground. It gasped, slobbered, spun, doubled, clawed the air frantically; finally its mouth gaped and its pink-white tongue shot out stiffly. I tied the rope to a nail and went to find my brother. He was crouching behind a corner of the building.

"I killed 'im," I whispered.

"You did bad," my brother said.

"Now Papa can sleep," I said, deeply satisfied.

"He didn't mean for you to kill 'im," my brother said.

"Then why did he *tell* me to do it?" I demanded.

My brother could not answer; he stared fearfully at the dangling kitten.

"That kitten's going to get you," he warned me.

"That kitten can't even breathe now," I said.

"I'm going to tell," my brother said, running into the house.

I waited, resolving to defend myself with my father's rash words, anticipating my enjoyment in repeating them to him even though I knew that he had spoken them in anger. My mother hurried toward me, drying her hands upon her apron. She stopped and paled when she saw the kitten suspended from the rope.

"What in God's name have you done?" she asked.

"The kitten was making noise and Papa said to kill it," I explained.

"You little fool!" she said. "Your father's going to beat you for this!"

"But he told me to kill it," I said.

"You shut your mouth!"

She grabbed my hand and dragged me to my father's bedside and told him what I had done.

"You know better than that!" my father stormed.

"You told me to kill 'im," I said.

"I told you to drive him away," he said.

"You told me to kill 'im," I countered positively.

"You get out of my eyes before I smack you down!" my father bellowed in disgust, then turned over in bed.

I had had my first triumph over my father. I had made him believe that I had taken his words literally. He could not punish me now without risking his authority. I was happy because I had at last found a way to throw my criticism of him into his face. I had made him feel that, if he whipped me for killing the kitten, I would never give serious weight to his words again. I had made him know that. I felt he was cruel and I had done it without his punishing me.

But my mother, being more imaginative, retaliated with an assault upon my sensibilities that crushed me with the moral horror involved in taking a life. All that afternoon she directed toward me calculated words that spawned in my mind a horde of invisible demons bent upon exacting vengeance for what I had done. As evening drew near, anxiety filled me and I was afraid to go into an empty room alone.

"You owe a debt you can never pay," my mother said.

"I'm sorry," I mumbled.

"Being sorry can't make that kitten live again," she said.

Then, just before I was to go to bed, she uttered a paralyzing injunction: she ordered me to go out into the dark, dig a grave, and bury the kitten.

"No!" I screamed, feeling that if I went out of doors some evil spirit would whisk me away.

"Get out there and bury that poor kitten," she ordered.

"I'm scared!"

"And wasn't that kitten scared when you put that rope around its neck?" she asked.

"But it was only a kitten," I explained.

"But it was alive," she said. "Can you make it live again?"

"But Papa said to kill it," I said, trying to shift the moral blame upon my father.

My mother whacked me across my mouth with the flat palm of her hand.

"You stop that lying! You knew what he meant!"

"I didn't!" I bawled.

She shoved a tiny spade into my hands.

"Go out there and dig a hole and bury that kitten!"

I stumbled out into the black night, sobbing, my legs wobbly from fear. Though I knew that I had killed the kitten, my mother's words had made it live again in my mind. What would that kitten do to me when I touched it? Would it claw at my eyes? As I groped toward the dead kitten, my mother lingered behind me, unseen in the dark, her disembodied voice egging me on.

"Mama, come and stand by me," I begged.

"You didn't stand by that kitten, so why should I stand by you?" she asked tauntingly from the menacing darkness.

"I can't touch it," I whimpered, feeling that the kitten was staring at me with reproachful eyes.

"Untie it!" she ordered.

Shuddering, I fumbled at the rope and the kitten dropped to the pavement with a thud that echoed in my mind for many days and nights. Then, obeying my mother's floating voice, I hunted for a spot of earth, dug a shallow hole, and buried the stiff kitten; as I handled its cold body my skin prickled. When I had completed the burial, I sighed and started back to the flat, but my mother caught hold of my hand and led me again to the kitten's grave.

"Shut your eyes and repeat after me," she said.

I closed my eyes tightly, my hand clinging to hers.

"Dear God, our Father, forgive me, for I knew not what I was doing . . . "

"Dear God, our Father, forgive me, for I knew not what I was doing," I repeated.

"And spare my poor life, even though I did not spare the life of the kitten . . . "

"And while I sleep tonight, do not snatch the breath of life from me . . . "

I opened my mouth but no words came. My mind was frozen with horror. I pictured myself gasping for breath and dying in my sleep. I broke away from my mother and ran into the night, crying, shaking with dread.

"No," I sobbed.

My mother called to me many times, but I would not go to her.

"Well, I suppose you've learned your lesson," she said at last.

Contrite, I went to bed, hoping that I would never see another kitten.

In your journal, respond to the following questions:

Thinking About Content

1. In your own words, characterize the main characters: child, father, mother. What specific details in the story led you to these characterizations? What is the nature of the family relationships? How did you form these ideas?

2. Do you believe the boy is portrayed as a victim? Is Wright looking for sympathy from his readers?

Thinking About Writing

1. Wright provides both a physical and a psychological description for his readers. List words, phrases, and so on that provide us with these descriptions.

2. How is the use of dialogue essential to this story? Would you have the same reactions if there were no dialogue?

3. From whose point of view is the story presented? How might the story change if another person related the incident?

Personal Connections

1. Children and adolescents often feel victimized by adults, people in authority (e.g., parent or caretaker, teacher). Have you ever been in a situation where you believed you were treated unfairly, picked on, victimized? What, if anything, did you do?

2. Do you believe Wright's action was justified? Do you know of situations where children had to take desperate measures to preserve themselves? Do you know of situations where children manipulated adults for the sheer pleasure of it?

3. As a child or young adolescent, were you ever in a situation where you could push an adult into a corner? What did you do?

4. What are your beliefs on disciplining children and adolescents? Is parent as lawgiver an appropriate and necessary role?

Before you read the following excerpt by Sandra Cisneros, reflect in your journal on your early childhood for a moment. Are there memories of what it felt like to be safe? Are there "sense" memories—smells, sounds, sights that even today bring back feelings of safety, of home (and *home* may be someone or somewhere other than your street address)?

HAIRS

Sandra Cisneros

"Hairs" is from Sandra Cisneros's best known book, The House on Mango Street.

Everybody in our family has different hair. My Papa's hair is like a broom, all up in the air. And me, my hair is lazy. It never obeys barrettes or bands. Carlos' hair is thick and straight. He doesn't need to comb it. Nenny's hair is slippery—slides out of your hand. And Kiki, who is the youngest, has hair like fur.

But my mother's hair, my mother's hair, like little rosettes, like little candy circles all curly and pretty because she pinned it in little pincurls all day, sweet to put your nose into when she is holding you, holding you and you feel safe, is the warm smell of bread before you bake it, is the smell when she makes a little room for you on her side of the bed still warm with her skin, and you sleep near her, the rain outside falling and Papa snoring. The snoring, the rain, and Mama's hair that smells like bread.

⎯ Thinking About Content ⎯

1. Why do you think Cisneros has written about the different types of hair in her family?
2. What, for you, is the center of Cisneros's narrative? What captures your attention? Why?

⎯ Thinking About Writing ⎯

1. Reread Cisneros's description of hair. What senses are touched with her words?
2. What other sense images does she bring to us?

⎯ Personal Connections ⎯

1. Did Cisneros's narrative bring back any childhood memories you hadn't thought of before you read it?
2. As adults, do we need positive childhood memories?

Before you read the following piece, write in your reading journal whatever words come to mind when you think of *mirrors*. What associations does this word bring to mind?

MIRRORS

Susan Kenney

Susan Kenney is a contemporary professional writer. This excerpt is taken from her book In Another Country.

My father died suddenly when he was forty and I was twelve. For years after his death I was bitterly resentful of his abrupt departure: I tried to keep the memory of him, his voice, his face, the color of his hair, the way he moved, the clothes he wore, and noted the anniversary of his death each year as it came around. Five years, ten years, twelve, and he had been dead as long as I knew him; fifteen, twenty-five, the years passing so quickly that soon he would be dead as long as he had been alive. I regarded that anniversary with an almost physical dread; we are

: alive so little and dead so long, and even in the memories of those who
: want to keep us we fade away.

Thinking About Content

1. We have a tendency to distort our memories, making them better or worse than the actual event or person. Do you think Kenney's memory has distorted her father's image? Explain.

2. "Mirrors" is a very suggestive title. Why might Kenney have used it for this section of her childhood memories?

Thinking About Writing

1. Notice how Kenney uses lists after "I tried to keep the memory of him" and for counting time. Why is this an effective method for her purpose?

2. The sentence "we are alive so little and dead so long" is a very effective one. What did Kenney do to achieve such a nice balance between the ideas?

Personal Connections

1. Anger directed at a person who has died is not an uncommon response among children, adolescents, and adults alike. Have you ever experienced this type of anger or known someone who has? Analyze why it occurs and why it can be considered a natural response.

2. Reflect on times when, as a child or young adolescent, you have been most angry with an adult. Is there a pattern?

3. Kenney notes "even in the memories of those who want to keep us we fade away." Do you believe such fading away is natural and good? Have you ever experienced a fading away? How did you finally deal with it?

4. If you were reflected in mirrors by someone who knows and cares for you deeply, what might the reflections be?

5. Sometimes, people view us as the "very image" of a parent or grandparent. Has this ever happened to you, and if it has, how did you feel about it? How would you feel if someone said this to you? In what ways could you be "the very image"?

Jennifer Urman wrote the following personal-experience essay in freshman composition when she was 19 years old. In it, she reflects on another kind of anger and resentment at losing a father.

Before you read the following essay by Jennifer Urman, respond to the following in your journal:

Divorce is _____ .

Second families are _____ .

Passage

I distinctly remember my father stopping by the roadside to teach me about cotton fields. "This is how thread is made," he would explain, and "How do you think these plants get water way out here in the desert?" He loved to play Master Educator; I was his doting pupil. He took me to Encanto Park on Sundays, where we sailed my plastic sailboat and raced rocket ships and chased geese that pestered us for bread crumbs and popcorn. I ran to my father when the geese bit my fingers because he was all that was strong and good and great in my life. My father was my teacher, my playmate, and my refuge.

My fourteenth summer shattered my world. I was an hysterical adolescent, melodramatic and demanding. Because of my parents' divorce, I was caught between two families, belonging to neither. I was probably looking for some reason to choose between the two. I am not quite sure. In any case, my father became my scapegoat. His hurt looks when I pulled away from his embraces, his fury when I lashed out at my half-sister in a jealous rage, and his uncomprehending anger when I matched my stubborn will with his own; all of these are imprinted on my mind as pre-emptory to our eventual parting of the ways. We topple our childhood gods from their lofty pedestals farther than they ever deserve to fall. That summer I was stony-faced and unforgiving, not realizing, too young to understand the failings of human nature. Youth is willing to sacrifice so much for its impatient ideals. . . .

Five summers have passed. But I am there again and again, reliving the final moments of my fourteenth summer. The airplane cabin is a little world all itself, a pressurized corridor muffling voices and sti-

fling engines at take-off. It is a good place to
think. Leaving the heat of Arizona for my family in
cool, green Wisconsin seems momentous to me. My father
stands outside the fence, one hand in his pocket,
the other dangling a cigarette. He wears sunglasses
against the scorching Arizona sun. They hide his eyes
and all expression. Seeing him standing there, all
alone, I feel regret, sorrow, pity, anything but the
tension and frustration of the wasted summer. These
are useless tears. It is suddenly clear he is lonely
and lost. There are so many hard lessons to learn, all
of this growing up to do.

Jennifer Urman

▬Thinking About Content▬▬▬▬▬▬▬▬▬▬▬▬▬▬

1. Is this essay about the father or the daughter? Why?

2. Compare Jennifer's anger and resentment with that of Susan Kenney. Are they similar or different? Explain your response.

3. Is this essay just about anger or about something more universal to our experience, to growing up? Refer back to sentences or passages that support your view.

▬Thinking About Writing▬▬▬▬▬▬▬▬▬▬▬▬▬▬

1. Quickly review the content of each of the three paragraphs. What has the author done in each and why? How does each serve her purpose in writing this essay? Note the time frame in each paragraph. Why does Urman write the third paragraph as though she were still 14 years old?

2. What is the tone of this essay? Do you think Urman was trying to evoke sympathy? Do you think she was merely recording?

3. List some words, phrases, or sentences that you found to be especially effective.

▬Personal Connections▬▬▬▬▬▬▬▬▬▬▬▬▬▬

1. Do you believe young adolescents often become, as Urman describes herself, "melodramatic" or "demanding" when faced with some crisis? Can you recall a time when you could have been described in this way?

2. Have you ever been in a situation where, like Urman, you realize as an adult that your adolescent response was "youth sacrificing so much for its impatient ideals"?

3. With an American divorce rate at 52 percent in the 1990s, the chances of children experiencing a sense of abandonment by one parent or facing remarriage and subsequent half-siblings are greatly increased. What are your thoughts on these critical family situations?

4. Urman believes, "We topple our childhood gods from their lofty pedestals farther than they ever deserve to fall." Do you agree with her? Explain your response.

Writing Activity

In your journal, explore further one of the ideas in "Personal Connections": adolescent demands, unrealistic expectations, sibling rivalry, melodrama, impatience, anger.

Like Jennifer Urman, Marjorie Harnden wrote the following essay, "Christmas Time," as her personal-experience essay in a college composition class. When she wrote this essay, Harnden was in her early twenties, looking back to a family incident that happened when she was still in high school.

Before you read this essay, write in your journal the name of some holiday or ritual that has special meaning for you. Quickly list all the things associated with this holiday or ritual, including family members and any specific roles they play—or you expect them to play.

Christmas Time

The Christmas of my junior year in high school is one I will never forget, not because I got a lot of presents or all the relatives came down, but because of what happened. My father went to jail on Christmas Eve. He was not a bad man, just sometimes a careless one. He was on probation for writing bad checks, and he must've done it again on Christmas Eve. He was apprehended at Shopko just before supper time, and his car was left in the parking lot, full of Santa's surprises for the wonderful morning.

When we found out what happened, we four kids were furious. How dare he ruin Christmas for everyone? What kind of father goes to jail on Christmas Eve? Nobody would get any presents. I looked to my mother just in time to see her wipe away a painful tear, and then it occurred to me. I faced my siblings and said, "I know we all feel bad, but how do you think Dad feels? I bet he feels like a real failure right now. How would you like to spend Christmas in jail? He's probably worrying about what we're going to think of him. And we all know he wouldn't do something like this on purpose. Accidents happen."

I paused for their reaction. Mom held her breath, looking first from one thoughtful face to another. My sister Mary spoke first. "She's right. He probably feels terrible." Amy began to cry. Mary continued, suddenly inspired. "Let's wait for Christmas! We can have it when Dad gets home. It's only a couple of days, and we can have it like he never was gone!" She was overwhelmingly supported.

When Dad got home two nights later, walking in the door with a tired and apprehensive look on his face, Christmas Eve dinner was steaming on the table. His four daughters came roaring downstairs to greet him, a massive flurry of hugs and kisses. Tears of joy and relief brimmed in his eyes, and he exclaimed, "I'm the luckiest father in the world!"

For the first time I had realized that my parents aren't just my father and mother; they are real people with dreams of their own. Parents also make mistakes, and they can feel just as bad as any kid. The lesson I learned became a valuable one as I grew up understanding why they did things the way they did. That gave me respect for their decisions, a respect I might not have had otherwise.

Marjorie Harnden

Thinking About Content

1. Do you think the four daughters are typical? Why or why not?
2. In your experience, are teenagers generally so forgiving?

3. Are parents under pressure to "do the right thing"? In this case, has the father done "the right thing"? How many different ways can you view his action?

4. How would you characterize Harnden's relationship with her father? What leads you to this characterization?

Thinking About Writing

1. In the final paragraph, Harnden makes a number of assertions about parents: "they are real people with dreams of their own"; "parents also make mistakes"; "they can feel just as bad as any kid." Do you have enough information to accept these statements? Are there too many of them?

2. In that same paragraph, Harnden says of herself: "I grew up understanding why they [parents] did things the way they did." Does this conclusion match the story she related? Where might she have concluded her essay?

3. If Mrs. Harnden, Marjorie's mother, had written this essay, how would it change?

Personal Connections

1. Harnden says, "Accidents happen," with reference to her father's lapse of judgment in writing more bad checks. Do you think his deliberate violation of the law and probation was justified? Have you ever faced a situation where you "did wrong" in order to "do right"?

2. Many people believe that Christmas has lost its original significance, has become little more than a commercial event, and has increasingly brought stress to people, especially those struggling financially. Do you agree with this judgment? Why?

3. Think of a holiday or ritual most celebrated or held in high regard by your family or culture. What would ruin it for you?

4. How do children learn to be as forgiving and generous as Harnden and her sisters? Do you think it is difficult to respond as they did?

5. Holidays, whether religious or cultural, carry expectations for those who have grown up with them. What expectations do you have for a particular holiday or ritual? Have you ever been angry or frustrated when those expectations weren't met?

BLUE WINDS DANCING

Thomas Whitecloud

Whitecloud, a Chippewa Indian, wrote this essay while a student at the University of the Redlands (California) in 1938. He later earned a medical degree, served as a military surgeon in Europe during World War II, and practiced medicine in the West.

There is a moon out tonight. Moon and stars and clouds tipped with moonlight. And there is a fall wind blowing in my heart. Ever since this evening, when against a fading sky I saw geese wedge southward. They were going home. . . . Now I try to study, but against the pages see them again, driving southward. Going home.

Across the valley there are heavy mountains holding up the night sky, and beyond the mountains there is home. Home, and peace, and the beat of drums, and blue winds dancing over snow fields. The Indian lodge will fill with my people, and our gods will come and sit among them. I should be there then. I should be at home.

In my Wisconsin, the leaves change before the snows come. In the air there is the smell of wild rice and venison cooking; and when the winds come whispering through the forests, they carry the smell of rotting leaves. In the evenings, the loon calls, lonely; the birds sing their last songs before leaving. Bears dig roots and eat late fall berries, fattening for their long winter sleep. Later, when the first snows fall, one awakens in the morning to find the world white and beautiful and clean. Then one can look back over his trail and see the tracks following. In the woods there are tracks of deer and snowshoe rabbits, and long streaks where partridges slide to alight. Chipmunks make tiny footprints on the limbs; and one can hear squirrels busy in hollow trees, sorting acorns. Soft lake waves wash the shores, and sunsets burst each evening over the lakes, and make them look as if they were afire.

That land which is my home! Beautiful, calm—where there is no hurry to get anywhere, no driving to keep up in a race that knows no ending and no goal. No classes where men talk and talk, and then stop now and then to hear their own words come back to them from the students. No constant peering into the maelstrom of one's mind; no worries about grades and honors; no hysterical preparing for life until that life is half over; no anxiety about one's place in the thing they call society.

I hear again the ring of axes in deep woods, the crunch of snow beneath my feet. I feel again the smooth velvet of ghost-birch bark. I hear the rhythm of the drums. . . . I am tired. I am weary of trying to keep up this bluff of being civilized. Being civilized means trying to do everything you don't want to, never doing anything you want to. It means dancing to the strings of custom and tradition; it means living in houses and never knowing or caring who is next door. These civilized white men want us to be like them—always dissatisfied, getting a hill and wanting a mountain.

Then again, maybe I am not tired. Maybe I'm licked. Maybe I am just not smart enough to grasp these things that go to make up civilization. Maybe I am just too lazy to think hard enough to keep up.

Still, I know my people have many things that civilization has taken from the whites. They know how to give; how to tear one's piece of meat in two and share it with one's brother. They know how to sing—how to make each man his own songs and sing them; for their music they do not have to listen to other men singing over a radio. They know how to make things with their hands, how to shape beads into design and make a thing of beauty from a piece of birch bark.

But we are inferior. It is terrible to have to feel inferior; to have to read reports of intelligence tests, and learn that one's race is behind. It is terrible to sit in classes and hear men tell you that your people worship sticks of wood—that your gods are all false, that the Manitou forgot your people and did not write them a book.

I am tired. I want to walk again among the ghost-birches. I want to see the leaves turn in autumn, the smoke rise from the lodgehouses, and to feel the blue winds. I want to hear the drums; I want to hear the drums and feel the blue whispering winds.

There is a train wailing into the night. The trains go across the mountains. It would be easy to catch a freight. They will say he has gone back to the blanket; I don't care. The dance at Christmas. . . .

Northward again. Minnesota, and great white fields of snow; frozen lakes, and dawn running into dusk without noon. Long forests wearing white. Bitter cold, and one night the northern lights. I am nearing home.

I reach Woodruff at midnight. Suddenly I am afraid, now that I am but twenty miles from home. Afraid of what my father will say, afraid of being looked on as a stranger by my own people. I sit by a fire and think about myself and all the other young Indians. We just don't seem to fit in anywhere—certainly not among the whites, and not among the older people. I think again about the learned sociology professor and his professing. So many things seem to be clear now that I am away from school and do not have to worry about some man's opinion of my ideas. It is easy to think while looking at dancing flames.

Morning. I spend the day cleaning up, and buying some presents for my family with what is left of my money. Nothing much, but a gift is a gift, if a man buys it with his last quarter. I wait until evening, then start up the track toward home.

Christmas Eve comes in on a north wind. Snow clouds hang over the pines, and the night comes early. Walking along the railroad bed, I feel the calm peace of snowbound forests on either side of me. I take my time; I am back in a world where time does not mean so much now. I am alone; alone but not nearly so lonely as I was back on the campus at school. Those are never lonely who love the snow and the pines; never lonely when the pines are wearing white shawls and snow crunches coldly underfoot. In the woods I know there are the tracks of deer and rabbit; I know that if I leave the rails and go into the woods I shall find them. I walk along feeling glad because my legs are light and my feet seem to know that they are home. A deer comes out of the woods just ahead of me, and stands silhouetted on the rails. The North, I feel, has welcomed me home. I watch him and am glad that I do not wish for a gun. He goes into the woods quietly, leaving only the design of his tracks in the snow. I walk on. Now and then I pass a field, white under the night sky, with houses at the far end. Smoke comes from the chimneys of the houses, and I try to tell what sort of wood each is burning by the smoke; some burn pine; others aspen, others tamarack. There is one from which comes black coal smoke that rises lazily and drifts out over the tops of the trees. I like to watch houses and try to imagine what might be happening in them.

Just as a light snow begins to fall, I cross the reservation boundary; somehow it seems as though I have stepped into another world. Deep woods in a white-and-black winter night. A faint trail leading to the village.

The railroad on which I stand comes from a city sprawled by a lake— a city with a million people who walk around without seeing one another; a city sucking the life from all the country around; a city with stores and police and intellectuals and criminals and movies and apartment houses; a city with its politics and libraries and zoos.

Laughing, I go into the woods. As I cross a frozen lake I begin to hear the drums. Soft in the night the drums beat. It is like the pulse beat of the world. The white line of the lake ends at a black forest, and above the trees the blue winds are dancing.

I come to the outlying houses of the village. Simple box houses, etched black in the night. From one or two windows soft lamp light falls on the snow. Christmas here, too, but it does not mean much; not much in the way of parties and presents. Joe Sky will get drunk. Alex Bodidash will buy his children red mittens and a new sled. Alex is a Carlisle man, and tries to keep his home up to white standards. White standards. Funny that people should be ever falling farther behind. The more they try to imitate whites the more tragic the result. Yet they want us to be imitation white men. About all we imitate well are their vices.

The village is not a sight to instill pride, yet I am not ashamed; one can never be ashamed of his own people when he knows they have dreams as beautiful as white snow on a tall pine.

Father and my brother and sister are seated around the table as I walk in. Father stares at me for a moment, then I am in his arms, crying on his shoulder. I give them the presents I have brought, and my throat tightens as I watch my sister save carefully bits of red string from the packages. I hide my feelings by wrestling with my brother when he strikes my shoulder in token of affection. Father looks at me, and I know he has many questions, but he seems to know why I have come. He tells me to go on alone to the lodge, and he will follow.

I walk along the trail to the lodge, watching the northern lights forming in the heavens. White waving ribbons that seem to pulsate with the rhythm of the drums. Clean snow creaks beneath my feet, and a soft wind sighs through the trees, singing to me. Everything seems to say "Be happy! You are home now—you are free. You are among friends—we are your friends; we, the trees, and the snow, and the lights." I follow the trail to the lodge. My feet are light, my heart seems to sing to the music, and I hold my head high. Across white snow fields blue winds are dancing.

Before the lodge door I stop, afraid. I wonder if my people will remember me. I wonder—"Am I Indian, or am I white?" I stand before the door a long time. I hear the ice groan on the lake, and remember the story of the old woman who is under the ice, trying to get out, so she can punish some runaway lovers. I think to myself, "If I am white I will not believe that story; if I am Indian, I will know that there is an old woman under the ice." I listen for a while, and I know that there is an old woman under the ice. I look again at the lights, and go in.

Inside the lodge there are many Indians. Some sit on benches around the walls, others dance in the center of the floor around a drum. Nobody seems to notice me. It seems as though I were among a people I have never seen before. Heavy women with long black hair. Women with children on their knees—small children that watch with intent black eyes the movements of the dancers, whose small faces are solemn and serene. The faces of the old people are serene, too, and their eyes are merry and bright. I look at the old men. Straight, dressed in dark trousers and beaded velvet vests, wearing soft moccasins. Dark, lined faces intent on the music. I wonder if I am at all like them. They dance on, lifting their feet to the rhythm of the drums, swaying lightly, looking upward. I look at their eyes, and am startled at the rapt attention to the rhythm of the music.

The dance stops. The men walk back to the walls, and talk in low tones or with their hands. There is little conversation, yet everyone seems to be sharing some secret. A woman looks at a small boy wandering away, and he comes back to her.

Strange, I think, and then remember. These people are not sharing words—they are sharing a mood. Everyone is happy. I am so used to white people that it seems strange so many people could be together without someone talking. These Indians are happy because they are together, and because the night is beautiful outside, and the music is beautiful. I try hard to forget school and white people, and be one of these—my people. I try to forget everything but the night, and it is a part of me; that I am one with my people and we are all a part of something universal. I watch eyes, and see now that the old people are speaking to me. They nod slightly, imperceptibly, and their eyes laugh into mine. I look around the room. All the eyes are friendly; they all laugh. No one questions my being here. The drums begin to beat again, and I catch the invitation in the eyes of the old men. My feet begin to lift to the rhythm, and I look out beyond the walls into the night and see the lights. I am happy. It is beautiful. I am home.

Thinking About Content

1. Whitecloud, a Chippewa Indian, lived in both the white and Native American cultures. How does he give his readers a sense of being between two cultures? How do we learn what each culture is like, at least according to Whitecloud?

2. Why does Whitecloud both long for and fear going home to northern Wisconsin, ancestral home of the Chippewa?

Thinking About Writing

1. Like Richard Wright, Whitecloud provides both a physical and psychological description of this environment. Choose one example of each and explain how Whitecloud brought you into the description, allowing you to share his environment and himself.

2. Whitecloud writes in the first person, *I.* What is the advantage of using *I?* The disadvantage?

Personal Connections

1. Whitecloud describes his Wisconsin home in vivid detail, letting us see and hear it. We can then better understand his emotions upon returning home. Do you have a place that is special, where you feel in touch with yourself?

2. Have you ever felt caught between two worlds—not necessarily of race or ethnicity, but also the worlds of child/adult, home/school, country/city? Explain.

As a student from a war-torn Central American country, Ruth Aida Cañas had family memories unlike most of her classmates. For her personal-experience essay she chose a positive one, but one born of tragedy.

Before you read this piece, reflect in your reading journal on a family member or friend who is especially dear to you. Have you ever told this person how deeply you care, how important he or she is to you?

"I Love You, Chava"

"Your brother is going to the mountain," my mom said on an unforgettable 30th of December, 1980. I was just a little, shy, ten-year-old girl who did not know anything about the war in El Salvador, my country. How could I have understood the peril of my brother's leaving?

My brother could not avoid being active: he thought that the war in El Salvador, his country, needed to stop immediately. He could not stand looking at the starvation, exploitation, and poverty that most Salvadorans suffered. An enthusiastic, straight-A student, Chava left his studies, family, comfort, friends--everything--to fight and stop the hated war.

We did not hear from him after he left. My mom missed her only son. She was proud of him because Chava was not just a great student, but also an excellent son and a fantastic brother; he used to help my mom clean the house, wash the clothes, and take care of us, his sisters. He even took a job on a farm to earn a little extra money; one Christmas with that money he bought presents for each member in our family instead of buying things for himself. I learned from him to be courageous because he chose to fight with the Salvadoran's guerrillas, even though he knew that going to the mountain was dangerous.

However, his dreams of an El Salvador without strife never came true; he was killed in 1981. No one knows where his body rests, or how he was killed. His precious life was taken; all his ideals were stolen with his death. I did not understand that he was not going to come again because I was not old

enough to realize all the consequences that his
death had.

My mom and sisters cried when they found out about
the murder of my brother, but I could not cry. I re-
proached myself for not reacting as a sister who loved
her brother. Yet, there is something for which I re-
proach myself even much more: I never told him how
much I admired him and what I felt for him.

Now, I have lost him, and there is nothing I can
do. Nevertheless, I have understood what his departure
meant: I know how generous he was by giving his life to
building an El Salvador where everyone would have a
dignified life. Sometimes I have wanted to be sure he
can hear me from the divine place where he is, and tell
him: "I love you Chava; I have missed you all my life."

Ruth Aida Cañas

▄ Thinking About Content ─────────────

1. What portrait of Chava emerges from Cañas's essay? Can we trust her memory? Why?

2. How do you picture Ruth Cañas? Why? Is the significance of this essay found in Chava or in Ruth?

3. Cañas never mentions her father. What will the reader assume? Is that assumption justified?

▄ Thinking About Writing ─────────────

1. Is Cañas looking for sympathy in this essay? How does she control the tone?

2. Could Cañas have provided the reader with more detail about the state of El Salvador when Chava left for the mountain?

▄ Personal Connections ─────────────

1. Did Ruth Cañas's narrative nudge your thinking about what's important in life, in families?

2. Even if you have never had to face war in America or in your country, through television war has been brought into every home. In America, we have also witnessed "civil war" born of urban poverty and hopelessness. Reflect on those images.

As a young girl, Catalina Ruge, the author of the following essay, experienced her first sense of betrayal. Looking back as a college freshman, she shares that moment.

Diary

When I was 13 years old, I kept a diary. All of my personal thoughts, feelings, and experiences were secure in between the hardcover of my Hello Kitty Personal Diary, or so I thought. I came home one afternoon after ballet lessons, my knees weak and my heart racing, I had just seen Felipe, my future husband. No one was aware of my wedding plans yet, not even Felipe. "I have to make a note in my diary to change the best man; Camilo is Felipe's best friend now," I said to myself.

I walked into my room and headed straight for my desk. The light shining off the brass handle of the third drawer always made me think of the invaluable treasure that lay in there, my wedding plans. But today there was something in between me and that gleaming handle. Laughter made me look up only to find my Hello Kitty Private Diary in the hands of my cousin. He had read it all. The only gleaming I could see now were the tears in my eyes.

I felt betrayed that day, as if someone had trespassed the boundaries of my privacy. My cousin's hurtful words made it all the more painful. The life spelled out in the pages of the diary was no longer mine. It became the object of a big joke. Although the whole incident is now a joke, thinking back, I realize how much of who I am today is a result of that occurrence.

Since then, I have been afraid to tell people what I'm feeling. Afraid that they will take my feelings and turn them into a big joke. I haven't kept a diary since.

Catalina Ruge

Thinking About Content

1. Was Ruge's daydream unusual? Her need for privacy?

2. Is there a gender difference here? Do both male and female adolescents have private hopes and dreams? The same type of hopes and dreams?

Thinking About Writing

1. How has Ruge organized her essay? Why?
2. Ruge tells us that her "cousin's hurtful words made it all the more painful." What might be the effect on the reader if those "hurtful words" had been revealed?

Personal Connections

1. Have you ever felt betrayed by a family member or close friend? Has anyone ever revealed your secret thoughts, things said in confidence? How did you feel? Are there lasting effects, like those Catalina Ruge relates?
2. Ruge tells us "the life spelled out in the pages of the diary was no longer mine." Have you ever felt as though your life was no longer yours?

Writing Activity

In your journal, you have already explored many ideas growing out of your experience as a member of a family, a community, a culture, including some of the following:

✦ Relationships between child and parent or caretaker

✦ Adult as lawgiver

✦ Child as victim

✦ Anger at abandonment through death or divorce

✦ Fading memories

✦ Growing up

✦ Adolescent self-righteousness

✦ Adolescent demands

✦ Expectations and regrets

Review your journal and put an asterisk (*) next to those that offer the most potential for your personal-experience paper. Then go back to the starred entries and choose one. You will use this entry to develop a discovery draft. But first, you need to think about the significance of that choice.

THINGS TO CONSIDER: THE "SO WHAT?" FACTOR

When readers finish our narrative, we want them to understand why we have written it. We don't want them to finish reading and think, "So what?" We want them to know the significance of our narrative. Keeping these questions in front of you is important as you consider your subject from a reader's viewpoint:

✦   Why is this event or person significant to me?

✦   Will my reader understand this significance?

✦   Will I be able to convey my thoughts and feelings on this topic?

As you read the next two student narratives, think about their significance. Why did David Schwartz and Tom McDonald focus their narratives on these people?

David Schwartz was "forty-something" when he wrote this piece in freshman composition. Out of all his life experience, he chose to write about a special "father." Why?

Unforgettable Father Rossiter

My first encounter with the man was early in my freshman year at Regis High School. As usual, I was late for homeroom and was trying to retrieve books from the chaotic mess of my locker. With my familiar breakfast carrot hanging from my mouth, I really was trying to hurry when out of nowhere came this booming voice proclaiming "YOU BOOB!" Only one voice existed that could strike terror amongst the masses like that--our principal, Father John Rossiter, affectionately known as "Rock." There he was, an imposing figure with fire in his eyes, lumbering toward me with a half limp, a constant reminder of the Korean War. Ranting and raving, he let me know that being late wasn't tolerated. As terror stricken as I was, I continued to chomp on my carrot and tried not to convey fear. Seeming somewhat amused at my half-hearted attempt at calling his bluff, he shooed me off to class. Psychology books tell us how impressionable we are in youth, but I had no idea just how big an impact this chance encounter would have on the rest of my life.

Our relationship began to develop from that moment on, spanning over twenty years. I soon learned that beneath his tough rocklike exterior beat the unselfish heart of a man with immense compassion. Behind the scenes at Regis, he never denied a Catholic education to a student unable to pay for it. Something could always be worked out, from part-time work at the school or in the private sector, to a ten-year payment plan. If all else failed, he anonymously made tuition payments himself.

Tuition wasn't the only reason for reaching deep into his own pockets. Like today, the sixties were troubled times. For the less fortunate, that meant struggling to make ends meet. In his Buick we had dubbed the "Green Hornet," he made the rounds more than once to Regis families in need, delivering bags of groceries--anonymously, of course.

Haircuts were a similar matter. Part of a Catholic education was discipline, and one of the rules was that students' hair had to be cropped so close that bristles, as he called them, had to be visible on the back of the neck. Long hair, sported by that new singing group the Beatles, didn't fit with the program. Here again, if an occasional haircut was out of our price realm, he would foot the bill. I wore a regular path driving the Green Hornet between Regis and Tony's Barber Shop, shuttling classmates back and forth to get their locks shorn--on his tab.

Looking back, it comes apparent his niche was being there when you needed him. He readily identified with students like myself, who always seemed to have an uncanny knack for sniffing out trouble. In later years, he told me what a hellion he had been in his youth and how a teacher he had never forgotten had reached out to him. Likewise, he inspired us with nurturing, understanding, and support. Rock strongly encouraged us to always do our best as we traveled through life. In that respect, he was more like a father figure.

As with my own father, I sometimes wondered what life would be like when he no longer walked this earth. I found out all too soon. Six years ago, on a cold, snowy January day, a deranged individual entered his church and ended his life. I wasn't prepared. He had always been there; I couldn't imagine him not being there.

Reflecting after the funeral, I reassessed my own life and realized it was time to follow a path I had planned long ago but never finished--the pursuit of a teaching degree. It was as if his death held his final inspiration for me--to pass the torch.

David Schwartz

Tom McDonald, writing as an 18-year-old freshman, also reflects on a person who made a difference in his life.

Shaking Hands with God

Isn't it funny how life, when we're least expecting it, throws people or events our way that teach us that it is not all about us? Or that we don't have it so bad? The 1988 ELCA San Antonio youth gathering did that for me. Ron did that for me.

In the summer of 1988, my church shared buses with other area churches to go to the great Lutheran youth gathering held in San Antonio, Texas. My true reasons for going weren't religious, and when you get right down to it, weren't very respectable. Simply put, I went for the girls. Upon boarding the bus, I was more than pleasantly surprised to see that there was a great selection of available females to choose from. In fact, I was so busy scoping, I didn't even notice him.

In about the fifth hour of the first day of our ten-day trip, our pastors, always looking to "broaden our horizons," paired us with a complete stranger from a different church. Their task for us was to introduce ourselves and essentially make friends with our fellow Lutherans. "No problem," I thought, "Maybe I'll end up with one of the girls I've been watching."

To my dismay, I was not only paired with a male but he was a somewhat disfigured, unhealthy vision of a male. Smiling with a hairelip as he approached me, he winked at me with constantly watery eyes through Coke-bottle glasses. Then the scrawny figure that made me so uncomfortable to look at held out one of his three-fingered hands in greeting.

"Hi. I'm Ron," he said with a smirk, "but you can call me Ron." He followed this tension breaker with a boyish smile that drew me in.

"Hi Ron," I said, trying to ignore his deformities at all costs. "I'm Tom."

Putting one of his odd-looking hands on my knee he again offered his free hand for me to shake. Uncomfortably, my hand met his, and I was forced to look at him. Despite my typical teenage male attitudes, I began to see in front of me a very able, accepting person.

As we moved on, from day to day, Ron and I became very close, playing dumb bus games together and comparing notes on the girls on the bus, some from my town and some from his. Despite myself and my poor intentions, I was beginning to change my focus from strictly girl-watching to learning how to have and be a friend. This change was all Ron's fault, but he wasn't done yet.

On about the third day of the gathering, Ron and I attended a youth dance held at the local college, where we would be spending the night. I have never danced before, and assumed the same of Ron. I thought that we could hang out around the sides and watch the more confident people dance. To my surprise, Ron left me at the side and wove his way through the crowded dance floor, cracking jokes about his six fingers and making friends as he went. I couldn't make myself go out onto that dance floor, no matter how much I really wanted to, bringing to mind a stirring question. Who was the handicapped one now?

Yes, life taught me a huge lesson over those ten days. Through Ron, who excelled at things that at first-appearance seemed impossible for such a seemingly defective body, I learned that the only handicaps are those of the mind. Now, when I see Ron at a ball game or showing off his skills on the latest video game or piano keyboard (which I recently found was another of his innumerable talents) I realize how lucky I was to meet him and learn the lesson he had to teach. Now, I realize what an honor it is to know him and to shake his hand.

Tom McDonald

ON YOUR OWN

Developing a Personal-Experience Essay

Why are we so interested in stories? Is it the topic that draws us in? Or is it the people who interest us? Perhaps the setting or sequence of events? Or could it be the perspective that narrators bring to the story? Any or all of these may be the reason why narratives continue to be central to our lives—whether at home, school, or the workplace.

Because narratives are basic to many other kinds of writing, you need to develop skills of narrating and describing. Although you have been narrating and describing in oral language for a very long time, you do so there with little conscious thought about the process. In writing, you must consciously attend to the elements of effective narration and description.

All narratives have common elements. News writers refer to them as the 5 W's and an H: who, what, where, when, why, and how. As you explore topics for your personal narrative, ask yourself questions:

◆ **Turning points.** When did I "grow up" in some way? Where was I? Who was involved? How did I change? Why did it happen this way? How do I feel about it now, looking back over time? What is its significance?

◆ **Wins and Losses.** What did I gain or lose? Where was I? Who was involved? When and how did the "win" or "loss" occur? What is its significance to me? How did I resolve or recover from a "loss"? Were there unpleasant effects from a "win"?

◆ **Everyday Life.** What gives meaning to my life on a daily basis? Why? What routine thing is important? Why? What do I count on? Why? What would I miss? How would my life change if _____ ?

The list of topics and questions in Chapter 1 (Tell Me About . . .), as well as the those in Chapter 5 (Tapping into Personal Experience), may help you. If you have saved notes from exercises and maintained your reading journal responses, you have additional resources for finding a good topic.

DRAFTING AND REVISING

Your discovery draft should capture the essence of your narrative; you should know why you chose this particular piece of experience as your topic. The revising process will help you with the details and examples, the organization, and other aspects of writing a clear and effective narrative. When you have a second draft, question yourself.

Storytelling

✦ Do I have a beginning, middle, and end?

✦ Does my narrative build to a point?

✦ Where do I lose intensity?

✦ Where is there too little detail? Too much?

✦ Where am I telling rather than showing?

✦ Would dialogue help move the story along?

✦ Where do I need more or better transitions?

Describing

✦ Do I use enough sensory words (sight, sound, touch, smell)?

✦ Do I use comparison when appropriate?

✦ Do I give enough descriptive detail?

✦ Do I go "overboard" with detail?

✦ Have I let dialogue do the describing?

✦ Have I done too much telling and not enough showing?

Organizing

✦ Is my arrangement sensible?

✦ Does my organization move the story along?

✦ Is there any place where something is out of order?

✦ Should I eliminate anything?

Answering "So What?"

◆ Have I answered "so what?"

◆ Will the reader understand the significance?

Beginning and Ending

◆ Does the opening create interest?

◆ Does the ending bring a sense of closure?

Having a Voice

◆ Will a reader hear me through this essay?

◆ Will my voice (my sentences, vocabulary, way I handle language) be clear?

Adding Dialogue

In your draft review, you might have realized that adding dialogue would liven up the narrative considerably. Often, when we hear people talking, we get a better idea of what they are really like; dialogue demonstrates characteristics and attitudes in a way that simple restating cannot. In addition, the use of dialogue gives our writing a variety of sentence types that again adds interest to the narrative.

◆ **Breaking the rule of "complete" sentences.** When you use dialogue, you can use fragments; we often speak that way. Your goal is "real world" talk when you write dialogue, so using short, non-sentence sequences is appropriate.

"Where'd you go?" my mother asked.

"Out," I replied uneasily.

◆ **Enclosing the words in quotation marks.** Always enclose the exact words spoken by a person in a set of quotation marks. Quotation marks are like mittens or gloves: they come in pairs.

My teacher looked at me with narrowed eyes and asked, "What's your excuse?"

"Huh?" I responded, desperately searching for any excuse.

◆ **Putting quotation marks before and after exact words.** Because the marks set off only the exact words of each speaker, they do not always match the beginning and ending of a sentence. Several sentences or parts of sentences may be included in one set of quotation marks.

"I don't have an excuse. I mean I don't have a regular kind of excuse. My computer sort of blew up," I finally mumbled.

◆ **Using punctuation correctly.**   One of three punctuation marks separates the quoted words from the person speaking: comma, question mark, or exclamation point. The comma is used where we would normally use a period.

Mrs. Axeruler quickly responded, "What do you mean by that?"

"I can explain," I said.

"Can you indeed?" Mrs. Axeruler asked.

"Yes, it blew up, really blew up!" I said, hastily inventing my excuse.

◆ **Capitalizing correctly.**   The first word of the quotation is capitalized.

◆ **Paragraphing correctly.**   A new paragraph begins and ends with each speaker. Even if the speaker utters only one word, it is handled like a single paragraph. Changing speakers means beginning a new paragraph.

Revising for Problems

A double-column chart may help you see and solve problems in your draft.

Area	Solution
Storytelling	
losing steam, intensity	Cut some parts down or out
too much "telling"	Add descriptive words, action, dialogue
Describing	
mood isn't right	
too much "telling"	Check thesaurus
Organizing	
takes too long to get to point	Eliminate a couple of events
So what?	
not sure this is clear	Be more up front/honest
Beginning and ending	
first paragraph weak	Ask question, use quotation

__Group Activity__

With your writing partner or group, exchange drafts of your personal-experience essay. For the first reading, pay attention to the content only. When you respond, point out the strengths of the piece first. Praise anything that really merits it, but don't give praise where none is due; being genuine is the first rule of response. Ask questions whenever you can. And focus only on major problems at first: What really derailed you as a reader? Why? Where did you need more or better information? Where did your interest lag? Where did you lose the sequencing? Is better description needed? Where? Is the "so what?" factor answered? Is there a sense of the author, a voice?

Your instructor might prefer that you use a specific response form. For example:

Responding to Personal-Experience Essay

Author _____

Peer Reviewer _____

1. What is the "heart" of the story?
2. Has the author answered the "so what?" factor?
3. Is the narrative easy to follow? If not, where did a problem occur?
4. Is there enough information? If not, where should some be added?
5. Is there too much information? If so, where could some be deleted?
6. Where does your interest lag? Pick up?
7. Are the descriptions clear? Interesting?
8. Do you hear the author's voice in the narrative?

If you can offer specific suggestions to improve the narrative, do so. The author will decide whether or not to act on them, but providing good response as a first reader will help the writer.

For a second reading, pay attention to the "technical" aspects of the writing:

✦ Sentences: complete, clear in meaning, varied in structure

✦ Usage: subject and verb agree, noun and pronoun agree

✦ Punctuation: commas to separate word groups, quotation marks correct, apostrophes

✦ Spelling: double-check on sound-alikes (e.g., there, their, they're) and easily confused words (e.g., affect and effect)

Put a check mark in the margin to indicate that there is an error in that line. Talk with the author about problems or errors, but don't make any corrections on the paper.

REFLECTING

One of the most important things we do as writers is to reflect on the process of developing a piece of writing. What worked? What didn't? Why? In a brief paragraph, tell your instructor what you learned in the process of writing your personal-experience essay. The questions that follow are merely a guide.

✦ Where in the process did I have trouble?

✦ How did I get myself out of trouble? What strategies helped me?

✦ What part of the process went really well? Why?

✦ What still seems hard to do? Why?

✦ What would I do differently?

✦ What do I like best about this essay? Why?

✦ How did peer response help me?

✦ How could peer response be more helpful?

CHAPTER 7

Writing to Inform, Writing to Analyze

Expository writing, writing whose purpose is to inform or explain, is the type of writing found most often in school, the workplace, and the community. It differs from narration in that the writer's emphasis is on the subject matter in exposition. And where narration is often in chronological order, expository writing uses many different patterns of organization, including chronological. Comparing and contrasting information or exploring a cause and effect relationship, for example, will lead us to a specific organization pattern or strategy. Expository writing often seems very utilitarian: it helps us get the job done or it helps us understand some issue or situation. Expository writing is characterized by a controlling idea or thesis that is then developed through facts, reasons, examples, and illustrations. Expository writing is also characterized by analysis, which means the writer has broken down the information, studied its parts, and then commented on the significance of that information. We'll work with analysis a little later in this chapter.

Reports are a common expository writing task, one that is important to most businesses. Essays, on the other hand, are more common in academic settings. These two forms of writing differ in their purpose. Reports present accumulated information but, generally, do not contain the writer's opinion on that information. Essays, by contrast, incorporate the writer's personal point of view or opinion on the information presented. Quite often, however, writing tasks are a mix of report and essay. The writer may provide the information common to reports but accompany it with analysis that reveals a personal perspective or opinion.

Although we tend to think of such writing tasks as school work, a discussion with business people will quickly reveal the importance of informing and analyzing in the workplace. Hundreds of daily decisions depend upon information and thoughtful analysis, accurately and clearly presented. This important skill is also needed in our personal lives. Buying a car, for example, demands thoughtful analysis, at least if we want to get the best car for our budget. Although it's true that we can depend upon "experts" to provide analysis for us, on everything from the best brand of athletic shoes to the most able politician, we really need to rely on ourselves.

CRITICAL STRATEGIES FOR ANALYSIS AND WRITING

Whether you read or write, analysis is the basis for most academic work; it is a skill all students rely on. But what exactly is it? What do we do when we analyze something? Analysis occurs whenever we break down an idea or event, separate it into its parts, examine the parts, and then explain how these parts fit into a whole. For example, in history class you could be asked to explain the rise of industrialism in England. This is a complex subject, with many parts to it. So, you would look at those parts: the historical time and setting; the economic, political, and social situations; influential or creative people. What separate parts contributed to industrialism? What made it possible at this time and not earlier? How did these parts interact with one another? To answer the question, then, you would take the parts and weave them into a whole to explain the rise of industrialism. Analysis always involves a close look into what makes an idea, an event, a situation, or even a person, "tick." Fortunately, we have many different strategies to help us with this essential task.

Types of Analysis

Cause and Effect.   Examining the cause and/or effect of an event, an action, or situation is one form of analysis, one that is used often in school and the workplace. When we examine causes, we are trying to get at the root of "why and how did this happen?" When we examine effects, we are trying to figure out the results or consequences. Because life is complex, cause and effect is most often complex. Thus, when you think about "cause," you need to think in terms of the plural, "causes." A war, for example, usually has multiple causes, not just "a" cause. Similarly, "effect" is most often a plural. A war may have a major effect, but it most certainly has many effects, and we would have to explore them in our analysis. There may also be a chain reaction, where the effect of one cause becomes the cause of another. For example, the effect of a war was widespread hunger, which then became the cause of riots, the effect of which led to a new government. As you work with cause and effect, think in terms of multiples when you start out. You can always sort things out into major and minor later, but you need a good base of information to begin your analysis.

Group Activity

A. With your partner or group, identify and analyze causes for the following:

failing an exam   getting a sales job at a sporting goods store
stress among students   losing a job at McDonald's

B. Identify and analyze effects of the following:

smoking   losing your wallet
divorce   working 11 P.M. to 6 A.M.

C. Analyze a chain reaction:

Your alarm clock fails to go off.

D. Television has changed life in the late twentieth century. List a number of the effects of television in the last 10 years and analyze their significance. If you were to write on this topic, what might your controlling idea be? What order would you use for discussing the effects? Why?

E. American children are reported to be headed for health problems as adults. Analyze potential causes for this threatening situation. What would your controlling idea be? What order would you use for discussing the causes? Why?

Comparison and Contrast. Comparison and contrast is another form of analysis in which we break down two or more ideas, events, or situations. When we have the major characteristics of each, we line them up side by side to see how they are alike or different. Once we have the similarities and differences isolated, we can explain the significance of what we have found. Just lining things up, showing that there are similar or dissimilar characteristics, is only the first step in the process. If we don't go on to discuss why the similarity or difference is important, we have not completed the analysis. For example, suppose you noticed that movie heroes have changed in the past 50 years. Your grandparents noted that the Western hero, like John Wayne and Gary Cooper, was their idea of a hero; your uncle, however, said the James Bond superspy was his. When you started to think about more recent Terminator "hero" types, you started to wonder about movie heroes over the years. So you watched a few videos, made a list of the characteristics of these heroes, and lined them up for a comparison. If you didn't go any further, you would not have done the analysis. Analysis comes in when you think about what the comparison shows and suggests about our society over 50 years. Have Americans changed their idea of what "hero" means? If so, why might this be so? Once you think about these questions, you are on your way to finding the significance of the comparison and contrast, and the heart of your writing task.

Group Activity

With your partner or group, choose a type of television show (sitcom, drama, talk show) to analyze through comparison and contrast. Be sure you have a point to your analysis: What can we learn from the comparison? What does it tell us about ourselves, our society, life in the 1990s?

Process.   When we want to know how something works, how some event unfolded, or any kind of life cycle, we analyze its process. Process analysis is basic to many academic fields. In business, we look at how information flows or how products get to market. In science, we look at the development of life forms and the processes involved in chemical or physical reactions; in history and government, we trace the evolution of power and governing structures. In dance and sports, we examine the mechanics of a successful physical movement. Process analysis is commonplace, and as such, an important skill. But as with other forms of analysis, it must have a point to it. For example, you might analyze the flow of information in a corporate setting because there is a problem: the process has broken down, people are not getting vital information, and mistakes are made. Or you might be interested in how successful companies market their products: What processes contribute to effective marketing and increased sales? The ability to study the parts of a process, to report on them as both parts and a whole, is a good academic and workplace skill.

Group Activity

With your partner or group, analyze one of the most common, and often frustrating, student processes: registering for classes. Be sure to note your purpose for the analysis.

Taking a Position.   Analysis to present your side of an issue demands more than your personal opinion. Rather, you gather evidence (e.g., facts, statistics, expert opinion, direct observation) to support your point of view. Your analysis must also include investigation of all sides of the issue, especially those that differ significantly from your own. Suppose you believe that the drinking age in your state should be lowered. The opposite view, of course, says it shouldn't, so your analysis would have to provide evidence that lowering the age would not have harmful effects. This would involve taking each of the opposition's objections and responding to them: increased car accidents, rowdy behavior, increased risk of pregnancy or sexual diseases, potential alcoholism from lack of control and good judgment, and so forth. In fact, your ability to analyze the opposition's argument would be a critical factor in how well you present your own.

Group Activity

With your group, choose a position for or against the following issue: students working more than 20 hours per week while in high school. Analyze both sides well, taking into account what the opposition would say, but present only your position and how you would defend it if you had to write an essay.

Proposing Solutions.   When we propose a solution to a problem, we are not only analyzing the problem; we are analyzing reasonable responses to it. After we identify the problem, we explore possible solutions, analyzing each one for its workability. As we do this, we are also comparing and contrasting them. Our analysis will lead us to the best solution, and then we argue that it *is* the best solution. For example, you may be frustrated with the lack of computer time at your school. You know that simple complaining about it won't get you anywhere, so you decide to analyze the problem and come up with a reasonable solution. You observe the times when computers are heavily used, and for what purposes, and you chart this information. From this, you note that many students are simply using e-mail and "chatting" with friends. One solution, then, would be to designate a few computers for e-mail only, thus freeing up the majority for academic writing. Another solution would involve purchasing more machines, and you can suggest it, even though you suspect costs would be prohibitive. Your analysis, however, would include any reasonable solution. Your proposal/solution essay would address every reasonable solution: what it is, why it would work, how it would work, what its benefits are. From all that are reasonable, you would choose the best, showing it to be preferable to all the alternatives.

▬Group Activity▬▬▬▬▬▬▬▬▬▬▬▬

With your group, propose a solution to a common school problem: not enough parking spaces. Be sure you consider what others may have proposed and why this problem has not been solved to date.

▰▰ SUPPORTING OUR IDEAS ▰▰▰▰▰▰

Analyzing our ideas, data, and materials is one part of the process when we write to explain something. Offering good support for what we say is another. You have already explored some of the ways in which we provide support. In writing a personal-experience essay, you drew upon your experience, including observations, details, and descriptions. You may also have provided reasons and examples. All of these are used in supporting explanatory or informational writing as well, especially reasons and examples.

Using Reasons

We use reasons in our daily lives, regardless of whether or not these reasons are actually good, accurate, or fair. In academic or workplace writing, however, we need to analyze our reasons and be certain that they will stand up to questions, skepticism, or attack. Our reasons support our ideas or proposals, and if they fail the reader's expectation of "good, sensible, logical," they will be rejected. Just stating a reason is not enough; we have to add details or examples. Suppose you asked a friend to give you a ride to school, and he or she simply said, "I can't." You would probably ask, "Why not?" And your friend would then have to supply an acceptable reason. If the next words you heard were "I'm busy," you would probably reject them. However, if your friend followed up with "I promised to show my brother how to use a new computer program, and this is the only time we can do it," you would accept the situation. The reason had substance because it had detail. Similarly, examples provide substance for reasons. If your boss asked you to work with someone who you knew was lazy, you wouldn't be able to object or refuse without giving examples. Just saying that you don't want to isn't good enough. Rather, you would supply specific examples: she takes breaks every five minutes; she doesn't help with the paperwork; she makes mistakes on purpose, just so we won't ask her to take on different jobs. Giving reasons is an important part of academic and workplace writing, and backing up those reasons with specific details and examples must become part of your analysis.

▬ Group Activity ▬▬▬▬▬▬▬▬▬▬▬▬▬▬▬▬▬▬▬▬▬▬

With your partner or group, back up the following with specific reasons:

A. "I need a car."

B. "I won't take this apartment."

C. "We shouldn't have that exam on Friday."

D. "This school needs better food service."

E. "We can't have that report ready by next week."

Using Examples

Giving examples comes naturally to us; it is usually our first response when someone asks a question or asks for clarification. If someone asked you why you like a specific teacher, you might start with a reason (because he makes learning fun) but go on to specific examples (he uses skits; he took us to a field site). If you told someone that Leo was so stingy that you won't go out with him again, you would no doubt be asked to explain what you mean by "stingy"—and the examples would flow. Or if someone told you Kitty's outfit cost more than your computer, you would want specific examples to "prove" it.

Where do we get specific examples? From many places: many are "real world," from our personal observations; some are anecdotes from direct experience or from others' experience; still others come from research, such as facts and statistics or case studies; and others come from expert opinion based on experience and/or research. Getting examples is seldom difficult; selecting just the right one offers more of a challenge.

Whatever you choose must be relevant, accurate, and representative. You must be careful with statistics, for example. If you are using research, you need to know how the study was carried out. An example stating that 75 percent of working mothers were unhappy would be misleading if there were only four mothers involved and all of them worked in a single business. Similarly, if you stated that piano lessons increased math skills and had only a single example, one child, you would be misrepresenting the importance of the study.

You can use variety in your personal examples; it is not necessary that you have experienced everything yourself. You could present a typical example, not your own experience, but something you read about in a newspaper or magazine or heard on television or radio. You could also use a hypothetical example, a "suppose _____," as long as your readers understand that you invented it. And you can generalize, such as "when college students face tuition increases, . . . "

Your examples must support your controlling idea. Asking yourself questions about each example will help you decide which stay and which are discarded: (1) Does it really support my controlling idea? (2) Is it convincing? (3) Will it get the attention of my readers? (4) Will it really help me explain my idea or position? Developing the example also depends upon detail, upon being very specific. There's a significant difference between a general example and a specific one: a drink/water/Perrier; food/pizza/gourmet sun-dried tomato and charbroiled duck pizza; vehicle/truck/black '95 Ford 150 with gun rack. And if you are using more than one example, you need to decide the order in which to present them. Would it be best to start with the most simple example and move to the most complex? Or is there a spatial order that must be followed?

Activity

A. Read the following introductory paragraphs to a newspaper article on discipline. How has the author both caught our attention and supported her controlling idea?

DON'T BECOME A CHILD TO MAINTAIN DISCIPLINE

Sometimes parents resort to the same inappropriate behaviors as their youngsters. They hit, bite, name-call and even throw tantrums. From a distance it can be hard to tell who's the child and who's the adult. It starts when parents forget their innate positions of leadership and feel they must compete with their kids for control.

For example, when 5-year-old Wylie calls his mother "dummy," and she defensively responds, by saying "Hey, you're the dumb one around here." Or when 12-year-old Jay smacks his unsuspecting father on the head with a snowball, his father picks up an even bigger piece of ice to throw back, yelling, "Maybe this will teach you a lesson!"

What these parents fail to realize is that such negative behaviors are wrong—no matter who does them. Becoming ensnared in a youngster's childish actions not only fails to improve the situation, but usually makes it worse. Let me give you another example. Elisha, 6, grabs a cookie from her mother's hand, protesting, "That's the last one and it's mine." Her mother, stunned, grabs it back and scolds, "Don't you grab things, you little brat. You need to learn to share." Elisha then hits her mother, crying, "Give me my cookie!" Mother, in desperation, spanks her daughter and yells, "Don't hit me!"

Lisa Lewis Griffith

B. Evaluate these opening paragraphs from a *Newsweek* article on teens working. Do the authors hook us? Why are the specific details and examples so critical?

TOO OLD, TOO FAST?

Anyone who thinks teenagers spend their afternoons playing hoops, hanging out at the mall—or, for that matter, studying—should meet 18-year-old Dave Fortune of Manchester, N.H. He wakes up at dawn, slurps some strawberry jam for a sugar rush, goes to the high school until 2:30 P.M., hurries home to make sure his little sister arrives safely, changes and goes off to his job at a clothing store. He gets home around 10:30, does maybe an hour of homework—"if I have any"—and goes to sleep around midnight. The routine begins anew five hours later. Fortune knows he's sacrificed some of his school life for his job. He misses playing soccer and baseball as he did in junior high, and he had to give up a challenging law class because he had so little time for studying. "I have to work," Dave says. "I *have* to work."

A peek into Fortune's closet suggests otherwise. His back-to-school wardrobe: two leather jackets, six sweaters, 12 pairs of jeans, four pairs of shoes, two pairs of sneakers, two belts, "loads of shirts," and a half-dozen silk pants and shirts that would make a jockey proud. Price tag for this spree (with his store discount): $550.

Steven Waldman and Karen Springen

C. Alison Bass states up front that her example is hypothetical. How does she use it to set up her article on "Make Use of Your Anger"? What is she promising?

Take a hypothetical but familiar situation: Anita Jones and Richard Hughes are angry. Their employer has just announced layoffs, telling 40 of their co-workers to clean out their desks and leave. Jones is so furious that she storms into her boss's office and complains loudly. That night she blows up at her husband. He retorts, "If you keep flying off the handle like this, you're going to have a heart attack."

Hughes is equally upset. But fearing that criticism could hurt his job, he says nothing. At home he opens a beer and stews silently in front of the TV. His wife says, "If you keep your anger bottled up like that you're going to have a heart attack!"

So, who's right? Is it better for your health to vent anger or to put a lid on it? Is it good for your career or bad? And what about your marriage? New research is producing some answers.

Boston Globe Magazine

Group Activity

With your partner or group, generate and select examples for one of these topics:

The best things in life are *not* free.
The best gift may cost the least.

Not all fast food is bad food.
Pro athletes make poor (good) role models.

When you have a good list of examples, be sure to ask questions about their effectiveness for your controlling idea. Also consider the best order for their presentation to a reader.

Activity

Evaluate this student essay for its use of examples and details. Determine the controlling idea and offer specific suggestions to improve the content and organization.

Life in the Fast Food Lane

There are many different jobs but one of the hardest has to be working at a fast food restaurant. One thing that is hard is that you're supposed to be kind to the customers. That's hard when you were going out that night but were called in five minutes before you were leaving to meet friends. Another problem is you don't know your hours from week to week. They're always changing.

Not only are the days you work bad, but the hours are worse. Some nights you work only enough for the gas money to get there. Other nights you work until the sun comes up.

The third thing that's bad about working at a fast food place is the rushes. You can't ever work fast enough to suit your boss. Another bad thing about rushes is that people seem to be attracted to your cash register. I think you should be paid by the number of customers you serve during this time, not by the hour.

That brings up another point. The pay for the work involved is too low. Fast food workers should be one of the highest paid occupations. But if that was the case, I wouldn't have to write this paper for school.

ORGANIZING EXPOSITORY WRITING

At the heart of expository writing is a general organizational pattern:

Introduction or lead

The hook—something to get the reader's attention

Background or context—something the reader needs to know in order to follow or appreciate your points; the importance of your topic

Thesis or controlling idea—of the entire essay

Development of first major point

Topic sentence—main idea of this paragraph

Explanation of the main idea

Concluding sentence or a lead into the next paragraph

Development of second major point

Development of third major point (and so on)

Conclusion

Summary—sometimes provided, a brief review of all major points just presented in essay

Significance—usually provided, a brief statement of why readers should be concerned

Implications—usually provided, a brief statement of what may or may not occur

Read Eric Betthauser's expository essay on the video generation. What was Eric's purpose? What was the significance of his essay? Why is Eric's topic a good one for informing and analyzing? How did Eric organize his essay?

Super Mario: A Member of the Family

If you happen to meet a child who spends more time with Super Mario than his or her father, don't be too surprised. This is the generation of Pac-Mania, of "my score is higher than yours," of kids with frazzled hair and glazed eyeballs. It is the video game generation, and the more time children spend with Donkey Kong, that ape of video game fame, the less time they spend with real people.

It's a phenomenon that begins before children can even read. They go for the glory of the high score of their favorite VG, a score that wins approval of peers, or maybe even a shot on a video game TV show! Parents rarely share the enthusiasm.

Even so, parents are often to blame. They dump off their children at the arcades, especially when the folks are out for Tuesday night bowling. Parents give their young ones a roll of quarters: "Go amuse yourselves." They later wonder why they're caving in to buying a Nintendo for the kids.

Once that Nintendo is bought, look out! Children somehow metamorphasize to blank-faced, jittery video warriors often complaining of "fire-button thumb." As soon as school ends--zoom! Right in front of the screen they go. Taking a short break for dinner, they continue the battle in early evening. "I've got to get to level six," they are often quoted as saying. The dinner conversation, incidentally, is not how English was, but how we killed the vampire on level three.

All night the battle in videoland drags on. Once bedtime comes, these children are not read a book before slumber; rather, they are lulled to sleep by the memory of little beeps indicating that the hero has conquered yet another foe. When the day comes, the same cycle repeats itself. The games often last most of the day on weekends.

As these children grow older, many have thoughts that turn to love, which can mean dating. Not the video children; they'd rather master Tetris. Spending time with their parents when they were younger wouldn't drag them away, so why should members of the opposite sex? Read a book? Play a school sport? Nope, they're content in front of their video screen.

This behavior, of course, has to result in something. Quicker reflexes? Maybe, but these people also spend no time developing social skills or family ties. They live in a fantasy world with few friends besides other VG maniacs. They've spent so little time with their families that they barely know each other. In times of trouble, they have almost nowhere to turn for support, and if they do, they don't know how to interact. Technology, such as in video games, often yields great results. It can also cause us to forget ourselves and those around us.

Eric Betthauser

Eric was interested in a cause, video games, and their effects on children and families. Skim Eric's essay and fill in the effects he attributes to video games.

Cause: Children playing video games excessively

Effect 1 _____

Effect 2_____

Effect 3_____

How did Eric organize and support his main points?

Development/major point 1 _____

Support _____

Development/major point 2 _____

Support _____

Development/major point 3 _____

Support _____

Now examine Eric's introductory paragraph or lead:

Hook _____

Background _____

Thesis or controlling idea _____

Examine his concluding paragraph:

Summary _____

Significance _____

Implications _____

In addition to figuring out his general organization, Eric also had to develop adequate support. What kind we use depends a great deal on our audience and our purpose, as well as on the main idea we're presenting and whether or not we are using research or other outside sources. Eric was not required to use outside sources for this assignment. Consider the following list and decide what Eric used as support.

Ways to Support Ideas

Personal experience, anecdotes, observation

Examples

Reasons

Effects

Description/specific details

Step-by-step explanation

Reference to authorities or expert opinion

Facts and statistics

What other support might have been helpful in Eric's essay? Why? Would expert opinion be available? If so, where would you advise Eric to look for it?

Selecting supporting material for an expository essay involves two other important questions: (1) Is this material relevant, on the topic, and to the point? (2) Is there enough information? If you've ever read something and a voice in your head was saying, "Get on with it!" you know the meaning of relevant. Sometimes we get a sense of "beating around the bush" when writers get off the topic or fail to make the point efficiently. As readers, we get pretty annoyed when information isn't relevant to the point being made.

As readers, we expect *unity;* we expect everything to be relevant, on the topic, and appropriate to the point being made. Whether we refer to the entire essay or a single paragraph within it, unity is critical to the success of that writing.

Is Eric's essay unified? Does he present relevant supporting material? Does he provide sufficient material? If a voice in your head was saying, "This isn't complete enough," or, "I need more information," the writer has failed to provide you with sufficient material. Rather than being annoyed, we may simply stop reading altogether.

The aspects of writing that we have been looking at thus far are somewhat mechanical; that is, we can go back to the essay, pick them out, and display them graphically. There are two other aspects, however, that don't lend themselves to that type of display: the writer's voice and the significance of the piece of writing. You were concerned with voice and significance when you wrote your narrative essay; they were at the heart of your personal-experience writing.

They are similarly important in expository writing. Despite the emphasis being placed on the subject matter, we want a sense of the writer to come through. We want the feeling that one human is talking to another. In short, we want *voice*. And without a sense of significance, the entire point of the writing is lost. As readers, we need to feel that our time, as well as that of the writer's, was well spent on this piece of writing. We want to come away thinking, "That was interesting," or, "I learned something."

Did you get a sense of Eric in the video games essay? If you did, how did he manage to connect with you? What was the significance of his essay? Why should we be concerned with his topic? How has his analysis of the effects of video games expanded our knowledge or enhanced our thinking?

In the next student example, Tom McDonald, because he was interested in exploring two different comic book eras, used a different organizational pattern. As you read Tom's expository essay, think about the significance of what he is saying. How does he link comic books with a much larger issue?

Comic Books: Then and Now

Early in its life, the comic book was a simple, somewhat mindless creation to keep children happy on family trips, in the backs of cars, and during other occasions when they should be seen and not heard. Now, comic books have an adult audience, with intricate plots, less than super heroes, and portrayals of graphic violence.

Comic books--before the 1980s--consisted of characters like Daffy Duck and Batman. Although entertaining, these fictional subjects were hardly realistic, having no real life problems. Batman was never drunk,

never sad, and basically never anything less than superb. All Daffy was meant to do was make us laugh,
taking us away momentarily from the drudgery of our
daily lives. Batman was equally simple, never having
any question of purpose of motivation. He was the
perfect patriot, the perfect white, middle-western,
middle-class, heterosexual gentleman, and a perfect
scholar, knowing a good deal about everything.

The art of this old breed of comic book fit its
message, simplistic and clear-cut. The reader isn't
made to work or interpret this production line art at
all. That's the way artist teams did things, and the
reader had no choice but to accept it. Now, a very
different picture is painted.

In the graphic novel <u>The Dark Knight Returns</u>,
Batman is portrayed as an over-the-hill alcoholic,
haunted by his past. With violent crime in Gotham City
in a frenzy, the aged Bruce Wayne dons his black cloak
again, not by his own choice, but driven by some mysterious dark force he cannot control. Ultimately, the
Dark Knight has become so sickened by this new crime
wave in Gotham that he has become violent. This time
it's kill or be killed and Mr. Wayne chooses the former, victimizing street gangs with an extremely physical edge. Finally, it seems, the authors are trying
to confront the fact that the world isn't a bowl of
cherries.

The writers of this new breed of comic book are educated, thinking men who manage to throw political and
social commentary into their twisting, dancing story
line. A current issue of Spiderman deals exclusively
with the issue of cruelty to animals, making a powerful point to the reader that we may be wrong to torture these animals in the name of science. In today's
comic book, it's not uncommon to see Shakespeare
quoted. For example, in a recent issue of <u>X-Men</u>,
Storm, the leader of the renegade gang of mutants
known as the X-Men, quoted MacBeth in her dialogue
in which she grieved over the loss of an innocent man
by her own hands. The readers of this new comic are
actually made to think, and demanding thought is often

a characteristic of a productive, useful piece of fiction.

The art in this thoughtful new creation surpasses its writing in the provocation of thought. Awarded for its imagery and artistry, <u>The Dark Knight Returns</u> portrayed a macabre vision of the same Gotham City that had earlier been shown to us through rose-colored glasses. No longer was Batman slim and trim--his new portrayal can only be described as a demonic heap of brutish flesh. Again the simplicity and wholesomeness of the comic book of yesterday is made into something complex and sometimes lurid. This change isn't to shock the audience; it's to urge them to look beyond the black and white outline that we're presented with so often in everyday life.

Finally, the change in comic books can be seen in the vocabulary used. The words used for description went from "BIFF, BAMM, WHAMMO" to somewhat intellectually stirring words and phrases, worthy of Hemingway, like "adamant," "boisterous," or "deviously."

As you can see, the world of comic books has undergone a certain Renaissance or rebirth, changing in script and illustrations from idealistic to realistic, simple to complex and thought-provoking. It could, in fact, be argued that comic books are a mirror to society's change and will continue to parallel our lives.

Tom McDonald

Tom used comparison and contrast as the organizing strategy for his essay. Before you look back to see just how Tom used this strategy to explore his topic, examine the following chart. Then, as you skim Tom's essay, decide which of the three options he used.

Method 1	Method 2	Method 3
Introduction	Introduction	Introduction
Discuss A	Show likenesses between A and B	Discuss A and B on one point or topic
Discuss B	Show differences between A and B	Discuss A and B on second point or topic
Conclusion	Conclusion	Conclusion

Your topic and thesis or controlling idea will determine which of these patterns is best for you. For example, if it's important to emphasize the individual points, as is often the case with a more complex topic, Method 3 will be best. If you are interested in a general, overall comparison, then Method 1 or 2 is best. Sometimes, writers mix these patterns.

When you use comparison and contrast as a way to explore and analyze your topic, you need a strong controlling idea or thesis and careful organization. You have two subject areas instead of one, and you must have a point beyond mere comparison/contrast. If you omit your point, the reader will wonder why you are doing the comparison/contrast in the first place. Tom McDonald, for example, used comic books to make a point about changes in our society, and by implication, changes in today's kids.

In addition to deciding that comparison and contrast would be his organizational strategy, Tom also had to decide how to arrange his support material in each paragraph.

Arrangement

Topic sentence
Example (and/or)
Fact (and/or)
Personal experience (and/or)
Illustration (and/or)
Reason (and/or)
Expert opinion

Topic sentence
Example (and/or), etc.

After grouping material for each paragraph, Tom had to make a few more decisions. What point and material should be first? Last? And why? The following are typical ways we arrange the overall order in the essay:

Least important to most important: We build momentum and leave our reader with the most powerful point and material.

Most important to least important: We get the reader's attention immediately. In essay exams, we need to use this order, or we might run out of time before getting to the most important point. Newspapers and business reports use this order, mainly as a time saver for busy readers.

Known to unknown: In most learning situations, we need to move from what we know to what we need to learn. In writing, we also may need to establish a common ground, things our readers know, before presenting new material. The "known" then provides the context and foundation for new material.

Accepted to controversial: Again, establishing a common ground with our readers allows us to pursue new, debatable material.

Step by step: Sometimes our material can be explained only through chronological order. Everything from how-to books to historical accounts relies on this order.

Spatial: When we describe things or people, we rely on spatial order; we move from a set point to another set point. In biology labs, as well as art studios, we are often confronted with the need to order observations spatially.

Return to Tom's essay and note how he arranged it. Then skim Eric's essay and note his arrangement. Did they use the same arrangement? Were they limited to certain arrangements because of their subject matter?

WRITING INTRODUCTIONS AND CONCLUSIONS

Students often report that the most difficult part of their writing task is the introduction or the conclusion. For this reason, they are sometimes advised to leave the formal introduction until last, until they can review their entire paper and write an introduction that matches it. Conclusions can also be troublesome, mainly because we want to leave the reader with our main point and yet not repeat what we just said in the body of the paper. Fortunately, we have some strategies to help us with this writing.

Introductions

Introductions, also called leads, are critical to the success of the essay. Effective introductions do two things immediately: focus our attention on the subject and provoke our curiosity or interest.

Group Activity

Select a favorite magazine or newspaper, read through several articles, and then, from separate articles, choose two leads that interest you and two that you find boring. Bring them to class.

In your group, read your leads and discuss their effect—positive or negative—and why. As a group, choose one that you agree upon as effective, and be prepared to discuss your lead in whole-class discussion. As a class, list characteristics of effective leads.

Strategies for Introductions

Quotation: An appropriate quotation is a common strategy for introducing academic essays. The quotation may come from an expert on the subject you are exploring, an "ordinary" person with related experience, or any number of well-known sources (e.g., literature, religious or philosophical writings) or well-known people (e.g., educators, scientists, journalists, politicians). The quotation helps focus the reader on your subject. For some topics, music lyrics may provide a wonderful introduction to your subject and point of view.

Illustration: An example illustrating your topic may give the reader a sense of "being there." Allowing people to sense the situation or issue (showing rather than telling) may be essential in drawing them into the points you will explore or argue.

Anecdote: Providing a brief story is a good way to raise interest in your topic. If you are the main character in the story, you might also be showing your reader why this topic is important to you. Your relationship to the topic becomes immediately clear.

Historical background: Sometimes, a topic needs a bit of background in order for readers to understand why things are as they are or why a problem occurred.

News stories: If your topic is on a current or controversial subject, you may find a local or regional newspaper article that can serve as an introduction to your discussion.

Statistics: Facts and figures may surprise your reader and gain interest in the topic. For example, many people associate homelessness with single, older males. Current statistics, however, show families comprising 40 percent of the homeless.

Questions: Asking a question or a series of questions in the introduction may draw the reader into the main text, where you will answer those questions.

Controversial statement: Saying something shocking is another way of getting readers into your discussion. You have to use good judgment, of course, as to the degree of shock value.

You may use several of the strategies at the same time, especially if the essay will be somewhat lengthy. And you may end up writing your introduction after the essay is completed. Don't feel that you have to get the introduction "right" before you can go on with the essay. In fact, learning to let go of the introduction is important. In early drafts, you may end up with false introductions, a fair amount of text that should be crossed out. All of us repeat and spin wheels as we try to get into the subject. All writers, no matter how experienced, generally end up throwing out many paragraphs of false introductions.

Some strategies for writing the introduction:

✦ Find your favorite line or lines from the body of the essay, write it at the top of page 1.

✦ Consider once more your purpose, your audience, and your own personality.

✦ Then review the strategies, and pick one that appears to be the best match with your purpose, audience, and personality.

✦ Try at least four potential introductions using that strategy.

✦ If nothing works or appeals to you, pick a different strategy and repeat the process.

Conclusions

Students often report that writing a conclusion, however short, is nearly as difficult as writing an introduction. They know that the conclusion is supposed to leave a lasting impression on the reader. However, they also know that just repeating the main idea has been overworked as a strategy. What are the options then? In some cases, the same strategies used in introductions also work well in conclusions. There are other strategies that are particularly well suited for conclusions, however.

Strategies for Conclusions

Question: Posing a question for further consideration on the topic can be very effective.

Quotation: Sometimes, the right quotation acts as a summary statement of the discussion.

Image: Leaving the reader with a physical image, a picture, is another way of reinforcing our main point.

Back to lead: When writers refer back to something in the introduction, they bring the reader "full circle." The entire discussion has then been framed by opening and closing statements focused on the very same words or image.

Resolution: The writer can answer the question posed or problem raised in the introduction.

Summary: This strategy must be used sparingly. A summary is a restatement of the main points. Since the writer has just presented these points, the reader might be turned off by a restatement, especially in a short essay. Unless the essay is very long, it's better to avoid anything that even hints at "This is what I have just told you."

Return to the two student essays and evaluate the introductions and conclusions. What strategies did Eric and Tom use? What other strategies might have strengthened their essays?

Group Activity

Evaluate another of Tom McDonald's essays, "In Search of a Good Scare."

◆   Is his purpose clear?

◆   Does he show awareness of his audience?

◆   Is his controlling idea clearly stated?

◆   Is his material well organized?

◆   Does he provide enough material?

◆   How does he support his points?

◆   Are the transitions appropriate?

◆   Does his voice come through?

◆   Are the lead and final paragraphs strong?

◆   What is the significance of his essay?

◆   Why is this an expository essay?

In Search of a Good Scare

Despite some popular misconceptions about fear, America thrives on it. From movies to amusement parks or skydiving to ghost stories, fear is a need for many of us that demands to be fulfilled.

Freddy Krueger. His name is as common to us as Superman. In A Nightmare on Elm Street, parts one through five, Freddy can be found viciously and sadistically murdering teenagers, plucking them from their slumbers and ruling their dream worlds. And in the end, the newly petrified moviegoer is horrified to find that Freddy is far from finished. Often, that viewer is so petrified that sleep for the next few weeks is either unattainable or very restless. However, when the next one comes out, save our petrified viewer a spot somewhere near the front.

Many people have fond memories of days spent at amusement parks. Perhaps a more appropriate label for these places would be "Please scare the hell out of me" parks. The longest lines are invariably for the biggest, fastest, scariest roller coasters in the park. Every time the rider starts out, part of them is screaming, "I don't want to do this! Please, please make it stop!" But when the ride is over the terror-stricken participant goes inexplicably to the back of the line to ride this nightmare once more.

Somebody . . . anybody . . . <u>please</u> tell me what is fun about jumping out of an airplane! As the plane ascends and the ground is just a memory, second thoughts abound. As the parachutist approaches the door he will soon fling himself out of, his heart is hammering in his chest, ready to explode. Yet the thrill seeker still jumps. WOW!

Finally, our taste for fear can be shown in the infamous ghost stories told in the dark or around a campfire. With hearts beating and imaginations running wild, the listener wants to cover his or her ears, but is afraid to miss the next eye-watering plot twist. Why do we submit ourselves to this torture?

When we are scared in certain ways, our minds and bodies react electrically. The adrenalin "kicks in" and we feel alive and excited. It's almost like a natural high. And we like the feeling. So, we overcome our fear to feel its effects, and the rush we feel becomes almost addictive. Ultimately, fear is a whirlwind of excitement that we often willingly take part in for the sake of its surging, powerful effects.

Tom McDonald

The next student essay needs work. Although the writer had some good ideas, she had trouble trying to clarify, organize, and develop them. Consequently, as readers we are left to piece things together. In addition, we are distracted by sentence, punctuation, and spelling errors. Read through the essay quickly, to get an overall idea of its content and intended purpose. Then, go through it slowly, evaluating it as you go. How would you help the writer turn this into an acceptable essay? Be specific and constructive in your advice.

Movies

There are basically three types of movies which attract the viewers attention, in other words its purposes and effects: crime, horror, and comical.

Crime movies have a way of capturing our interest to focus on the exciting detective aspect of catching the criminal. The cops and detectives seem to go through a lot of grief and frustration at the lose of more victums when the evidence is thin. Nevertheless, the good guys always finish off bad guys whether or not it's a shoot out to the end or a sentence of death or life imprisoned. This was the adventurous purpose of crime movies. The educational part shows viewers that crime doesn't pay and sooner or later the truth will come out, and justice will punish the wrong. Crime movies also have fast paced action when the presure begins and at the climax of the solution. For example, "Lethal Weapon" was about two cops, vets, who were after the main mafia men, were selling drugs laced with poison. These cops were tortured and still they hung on. To make a long story short, the cops beat the mafia at their own game and shut them down. Another case, "The Godfather" the mafia takes the law into thier own power.

A horror movies purpose is to thrill and frighten the veiwer with scary, gruesome scenes and exaggerated sounds. It is intensified by a stalking of some crazy person or thing, which keeps coming back to life for series after series. To illustrate, "Halloween I, II, III", "Friday The 13, I, II, III, etc., "Jaws", "The Shining", and "Nightmare on Elm Street I, II, III".

Comical movies are for entertainment, moreover, enjoyment. Since we all have a serious side to ourselves, the effects of a comical movie can help us maintain our sense of humor about life. laughter is good for the body and mind. Some examples are "Private Benjamin" starring Goldie Hawn, "The Glass Bottom Boat" with Doris Day, and Rod Sterling, and a musical comady by Walt Disney "The Sound of Music" of the Vantamp Family.

In conclusion, the purpose and effects that crime, horror, and comical movies have on veiwers depends on what attracts them in the first place. Each movie has a way of exaggerating its characters somewhat to emphasize a point.

For his expository essay, Stephan Severson explored similarities between two of his favorite television shows, *The Flintstones* and *The Honeymooners*. Note the changes Stephan made between his first two drafts:

Revision	Changes in content
	Changes in organization
	Changes in sentences
Editing	Complete sentences
	Punctuation
	Spelling

Read through each draft quickly to get an overall sense of each. Then read through each draft slowly, noting the changes he made. Comparing paragraph to paragraph might help you see how the changes improved or, in some cases, didn't improve Stephan's essay. Did he eliminate good material from his first draft? Did he add material that is essentially irrelevant to his point? Be specific in your response to changes he made and changes he might have made.

Stephan had a good expository subject. What suggestions do you have for taking better advantage of the subject, for improving it, and for making a significant statement about it?

DRAFT 1

Copycat

Have you ever noticed how much two television shows can seem alike. Growing up with television I have wit-

nessed this many times before. But there are two shows
that compliment each other The Flintstones and The
Honeymooners. The main reason why these two shows seem
identical is because of the main characters, Fred
Flintstone from the Flintstones and Ralph Cramden from
the Honeymooners.

First of all, Fred's and Ralph's attitudes are very
similar. They both have an explosive temper always using it to its full potential. Both of these characters
have best friends (Fred's being Barney Rubel, and
Ralph's being Ed Norton) Which they always seem to say
that their friends are no longer welcome in their
house. Ralph always using the trade mark "out, get
out!" and Fred using insulting swear words such as
"fricking reckun runbk ruk."

Another aspect of this relationship is that both
characters share an enormous figure, which distinctly
alientes them from the crowd. In each episode the boys
are always being put down because of their weight. It
doesn't help the fact that Alice and Wilma slave to
prepare a hardy meal for their hard working husbands.
Guest appearances always seem to poke fun a Fred and
Ralph, usually ending up in some sort of trouble.
Along with the weight issue comes their mothers-in-
law, both women have no time for their sons-in-law.
These women really know how to get a rise out of Fred
and Ralph. During the end of the season the boys are
always in a conflict where their mother-in-law is visiting and has to stay overnight, which leads to both
Fred and Ralph's humble temperment.

Adding to the list of likenesses is the fact that
both men in the show always find a way to get into an
excessive amount of trouble, later having to explain
the whole story to their loving wives. Wilma Flinstone
and Alice Cramden. Usually every show is dedicated to
the mayhem revolving around Fred and Ralph's interaction with trouble, always bringing Ed and Barney into
the picture. Usually the trouble takes place outside
the homestead, in a pool hall or when the boys go
bowling.

Finally Fred and Ralph always find a way of entertaining the audience, even though to very distinct age groups. When saying this I mean that the Flinstones is a cartoon, and the Honeymooners is a classic black and white. After watching both of these great shows I have come to a conclusion. The Flintstones was created in regard to the Honeymooners success.

DRAFT 2

Copycat

Have you ever noticed how much two television shows can seem alike? Growing up with television I have witnessed this before. When saying this, two shows come to mind: the Flintstones and the Honeymooners. These two shows compliment each other with the uncanny mannerisms of the characters. There is distinctly one main reason why the two shows seem identical: the characters.

After watching both the Honeymooners and the Flintstones, I sense that the main characters from the Flintstones are identical to those in the Honeymooners. Fred Flintstone, for example, is much like the character Ralph Cramden. They both possess violent tempers that explode like blood-gushing volcanoes. Also they both have a pretty big frame of a body, due to their voracious appetites. Another quality that brings Fred and Ralph closer together is their mothers in law. Fred and Ralph are always in some kind of trouble when these women appear. This interaction with their mothers-in-law creates another quality in Fred and Ralph: the famous out burst. Fred's outburst is "frikn rakun ruchin . . . ", and Ralph's famous outburst, "to the moon."

One of the biggest similarities of the shows is Fred and Ralph's best friends, Barney Rubbel from the Flintstones and Ed Norton from the Honeymooners. Both Barney and Ed share qualities of zany humor, brainless ideas, and countless hours of tormenting Fred and Ralph. This has been displayed by both shows whenever

Fred and Barney, or Ed and Ralph, participate in bowling, pool, or attend a boxing match. Plus Barney and Ed are always an accomplice to whatever mischief Fred and Ralph create.

Another aspect of similarity in character is the women in both shows--Fred's wife, Wilma and Ralph's wife, Alice. Both Alice and Wilma slave for their husbands throughout each entertaining show. Cooking and cleaning are a must for these women; neither one has a job. The Flintstones and the Honeymooners both had episodes in which Wilma and Alice insisted that they have jobs. But according to Fred and Ralph, the women were to stay at home.

Not only do Fred and Ralph have similar wives, but so do Ed and Barney. Their names are Betty Rubbel and Trixie Norton, but neither woman has a very big role. The only time these two women can be seen is when Alice or Wilma is the focus of the episode. The only other time that Betty and Trixie are involved is when all four characters are need for an special occasion such as going out to eat.

After watching both shows, the viewer can draw only one conclusion, that the Flintstones was created because of the Honeymooners success. In no way is this a rip on either show; my personal belief is that the television industry was looking to created a successful show with a general plot that would have an enormous effect on a diverse audience.

Stephan Severson

Apply the evaluation criteria to Stephan's second draft:

- ✦ Is his purpose clear?
- ✦ Does he show awareness of his audience?
- ✦ Is his controlling idea clearly stated?
- ✦ Does he provide enough support for his points?
- ✦ Does he provide good support?
- ✦ Is his material well organized?
- ✦ Are his transitions appropriate?
- ✦ Are the lead and final paragraphs strong?

✦ Is the significance (the "so what?" factor) clear?

✦ Does his voice come through?

✦ Are his sentences clear, effective?

✦ Do grammar and mechanics (punctuation, spelling) conform to Standard Written English?

You may have already touched on some of these criteria, but going through them point by point provides a clearer view of the essay's strengths and weaknesses.

Writing Activity

Informative writing focuses on the subject matter, and its aim is the reader's intellect rather than the imagination. It is essentially instructive, and the writer becomes the teacher. Although this role may be somewhat uncomfortable at this point in your development as a writer, think about the many subjects where you do have considerable knowledge. Also think about writing for an audience that does not share your knowledge or level of expertise on a subject. Add your personal interest in a subject, and you have a good base on which to build an interesting and informative essay.

Choosing and Developing a Topic.   Using one or several strategies, generate and explore potential topics for an expository essay. Remember, your purpose is to inform or explain—not take a position or propose a solution to a problem.

When you have two or three potential topics, turn to the analysis strategies and explore the topics in more depth: Does the topic deal with cause or effect? Would the topic involve comparison and contrast? Is there a process involved? What intrigues you about the topic? What would readers learn? Why should they learn this, or for that matter, care about learning it?

Once you have selected the topic, take some time to write down what you already know about it. Don't worry about how you write, just get down some information in whatever form is easy and useful (e.g., lists, phrases, sentences), including simple graphics. Then, list questions that you want to answer with your essay. Next, think about your readers. Take at least five minutes to ask yourself what they would already know and how you would add to that information.

Write a discovery draft. Don't worry about "how" you write at this point; just get the ideas from your head to paper or disk. Through the processes of drafting, revising, and editing, you will deal with the "how." Right now, just concentrate on the "what."

Drafting.   Read your discovery draft and ask yourself some questions:

- ✦   Do I have enough information?
- ✦   Do I know enough about this topic to write well on it?
- ✦   Will this topic interest my readers?
- ✦   What will my readers already know?
- ✦   How can I build on what they know?
- ✦   What is the best strategy for analyzing and organizing?
- ✦   Am I dealing primarily with cause and effect? Comparison? Process?
- ✦   What order best suits my purpose?
- ✦   What examples and details will make my writing more concrete?

Circle the information that you decide to keep; if possible at this stage, put numbers in the circles to indicate a tentative order for each chunk of information. Make a scratch outline—nothing fancy, and always consider this outline as tentative. It is merely one way of seeing the major parts and a possible order of presentation. Write your next draft. Try to allow a couple of days between your completion of this draft and the start of the revision process. You'll bring "new eyes" (and probably better motivation) to the process if you have had a break.

Revising.   Read your entire draft quickly to gain a sense of the overall "sense" and effect. Then, in one sentence, write down what the draft says. Finally, write down anything else that you noticed in your reading. Now read the draft once more. Why all this reading? It's very easy to read over and through problems in our own writing. We know what we want to say, and our brain sometimes fools us into thinking what's in our head is actually on the paper. What's more, we need a very good sense of the draft before we take on the "big" revision questions.

Questions about the heart of the draft

- ✦   Where is the real life of this draft?
- ✦   Where is it most energetic and engaging?
- ✦   Would anyone say "so what?" after reading it?
- ✦   What is my point? Why have I written about this subject?
- ✦   Where can I go with this draft to make it more interesting?

Questions about purpose

- ✦   Is my purpose clear?
- ✦   Is my controlling idea clearly stated?

Questions about content and organization

✦ How do I develop or support my controlling idea?

✦ Are my examples and details relevant and adequate?

✦ Does my organization make sense? Is it easy to follow?

✦ Is my beginning strong and interesting?

✦ Is my ending concise yet satisfying?

Questions about structure

✦ Do I have large chunks that could be dropped out?

✦ Do I have gaps that need filling?

✦ Is any part too long or too tangled?

Assessing Paragraph by Paragraph

Author Ann Lamott recounts a family story about her brother:

> Thirty years ago my older brother, who was ten years old at the time, was trying to get a report on birds written that he'd had three months to write. [It] was due the next day. We were out at our family cabin in Bolinas, and he was at the kitchen table close to tears, surrounded by binder paper and pencils and unopened books on birds, immobilized by the hugeness of the task. Then my father sat down beside him, put his arm around my brother's shoulder, and said, "Bird by bird, buddy. Just take it bird by bird."
>
> *Bird by Bird*

Her father's advice works equally well for tackling revision: substitute "paragraph" for "bird," and you have a plan. Read and revise the essay paragraph by paragraph. Not only will you do a better job of assessing the draft, but you will have specific start and stop points and a plan for systematically checking the draft.

Structure/Unity

✦ Number each paragraph in the left margin.

✦ Read each paragraph and, in a word or short phrase, write down its main point.

◆ If you can't "boil it down" to a few words, you probably have more than one point.

◆ If you have more than one point per paragraph, you have located a problem.

◆ Scan each paragraph again: Why is it here? How does it help develop my point?

◆ If you end up writing down what it says, go back and fill in this sentence to keep you on track with its function: This paragraph is here because it _____ .

Structure/Coherence

◆ Scan the entire essay, paying attention to movement from paragraph to paragraph.

◆ How does each paragraph connect and build upon the previous one?

◆ Would more explicit transition words help the reader?

◆ Read each paragraph separately, paying attention to connections between sentences.

◆ Would repeating key words or pronouns help?

◆ Would the addition of transition words help?

Style

◆ Read each paragraph, concentrating on the sentences and specific words.

◆ Are the sentences all alike or are they varied in structure?

◆ Are the sentences complete and clear?

◆ Does every word serve a purpose or is there repetition?

◆ Are there too many "it is" and "there are" sentences?

◆ Are there unnecessary, meaningless phrases?

◆ Is there a sense of you, the writer? An appropriate tone?

A Revision Plan

Locating the problems is, of course, the first step in revision. Deciding on how to fix them is the next and equally demanding step. Using a chart may help you to take it with increased confidence and efficiency. For example:

Area	Problem	Solution
Content	Too long Dull opening	Cut paragraphs 3 and 5, find anecdote or quotation
Organization	Process not clear	Make scratch outline, review each step in process
	Transitions	Use more direct connectors, check list of transitions

Peer Response

With your partner or group, exchange papers. Read through quickly for the overall impression; then, read the draft slowly. If your instructor provides specific instructions or a form for peer response, follow those directions. If not, respond to the major categories you have worked on during revision. The author should point out areas where he or she has had trouble and is still not satisfied with the result. Be sure to point out the strengths of the draft and to offer specific, concrete suggestions for improvement.

Editing

You may have corrected some obvious errors as you worked on the draft, but now it is time to systematically check for errors in usage, mechanics, and spelling. Before you check for these errors, be sure each sentence is complete. Also check your personal error log for areas that have been a problem in the past.

Usage

✦   Do nouns and verbs agree in number (singular/plural)?

✦   Do nouns and pronouns agree in number?

✦   Are any double negatives present (he can't hardly)?

✦   Are any double subjects present (my brother he left)?

Mechanics

✦ Are commas used between sentences with coordinating connector (and, or, but)?

✦ Are semicolons used between two complete sentences?

✦ Do commas separate items in a series, dates, or places?

✦ Do commas set off word groups used descriptively?

✦ Are capitals used on names, products, specific places?

Spelling

✦ Are sound-alikes (there, they're) used correctly?

✦ Are typos that form words (fro when mean for) deleted?

✦ Are easily confused words (affect, effect) used correctly?

✦ Are new terms or vocabulary correct?

Reflection

Write a brief paragraph in which you explore the development of your expository essay. The questions are merely a prompt. Feel free to discuss whatever aspect is important to you.

✦ What was most challenging?

✦ If you had a problem, how did you solve it?

✦ What seemed easier with this paper? Why?

✦ What part of the writing process still gives you the most trouble?

✦ What do you like most about this paper? Least? Why?

✦ What would you do differently on the next expository essay?

ANALYZING

When we analyze, we are really asking many questions: What's going on here? What is this all about? How did this occur? Why did it occur? Who's involved? What's involved? We are interested in examining the parts that make up the issue, situation, or problem. Our analysis will lead us back to consideration of the whole once more, its overall meaning or function. If you watched the news during the Persian Gulf War, you no doubt heard many military analysts. They would comment on the progress of the war by looking at the various parts of it: what the armed forces were doing, what military commanders were saying, and what the Secretary of Defense was saying, for example. From these various points of view, the analysts would study the war, draw conclusions about its progress, or speculate about future action. Their task was to present viewers with, presumably, a coherent statement or picture of what was happening at that time. Suggesting or stating the significance of the event or issue is the logical outcome of analysis.

During national political campaigns, we are surrounded by political analysts who seem to have analyzed everything that moves. They listen to the candidates, the campaign staffs, and people across America. Like military analysts, they then analyze all the parts and present their view of the situation. During the 1992 presidential election, some television stations and newspapers analyzed political ads in an effort to let voters know whether or not a candidate was being honest. And most of us have listened to sports analyses by ex-athletes, some on national television and some in the local coffee shop or corner bar. Analysis, then, is a familiar way of dealing with our world.

Analysis Project

Recent national elections saw an upsurge of interest in the "women's vote," and many politicians went after this segment of the voting public, including women who sought public office on local, regional, state, and national levels. What's more surprising, however, are the results of a 1997 poll conducted by Bruskin Goldring Research: one in four Americans believes a woman will be elected president within the next two election cycles, with slightly more men than women saying it will happen; four out of five Americans believe women will play a larger part in U.S. politics in the next 10 years. And more men than ever (61%) say it is no longer important to them whether a male or female represents them in Congress (*Eau Claire Leader-Telegram* 21 June 97:7A).

Because differences in male and female perspectives have been talked and written about for years, journalists have long been intrigued with the idea of "what if women ran America?" One major result of that interest was a scientific poll and a major publication exploring that "what if?"

IF WOMEN RAN AMERICA . . .

Lisa Grunwald

FAMILY

If women ran America, would child care be more available and maternity leave guaranteed?

A majority of Americans—but more women than men—favor government support of programs that help working parents. The greatest gender gap exists between younger women (ages 18–45) and older men (46 and up). Eighty-four percent of younger women favored paid maternity leave; just half of the older men agree. And 86% of the same women want the government to help develop childcare programs; only 58% of the men concur.

POVERTY

If women ran America, would government be more attentive to the needy?

Fifty percent more women than men (44% vs. 29%) believe the double-edged problem of poverty and homelessness should be an "extremely important" government priority. But neither women nor men condone a free ride. Since 88% overall support laws requiring welfare recipients to work if they can, It's no surprise that 91% of men and women favor increased spending for child care so parents on welfare can work or attend school.

CRIME

If women ran America, would there be stricter gun control?

Seven out of 10 women favor making it harder to buy firearms; half the men agree. The verdict on capital punishment is less clear. Women more than men choose life imprisonment for murders (40% vs. 33%), while more men than women prefer the death penalty (54% vs. 46%). Three out of five people believe that addressing social problems is a better way to reduce crime than beefed-up law enforcement, but women believe it more strongly than men.

VIOLENCE

If women ran America, would they be tougher on crime?

Twenty percent more women than men (55% vs. 46%) say the government should make fighting crime and violence an "extremely important" priority. More women than men say the system is "not tough enough" on drug dealing, rape and sexual assault, and wife abuse. A sizable gender gap relates to drunk driving: 76% of women as opposed to 58% of men say that the criminal justice system should be tougher on offenders.

WORKPLACE

If women ran America, would there be greater equality for working women?

Women take workplace equality issues more seriously than men do. Unequal pay for equal work, sexual harassment, discrimination in hiring and promotions, child care—all are rated by more women than men to be "very serious problems" for women. Men are more likely to label most of these issues "somewhat serious." Women's top concern? Pay inequity. Two thirds rate it a very serious problem; half the men agree.

ABORTION

If women ran America, would abortion be legal?

Judging from the poll, the legal status of abortion would be no different if the reins of government were in the hands of either women or men. It would be legal—with some restrictions. Overall men are slightly more supportive of legal abortion than are women. Age—rather than sex—is a telling factor and could change the politics of abortion in the future: 53% of younger women, ages 18–45, favor access to legal abortions "always" or in "most" circumstances, while just 36% of the women over age 45 agree.

PRESIDENT

If women ran America, would America be a better place?

Nearly six in 10 people say it would not make much difference whether men or women ran the government. Still, about one out of three believe government would be better if women were in charge. (Says one woman: "Men have been in so long, let's see what the gals can do.") Sixty-one percent hope to see a woman elected President in their lifetime. More women than men hope for a woman President (young women are especially intent on this), but more men than women believe they'll see it happen.

Note: At the time this poll was taken, there were only two women in the United States Senate, only three states with female governors, and only one female Supreme Court justice. In the 1992 elections, 186 women declared their candidacies for congressional offices. As a result of the 1992 national election, 6 percent of the U.S. Senate and 11 percent of the House of Representatives are women; however, 54 percent of the American population are women. (Statistics from the Center for American Women and Politics, Rutgers University)

Your Analysis of Poll Results.

A. Which issues are women most committed to? Why do you think this is so? Men? Why?

B. Which issues appear to be rather evenly supported by both men and women? Why?

C. Which issues have an "age gap," where the age of the respondents made a difference in their views? Why?

GRUNWALD'S CONCLUSION

It is no surprise in a year that saw vexing recession, unacceptable scholastic test scores, unaffordable health insurance and the breakup of the Soviet Union, to find men and women agreeing that the economy and health care should come before foreign affairs . . . but where women's views differ from men's, those views seem to lend particular insight into what the agenda of women in power would be. [p. 41]

A. Based on your reading of the polls, what do you think this agenda might be?

B. Does this suggest that American men don't care about these issues?

C. Or does it only suggest women care more?

D. How can you be fair in your analysis?

Lisa Grunwald's Analysis of Poll Results.   As you read Grunwald, notice how she presents her analysis. She draws conclusions from her reading of the polls, but she neither says nor implies that hers are the only conclusions. She adds to our knowledge without insisting that her analysis is the only one to interpret the polls. Notice how she uses questions in her analysis.

FURTHER EXCERPTS FROM GRUNWALD

Women, for example, are far more committed than men to cushioning the hard corners of the country, to making it simply a safer place. Women want stricter law enforcement against drunk driving and firearms and drug dealing, which may be another way of saying that they want to keep their children alive. It's not that men don't care about these issues. It's simply that women care more. Is it because womanhood has never been measured by the length of a pistol? Because manhood and cars and risk taking have so often gone hand-in-hand? Or is it because, as any woman who's carried and borne or cared for a child will tell you, the act of mothering takes a little more time than the act of fathering? . . .

Motherhood may be one way to explain why a woman's world would be crisscrossed with safer streets, but there is a less lovely reason as well, which is women's history as victims. . . . In 1990 an estimated 683,000 American women were raped; at least two million are abused each year by husbands and boyfriends. . . . "Even those of us who have not been victimized by crime are often victimized by the fear of crime," says former Dukakis campaign manager Susan Esterich. "It limits our lives—limits our choices, limits where we work, and when we go out, and where we live."

Safety first. But fairness also, especially for women at work. Not so long ago, prospective female employees were regularly asked to promise they wouldn't get pregnant. In 1990 women who worked full-time were still earning an average of 71 cents per male-earned dollar. [pp. 41–42]

[Regarding the workplace], as Colorado Rep. Patricia Schroeder puts it, "The most stressful thing is that we have a workplace where people are not allowed to mention their caregiver role. We tolerate a car breaking down more than a sick child at home." Only 3% of the nation's businesses offer day care.

Eighty-five percent [of the women] say they would approve of a law requiring businesses to allow employees an unpaid, 12 week family medical leave. . . . Behind that number are dying parents, spouses in surgery, new babies, sick children. Of those who support family leave, nearly 30 percent more women than men want it available for gay couples too; behind that number are the slow and awful ravages of AIDS. [pp. 42–43]

As she concludes her analysis, Grunwald focuses on an important question: If women ran America, if they had power, would they really be any different from the men who run America? As you read her commentary, note how she challenges us to think about this question.

If women ran America . . . they would not just run the Congress; they would run the special interests as well. Is there any reason to think that a female head of an insurance company would lobby any less vigorously than a man against a national health plan? Women would hold the federal purse strings and would have to decide if a peace dividend was worth laying off the thousands of workers who feed their families by making B2s. And with women having most of the power, they would have most of power's temptations: not just the perks of higher office, but also the lust to maintain those perks. Would women, once they had left behind their status as outsiders, really be able to defy not only the stereotypes about themselves but also the stereotypes about power?

Then, Grunwald responds to her own question, suggesting that perhaps women are different from men:

One way to answer the question is to admit—as feminist groups of two decades ago were not inclined to do—that there is something inherent to women's experience that makes them different from men. [pp. 44–45]

Examining Other Sources

If you were interested in pursuing Grunwald's question about women and power, you would need to search out other sources.

Read the excerpt from Carol Gilligan, whose research examines psychological differences between males and females. How does Gilligan add to our knowledge?

IN A DIFFERENT VOICE

Carol Gilligan

Sensitivity to the needs of others and the assumption of responsibility for taking care lead women to attend to voices other than their own and to include in their judgment other points of view. [p. 16]

Thus women not only define themselves differently in a context of human relationships but also judge themselves in terms of the ability to care. Women's place in man's life cycle has been that of nurturer, caretaker, and helpmate, the weaver of those relationships on which she in turn relies. [p. 17]

The discovery now being celebrated by men in mid-life of the importance of intimacy, relationships, and care is something women have known from the beginning. [p. 17]

How is Gilligan's research reflected in the poll results? In Lisa Grunwald's analysis? How does a writer benefit from his or her ability to search out relevant research?

If you were interested in pursuing the question of why there have been so few women "running America," you might find some material from *20/20* helpful as a starting point. On May 29, 1992, ABC News correspondent John Stossel reported on the research of Harvard University educator Carol Gilligan and others: Girls confident at age 11 end up confused and unsure of themselves at age 16. Researchers concluded that hormonal changes in adolescence may be generally positive for males and less so for females. That is, males become bigger, stronger, and more confident as a result of the physical changes they undergo. Girls, by contrast, become less confident as they pass through the many physical and emotional changes characteristic of early adolescence.

Stossel also reported on the work of Catherine Krupnick, another Harvard researcher: Teachers call on boys more than they do girls. Boys are generally more noisy and aggressive, vie for attention, and get it. As a result, girls end up in a "silence ghetto" within the classroom.

Stossel visited a classroom of five-year-olds where he found the research "acted out" in front of him. The boys cared little for responding in an orderly fashion, often shouting out answers without being called on. When Stossel asked the girls why they thought the boys did that, one little girl told him, "Because they don't care if they know the answer or not. They just like to talk."

The following readings might also be useful to you in analyzing the situation of women in American society.

BACK TO THE BASICS: TEST SCORES DON'T LIE

Diane Ravitch

When I was in public high school in Texas in the 1950s, one of the last things a girl wanted was a reputation as a good student. Girls who got good grades were "brains," and brains were socially handicapped. Most girls strived to cultivate the June Allyson image: a follower, not a leader; cute and not too smart; or at least not so smart that the guys felt threatened.

Apparently—despite the women's movement and the presence of significant numbers of successful women as role models—it is still considered inappropriate in most schools and colleges for girls to seem "smart." As a female student at Hunter High School in New York City recently explained, "I make straight A's but I never talk about it. . . . It's cool to do really badly. If you are interested in school and show it, you're a nerd." In elite institutions where students are chosen for their academic ability, girls are more willing to challenge the boys academically than they are in nonselective schools and colleges. But with the demise of most single-sex girls' schools and colleges, there are now even fewer institutions where girls can be leaders and achievers without feeling like freaks. The popular culture—through television, movies, magazines, and videos—incessantly drums in the message to young women that it is better to be popular, sexy and "cool" than to be intelligent, accomplished, and outspoken: Madonna has replaced June Allyson.

AUTHOR SAYS GIRLS LOSE SENSE OF SELF

Los Angeles—At 7 going on 8, Lacy Bird likes baseball and ballet and riding bikes with her best friend, Whitney. School is fun; reading is her best subject.

Boys are barely a blip on the radar screen.

And Lacy knows just what she wants to be when she grows up.

"I think about being a doctor and a waitress and a linguist," she says without hesitation.

The contradictions in the list don't make a difference to the suburban Simi Valley second-grader. It's what she wants and, for now, she believes she can have it.

Hang onto these memories—life won't always be so sweet, says Emily Hancock, a psychologist whose work at Harvard University led to her book, "The Girl Within" (Fawcett; $10). The clear thought and solid sense of self present in 9-year-old girls often erode at adolescence, her book suggests.

At puberty, the girls swap their blue jeans for a skirt and their independence for a more clearly defined female role, Hancock said. In fact, the Berkeley resident says she believes that a woman's best years may be over by the time she is 11 or 12 years old.

"Girls get buried. The loss of their sense of self doesn't depend on adolescence—it happens before then," Hancock said. "As girls get bigger, they get taken out of the tree house and asked to come inside. You lose something essential when you're no longer an adventurer pursuing your own interests."

Hancock stumbled on her theory while researching grown women's reactions to their own adult development. In studying 20 women, she found that each participant's true identity emerged when she remembered who she had been at age 7, 8 or 9.

"By reaching back to the girl within, the women were on their way to reclaiming their independence," Hancock said. Once that girl is unearthed, Hancock believes a woman can recover her true identity.

Independent research backs up the theory. A study by the American Association of University Women, a national organization of college students and graduates that promotes equity in education for women and girls, found that girls' self-esteem erodes dramatically between fourth grade, when they are 8 or 9, and the time they enter junior high school.

"AAUW did a study in the fall of 1990 . . . showing that girls' self-esteem drops off two times as much as boys' in adolescence," said Sharon Schuster, president of the organization. "Boys' self-esteem falls off some, but not nearly as much as the girls'."

The information parallels prior findings in the organization's acclaimed study about how girls fare in American classrooms.

How might Stossel's television news report contribute to our understanding and interpretation of the poll results? Ravitch's? Hancock's? AAUW's?

__Group Activity__

Analyze the categories and percentages in the chart below. What is the significance of this information? What are its dangers? How might you use your analysis?

Teens in Two Societies.   In different cities, here's where teenagers get their money and how they spend their time. (Source: University of Michigan in *Newsweek*)

WORKING TEENS		
Sendai, Japan	**Minneapolis, U.S.**	
Percent working	21%	74%
Mean number of hours worked weekly	9.8 hours	15.6 hours
Percent feeling stress at least once a week	43.4%	71.2%
Portion of spending money from parents	94.7%	47.5%
Weekly amount received from job and parents	$86	$205
Percent dating	38.8%	84.5%
Weekly TV watching	16.7 hrs.	12 hrs.

__Group Activity__

Study the two graphs carefully. When you are familiar with the factual information presented there, analyze what it might mean for American society as a whole. Why are people interested in family changes and family values? What impact do they have on economics, education, and other areas? Think in these terms: What's going on? Why? What might happen? Why?

Changing Families

The facts of family life today mean fewer children live with two parents; 25.5 percent live with just one, usually their mother. And while married-with-children remains a prominent living arrangement, a growing number are blended stepfamilies.

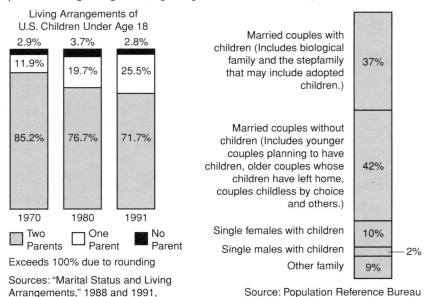

Living Arrangements of
U.S. Children Under Age 18

1970	1980	1991
2.9%	3.7%	2.8%
11.9%	19.7%	25.5%
85.2%	76.7%	71.7%

☐ Two Parents   ☐ One Parent   ■ No Parent

Exceeds 100% due to rounding

Sources: "Marital Status and Living Arrangements," 1988 and 1991, Eau Claire Leader-Telegram 11 Oct. 92.

Married couples with children (Includes biological family and the stepfamily that may include adopted children.) — 37%

Married couples without children (Includes younger couples planning to have children, older couples whose children have left home, couples childless by choice and others.) — 42%

Single females with children — 10%

Single males with children — 2%

Other family — 9%

Source: Population Reference Bureau

America's Family Values

Study after study suggests that Americans still cherish the nuclear ideal, a model of family life that stretches back generations. People long for a sense of commitment to community and family ties.

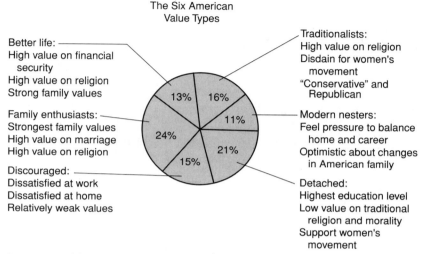

The Six American
Value Types

Better life:
High value on financial
  security
High value on religion
Strong family values

Family enthusiasts:
Strongest family values
High value on marriage
High value on religion

Discouraged:
Dissatisfied at work
Dissatisfied at home
Relatively weak values

Traditionalists:
High value on religion
Disdain for women's
  movement
"Conservative" and
  Republican

Modern nesters:
Feel pressure to balance
  home and career
Optimistic about changes
  in American family

Detached:
Highest education level
Low value on traditional
  religion and morality
Support women's
  movement

Source: *Eau Claire Leader-Telegram* 11 Oct. 92.

AMERICA'S MOST IMPORTANT VALUES

Rank order of 10 values on three different questions	How important	Learned in family	A "family value"
Being responsible	1	1	1
Emotional support	2	2	3
Respect for others	3	3	2
Happy marriage	4	5*	4
Faith in God	5	8	5
Live up to potential	6	5*	7
Follow moral code	7	4	6
Earn good living	8	5*	8
Help community	9	9	9
Being free	10	10	10

*Three values were tied for fifth place ranking in the proportion who say they learned the value in their family.

Source: *Eau Claire Leader-Telegram* 11 Oct. 92.

Life on the home front

According to a poll conducted by USA TODAY, CNN and Gallup,
this is how attitudes have changed in the past 40–50 years:

What has changed a lot

At family meals at home, does anyone say grace or give thanks aloud before meals?

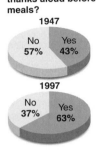

1947
No 57%   Yes 43%

1997
No 37%   Yes 63%

Do American women dominate their husbands, or do husbands dominate their wives?

■ 1952   ■ 1997

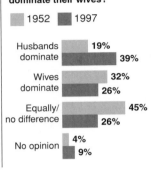

Husbands dominate   19% / 39%
Wives dominate   32% / 26%
Equally/no difference   45% / 26%
No opinion   4% / 9%

(Asked of mothers) Will your daughter's opportunities to succeed be better than or not as good as those you've had?

■ 1946   ■ 1997

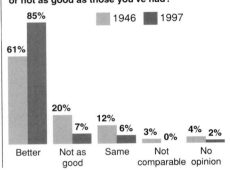

Better: 61% / 85%
Not as good: 20% / 7%
Same: 12% / 6%
Not comparable: 3% / 0%
No opinion: 4% / 2%

Does the man of the house help with the cooking?

1949
No 60%   Yes 40%

1997
No 27%   Yes 73%

Does he help with the housework?

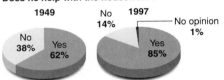

1949
No 38%   Yes 62%

1997
No 14%   Yes 85%   No opinion 1%

Who has the more interesting time: the woman who is holding a full-time job or the woman who is running a home?

1946
8% 12% 30% 50%

1997
9% 8% 42% 41%

□ Full-time job
■ Running a home
■ Same
■ No opinion

What is the ideal number of children for a family to have?

	0-2	3	4+	No opinion
1945	23%	28%	49%	0%
1997	54%	23%	8%	15%

What has changed a little

Do you approve or disapprove of spanking children (parents only)?

■ Approve
■ Disapprove
■ No opinion

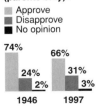

1946: 74% 24% 2%
1997: 66% 31% 3%

Who made the marriage proposal — you or your (husband/wife)?

■ 1952   ■ 1997

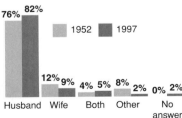

Husband: 76% / 82%
Wife: 12% / 9%
Both: 4% / 5%
Other: 8% / 2%
No answer: 0% / 2%

(Asked of fathers) Will your son's opportunities to succeed be better than or not as good as those you have had?

■ 1946   ■ 1997

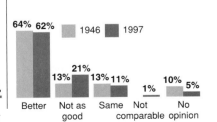

Better: 64% / 62%
Not as good: 13% / 21%
Same: 13% / 11%
Not comparable: 1% /
No opinion: 10% / 5%

Source: Copyright 1997 *USA Today*. Reprinted with permission. 11 Mar. 97: 6D.

What hasn't changed much at all

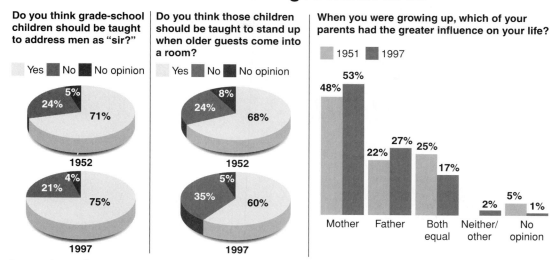

Do you think grade-school children should be taught to address men as "sir?"

Yes ▨ No ▨ No opinion

1952
71% Yes
24% No
5% No opinion

1997
75% Yes
21% No
4% No opinion

Do you think those children should be taught to stand up when older guests come into a room?

Yes ▨ No ▨ No opinion

1952
68% Yes
24% No
8% No opinion

1997
60% Yes
35% No
5% No opinion

When you were growing up, which of your parents had the greater influence on your life?

▨ 1951   ▨ 1997

Mother: 48%, 53%
Father: 22%, 27%
Both equal: 25%, 17%
Neither/other: 2%, 5%
No opinion: 5%, 1%

Source: Copyright 1997 *USA Today*. Reprinted with permission. 11 Mar. 97: 6D.

Writing Activity

Write a brief expository piece in which you analyze information from *one* graph on American families. Follow the process you went through in working with "If Women Ran America." Use the information in the graph as your starting point. For example, if the graph shows an increase in single-parent families, you could analyze possible causes or possible effects or both.

Reading and Responding to Arguments

In both school and the workplace, we face issues to be studied and addressed. And even though we often give oral responses, we are just as often required to present our opinion in writing. Consequently, writing a position statement or paper is a fairly common writing task. This type of writing requires us to analyze the issue, formulate a clear statement of our position, and defend that position with support that is both relevant and adequate. Responding to an issue also requires that we write somewhat dispassionately, regardless of how passionately we may feel. We may argue fiercely in our homes or the student union, but for academic or business purposes, we are required to remove some of the emotion and replace it with logic.

With its emphasis on logic, the position paper requires a careful structuring of information as we build a case. However, we can't merely state our view and expect that a reader will accept it. We must provide both solid evidence and sound reasoning. An important part of that reasoning includes figuring out what the opposition would say, and either accommodating or refuting that view. This practice does not weaken the position paper; rather, it strengthens it. We want to appear reasonable, and agreeing with reasonable arguments from the opposite side is one way of doing so. Counterarguments that we can't accept have to be refuted, that is, have to be shown as wrong, illogical, or unreasonable. Similarly, because we want our readers to take us seriously, we must write with a tone that is likely to gain the reader's respect. If you have ever observed an argument in which people are shouting at one another, you know what happens when tone and language are ignored. You don't want someone mad; you want someone listening. One of the real advantages to writing rather than speaking is our increased ability to control the tone and remain reasonable.

Before you write a position paper, you'll explore some pieces that confront and analyze an issue. As you work your way through these pieces, you'll be discovering strategies that will help you with your own writing.

Although you will be working with academic arguments, we'll start with the kind of everyday issues that lead us into discussion and opposing sides.

THE DAILY NEWS: OFTEN DEBATABLE

One of the places where we often find ideas, events, persons, or situations that we have strong feelings about is the daily news. Editorials aside, the news should be presented in such a way that we can make up our own minds about it. However, the skill of a journalist can tip our sentiment into one camp or another quite easily. As you read the following articles, decide how you feel about each situation and why you find one side more "right" than the other—or perhaps, neither of them "right."

✦   Sort out both sides of the situation, which has escalated into an argument over "whose rights are violated here?"

✦   Is the situation absurd or is simple justice at issue?

✦   Are Americans obsessed with lawsuits (another debatable topic)?

JEREMY, 9, FACES FELONY TRIAL

He's been arrested, strip-searched, charged with a felony, and now 9-year-old Jeremy Anderson is headed for trial April 21—all because he wrote his name in wet cement.

Jeremy's lawyer, Robert Kossack, entered a not guilty plea yesterday on behalf of his young client, charged with malicious destruction of property valued at over $5000.

"I think it's outrageous. I think the charge is ludicrous. The whole thing has been mishandled," said Jeremy's mother, Barbara Anderson, 34.

In November, Jeremy and some friends were on their way home from school when he says a construction worker showed them a freshly poured sidewalk and asked if they wanted to write their names in it. "The man said I could, so I did," said Jeremy, who has won citizenship awards at his elementary school. He and his friends wrote their names and made hand and footprints in about 20 feet of sidewalk near Jeremy's condominium complex in northeast Las Vegas. A few weeks later, a contractor from Plaster Development Co. contacted Anderson saying she owed "$11,000 because the company would have to re-lay the side-walk.

"Had he not been invited, he wouldn't have written his name and identified himself," she said.

Anderson [who refused to pay] forgot about the incident until Jan. 28 when Jeremy didn't come home on the school bus. She called McMillan Elementary School and was told Las Vegas Metro Police had taken Jeremy. Anderson went to Juvenile Hall and watched as her son was read his rights. She was told a bench warrant had been issued for Jeremy's arrest and that her son signed an admission-of-guilt form and waived his rights to an attorney.

"He has no idea what an attorney is," Anderson said.

"A child of that age cannot consent to waive his constitutional rights," said Kossack, a civil rights attorney.

Cranford Crawford, assistant director of Clark County's Family and Youth Services, said the other children cannot be charged with a crime because they are younger than 8. In Nevada, police can legally arrest anyone 8 years and older for a crime, and property crimes above $5000 are considered felonies.

Jeremy was also strip-searched before being placed in a holding cell with older juveniles. Punishment could range from probation or a treatment plan for him and his family to paying restitution to the company, Crawford said. "The ultimate would be removal from his home and placed in a correctional institution."

Angie Bluethman, *San Diego Union-Tribune*

CATTLEMEN SUE OVER COMMENT ON "OPRAH" SHOW

Texas cattlemen have a serious beef with Oprah Winfrey. During an "Oprah Winfrey Show" broadcast last year, an expert said that feeding ground-up animal parts to cattle could spread mad cow disease to humans in the United States. To applause from the studio audience, Winfrey said: "It has just stopped me from eating another burger!" Within weeks, cattle prices plunged. Amarillo cattle feeder Paul Engler and a dozen cattlemen are now suing under a 1995 Texas law that protects agricultural products from slander.

"I couldn't help but be infuriated," said Engler, who flipped on the program while visiting Chicago, Winfrey's home base. "I sat there and couldn't hardly believe what I was seeing."

Engler's year-old federal lawsuit appears to be the biggest test of the so-called "veggie libel" laws, which sprouted after a "60 Minutes" report in 1989 on apple growth regulator Algar sent prices plummeting. Winfrey's show came at a time when drought, high feed prices, and oversupply were crippling cattlemen. While her recommendations have made best sellers out of books, Engler said, that same power cuts both ways. Mad cow disease, or bovine spongiform encephalopathy, has not been reported in the United States. It is a brain-destroying disease that has ravaged cattle in Britain since the late 1980s, where it is believed to have spread by cattle feed containing ground up sheep parts.

Cattle prices dropped 10 percent by the end of the month following the [Winfrey's] show, from 62 cents per pound to 55 cents. They rose later. Engler said he lost $6.7 million.

Associated Press

TO HUNT OR NOT TO HUNT

The following student essays illustrate two views on deer hunting. Even if hunting is not part of your world, you no doubt have views on conservation of the environment, firearms, and rituals associated with growing up. Read through both essays for an overall, first response. Then, read slowly and carefully, and respond to the questions that follow the essays. These are first-draft, unrevised student essays.

ESSAY 1

Many people believe that deer hunting is a mindless slaughter but in reality it is a challenging sport and is necessary for the preservation of the species.

A deer has many advantages over a hunter in the woods. For example, their senses are much keener than that of the hunter. A deer may smell a hunter before he even gets close. The deer can then walk around the hunter and the hunter will never see the deer. The deer also have a sharp sense of hearing so the hunter has to be very quiet or the deer will hear him and flee from him. Their sense of sight is poor and they cannot define colors, so they rely on being able to see movement well. So the hunter must remain motionless while hunting.

A natural camouflage and speed are also advantages the deer has. A deer is very difficult to spot in the woods due to its natural grayish brown fur that blends very well with the trees and fallen leaves. A deer is also very swift and quiet. For example it can be there one second and gone the next and the hunter never saw or heard him. Once spooked, a deer can run for miles through the thickest forest so quick you will never see him.

With all these advantages that the deer has over the hunter, it makes it a fair sport for the hunter to get his deer. If a hunter is lucky enough to shoot a deer he may be killing a deer but allowing for a chance for more to live. It's like a harvest, by taking a few you allow many more to live. If you didn't harvest the population, it would grow and there would be a lack of food. Because of the lack of food many many more would starve to death over the long winter months, which seems more cruel and mindless than killing them instantly with a bullet. This may not follow the rule of nature, that only the strong survive, but it allows for many more of the species to survive the winter months.

ESSAY 2

The deer hunters are at it again. I know for a fact that a certain percentage of deerhunters only stalk these animals because they perceive it as the "manly" thing to do. I find it amazing to think of these guys trudging through the forest, feet freezing, frustrated, toting an expensive, accurate, high-power rifle that they could scarcely hit the broad side of a barn with. These are the men who carry semiautomatic rifles that will pound out projectiles of hot lead as fast as you can pull the trigger. Sometimes they even kill a deer with one, but usually just a sapling or their self-esteem fall prey.

These men are not hunters, they are one of the boys paying their dues for acceptance or self-assurance. They are not marksmen these sportsmen. They are not hunters, they are laborers. They most often don't even like venison, they merely think they do because "men are meateaters Men like venison." The semiautomatic rifles are a real farce. If you don't hit a deer with one shot, it is only by sheer luck that you will hit it with a rapid succession of shots to follow. All the good marksmen I know hunt with a bolt-action rifle,

they are unlikely to get a second shot. Also, these in-
voluntary hunters I have mentioned seldom butcher their
own deer, but rely on a locker to do all the cutting
because they don't know how and don't want to know how.

These guys are a rather small minority I'm sure,
but they are not out to enjoy a sport and obtain a
greatly prized foodstuff. They are out to prove something to themselves and their friends and family. I
sound like I'm condemning this practice but I'm not. I
am, perhaps, making fun of it but I know people who
deer hunt for the reason's I've mentioned. They have
as much right to be out there, it's just sad to see
them gauge manhood by what you do, not what you are.

Responding to the Arguments

State the position taken:

Essay 1 _____

Essay 2 _____

Although these two writers are not directly arguing with one another, each does present a different point of view: (1) Deer hunting is
not only a sport but also a necessary conservation effort. (2) Deer hunting is not a sport but rather a male ego trip or ritual.

How did each writer support his position? Consider the strategies
each used: examples, expert testimony, pointing out consequences or
important implication, responding to opposition.

Put a check mark next to each strategy used:

Strategy	Essay 1	Essay 2
Examples	_____	_____
Expert testimony	_____	_____
Consequences or implication	_____	_____
Responding to opposition	_____	_____

Examples.   Examine the examples that the writer of Essay 1 used:
What were they supposed to prove? Did they work? Even if you know
nothing of deer hunting, could you relate to them?

Examine the examples used by the writer of Essay 2: Why is the type of rifle an issue? What's the implication of semiautomatic rifles? Did this writer use examples or present reasons? Look at the descriptive words for the rifle in paragraph 1. Why did the writer choose these particular words? What is he implying?

Expert Testimony.   Neither writer used expert testimony. Could each have done so? Would expert opinion strengthen Essay 1? Where would you bolster the argument with expert opinion? Where would you turn to find the right kind of experts for this essay?

Would expert testimony strengthen Essay 2? How and where would you suggest it? Where would you find experts to strengthen this essay?

Consequences.   What consequences or implications did Essay 1 note? Did you find them effective? Could the writer have made a stronger case for conservation and animal control?

In Essay 2, does it make any difference whether or not these hunters eat venison? Does it make any difference whether or not these hunters hunt because they like to or because they think they must? What is the implication suggested by "gauging manhood"? Could the writer have made a stronger case?

Responding to the Opposition.   In Essay 1, the writer is sensitive to the charge that hunting isn't a sport, precisely for the reason brought out in Essay 2: weapons used today may give hunters the edge. Should he have been clearer in his defense of the rifle or addressed the various types of rifles available and used? The second point addresses "mindless slaughter," refuting it by saying that hunting is a conservation measure and that it is humane in the face of starvation. The writer also notes that starvation "seems more cruel and mindless than killing them instantly with a bullet," even if this act goes against a law of nature that only the strong survive. Was this an effective point to include? Why?

In Essay 2, does the writer make any concessions to the opposition? Is he clear about it? In other words, would most readers understand that he is not condemning all hunters?

Group Activity

These essays were very early drafts, unpolished but clear enough in the positions taken. What specific suggestions would you have for each writer as he continues drafting and revising?

Examples (add or subtract): _____

_____

Expert opinion (add): _____

_____

Important consequences or implications of position: _____

_____

Response to opposition: _____

_____

Organization of major points: _____

_____

Tone/language: _____

_____

Group Activity

Even if you know nothing about deer hunting, you can respond to one of these essays, mainly because they touch on larger issues:

✦ Conservation and management of wildlife

✦ The definition of what's sporting

✦ The definition of manliness (with a side issue of females who hunt)

✦ Rituals of growing up and being accepted

✦ Family tradition

Discuss these issues, reach a consensus, and formulate a thesis statement that clearly states the position you will defend. Then state your major points and how you would support each. Formulate your response to the opposition. Where do you think you would place it: first, woven into your major points, or last? Why?

PSYCHOANALYZING LITTLE ARTISTS

The next student essay makes a link to a larger societal issue more directly. Marge Harnden, an art major, responded to a television program with "A Sign of the Times."

A Sign of the Times

Over Easter vacation, I happened to catch a show on TV that was featuring children's art in our major museums. The work was being displayed because children have the unique freedom to express themselves in any way they see fit. They don't have the limitations and control adult artists do. Children needn't follow the "rules" to making good art, such as color, coordination, perspective, subject material and imagery. Adult artists (to be taken seriously) must follow such "rules"; children draw however and whatever they fancy to draw.

Near the end of this interesting program, a prominent museum director walked along the walls of work, pointing out different pieces. To my surprise and dismay, she began to analyze the work! "The children must have used blue here to convey their feelings of peacefulness. And this one used gray very effectively to exaggerate the bleakness of his city scene. The bright yellow sun, however, symbolizes hope for a better world."

EXCUSE ME? I have yet to see such a symbolic six year old. Why was this woman applying adult concepts to a child's simple (and beautiful) drawing? Hadn't the whole show just said this stuff was great because it contained no hidden messages, no limitations? Maybe the little girl used blue because she liked that color, maybe she couldn't find the green crayon, and settled for second best. How could the museum director even know?

This woman was not viewing art. She was practicing psychology, analyzing and picking the work apart to discover the how and why. In the adult world, we are all guilty of such senselessness. There always needs to be a deeper meaning, the conveyance of some ingenious (and usually social) idea within the work of art, or it is written off as merely "illustration." Adults cannot enjoy the freedom children have in art because we don't let ourselves.

Perhaps it is reflection of our society. Haven't we built ourselves a complicated world, one where the reason we do things is almost as important as what we do? (Inquiring minds want to know!) How many millions of dollars does corporate America spend in marketing research, delving into such things as why one may prefer the blue over the green? Our adult world is self-analyzing and critical. The calculating, controlled environment we have created has taken away the wonderful spontaneity we admire in almost everything children do.

Perhaps we have much to learn from those children. Maybe if we could just learn to accept things for what they are and resist our urge to analyze life, our world would be a much less complicated, more free and enjoyable one.

Marjorie Harnden

Responding to the Arguments

Summarize (present the main points only of) Harnden's argument:

_____

_____

_____

What strategies did she use to present her position?

_____

_____

_____

What was her most convincing point and why?

_____

_____

What was her least convincing point and why?

_____

_____

If you disagree with Harnden's position, offer a contradiction through one or more of the following:

Fact _____

Observation _____

Statistics _____

Explanation _____

Causes or effects _____

If you agree with her position, provide additional support through one or more of the following:

Example _____

Explanation/reason _____

THE FUR FIGHT

When we deal with issues, we have to pay close attention to the language used and whether the writer was appealing to logic or to emotions. In academic writing, we need to appeal to logic rather than to emotions. Does this mean we have no emotion about the issue? No, of course not. But it does mean we hold strong emotions in check when we respond. Certain ideas or words strike us emotionally, and are meant to, and therefore we have to be on guard both as a writer and a reader.

The following student essay deals with an issue that was close to the writer's heart. Jay's family were mink ranchers, and his perspective on animal rights activists arose from family. Given this, he had to be careful that logic, not emotion, guided his argumentative essay. As you read, pay particular attention to the major points, support, and logic of Jay's essay. He used outside resources to substantiate his claims, so also note to what degree these resources bolster his argument.

The Facts About Fur

On a cold December afternoon, a woman wearing a beautiful black mink coat walks down a New York City street. She stops to look in a store window, and the two men who have been following her for several blocks make their move. Without warning, they appear out an alley, each carrying a silver bucket of paint, and charge toward the woman. Still browsing the store window, the woman doesn't notice her attackers until it is too late. The two men dump the red-blood paint all over the fur coat and quickly run away.

The assailants are not muggers, or even felons; they call themselves "anti-fur activists" or "environmentalists." And they believe that wearing fur is wrong. These people are very misdirected and have blinded themselves to the actual truth about commercial fur. If these "environmentalists" were to listen to the facts about fur, perhaps they would realize that opposing the fur industry is wrong. Commercial fur farming, particularly mink ranching, is a humane and beneficial industry.

The definition of fur as I mean it here is any garment made of the soft, thick hair of an animal raised domestically on a fur farm. Fur is the most natural way for mankind to keep warm. However, organizations such as the People for the Ethical Treatment of Animals (PETA) say that wearing fur is wrong because killing any animal is cruel and inhumane. Don Mathews, the twenty-six year old director of PETA's anti-fur campaign says, "If people are still wearing fur coats after all the years of our movement, they're ignorant"

(Darnton 49). Well, PETA, the facts on fur tell whose opinion is truly ignorant.

Death happens anyway, and it's never pretty. Ranch mink are killed in a manner that is as humane as possible, and they do not suffer very long. Mink are very well cared for on a fur farm. The animals are vaccinated, baby-powdered, and well fed. If a rancher did not take good care of his mink, they would be worthless due to poor pelt condition. Like cows and sheep, mink have become domesticated over the years and could not live well in the wild. By the way, what happens to cows and sheep after they are no longer of any use to man? They are butchered for meat and leather. However, animal rights activists mostly choose to attack the mink industry because it is an easier target. Most people, environmentalists included, see nothing wrong with swatting a mosquito or spraying for termites. "That's different," they say. By that rationale, an animal's right to live is based on how large, furry, and appealing it is. It's okay to kill a cockroach, but not a big, furry mink. Saying that the cockroach is "lower" than the mink is admitting to an hierarchy of animals. Presumably, man would sit on top, so humans have a right to kill and use the mink, as the mink would kill and use the mouse. On the surface, killing a mink may seem cruel, but it is necessary in the order of the food chain. It is far crueler to ruin our environment and pollute our air with factory smoke caused by the anti-fur movement's number one solution: fake fur.

Opponents of the fur industry believe a garment made of fake fur is a fine alternative for those who love the feel of fur. Fake fur and other synthetic garments, which are made from petrochemicals, come from an oil well and a factory ("Furriers Fight Back" 82). Thus the production of fake fur wastes valuable oil and pollutes the air at the same time. Oil is a non-renewable resource, and petrochemical garments are non biodegradable, meaning they will sit in a landfill forever ("Furriers fight Back" 82). Synthetic fur disrupts the earth's natural cycle and contributes to ruining habitats for all animals, mankind included. Real fur is a natural, renewable resource. Fur will rot in time and go back to the ground, which is nature's cycle.

Also, fake fur does not stimulate the economy as well as natural fur. The fur industry is very beneficial to the economy. Mink eat leftover animal parts and other food that is inedible for humans. A rancher must buy inedible food from butchers and other food sources. If the rancher stopped buying mink food, meat prices would go up. For example, if a butcher slaughters a chicken, he can sell the inedible parts to a fur farmer. If the butcher had no market for the head and feet of the chicken, prices of the desirable meat favored by humans would rise. People who wish to ban commercial fur could not complain, then, when prices on chicken rise at the corner grocery.

Finally, virtually no part of a slaughtered mink is wasted. The carcass is used for research, and the mink fat is a key ingredient in cosmetics, certain oils, and soap (Zimmerman). Carcasses can also be shipped to meat by-product or pet food plants. It's a good possibility that every time you feed your dog, animal lovers, you are supporting the fur industry, whether you like it or not. The uses of mink beyond fur are invaluable to many industries important to our lives.

These facts add up to the undeniable truth that commercial fur farming is a humane and beneficial industry. It is time these so called "environmentalists" stopped harassing their fellow human beings and wake up. Wearing fur is natural and beneficial to our economy, our lives, and our planet.

Jay Zimmerman

Works Cited

Darnton, Nina. "Revolt of the Fur Bearers." <u>Newsweek</u> 6 Jan. 1992:49

"The Furriers Fight Back." <u>Newsweek</u> 18 Dec. 1989:82

Zimmerman, Myrle. Telephone interview. 10 Nov. 1996

Works Consulted

Beinart, Peter. "The Fur Flies." The New Republic.
    18 Dec. 1995:11-12
Menkes, Suzy. "Is There a Future for Fur?" Vogue.
    Aug. 1994:28-29.

Responding to the Arguments

A. Briefly summarize the writer's position:

_____

_____

B. If we think about the larger issue, animal "rights" versus human "rights," is this an issue of importance? Why?

_____

_____

C. What strategies did the writer use? On a separate sheet of paper, list each major point and the strategy used to support it.

Examples	Explanation/reasons
Facts	Observations
Statistics	Expert opinion

D. How would you rate the effectiveness of the support? Why?

_____

_____

E. What kind of support would you use if you wanted to convince readers that animals should not be "farmed" and used to supply women with fur coats or men with alligator boots?

_____

_____

F.   Acknowledging the opposition:

Major points	Opposition would say
_____	_____
_____	_____
_____	_____

G.   The writer makes a number of strong statements. Respond to each of the following:

Fur is the most natural way for mankind to keep warm.

. . . killing a mink may seem cruel, but it is necessary in the order of the food chain.

These people [anti-fur activists] are very misdirected.

H.   Does the logic of this piece—if this is so, then this must also be so—hold up? What flaws can you note in the following line of thinking?

Most people, environmentalists included, see nothing wrong with swatting a mosquito or spraying for termites. "That's different," they say. By that rationale, an animal's right to live is based on how large, furry and appealing it is. It's okay to kill a cockroach, but not a big, furry mink. Saying that a cockroach is "lower" than the mink is admitting to a hierarchy of animals. Presumably, man would sit on top, so humans have a right to kill and use the mink, as the mink would kill and use the mouse.

I.   Word choice and tone are critical when we discuss and debate issues. Evaluate the following sentences for their effect on the reader.

Well, PETA, the facts tell whose opinion is truly ignorant.

It's a good possibility that every time you feed your dog, animal lovers, you are supporting the fur industry, whether you like it or not.

It's time these so called "environmentalists" stopped harassing their fellow human beings and wake up.

Death happens anyway, and it's never pretty.

J.   What about statements that are so absolute that "it's this way or no way"?

These facts add up to the undeniable truth that commercial fur farming is a humane and beneficial industry.

Fur is the most natural way for mankind to keep warm.

. . . killing a mink . . . is necessary in the order of the food chain.

What about definitions? Does the reader know the difference, if any, between an "environmentalist" and an "animal rights activist"?

K.   This topic calls for expert opinion and library research. Has Zimmerman provided both enough and the right kind of research in this piece? Explain.

_____

_____

_____

_____

L.   Examine the structure of this essay. Briefly note how Zimmerman presented his information.

Introduction (first two paragraphs) _____

_____

Body paragraph 1 _____

Body paragraph 2 _____

Body paragraph 3 _____

Body paragraph 4 _____

Conclusion _____

Where and how does Zimmerman address the opposition?

_____

_____

What's the advantage of presenting your view and the opposing view at the same time?

_____

_____

Why might you address the opposing view in the introduction?

_____

_____

Why might you address the opposing view in the conclusion?

_____

_____

— Group Activity

Discuss opposing views in the "animal versus human rights" question. Where, besides wearing animal fur, are there serious conflicts? Why should anyone care? Is there a difference between using animals for research in AIDS, cancer, or other deadly diseases and using animals for testing cosmetics? Should activists who damage or destroy research labs be prosecuted as criminals? Should activists who destroy fur coats be prosecuted? Is fur farming similar to raising cattle or sheep? Is there something to Zimmerman's argument that people react differently when an animal is "cute and cuddly"? Is anyone concerned about ugly alligators turned into wallets and boots? Do activists have legitimate concerns about cruelty to defenseless animals? List both arguments and counterarguments as you discuss this topic.

When you have generated enough information and formulated a position for or against animal "rights," develop a rough outline for one position. Include each major point and its support (note if you would use example, facts, statistics, experts, etc.). Be sure to note where you would put in any concessions that you would make to the opposition. Who would be your audience? What do you know about them? What assumptions can you safely make? What must you be careful of? How do these considerations figure into your concessions? Why are emotions likely to flare with this topic?

Be prepared to discuss your thesis and outline in class.

THE BEAUTY QUEEN

In America, beauty is big business. The issue is, Who benefits? The next student position paper explores this question through the Miss America Pageant. Before reading the essay, record your responses to the following statements:

1. Beauty pageants are _____.

2. Beauty pageants provide a useful function.

_____

3. Beauty pageants degrade women.

_____

As you read Kevin Piper's essay, respond in your notebook or journal to the ideas being presented. Note your response to various words and phrases that may strike you as particularly vivid or abrasive.

Atlantic City, Again

"The greatest spectator sport in America is not football or baseball. It's watching pretty girls and that won't change." So says Albert Marks, chairman of the 1984 Miss America Pageant, and he's probably right. An estimated one-third of the nation's population--three quarters women--watched the 58th annual event this past Saturday. Some 75,000 smaller but similar contests involving millions of women are held each year. There can be no doubt about the popularity of such events, but what does all this say about our culture's view of women?

It is time to recognize the Miss America Pageant for what it is--a commercial and prurient exhibition of women as sex objects. It remains an enduring symbol of chivalry that by rights should have died years ago. The pageant degrades the collective female identity, perpetuates popularly held myths about sex roles, and maintains normative standards of women that have no place in the twentieth century.

From its beginnings in 1921 when Atlantic City business interests wanted a way to lengthen the tourist season, the annual Miss America Pageant has operated from the central premise that a woman's value in this world is directly proportionate to her proportions. Keeping in mind the massive commercial event the contest has become, I find little to distinguish it from pornography. Both industries view women as objects of sexual art, and both know that, simply put, sex sells. The only difference seems to be that pageantland prefers virgins, while the pornographers prefer experienced subjects.

The event sends a clear message to men, women, and children: attractive women are valuable property to be possessed, manipulated, and exploited. (God help those who, by reason of genetics or grooming, are designated as unattractive.) Nothing could be more ridiculous than the Miss America tradition of parading around in swimsuit and high heels. But the tradition exists to prove a point. The same kind of point was made at slave auctions not too long ago. A full viewing was necessary to properly evaluate the merchandise. We are just more legal and dignified about it today.

Pageant defenders maintain that the event is a noncommercial scholarship competition and not a beauty contest. True, the pageant itself is a nonprofit operation and has developed into the largest source of scholarship money for women. Yet, one would have to be blind not to notice the incredible commercialism involved. The promotional value of these contests is well tested. Seemingly every commodity and tourist trap in the republic has its own beauty queen. You name it and cleavage can sell it--and does.

On the issue of beauty versus intellect, it is clear that modern contestants must have both formal education and talent (usually singing ability) to survive the long journey to Atlantic City. A certain foundation of self-accomplishment has become an informal standard. However, half the competition still directly revolves around silently posing in swimsuit or evening gown. It's hard for me to see how this posing can be mistaken for academic promise. The reality is that if the posing events were dropped, nobody would watch and the whole process would become just a long "Gong Show." That is, if it hasn't already.

Finally, pageant officials and most contestants vehemently deny that participants are being exploited. They say they voluntarily choose the rugged, painful, and expensive road to the top of glitter world. This is true. What's more, these young women are not nitwits. They are bright individuals with firm ideas of where they want to go. Nonetheless, I can't help but feel that they are participating in a crass game which demands a price from all women. The offerings of cash, prizes, and publicity notwithstanding, these women owe their sex more respect than this. And society owes these women more recognition and opportunity than a flesh show can justly provide.

No longer can any of us tolerate the moral and social cost of these institutionalized pageants. Affording (supposedly) women equal legal rights while at the same time allowing indignities like the Miss America exhibition to continue is hypocritical. The battleground for human dignity goes beyond statute books and courtrooms. It's time that people wake up and realize that the Miss America Pageant went out with the chastity belt.

Kevin Piper

Responding to the Arguments

Summarize Piper's position:

_____

_____

_____

List the strategies (e.g., examples, facts, expert opinion, statistics, reasons) used to support his position:

_____

_____

_____

Piper also uses analogy, a strategy that compares one thing to another, in this case a very negative comparison bound to cause an emotional reaction in many readers. List it and then comment on whether or not he may have gone too far and risked alienating his readers.

_____

_____

List his responses to the opposition:

_____

_____

_____

How did he then turn the responses to opposition into his points once more?

_____

_____

_____

List at least one point that would require more substantial evidence before most readers would accept the point.

_____

_____

Comment on the tone of this essay.

_____

List specific words or phrases that you believe are "loaded," emotionally charged, and perhaps risky in terms of alienating the reader.

_____

_____

Group Activity

Formulate a response to Piper's essay. Divide up the writing task so that each person in the group has a specific point to make and write up. You may choose to agree or disagree with his point of view. Before deciding, read the following articles pertaining to the 1992 and 1997 Miss America Pageant. Until the 1997 controversy, the pageant remained very much the same, and contestants represented similar accomplishments and aspirations as those noted here. Use any information that is available and appropriate to support your response.

NO DUMMIES: MISS AMERICA HOPEFULS SMASH STEREOTYPES

Terry Mulcher

Atlantic City, NJ—The Miss America Pageant is a durable slice of Americana and probably will be as long as it survives its critics. The feminist movement calls it demoralization of the "second sex." The contest's sponsors defend it as a scholarship program that will award more than $10 million to about 80,000 women this year. No matter a person's opinion of the pageant, the contestants—at least this year's lot—smash the stereotype of the blond bimbo who smiles sensuously and shows a little cleavage in hope of winning the rhinestone crown, $35,000 and a little red sports car.

Many of the contestants are intelligent, articulate women with top-flight credentials. For example, Miss Wisconsin Stephanie Ann Klett is pursuing a master of fine arts degree from Moray House College in Scotland. Klett is a member of the National Organization for Women, describes herself as an "ardent feminist" and plans to push an AIDS platform if crowned. Carrie Lee Davis is a South Carolina doctor who has delivered 35 children, set up clinics and taught preventive medicine in rural South Carolina communities. Leah Hulan, Miss Tennessee, is a commissioned officer in the army, who has done undercover intelligence work in Panama. Patricia Ann Northrup, Miss California, is a graduating senior at California Polytechnic State University studying aeronautical engineering and music composition.

Why would they use duct or graffer's tape to push their breasts to the center to create cleavage? Why would they use a hemorrhoidal ointment to reduce swelling under their eyes, or glue their swimsuits to their buttocks for the strut down the runway in a pair of high-heeled shoes? Why would two contestants approach Davis, the doctor, and ask her to write prescriptions for diuretics which help them shed water weight? Even after she said no and stressed the dangers of diuretics, the women still wanted them. Contest promoters say one of the aspects of a "wholesome" woman is that she stays in shape physically.

Women's advocacy groups say the pageant forces women to fit a certain mold and to believe that to be successful, she must grow up to be thin, blond and beautiful. David Schleicher of the Anti-Sexist Mens' [sic] Network in New York calls the contest a meat market. "We all know it's really a forum to continue the whole brutality and sexual objectification process against women that reaches its culmination in forums like Playboy and Penthouse," Schleicher said.

• • •

LETTERS FROM *USA Today,* September 25, 1992

CHANGING IMAGE

As the executive director of a local preliminary pageant to Miss America, I have been trying to change what people think about pageants. With the Miss America program, the emphasis is placed on intelligence (interview is 30% of total score) and talent (40% of total score). Yes, beauty of the face and figure is part of it, but a small part.

—Sherrie L. Cottom, Centerville, OH

SENDS WRONG MESSAGE

Beauty pageants give a terrible message to little girls. I have two daughters, 9 and 11. They think you have to grow up and be a Barbie doll with a thin waist. I totally disapprove of these pageants.

—Nancy Smith, Tulsa, OK

WOMEN AS OBJECTS

Being a former contestant in the system, I have run across pageants where over three-quarters of the women had breast implants or reductions. The message the pageants continue to send out is that women are viewed as objects.

—Debra Grady, Notre Dame, IN

JUDGE DISAGREES

As a judge for last week's Miss America pageant, I disagree with your editorial which stated that "pageants shout that a woman's measurements matter most." For the record, as judges, we were never given contestants' measurements, let alone asked to judge them. The qualities we assessed were: intelligence, ability to inspire others, achievements, leadership, communication skills, confident presence and commitment to volunteerism. Let's not forget that the most impressive "figure" in the Miss America pageant is the $10 million in scholarships. Any program which empowers women with $10 million in scholarships gets my vote.

—Ann-Marie Bivans, Miami, FL

BUILDS CONFIDENCE

I never could have been what I am today without pageants. I participated at the local level and did a lot of preliminary pageants. I met a lot of friends, and it gave me a lot of confidence. Pageants are what you make out of them: helpful or not so helpful. If looked at realistically and allowed to help in educational pursuits, they can be very positive for young women today.

—Kim Huffman, Starksville, MS

HASN'T HELPED HER

I am a veteran of different pageants. In the long run, even though they claim that you gain poise and confidence, it can be defeating in today's society. I won several pageants. In the long run, it hasn't helped me in any job choices. In fact, I think it's been a deterrent. I don't even tell people anymore that I competed because they look at you like an airhead instead of looking at your degrees. It's irritating to see certain lines still be touted so highly, with a majority of women in society today still not getting the education they deserve.

—Layla Bryant, Kansas City, MO

MISS AMERICA PAGEANT, NBC SEPTEMBER 19, 1992

The following information was obtained from the live broadcast of the Miss America Pageant.

Jobs and Majors.   Included in this year's group are the following majors or professions:

Professions
Police officer
Physician
Sports broadcaster

Undergraduate Majors
Aeronautical engineering
Communication
    (16 contestants)
Music and theater
Education
Business
Psychology
Advertising
Political science and prelaw
Public management

Graduate School
Law (3 contestants)
Counseling
Marketing (2 contestants)
Music
Sports medicine
Biology
Communication
Central and
    South American Affairs
Chemistry
Business

Judging.   The criteria for the preliminary judging included talent, swimsuit, evening gowns, and interview. Finalists were judged on talent (30% of total score), swimsuit (15%), evening gown (15%), and interview (40%). The swimsuit category was noted as stressing "athletic ability, fitness, and nutrition." However, the contestants wore spike heels. Miss South Carolina, a doctor, won the swimsuit competition.

Commercialism.   The 1992 Miss America introduced commercials for Loving Care Hair Color, Vaseline Intensive Care Lotion, and Ultra Slim Fast throughout the television broadcast.

A major 1997 issue in the Miss America pageant is the two-piece suit. April Adamson of Knight-Ridder Newspapers stimulates some debate when she asks, "Is it freedom or just more flesh?" (*Milwaukee Journal-Sentinel*)

Longtime pageant producer Leonard Horn says he believes contestants can express themselves more freely without a piece of material covering their stomachs . . . [announcing] that he'd allow two-piece suits so contestants can "stress their individuality" and "be more themselves." But beneath the seemingly benign attempt to boost contestants' self-esteem, critics—and even a former Miss America—say the extra skin will inevitably lead to racier and more offensive get-ups.

The producer insists his decision had nothing to do with ratings or sexiness and everything to do with capturing the essence of the all-American gals who should take the stage wearing the same dresses and bathing suits they wear at hometown pools and proms. Though swimwear designers and trade organizations agreed that two-piece suits outsell one-piece styles 7 to 3 in the general population, they don't necessarily believe today's two piece styles are appropriate for television. Many designers and wholesale reps said contestants who pick two-piece styles will be killing their chances at exuding a wholesome look.

Michael Gross, writing for the August 28, 1997, issue of TV GUIDE provides more comment on the latest controversy.

In the "Beauty and the Bikini," Gross notes that age 77, Miss America is "nudging aside an old-fangled notion of beauty pageant decency. Miss A. still wants to dazzle us with her accomplishments; after all, she's running a scholarship competition that has doled out $150 million since 1945. But to fight off the most dreaded symptom of age, ratings droop, she's deploying her last defense: bikinis and bare belly buttons" (12).

This isn't the first time Miss Americrats tried to "update" their product image. Not long ago, the pageant renamed the segment [swimsuit competition], dubbing it a "display of physical fitness in swimwear." Then, during a 1995 broadcast, it let the public vote on whether it wanted a swimsuit competition at all. Seventy-nine percent of the voting public said "Keep it."

In the days after Miss America's bombshell was announced, some columnists harped on the hypocrisy, pointing out that bikinis are hardly consistent with other dictates pageant sponsors are asked to accede to. They must use the words *scholarly program* not *beauty contest* in their promotional materials; avoid words that reference royalty (such as beauty *queen*); and stress leadership, ambition, and education over poise, charm, and grooming. (15–16)

Gross also includes a "A Word from the Judges" in his article:

Capt. Scott O'Grady [former Air Force pilot shot down over Bosnia], Miss America Judge 1996: "I wasn't sitting there looking at who looked best in a swimsuit. It was about their poise. And I weighed the interview more than anything else. It isn't a beauty contest—they're out there for scholarships." (16)

Donald Trump, Miss America Judge 1989: "The swimsuit competition is essential because people greatly admire a beautiful woman and you can't totally judge a beautiful woman without seeing her in a swimsuit—or less." (16)

ON YOUR OWN

Judith Christ's position paper deals with censorship and warning labels in the music industry. Before you read, jot down your ideas about placing warning labels on records and tapes. As you read, make marginal notes of your responses to Christ's arguments.

Stop the Labels

For the past five years, censorship has been brought up in the music industry. Parents have been wondering what exactly their children are listening to and the meaning behind it. People have gathered together to join an organization called the Parents' Music Resource Center (PMRC). This organization consists of twelve members who originated the idea of warning labels. I feel warning labels should not be placed on records and tapes.

My reason is because warning labels are simply too expensive. It costs money to have the labels printed and the cost of having someone apply them. In today's world, the cost of printing thousands of adhesive stickers would be quite high. Besides the printing process, many hours would be spent having an individual put on the stickers or purchasing a machine to apply them. Even with an automated machine, a person would have to stand nearby to prevent machine malfunctions. From my experience, I have found that working with a labeling machine and putting on stickers by hand takes many hours of hard, tiring work.

Also, who should have the power to make the decision? I feel the answer is no one. Record companies and recording artists are too close to the product to pass unbiased judgments. Organizations such as PMRC should not have the right because their decisions are merely personal opinions. Basically, it comes down to the fact that no one or no group will be able to satisfy all people involved. Personal decisions will not work. One person can not determine what all others see as "offensive." What one person may call a crude statue of a naked body may be considered art by another person. It is simply not right for an invidual to decide what is right for others.

The PMRC and similar organizations are simply concerned about what children are listening to for entertainment these days. It is safe to say that there are many performers around who have put out some rather outrageous material. Parents have the right to worry about what their children are taking in, and it is nice to see some are concerned. However, if parents are truly doing everything they can to help their sons and daughters, they will not need the music industry to babysit. If parents are really communicating, they will know what their children are listening to and can talk to them about it. We should let record companies conduct their business and let the consumers decide if they want to purchase their products or not. A good parent will make it a point to be at least a small part of that decision.

Judith Christ

Writing Activity

Using strategies you have practiced in this chapter, analyze Judith Christ's position. Then, before you decide whether to support Christ's position or argue against it, try the following strategies:

1. In your journal, freewrite on what you've read. Allow yourself the freedom to respond and develop your own ideas.

2. Next, fill in the following outline:

   Christ argues_____

   _____

   because _____

   _____

Christ's Major Points	Your Response

Christ's Support/Evidence	Your Response

3. Finally, determine whether you will support her position or not. If you agree with Christ, offer additional support material. If you disagree, formulate opposing evidence.

Remember, no matter what position you take, you must defend it through logic, facts and reasons, statistics, or expert opinion. Add information gained from your own observations, firsthand experience, and reading. Concede valid points to the opposition. Keep your tone logical, rational, and calm. Do not go on the attack and risk losing your audience.

Developing and Organizing Your Response.   The following suggestion is only one way in which writers respond to issues. Your teacher may provide you with others or ask that you follow a different form.

Introduction.   Provide a brief summary of Christ's position, and then state your own position (agree or disagree). Use thesis format to show your position of agreement or disagreement; that is, don't say "I agree" or "I disagree." The thesis should make your position perfectly clear.

Paragraph 1.   Discuss Christ's first point, reminding your reader what Christ said, and then respond with your own point.

Paragraph 2.   Discuss Christ's second point, and so on. Follow this process for all the points you wish to present and discuss.

Conclusion.   Very briefly, remind the reader of your position and why you hold it. Be careful not to introduce any new material or unrelated issue in the conclusion.

Adding the Opposition's Valid Points.   You must decide where to place opposing views. Sometimes, it is advantageous to add them in the introduction; for example, if you suspect that many readers will disagree with your position, it may be better to concede their valid points immediately. At other times, the conclusion is the most likely place for them, especially if you know most of your readers will agree with you. And, at still other times, writers intertwine them in the body paragraphs, as Kevin Piper did. If the issue is particularly complex or controversial, placing the point and counterpoint together helps readers.

__Peer Response

As you respond to one another's essays, follow this process:

1. State the writer's position.
2. List the main points, with support and evidence.
3. Disagree with the points—even if you agree with the writer, list counterpoints or arguments.
4. Note any problem with organization.
5. List any words or phrases that strike you as "loaded."

Analyzing and Writing Arguments, Proposing Solutions

In the previous chapter, you may have found yourself defending your opinion quite often, and just as often, listening intently to an opposing point of view. One of the most interesting things about our world is its variety of people and opinions. Reasonable people can and do disagree on many issues, everything from the best way to provide health care to the most efficient use of a limited tax base. In fact, disagreement is one of the ways through which people expand their world. In considering positions other than our own, we learn something more about a complex issue or situation. This skill is a useful one, whether we are at school, work, or home.

Acquiring this skill requires us to put our emotions aside and rely on logic. Sometimes it is quite difficult to do so. For example, as you read each of the following statements, note your immediate response in your journal:

1. Abortion is murder.
2. Immigration is ruining America.
3. Welfare breeds lazy people.
4. Prayer belongs in public schools.
5. Gun sales should be outlawed.

Now think about why you responded as you did. Chances are your emotions took over. These statements go back to strongly held beliefs arising out of years of family and religious training. Consequently, when we face such issues we tend to respond emotionally rather than logically. Where personal moral and ethical beliefs are concerned, we simply believe we are right. However, when we construct academic arguments, we must set aside the strong emotions that accompany such beliefs and rely on logic to prove our point. This task, of course, is easier said than done.

PROBLEMS OF REASONING

We have already explored ways in which writers support their position in reasoned and logical ways, but we also need to take a closer look at problems of reasoning. People who disagree with our position are quick to point out where our reasoning falls apart or violates some principle of logic. What's more, in an academic setting, some teachers may be more interested in how you presented your argument than in the position you took. It's important, then, that you avoid the most common flaws in this type of academic writing:

- ✦ Oversimplification
- ✦ Generalization without evidence
- ✦ Exaggeration or distortion
- ✦ Faulty logic
- ✦ Slippery slope
- ✦ Inappropriate expert opinion
- ✦ Out-of-date material
- ✦ Emotionally charged vocabulary
- ✦ Attacking the person rather than the issue

Oversimplification

Oversimplification means that a complex issue or situation has been presented as though it were a simple one. For example:

A lack of education is responsible for inner-city riots.

Inner-city riots are a complex problem, and a lack of education for inner-city youth is only part of that problem. Jobs, the lack of economic opportunity, and family stability are just as important. The availability of drugs and weapons, as well as the growth of neighborhood gangs, also contribute to the problem. To place the responsibility on a single factor, education, is simplistic. As a result, the writer of this statement appears ignorant, incapable of analyzing a complex issue for relevant, supportable causes for this tragedy. To say money is the solution to this complex problem is equally simplistic. Economics is one part, but only one part of many.

Another form of oversimplification is the "either/or" proposal. You may have seen bumper stickers such as "America: Love it or leave it," a statement that denies any middle ground. Further, just because someone disagrees with some government policies or actions doesn't mean he or she doesn't love the country. Writers who make an either/or statement are trying to make the reader believe there are a very limited number of ways to look at an issue or situation. In the 1992 presidential election, some environmental issues were presented as an either/or choice: save the spotted owl and destroy jobs. The reality is somewhere in between, and environmental and economic issues are certainly more complex than either/or. Either/or sounds good emotionally, though, and that's why we run into it.

Generalizations

In constructing an argument, you will need to generalize from facts, examples, statistics, or other means of support. However, when you generalize, you must be very careful not to exaggerate the meaning of those facts, examples, or statistics. That is, you must have the evidence to back up your generalization. For example, if you have observed that married students appear to be better students, you cannot generalize that *all* married students are better students. You could investigate studies of married students, their achievements and grade point average, and you might find support for your observation. But if you then say that students would be better off to marry while in college, you're in logic trouble. You would have made a sweeping generalization and jumped to a conclusion that isn't valid. Some students cannot function with competing demands from a marriage and college work. Other students end up failing because their marital relationship is in trouble. Without evidence, then, you simply cannot make such a generalization.

Even with evidence, you might do well to use some qualification or limitation on your generalizations.

Unsupported/Sweeping Generalization:

Married students are better students.

Supported:

Of the ten married couples in my classes, seven are honor students.

A recent college survey shows over 50 percent of the married students have a GPA of at least 3.00.

Qualified:

Many married students appear to be top students.

Marriage seems to agree with some college students; many are honor students.

Exaggeration or Distortion

An exaggeration or distortion of the facts is another way in which writers destroy their own credibility. For example, if you observed that a couple of students regularly cheated in your math class and then reported that cheating was widespread, you would be guilty of exaggeration. Although it's possible that cheating was widespread, without solid evidence you cannot make the claim.

Faulty Logic

Arguing in a circle is a way in which writers can be illogical. For example: "Football players are unintelligent which is why they are football players." Besides being a ridiculous generalization, this statement is circular and proves nothing at all. The cause and effect simply don't work.

Irrelevant examples are also illogical. Whatever evidence you use must be clearly related to your position. For example:

Women demand equal pay, but they still want to be taken out to dinner. Therefore, they really don't want to be equal.

These two issues have nothing to do with each other. Equal pay is an economic and work issue; a dating practice is a social one. And even though one might argue dating does involve economics, in this case, the writer cannot make the leap from equal pay to going out to eat.

Another type of flaw is called a *non sequitur,* a Latin phrase meaning the conclusion simply doesn't follow from the evidence presented. For example:

A student fell asleep in class twice this week. The class is obviously boring, and that teacher should be fired.

There's no logical connection between these two sentences. The student may have fallen asleep because of working late, illness, drinking too much the night before, or a host of other reasons. There is no evidence that the class is boring, let alone that a teacher should be fired because a student fell asleep.

A similar flaw called *post hoc* occurs when a writer says one event causes another simply because it happened first. Sometimes people jokingly say something like: "Of course it rained; I just finished washing my car." The two events have nothing to do with one another: we can wash our cars all we want, and not assure anxious gardeners or farmers of rain. In writing, this flaw in logic is serious.

> Since MTV has been on television, the number of teenage pregnancies has increased. It is obvious that MTV is responsible for increased sexual activity and the resulting increase in illegitimate children.

There is no evidence that MTV is responsible for either increased sexual activity or pregnancies among teenagers. Without scientific studies linking increased sexual activity and pregnancies to MTV, no one can make this claim.

Slippery Slope

Yet another flaw is the "slippery slope." It occurs when a writer assumes that one problem inevitably leads to more and more serious problems. For example: "If we don't fight communism in Central America, it will spread to all of South America." There's no proof that communism in a Central American country would lead to communism in South America.

Inappropriate Experts

We've seen advertisements on television in which some celebrity tells us that we should drive a certain car or drink a certain soft drink. However, unless that celebrity also happens to be an expert on cars or soft drinks, there is no reason why we should pay any attention to his or her claims. When writers use expert opinion, they are calling upon someone's demonstrated excellence in a field. It's critical that someone we cite as "expert" really is, and what's more, that we are using that expert appropriately. An astronaut, for example, is an expert in engineering, but why listen when he or she tells us to drink a certain brand of orange juice?

Out-of-Date Information

In addition to making sure experts are experts, academic writers also have to use current facts in their defense of a position. In some fields, such as psychology, sociology, and chemistry, the use of outdated material might destroy the argument. Checking sources to ensure they provide the latest available information is an important part of defending a position.

Emotionally Charged Words

Some words can be counted upon to produce irrational reactions: *welfare, drugs, abortion, capital punishment,* and *patriotism,* to name just a few. In an academic argument, however, we do not want to produce an irrational, emotional reaction in the reader. Rather, we want to appeal to logic. Choosing words that are neither negatively nor positively charged is important to your defense.

Attacking the Person

Ad hominem is Latin for "to the man." It means the writer is guilty of attacking someone's character rather than the issue itself. For example, the mayor opposes building a new sports arena because he believes the costs are simply too high for the present tax base to support. Sports enthusiasts might charge that the mayor is a "wimp," never made an athletic team, and dislikes sports; therefore, he doesn't want the arena built. Personal attacks appear mean-spirited and most often turn people off.

▬Group Activity ▬▬▬▬▬▬▬▬▬▬▬▬▬▬▬▬▬▬▬▬▬▬▬

Read Mike Royko's piece on legalizing marijuana and decide

1. what his principal arguments are.
2. whether he uses logic or emotion.
3. if he violates any principles of logic.
4. how he supports his arguments.
5. if he addresses his opposition.

Then, defend the legalization of marijuana by citing arguments not used by Royko or by expanding (not just repeating) those he does use. When you have completed the defense, argue against the legalization of marijuana by responding to Royko's and your own arguments in favor of it. Be prepared to share your work in whole-class discussion.

Royko, incidentally, was a Chicago journalist. His column appeared in papers nationwide, and he is best known for his biting commentary on American politics and lifestyles.

LEGAL MARIJUANA—A POT OF GOLD

Mike Royko

I've been playing around with a fascinating number—14,000 tons. That's the amount of marijuana—foreign and domestic—that's said to be consumed each year in this country. Actually, the federal narcs think it might be even higher. A recent raid in northern Mexico turned up 10,000 tons. The narcs were stunned because they thought that Mexico produced only one fourth that amount. But for this column's purpose, let's stay with the 14,000-ton figure.

If you break that down, it comes to 448 million ounces. I'm told that one ounce of marijuana will produce between 20 to 40 joints, depending upon whether you are frugal and make skinny ones, or are self-indulgent and make them stogie-sized. There's also a waste factor—seeds, twigs, bugs, spillage and so on. So let's be conservative and figure 20 joints an ounce. That's just under 10 billion joints a year. If you divide that by the population of this country, it comes to about 40 joints for every man, woman and child.

Now, we can assume that millions of little toddlers and preschoolers don't smoke it. We can even assume that most of the kids in elementary school don't, since most of them don't have the purchase price. And we can assume that millions of old codgers in nursing homes or two-room flats don't use it.

So who's doing all this grass-smoking? Recent studies say that teenagers are smoking less and less pot. So the biggest users are the age groups that range from young adults to middle-agers. And they're a huge part of the population. If they aren't the majority, they're not far from it. That tells us something obvious: There's a great demand in this country for marijuana.

As any Harvard economist—or dry goods salesman—will tell you, when there's a great demand for something that isn't hard to supply, somebody is going to supply it. Obviously, that's happening. Whether you live in a big city, a suburb, or a small town, you can easily buy mari-juana. If you aren't sure where to get it, just ask the nearest teenager.

So I have a simple question: If so many Americans want and use marijuana, if they are already getting it so easily, if they insist on spending billions of dollars a year on it, why are we screaming at Mexico, why are hordes of narcotics agents floundering around in futile attempts to find it, why are the police and courts wasting time and money trying to put dealers in jail for selling it?

It ought to be obvious by now that the politicians in Washington can talk all they want about stamping it out, but they can't do it. It has become one of this country's biggest cash crops. It's a big part of Mexico's economy. So maybe it's time to give up trying to stamp it out, and consider legalizing it, thereby controlling it.

It would allow the narcs to stop wasting their time trying to stop it, which they can't do, and would let them concentrate on chasing far more harmful drugs, such as heroin and cocaine. And, best of all, it could be taxed. A $10- or $20-an ounce federal tax would bring in more than $5 billion or $10 billion a year. And every local government could slap on a little tax of its own.

Who would sell it? Private enterprise, I suppose. The day it became legal, we'd see nationwide pot franchises springing up. And we could stop feuding with Mexico, since our own needy farmers could grow enough to meet all local demands. Why, they would probably end up dealing in marijuana futures on the Board of Trade.

The sale could be regulated just as we now regulate the sale of booze. TV and radio advertising of pot would be banned, just as we've banned the advertising for liquor and cigarettes. Minimum age limits would be set. Sure, it would be impossible to enforce the laws 100 percent. But the fact that teenagers find ways to buy beer doesn't prevent the rest of us from drinking it.

And, yes, I'm aware that marijuana isn't good for us, although scientists still aren't sure what the effects really are. However, the scientists do know a lot more about the effects of even the finest scotches, the most elegant gins, the most regal cognacs. Even if you pay $5 a shot and tip the bartender a deuce, they will still quiver your liver and strain your brain.

So it might be time for us to stop pretending that we can do something to stop marijuana from being sold and consumed. In a country where the citizens—and even illegal aliens—have unlimited freedom of movement, and where there is almost no control of its own borders, we can't do it. Then why not try to at least regulate it and let our own farmers and businessmen make a buck.

Are we ready for a McJoint?

CONSTRUCTING A POSITION PAPER

Approaches

There are various ways in which we can construct a position paper. One way is to state our position and then defend and explain it point by point. This is a *deductive* approach. But we might also approach it in the opposite way: present and defend the points and then present our position as the conclusion. This approach is *inductive*.

Deductive Approach

I believe or feel this way because of

   this, this, and this.

You state your position in the introduction and then present the evidence that supports your position.

   Children should not play competitive sports—because of— physical injury, emotional trauma—lasting effects, on both child and family.

Introduction: Anecdote, background information, thesis stated:

   Children should not play competitive sports because of the threat of serious physical injury and emotional trauma.

Body: Evidence to support (facts, statistics, examples, expert opinion):

   Serious physical injuries—what they are, how often they occur, lifelong effects, etc.

   Emotional trauma—what it is, how often it occurs, effects on child and family, etc.

Conclusion

Inductive Approach

Because of this, this, and this

   I believe or feel this.

We present the evidence and lead up to our position, to our conclusion based on that evidence.

Introduction: Anecdote or background information. No thesis here.

Body: Evidence to support your position:

   Serious physical injuries—what they are, why they are serious, lasting effects, etc.
   Emotional trauma—what it is, how it occurs, lasting effects on child and family.

Conclusion: Statement of thesis:

   Because of the very real threat of serious physical and emotional trauma, young children shouldn't participate in competitive sports.

Expectations

Readers have certain expectations when they read an argumentative essay or position paper. One of these is recognition of the opposite point of view. Where you place the opposition's point of view is up to you, but readers look for it. You also have a choice as to whether you will simply admit the strength of an opposing point, allow it, and move on, or refute it. Both of these strategies work in your favor; both indicate that you have carefully considered the evidence on both sides of the issue.

Another expectation is that of appropriate background or history. Readers want a context for the issue or problem, so we have to provide them with it, even if we believe they already know something about the subject. A strong, clearly stated thesis is another expectation. Sometimes, we merely suggest our opinion, but in a position paper it is explicitly stated—leaving no doubt about which side of the issue we are on.

▬ Group Activity ▬▬▬▬▬▬▬▬▬▬▬▬▬▬▬▬▬▬▬▬▬▬▬▬

A. Refer back to the essays on the Fur Fight and the Miss America Pageant. How did these students deal with the reader's expectations relative to an opposing point of view? Now refer to Royko's editorial on legalizing marijuana. How did he deal with the opposition? In your opinion, which was most effective in addressing the opposition? Why?

B. How did Royko provide the reader with background information on marijuana? Was this an effective opening? Did the writer of the Fur Fight essay provide an effective context for his argument? And what of the Miss America argument? Do readers understand why this issue is important or a problem?

C. Do readers get a clear, well-stated thesis in these three pieces?

A Basic Format

Your instructor may provide you with other formats, and the following may be adapted. For example, you may decide to present your position before addressing the opposition. Or you may decide to present both your points and the opposing ones at the same time. Consider your audience. If you believe they might be hostile to your position, you might want to grant them the allowable points right away. You'd be saying, "These are valid and reasonable, and I accept them," thereby gaining some goodwill. Or you might decide to refute their points immediately. This strategy might stop the reader from arguing with you along the way. You want readers to think about *your* point of view. You can probably remember times in a verbal disagreement when instead of listening to the opposition, you were mentally on the defensive, conjuring up your argument and not fully listening to what the opposition was saying. In any case, your consideration of the audience and their likely response should guide your decision.

I. Introduction

A. Gain reader's attention and interest (e.g., a brief story, startling statistic, quotation)

B. Establish context, background for the reader (e.g., history of problem, how issues developed)

   C. Provide thesis, direct statement
II.   Address Opposition
   A. Grant allowable points
   B. State and reply to unallowable points
      Show they are
         untrue
         illogical
         dishonest
         absurd
         ambiguous (not clear, not defined)
III.   Present Your Position
   A. Present evidence
      Support through
         facts
         reasons
         statistics
         expert opinion
         examples
         analogy
   B. Use order of increasing interest or importance
IV.   Conclusion

Checking Resources

Often we choose to defend a particular point of view because we have already thought about the issue. Before consulting library or human resources, check the present status of your personal information:

- What do you already know about the issue?
- Why are you convinced of the truth of your position?
- What information do you have from firsthand experience?
- What have you observed that supports your claim?
- What have you read that supports your claim?
- What examples do you have to support your claim?
- Whom do you know that might be able to provide you with expert opinion?

Testing Evidence

In conversations, we can sometimes get by without offering substantial evidence for our opinions. When we write, however, we are expected not only to provide evidence but to ensure that such evidence is trustworthy. Test your evidence by asking the following questions of it:

◆ Is it accurate? It is your responsibility to verify that what you use is both accurate and up-to-date. You also need to check for bias.

◆ Is it reliable? Evaluate your evidence by comparing different sources. They all should say the same thing.

◆ Is it to the point, relevant? You must back up the exact claim you have made.

◆ Is it representative? The examples you provide should be very typical for the situation.

◆ Is it sufficient? You need to provide enough evidence.

EVALUATING A STUDENT POSITION PAPER

For your first reading of Lorie Hilson's paper, read rather quickly to get an overall sense of her position. Then write a few sentences indicating your initial reaction. Were you interested in this issue? What is your personal opinion of it? What was most convincing in the essay? Least convincing?

When you have finished your initial notations on Hilson's essay, read the draft again, this time slowly. Then respond to the questions that follow the essay.

FINAL VERSION

Wanting Winners

This boy of nine is up to bat, and his parents are in the stands watching. He strikes at the first ball that is pitched. His father yells, "How many times do I have to tell you to let the first ball go by?" We are in a generation where fun has been taken out of kids' sports because parents want winners.

According to what I have observed at ball games, parents want winners for their own selfish reasons.

One of these reasons is so they can brag to friends and neighbors what a great team their child is on. Also another reason is that some parents feel a child's performance is a reflection on themselves. These kinds of attitudes leave little room for the child to just enjoy the sport for the fun of it.

When winning becomes more important than the fun of the game, young children get serious injuries. Most of these injuries don't have a lasting effect; however, once in a while they may cause permanent damage to the muscle or bone tissues of a young girl or boy. Take, for instance, a young boy I know who was playing basketball when he fell, damaging his elbow and upper right arm. Now at the tender age of fifteen he can only run track. Another example is of a young boy whose father wanted him to be on the winning baseball team; therefore, he taught him to throw curve balls at too young of an age. Now the boy's right arm hurts him to a point that he no longer plays any type of ball. Was the sacrifice of the son's arm worth it so the father could say he had a winner? The answer is no.

Besides the physical injuries that kids get, they experience emotional pain that is caused by what parents say to them. Sometimes emotional pain is more harmful than physical pain ever could be. Once at a wrestling match, a boy of nine was wrestling out on the mat. Afterward his mother told him he could have done better; his tears started flowing down his cheeks like big raindrops. His mother had just taken the fun out of wrestling for him. I wonder if we as parents realize how important our approval is to a child.

There ought to be a class for adults only on how to lose gracefully. A kid, however, would have to teach this class because kids have an inborn grace for losing. We as adults lost our ability to accept losing somewhere in the process of growing up. I think we should just go to kids' sports and watch children play, and then maybe we could learn how to put the fun back into their sports. Then as parents we could say, "We had fun," instead of saying, "We have winners."

Lorie Hilson

Defining the Issue

Has Hilson provided enough information for the reader to understand both the issue and its importance? What questions still need to be addressed or answered? Is the issue really arguable (that is, can reasonable people have opposing views on it)?

Forming a Clear Thesis

Find Hilson's thesis. Is it appropriately stated? Should it be qualified in any way? Does she fill out her thesis promise? Stray from it? Add anything not covered in her thesis or introductory material?

Supporting the Thesis

Find Hilson's reasons for her claim and number them. Then consider each in terms of its evidence. How is it explained or supported? How clear or convincing is each? Have any important reasons been left out? Has she overemphasized weak reasons?

Check Hilson's reasoning. Has she made broad, unsupported generalizations or oversimplified anything, for example?

Handling Counterarguments

Has Hilson addressed the opposing view? If not, where and how would you deal with counterarguments: Where might be areas of potential agreement? Where would you anticipate objections? Why? How would you refute them? Be certain to think through the counterarguments, being careful to include some of the strongest and not just the weakest. Presenting only the opposition's weakest points weakens your own position.

Being Reasonable

Does Hilson maintain a reasonable tone? Note places where the tone appears thoughtful, believable, and trustworthy. Are there places where the tone becomes too emotional, sarcastic, and the like?

Organizing Effectively

Reread the opening and final paragraphs and evaluate their effectiveness. Does the opening give a good preview of the argument to - follow and provide a context for why it is an important issue? Does the conclusion leave one with a good sense of the importance of the issue?

Now reread the major points and determine if they should be re-ordered. Also check if any evidence is misplaced. Note topic sentences, transitions, and summaries, and determine if some should be added or changed for greater effectiveness.

Evaluating Overall

What is the strongest part of Hilson's essay? Why? What is the weakest part, the most in need of further thought and revision? What would you suggest for revision?

Look at Hilson's earlier draft of "Wanting Winners" and note the changes she made between it and her final draft on pages 287–288. How did Hilson strengthen her essay?

DRAFT 1

Wanting Winners

Kids sports are a common sight. *W*~~w~~e see them out on

football and base ball fields, in swimming pools, on

tennis courts and basket ball courts, and *on* parallel

bars just to list a few sports.

for children

When I go to a base ball game and hear a father

call out to his son or daughter because of an error

2

that they make. I stop to reflect ~~on~~ if the ~~kid~~ *child* is out for fun or were they told that winning was the whole idea of the game. I know this kind of action by either parent is an (embarrassment) to the child, for I have asked my own children about how they would feel if they were in ~~that~~ *this* kind of situation.

has been made

I feel that there ought to be a class on how to lose gracefully for adults only. We are the ones who remove the fun out of kids sports by wanting our children on the ~~best~~ *winning* team ~~or the winning team which ever you prefer.~~ Children have this inborn grace on how to lose, ~~us~~ *we* as parents have a habit of destroying it.

3

My feelings are based on experiences that I have encountered over the last year or two. For an example, at a base ball game one, in particular comes to mind. This boy is up to bat his parents are in the stands watching he strikes at the first ball that is pitched. His father stands up and yells "How many times do I have to tell you to let the first ball ~~pitched~~ go by". The boy is nine or ten years old, scared of the ball hitting him the way it is, without his father adding to it. The fun has just left the game for this boy.

When winning becomes more important then the fun of
the game or sport, we have young children getting
serious injuries. Most of the time these injuries
don't leave a lasting effect on the young girl or boy,
but once a great while the injury my last a life time.
Take for instance a young boy I know was playing
basketball, the boy fell damaging his elbow and (uper)
5 arm, he now can only run track, at the tender age of
fifteen. Another instance that I know of is a young
boy who father wanted him to be on a winning base ball
team, so he taught the boy how to throw curve balls,
now that boys right arm hurts him to a point that he
no longer can play any type of ball. Was it worth the
sacrifice of his son so he could say his son was on a
winning team? To that question in my opinion the
answer is a (defiant) no.

When at a wrestling match this last winter with my
oldest boy. I told my son that no matter what placing
he recived, I would still be proud of him. This is how
all parents should feel I thought, boy did I get my
mind changed in a hurry that day. The lady sitting
4 next to me also had a boy wrestling that day, as she

sat there watching her child wrestle, she started to
use such language that I was (ashame) to be sitting by
this lady.

~~When did~~ winning ᴡ ʜᴀˢ become so important that we as
parents seem to misplace the (emphasizes) on the whole

? concept of kids sports.(More and more children are

6 starting to enter sports at a much younger age then
ten years ago.) This points out ᵗᵒ ᵐᵉ that ~~the~~ parents ᵃˢ ~~what~~ ʷᵉ ʷᵃⁿᵗ
~~there~~ children to be ~~the best.~~ ʷⁱⁿⁿᵉʳˢ It's no longer left to
the child to decide if he or she is out for fun but
whether she or he is the best.

Lorie Hilson

| **Writing Activity** | Write a response to Hilson. You may either agree or disagree with her position. If you agree with her, provide additional support (not repeating her points). If you disagree with her, either take her points and refute them or develop an opposing point of view. Be sure to go through the list of resource questions for yourself (since you won't use library research or outside resources for this writing task) and test the evidence you supply. |

ON YOUR OWN

You have been responding to positions taken by others. Now you'll support your own position on some issue that interests you. You won't be using library sources for this essay, so you need to limit yourself to an issue where you feel confident about your firsthand knowledge or experience. For example:

Should college sports be dropped?

Should college students hold jobs?

Should day care be available on campus?

Should all students be required to take a common set of courses?

Should first-year courses be pass/fail?

Should first-year students be required to live on campus?

Should the student union be a smoke-free building?

Should extracurricular activities be dropped?

Should the library change its hours?

As you choose an issue, be sure it is one on which reasonable people might disagree; that is, there must be two sides to it.

Exploring the Issue

Freewrite on your topic for at least five minutes: what it is, who's involved, and so on. If you believe you have enough to write an essay on this topic, apply one or two of the generating strategies from Chapter 5. Since you have to deal with both sides of the issue, some sort of chart would probably work well. Even if you are already certain which side of the issue you will defend, laying both out will help you define the issue.

For	Against
_____	_____
_____	_____
_____	_____
_____	_____

Formulate the position you'll take in a very tentative, rough thesis statement:

_____

_____

State the purpose of your essay:

_____

Consider your audience: How would your readers define this issue? What assumptions would readers be likely to share with you? What kind of support would be likely to work with your readers?

_____

_____

_____

_____

▬ Group Activity ▬▬▬▬▬▬▬▬▬▬▬▬▬▬▬▬▬▬▬▬

Run your topics by one another. Help one another decide if you can write on this issue, and just as important, if you really want to.

Developing Reasons

When you're sure that you have a good topic, list every reason you can think of by using a base statement something like one of these:

I think this because _____

My position is this because _____

When you have as many reasons as you can think of, read through them with your reader's eye. Which of your reasons are the strongest? If you come to the conclusion that none of them is, perhaps you should find another topic.

When you have some strong reasons, brainstorm on each one. The brainstorming should turn up some good support. If it doesn't, move to the next reason.

Anticipating the Opposition

Take each of your reasons and list every opposing reason or point you can think of. Then review them and decide which you'll respond to. Use this format to help you think about it:

I'll respond to:

Opposing point: _____

_____

I'll respond to it because _____

I'll concede it because _____

I'll refute it _____

Now take each point you intend to refute. Brainstorm on each point and note for yourself why you are able to refute it: distorted, absurd, irrelevant, illogical, and so on.

I'll refute it because _____

_____

Before you begin to draft your essay, you might want to restate your thesis. Has the work you have done thus far led you to qualifying or changing your tentative thesis?

Organizing

One of the major decisions you make is organization. For this type of writing, preparing a scratch outline may save you time and energy later. The outline should be considered tentative, good enough to show what you plan, but not so good that you would be unwilling to throw it out. For example:

Introduction
    Thesis: Student union needs a fast-food franchise.

Body

    Major Point: Cafeteria inefficient

    Support: At noon, 20-minute wait in line for food

           Another 10-minute wait at checkout

           Result: miss class or bolt food

           Result: food often cold

    Major Point: Cafeteria expensive

    Support: Burger, fries, coke in cafeteria $3

           Burger, fries, coke in franchise $2.25

           Salad in cafeteria $1.75

           Salad in franchise $1.25

           Result: can add extra $5 per week

    Opposition: Fast food has fewer food options

    Refute: Depends on which franchise one gets

    Support: Example McDonald's vs. Hardee's

    Refute: Most students never order cafeteria's meat/potato dishes

    Support: Tally from cafeteria

Conclusion

    Make appeal for consideration of fast-food franchise

Drafting

Use your outline to guide you, but don't hesitate to diverge from it should something better occur to you. Sometimes our best ideas come in the process of writing, as well as from a momentum that directs us to things we hadn't considered earlier. If you get stuck, you can refer back to the outline for ideas and direction.

Revising

Use the analysis questions from Hilson's essay as a guide to evaluating your own essay. In order to see just where you need specific revision, make a chart that corresponds to the basic requirements or features of a position paper. As you apply the analysis questions to each part of your paper, make notes of the problems.

Features of My Position Paper	Problems
Introduction of issue (context, definitions, etc.) Thesis statement Reasons/support Opposition's points Organization Tone/language	

___Peer Response _____

Add comments from peer readers to the chart. Remember, their response to problems helps you revise.

PROBLEM SOLVING FOR REVISION

Once you (and your peers) have identified a problem, you need to systematically solve it. The following suggestions, paired to the general outline you just used, may help you do that. Add a third column to your chart where you will write your response—specific ideas for revising your draft. For example:

Feature	Problem	How to Solve
Introduction	No sense of why issue really is a problem	Use letter from student newspaper

Introduction of Issue.   Provide more information on how the issue arose and why it affects readers. Consider adding an example or anecdote.

Thesis Statement.   If readers don't recognize your thesis, you will have to rewrite it. It should be explicit, clearly stated.

If readers find the thesis won't hold up because there are legitimate exceptions or very strong counterarguments, rewrite it and modify it; add qualifying words.

Reasons and Support

Generalization Without Adequate Support.   Go back to your notes and brainstorm some more; come up with more examples.

Oversimplification.   Get rid of any either/or statements; qualify statements to show you understand that the issue is complex.

Vague or Weak Reasons.   Add explanation, examples, anecdotes.

Weak Evidence.   Review your brainstorming notes; if you can't find better support, consider eliminating that point.

Opposing View

Concessions.   Make some concessions to opposing view; show you recognize legitimacy of readers' views; let readers know you share some of their concerns, values, and the like.

Refutations.   Strengthen.

Acknowledging the Opposition.   Don't ignore counterarguments, especially strong ones—if you can't refute them, concede them.

Content and Organization

Introduction.   If the introduction is dull, try some startling fact, quotation, or anecdote.

Arguments and Major Points.   If the reader has trouble following your arguments, provide a blueprint of them in the introduction.

Support.   If support doesn't follow the main point closely, move it nearer the topic sentence.

Arrangement of Points/Counterpoints.   Reorder for better logic.

Conclusion.   Consider more striking language, an anecdote that sums up the situation or issue, a startling fact, and so on; make it briefer; don't just repeat main points; make an appeal for support.

Editing and Proofreading.   When you have completed revision, check for sentence- and word-level errors. Refer to your personal editing list.

Proposing Solutions

Often, we are called upon not only to address a problem but to suggest potential solutions to it. Problem solving is one of the most basic activities in our lives, whether we are students, workers, or citizens. As students, problems such as parking, access to classes, computer availability, and affordable housing are but just a few. As workers, we have to decide where to seek employment, what might happen if we change jobs, when to ask for a promotion or raise, what to do if a co-worker fails to produce on time. As citizens, we face problems in our community: taxes for new buildings or recreational facilities, street improvements, overcrowding in schools. In our relationships, as well, our ability to pinpoint a problem, find reasonable and workable solutions, and pursue the best solution is a critical skill.

▬ Group Activity ▬

Consider this editorial in which the writer, somewhat tongue in cheek but serious nonetheless, addresses a problem-solution. Tony Kornheiser, who has a 14-year-old daughter and 11-year-old son, is clearly unhappy with the Minneapolis School Board's solution to a problem. Read his remarks, and be prepared to respond with your own ideas of "solution."

SCHOOL BOARD GETS AN "F" FOR CODDLING SLEEPY STUDENTS

If you have children of middle-school age, now is definitely not the time to move to Minneapolis. Because starting in the fall, the Minneapolis middle schools are going to open at 9:45 A.M. Apparently, kids are falling asleep in class. The thinking behind this is that a later school day will rectify the problem.

What problem? Listen, kids have been falling asleep in class forever. I used to fall asleep in class all the time, and I turned out OK. I didn't turn into some stupid clown. Er. . . .

Maybe the problem is not the time of day. Maybe the Minneapolis School Board should consider hiring more interesting teachers, people who have grown up somewhere other than Minnesota. . . . Regardless, starting the school day at 9:45 is insane. At 9:45, most parents have left the house to go to work . . . The last thing in the world I want is for [my children's] schools to open at 9:45. The only way I can get my kids to bed at a reasonable hour now—and by "reasonable hour," I mean before the cable stations start showing *Nude Chicks in Prison* movies—is by convincing them that they have to get up by 7. Do you have any idea when they would go to bed if they didn't have to be in school until 9:45? . . .

Maybe this is no big deal in Minneapolis. Maybe kids there are apple-cheeked and when they're off from school, they volunteer at hospitals and wash cars to raise money for people to get heart transplants. But what are the chances that YOUR children would actually get up for school without someone there to wake them?

The only way I get my kids up for school now is because I shake them like snow globes—and I have to go in three and four times before they actually get up. When the sun explodes in a thunderous fireball and sends billions of tons of searing magma slamming into the Earth, my kids will sleep through it. Then, they will wake up and wonder aloud why it is so dark. . . .

What would your kids eat for breakfast if nobody were there to feed them? I mean, besides the leftover pizza from the night before, which your kids ordered at 3 A.M. because they didn't have to go to school until 9:45.

Milwaukee Journal-Sentinel

Analyzing the Problem-Solution.   One member of your group should be the recorder, keeping track of the potential solutions, reasons for them, and so on.

◆   What is the problem?

◆   Why is it a problem?

◆   Who is affected? When? How? Why?

◆   If not solved, who suffers?

◆   What are the facts in this problem?

◆   What are the most important facts or factors?

◆   Why should anyone be concerned?

◆   Who has the authority to solve the problem?

◆   Why hasn't it been solved until now?

◆   How could it be solved?

◆   What are possible solutions?

◆   What are advantages to each potential solution?

◆   What are disadvantages to each potential solution?

◆   What is the best solution?

◆   What is the best of the alternatives? Why?

Generate as many solutions as possible. Don't "edit" yourselves; sometimes, ideas that may seem far-fetched turn out to have the best solution. Go through your list and choose the best two or three. Then, list the advantages or strengths of each. Similarly, list the disadvantages or weaknesses of each. Discuss them, and choose one solution. In working with this, you will want consensus. That means that not everyone is equally enthusiastic about the choice, but can live with it. In two or three sentences state why this solution is the best alternative. Bring your solution to whole-class discussion.

In class discussion, decide who has the authority to take action on your proposed solution. How would you go about convincing this authority to do so? Then, imagine yourselves at a public hearing on this problem. What objections do you anticipate and how would you respond to them?

Thinking About the Process.   As you worked through this problem-solution, what difficulties arose? Why must alternative solutions be presented, carefully considered, before rejecting? Why or how is this form of writing going to be somewhat different from an argumentative essay? Is it the added requirement to get readers into understanding the problem? Is it related to people's normal resistance to change? Is it the need for people to believe that they are affected personally, that consequences of a solution are indeed both personal and critical?

Strategies.   There are three basic strategies to help you with this kind of writing, which you are already familiar with from writing argumentative essays:

1. Argue from consequences: we should (should not) do this because it leads to these good (bad) consequences.

    For example, suppose your 9:45 A.M. school start could result in fewer kids hanging around the streets from 3:30–6:00 P.M., when much of the petty crime from this age group occurs. Or from medical personnel, you know that kids this age simply do better scholastically when they start later in the day, that a late start actually works far better with their natural patterns. These are good consequences of the solution to a later start.

2. Argue from principle: we should (should not) do this because it is honest, ethical, fair (dishonest, unethical, unfair).

    For example, the 9:45 A.M. school start could be unfair when different groups of people are considered. Single parents might have little flexibility.

3. Argue from analogy: we should (should not) do this because _____ tried it, and and the results were excellent (terrible).

For example, if you know other school districts, similar to Minneapolis—urban, multicultural, economically mixed—tried the late start and had good results, then you have a reasonable comparison. It would be important not to mix "apples and oranges," however; be sure that the analogy is a fair one.

What was Tony Kornheiser using as his strategy?

Parts and Attributes of a Proposal-Solution Essay.   This kind of essay typically has these parts:

- ✦ Description of the problem
  - ✦ What is the problem?
  - ✦ What are the parts of the problem?
  - ✦ Who or what caused it?
  - ✦ Who is affected?
  - ✦ How long has it been a problem?
  - ✦ Why aren't obvious solutions satisfactory?
  - ✦ What are the effects of not solving it?
- ✦ Proposal-solution and justification
  - ✦ What is your proposal-solution?
  - ✦ Why do you believe it might work?
- ✦ Comparison with alternative proposals/solutions
  - ✦ Why do you believe alternative proposals won't work?
  - ✦ Why do you believe alternative proposals solve only part of the problem?
  - ✦ What are the advantages or strengths of your solution?
  - ✦ What are the disadvantages or weaknesses of your solution?

The attributes of a good proposal-solution essay or report are these:

- ✦ The writer informs people about the problem in such a way that they understand how it affects them or why it is in their best interests to care about addressing and solving the problem.
- ✦ The writer argues convincingly that this problem has significance.
- ✦ The writer proposes a solution that is both reasonable and achievable.

◆ The writer anticipates objections and prepares responses to them.

◆ The writer acknowledges that some readers may prefer alternative solutions.

◆ The writer uses a reasonable tone and shows respect for other opinions.

Group Activity

Consider the following problems/solutions that students generated about their schools.

A. Lack of parking space: enlarge the parking lot; give permits only to seniors; match number of permits to numbers of actual spaces; charge a higher fee; use a former softball diamond for parking; don't allow people living within a mile of school to use school lots

B. Lack of computer access: increase number of computers; limit e-mail access; enforce time limits

C. Public displays of affection: enact rules and enforce them

Apply the questions that need to be asked in each category.

Analyzing the Problem

◆ Is this really a problem? How do you know?

◆ What is the cause? Is the problem caused by a lack of resources? Lack of competence? Flaw in the "system"? Lack of leadership?

◆ Is there a history to this problem?

◆ Who is affected? How does it affect them?

◆ Does anyone benefit from leaving the problem alone?

◆ Are similar problems happening on other campuses?

◆ Who is in a position to do something about this problem?

◆ Why hasn't anyone solved this problem?

Finding a Tentative Solution

◆ What solutions may have already been tried?

◆ Why won't obvious solutions work?

◆ What solution might partially solve the problem?

◆ What solution might get rid of some of the bad effects?

◆ Would a series of solutions work? If so, which would be first, second, and so on?

◆ What would be a bold solution? A conservative one?

Choosing the Best Solution.   In one or two sentences, state your best solution.

Responding to Objections.   Since your proposal has to be reasonable and practical, you need to be prepared for people who believe it is neither. Respond to each of the following objections to your solution.

✦   Nobody will do it anyway.

✦   The school can't afford it.

✦   It takes too long.

✦   You're only saying this because it helps you.

✦   It won't work.

✦   Somebody tried this once; it didn't work.

✦   OK, so things aren't perfect; so what?

Rethinking Your Reasons.   Write down every "reasonable" reason for your solution. Be honest. Toss out any solution that really isn't achievable. Of those that remain, put a mark next to any that you believe are really strong. Then, explain in a couple of sentences why you believe each will be an effective point.

Considering Alternatives.   Alternative solutions are sure to come up, and you need to be prepared for them. List some, along with their obvious strengths and weaknesses. Then dig a little deeper and anticipate the less obvious in each. A chart might be useful for this activity.

Possible Solutions	Strengths	Weaknesses

Using Research.   In this context, we can consider research from both a library and real world perspective. Before you write up your proposal, you might need to learn more about the history or causes of the problem, as well as search out more information on implementing your solution. It is critical that you know what solutions have been tried, and failed, and why.

Review the student problems once more. What information must you have before you can offer your proposal-solution? Where will you get the information you need?

Group Activity

With your partner or group, evaluate this student essay on cultural diversity requirements.

Cultural Diversity Classes

College students must take many classes and acquire many credits while in school, including a variety that are required in language, natural sciences, social sciences, and humanities. Recently, the university added another requirement; students must take at least six credits in classes identified as "cultural diversity." These classes focus on American minorities, and every school has identified classes that fulfill the "ethnic studies" requirements for their majors.

It is believed by many students, myself included, that cultural diversity classes are a waste of time and are not needed to succeed in the world today. The university catalogue states that students in cultural diversity classes study the "discrimination and prejudice experienced by members of diverse cultural, ethnic and/or racial groups in the United States." This discrimination may be real, but ethnic people are not the only people being discriminated against in American society. Why should a class be taught only on ethnic minorities and not on all people experiencing discrimination?

Other questions also arise. Don't students experience "cultural diversity" everyday on campus? Isn't it possible that no matter what someone's color or ethnic background, students talk to one another? Isn't it possible that students learn about discrimination from watching what happens in public places? Or from watching the television news or reading newspapers? And what will make students change their minds about discrimination? Cultural diversity classes may give students some better insight into what minorities are all about, but I doubt the classes will change our minds about the way we do things.

> Some instructors believe that because we take these classes, our whole lives are going to change. I'm sorry, but I do not believe a couple of cultural diversity classes are going to change my way of thinking. If I am prejudiced in any way, I know six required credits are not going to have a major effect.

Although you may have strong feelings about what this student wrote, how would you address this serious campus problem? If students resent the requirement, will it work?

◆ **Problem:** Predominately white campus; few opportunities for Caucasian students to meet, work, and socialize with American minority students; limited knowledge about different ethnic and racial backgrounds

◆ **Solution:** Require courses that focus on American minorities (history, literature, sociology, language, art, music)

◆ **Your Solution:**   ?

ON YOUR OWN

You have worked through several proposal-solution situations; now it's time to work up your own proposal-solution. Although you will follow the same procedures you just practiced in defining and analyzing your problem, the following strategy might help you generate and choose a problem more quickly.

Divide your notebook paper or computer screen into two halves. On the left half, list all the places where you live or have lived (e.g., your school, your neighborhood, your hometown); all the groups that you belong to (church, sports, political, musical, hobby); all the places where you have been employed. On the right half, list the problems that you associate with these various places. For example:

My school   long waits for computer time
                 poor advising
                 not enough parking spaces
                 limited library hours on weekend
                 food service slow and unappealing
                 registration deposit for summer classes
                 no day-care center nearby

My hometown	no places for teens under 18 to go roads always in disrepair schools not equal in facilities, technology racial tension
My hobby	poor field conditions for soccer scheduling field time lack of sponsors
My job	unfair work assignments little training or supervision inflexible schedules

Review your list. Choose one problem that you believe can be addressed with a reasonable proposal-solution. You don't need to have the solution in mind right now, but you should be able to approach the problem with a firm notion that there are potential solutions—and that you are willing to discuss them in public.

Return to the list of questions for defining and analyzing a problem. When you complete them, and before you move on to finding a tentative solution, identify your audience:

♦ Who will be interested in this proposal? Why?

♦ How well-informed will my audience be?

♦ Are there different groups, perhaps with opposing views, interested in this problem?

♦ Which group is likely to share my view? Why?

♦ Have other proposals been forwarded in the past? By whom? Do we have common ground?

♦ Who has the authority to do something about this problem? Is this person or group likely to accept or reject my proposal? Why?

Now turn to the questions for finding and supporting your solution. When you have completed this activity, test your ideas with your writing partner or group.

Drafting

Review your notes and begin writing. When you have a first draft, you are ready to think about the organization of your proposal. Because this type of writing has a rather specific format, you might find it helpful to consider these segments as you prepare a second draft:

Opening Paragraph

✦ How can I gain my reader's interest? Anecdote? Statistics? Quotation? Raise questions? Challenge a common perception? Appeal to common good?

Definition of the Problem

✦ What will my readers already know about this problem?

✦ How much background or history is needed?

✦ How do I convey the seriousness or urgency of the problem?

✦ What is the primary cause? The major effect?

✦ If there are multiple causes or effects, how should I prioritize them?

Proposing a Solution

✦ What is my solution and why is it workable?

✦ If my solution could be implemented in stages, what are they?

✦ What are the advantages or strengths of my solution?

✦ What are the disadvantages or weaknesses of my solution?

✦ If my solution would be difficult to implement, how do I make a case that it's worth the effort to do so?

Preparing for Objections to My Solution

✦ What are the most likely objections?

✦ What reasons can I give for refuting them?

✦ How can I maintain respect for others' opinions?

Considering Alternative Solutions

✦ How many alternatives should I include?

✦ What reasons can I give for dismissing them?

✦ How can I reject alternatives without offending their proponents?

Closing Paragraph

✦ Should I simply restate the problem and my solution?

✦ Should I make a final argument that my solution is reasonable and achievable?

✦ Should I remind people of the consequences of ignoring this problem?

Peer Response

In the writing group, each person should present his or her proposal with a short statement of the intended audience and their background, followed by a statement of what he or she hopes will happen if the proposal is acted on.

Guidelines for Responding

1. Read through the entire draft for its first impression on you. Were you drawn in? Note any words whose tone or meaning turn you off or bring out hostility. Write a brief statement of the first impression. Do you think readers will be convinced? Are the arguments sound?

2. Is the problem clearly stated? Will readers grasp the cause(s) and effect(s) quickly and easily? Will readers identify with the seriousness of the problem? Is enough background provided? Too much?

3. Is the solution clearly presented? How might the writer strengthen it? Does the solution seem achievable and practical?

4. Is the solution supported by good reasons? Are there enough reasons? Can you suggest others?

5. Does the writer anticipate objections to his or her solution? Has the writer missed some objections?

6. Are the alternative solutions presented fairly? Has the writer respected their proponents? Are the alternatives either accommodated or rejected? Has the writer given convincing reasons to reject an alternative solution?

7. Is the writer's voice present? Has the writer kept the tone under control?

8. Is the organization of the proposal logical? Should any parts be moved? Are there any obvious gaps in information?

9. Is the opening interesting? Is the closing appropriate and strong?

Be sure to write comments telling the writer what you believe is the strongest part of the essay. Similarly, be sure to point out any part that needs more work.

Revising

Although your writing group's commentary is a key part of revising your problem-solution essay, your ability to shift from writer to reader of your own text is the most critical part of revision. Regardless of what a writing group or partner suggests, you are the one to make the revision decisions. Set the group's commentary aside while you get a good overview of your draft, reading straight through for an overall impression. Then, reread, this time applying good reading strategies and making notes in the margins. Return to the writing group's suggestions and match them with your own margin notes and ideas. Finally, make a scratch outline that shows the basic plan of your essay.

A Revision Plan.   Use the basic features of a problem-solution essay to guide your revision:

Features	Problems
Definition of the problem	
Background	
Seriousness	
Causes/Effects	
My solution	
Description	
Rationale/Argument	
Alternate solutions	
Objections to them	
Organization	
Opening and closing	
Awareness of audience	
Background	
Tone	

Responding to Problems.   Sometimes it is far easier to spot the problems than to solve them. However, the chart will help you focus on the major areas or features of this type of essay. In order to systematically address each problem, use the chart features once more. This time, put "solutions" in the right-hand column. For example:

Definition of problem—unclear	Add more background/history, compare to similar problem
My solution—sort of unclear	Redo steps to implement
My argument—easily attacked	Make consequences stronger
Alternatives—still too strong	Take good ones and incorporate into my solution
Organization—transitions	Look up better transitional words/phrases
Opening	Use anecdote
Closing	Shorten
Audience—check tone	Don't get "preachy"

An Editing Note.   One of the most common problems in proposal writing occurs when writers fail to provide "the actor." For example:

(1) Research should be done to find out if students do better when schools start later.

Who should do the research? The schools? The school board? A parent's group?

The Minneapolis Board of Education should ask researchers at the University of Minnesota to find out if middle school students do better with a later start.

(2) A survey should be taken at the end of the first semester.

Who should do this survey?

Each middle school should survey parents to learn how the late start affects them.

10

Writing from Research

WHY WE ENGAGE IN RESEARCH

Research begins with a question: What do I want to know about _____ ? This question leads us to think about not only what we wish to learn but how we might locate sources to help us answer that question. Once we have the information, we think about it; then, we respond to it. This process, thinking and responding, has too often been left out of research; consequently, many students rightly wonder why all the fuss about research. Sometimes, students believe they don't have the "right" to question or respond to what they find. And again, an important part of the research process is left out. Responding to what we find out is the essential part: What does this mean? What do I think about this? Your teachers will expect you to think about what you have found, respond to it, and convey these thoughts as part of your researched essay or report. They really don't want just a compilation of information from different sources. They want to know your response to it.

If you think about it, you ask and answer a research question every time you make a major purchase or decide on a vacation. Research is not just something academics do; it is a process that helps us make decisions in our lives: what car, what stereo system, what career path, where to live, what health regimen, what exercise program, whether or not to play sports. My students, for example, have researched everything from whether a physical condition excludes them from athletics to finding the appropriate nursing home for a parent, from the right child care-center to being the child of an alcoholic, from choosing the right major to learning where a career path really leads.

The student who researched his own cardiac condition needed to know which treatment would be best for him, and if he could return to varsity athletics. It would have been tempting to tell him that perhaps he wouldn't be able to read through the dense medical materials, but unnecessary. His motivation to learn the answer to his research question carried him through those materials: he needed to know; he wanted to know. At the end of the semester, on the basis of his research, he opted for surgery over winter break, and returned to the varsity tennis team that spring. The student who researched nursing homes was faced with a problem no 19-year-old should have: one parent with Alzheimer's and the other with multiple sclerosis. Through a carefully designed research plan, she matched her mother's personality and needs with care facilities and emerged with what she believed was the best place for her mother. In our daily lives, then, we use research to help us sort out the many important decisions. Knowing how to conduct research is a life skill, not just an academic skill.

OUR NAMES: A PERSONAL RESEARCH PROJECT

Regardless of the research question my students chose for their major research task, they all started with a search for their name. This project provided them with all the thinking, searching, writing, and documentation skills needed for later work. And they had fun in the process, most often learning something that even their parents or grandparents didn't know. Family members were important to this project, and students often spoke of interesting conversations that might never have taken place without it.

Why names? Names are integral to our sense of ourselves. How often as a child does someone play with his or her name, change the spelling, get a nickname, or try to lose a nickname? As an adult, a woman may decide to keep her name at marriage. Or a man may take his wife's name. What does our name say of our heritage? Why do families maintain certain first names? How do middle names turn up? Some religions ask that people add a name as part of a ceremony of coming of age. Some cultures believe names have magical powers and thus keep a child's real name a secret. And when we think about it, we most often have some feelings about our names.

Esperanza Cordero, Sandra Cisneros's young narrator in *The House on Mango Street*, says this of her name:

> In English my name means hope. In Spanish it means too many letters. It means sadness, it means waiting. It is like the number nine. A muddy color. It is the Mexican records my father plays on Sunday mornings when he is shaving, songs like sobbing. . . .

At school they say my name funny as if the syllables are made out of tin and hurt the roof of your mouth. But in Spanish my name is made out of a softer something, like silver, not quite as thick as my sister's name—Magdelena—which is uglier than mine. Magdelena who at least can come home and become Netty. But I am always Esperanza.

I would like to baptize myself under a new name, a name more like the real me, the one nobody sees. Esperanza as Lisandra or Maritza or Zeze the X. Yes. Something like Zeze the X will do.

"My Name" (pp. 10–11)

Like Cisneros's character, many of us have feelings about our names, even without knowing anything of their origin or journey through time and place. Our given names may be fairly common, and easy to locate, our family names less so. However, you may be surprised when you start your research and begin to see how certain combinations of letters or parts of names give away the meanings. You may also be surprised to see how your name has traveled. Some ingenuity on your part may be needed to break apart your name, search out its parts, change its spelling, or fuss with its sounds and the many ways it might have been changed when ancestors immigrated to America. Regardless of your ethnic heritage, you will find information through the school library, your public library, and the Internet.

WHAT YOUR RESEARCH PROJECT WILL INVOLVE

There are many steps in any systematic research project. For this one, you will probably follow these:

- Asking yourself what you already know
- Developing a list of questions to answer
- Asking family members for information
- Locating library and Internet resources
- Gathering available information from resources
- Documenting and giving credit to your sources of information
- Analyzing your information and keeping what is useful
- Synthesizing information from multiple sources
- Responding to your information
- Writing multiple drafts
- Formatting your final draft to meet researched writing requirements

Asking the Right Questions

Regardless of the research topic, the first question should always be this one: What do I already know about this topic?

◆ What has my family already told me about my name?

◆ What has some relative told me?

◆ What do I know from other sources, such as reading?

◆ What can I reasonably "guess at" in terms of my name's meaning or ethnicity?

◆ Why was I given this name? Family tradition? Favorite relative?

◆ Is there a story connected with my name?

◆ How do I feel about my name? Why?

The next question focuses the research task: What is the origin, history, and definition of my name? Within this question, you have three parts or topics to consider: origin, history, and definition. If you turn these into questions, you have specifics to work with. Most of these questions refer to the family name, but others work equally well for a given name.

◆ What is the origin of my name?

◆ What nationality or ethnicity is present in my name?

◆ Does my name have a counterpart in many languages?

◆ Has my name migrated through several countries?

◆ Has my name changed over the years?

◆ Did my name change as a result of coming to America?

◆ Does my name have an obvious meaning?

◆ Does my name refer to a place, something in the natural world, an occupation, a physical characteristic, a talent or skill, a disposition?

◆ Does my name indicate the lineage, from father to son?

When you have a list of questions, you need to sort them out. Are some questions repetitive? Which questions are important in terms of the origin of the name? Which ones relate to the name's history? Which ones relate to the name's meaning? Now refine your list, grouping similar questions.

Searching for Meaning

Although "what to name the baby" books abound with information about the meaning of given names, information about our surname's meaning is less common. Remember, however, that most surnames arose from rather practical situations: from a father's first name, occupation, dwelling place, or characteristic.

One of the most common ways in which surnames evolved was use of the father's name and addition of "son of _____." That golden arches place, McDonald's, is the Scots "son of Donald." And the giant pharmaceutical company, UpJohn, is a Welsh form of "son of John." Other nations also used this form of identification, but you may not recognize the forms: *-ski, -sky, -enko* in Slavic names; *-ap* in Welsh names (e.g., Ap Rhys = Price); *-az* in Spanish names; *-de* in French.

Another common way in which surnames evolved was through place names. Most Japanese surnames are place names; for example, a character translated in English as *-ta* or *-da* means "rice field." By contrast, one-fourth of all Chinese names are Chang (draw bow), Wang (prince), or Li (plum)—occupational or descriptive. Hindu names are most often linked to a profession or trade, or by adding the suffix *-kar* or *-wallah* the place of origin (Smith 199). The German *von* or Dutch *vander,* meaning of, directly link the name to a place. Some names translate directly into a place (German Berg = mountain) or occupation (German Meyer = farmer). Still others are purely descriptive: Rosenthall = rose valley. And some, like Cohen, descended from the Hebrew *Kohanim,* meaning priestly; this name, though, has many spellings in America, such as Cahn, Cohn, Kahn, and Kohn, or if from Russia, Kagan or Kogan (Smith 162).

Use these basic questions about an ancestor to guide your search for meaning:

✦ Where did he live (e.g., on a mountain, near a lake)?

✦ Where did he come from (place or area)?

✦ What did he do to earn a living?

✦ What was his father's first name (or mother's)?

✦ What was his most descriptive feature (e.g., white hair, dark complexion)?

✦ What was his characteristic feature (e.g., courage)?

Some Tips About Surnames: Beheadings, Clips, and Combos

There are a greater variety of surnames in the United States than in any other country, mainly because every other country in the world has contributed to it. Eldson C. Smith tells us that "not only are almost all of the important family names of all civilized countries found in the United States but there is a bewildering mass of variations of foreign names which would be unrecognizable to the inhabitants of the countries from which they have come" (93). Smith goes on to note that ignorant immigration clerks distorted names beyond all recognition; later, the "tongue-twisting names of people from eastern and southeastern Europe were altered and changed when Americans could not handle them" (93). Some immigrants changed their own names: to break with an old life or as the start to a new life; to satisfy a belief that a chance for success would be better with a new name; to reduce discrimination, to ease pronunciation; and in a practical sense, to accommodate American typewriters that had no accent marks.

Beheadings, of names, that is, happened fairly often as immigrants sought an easier or less foreign-sounding name. The German *Koenigsberger* became Berger or Berg, for example. Clipping off the second half of a name, where Koenigsberger became Koenig and *Alexopoulous* became Alex, was also common. With some Jewish names, acronyms evolved into an American surname: Ben Rabbi Kalman, BRK, added a vowel and became Brock. The surname *Wasservogel* (literally, water bird) was both shortened and Americanized into Waters (Hook 266). Japanese names with two parts, however, are parts not necessarily even related to one another and may be combined for reasons other than meaning (Hook 313).

In some cases, you will need to be inventive in your name search. When immigrants arrived on Ellis Island, customs officers often misspelled and twisted names. If the immigrant came from a country where the alphabet was not Roman, the clerk had to transliterate. The solution was to find a combination of letters close to what represented sounds in immigrants' native languages. A good example occurs in Slavic languages where letter combinations not found in English were changed to English. For example, *Derij* became Derry and *Walcsiar* became Walsh; the German *sch* became *-sh* or *-s*. Because the Greek *Ts* sounds like English *Ch*, one surname was spelled as *Chirakis*. People also dropped accent marks and modified or simplified spellings as they translated names into English. And in some cases, pronunciation caused changes in spelling: for example, *-kin* became *-kiss, -kes,* or *ks; -in* added a *-g* or *-gs* to become *-ing* or *-ings*. Contractions shortened names, such as Loftus for Lofthouse (Hook 322–23). Therefore, what appears to be a very American or British name may have a history that leads you to a surprising conclusion.

In this section, you have been reading researched material very similar to that you will be working with. And you have probably guessed that the names in parentheses were the authors and page numbers of my resources. To complete this process, I have to add the bibliography, called Works Cited, showing the title, place and year of publication, and the publisher. It looks like this:

Works Cited

Hook, J. N. *Family Names: How Our Surnames Came to America.* New York: Macmillan, 1982.

Smith, Elsdon C. *The Story of Our Names.* Detroit: Gale, 1970.

As you go through this chapter, you will learn to record your information accurately and completely, giving credit to your resources as you go. Academic research rests on our ability to do so, as well as our honesty in letting others know where we found and "borrowed" ideas from other writers.

As you think about your last name, try the following:

+ Various pronunciations
+ Various spellings
+ Breaking it into parts
+ Rearranging parts
+ Clipping or adding parts

A Wee Warning

Some names that appear to be traditionally from one country—aren't. In Scotland, for example, not all were original Gaelic names. Some were French (Frazer, Lindsay, Bruce); others were Norse (Maccauly, Macdougall). Peaceful and not so peaceful migrations have added many names to the roster of surnames associated with specific countries.

Determining Sources of Information

For the name project, your most obvious and probably first source of information lay in your family. If your name is not British or European in its origin (e.g., American Indian, African, Asian, Middle Eastern), you most certainly will need to consult family and perhaps other faculty. However, you may be surprised to see the number of books that do address non-European names and provide a wealth of information. If your name has British or European roots, you will find both general information books and those specializing in a single background, such as Irish. You should also consult the *Oxford English Dictionary,* found in the reference section of your library. Some students with European names have consulted dictionaries written in German, Spanish, Dutch, Italian, and so forth; faculty in foreign language departments have often helped them. You must use multiple resources, so making a list of potential sources is an important step:

◆ Family and relatives
◆ Community people
◆ Name books (on-line catalogue at school and public library)
◆ Dictionaries (reference section of library)
◆ *Oxford English Dictionary*
◆ Internet

Be sure to keep a record of your search for information. Some notes on the ease or difficulty of finding answers to your questions may be later incorporated into your essay. Especially if you have difficulty, the process itself becomes an important part of your essay. And in any case, your search for information, and the skills that are involved in this search, are extremely important.

Documentation

Documentation refers to your record of sources: you give credit to your sources, the words and ideas you borrow from others. You do this in two ways: (1) the bibliography that accompanies your paper; (2) your name and page references in the written text itself.

Works Cited.   This is the bibliography page, where you report the complete information about the source used in your essay or report. However, it lists only those sources actually used in the body of your essay or report. It does not include sources you consulted but did not actually use in writing your piece.

　　　　　　AUTHOR　　　　　　　　　　　　　*TITLE*

(1) Smith, Elsdon C. <u>New Dictionary of American Family Names</u>.
New York: Harper, 1973.

PLACE OF PUBLICATION   PUBLISHER   YEAR OF PUBLICATION

Citation.   This is the reference in your essay or report; it provides your reader with a reference to your Works Cited page.

　　　　　　　　TITLE　　　　　　　　　　*AUTHOR*

(2) In the <u>New Dictionary of American Family Names</u>, Elsdon C. Smith states that the name Christensen means "son of Christian." The Norwegian system of creating names takes the father's first name and adds *-son* to it (85).

PAGE

For this project, you will use the Modern Language Association's (MLA) system of documentation, commonly used in English classes. However, there are other systems, developed and used by different academic disciplines. One popular system is that of the American Psychological Association (APA), most often used in the social sciences, education, and nursing. Your instructors will tell you which to use.

What to Document

One of the important decisions you will make while doing research is exactly what to document. A general rule of thumb: anything that is not common knowledge, common history, or scientific record. For example, we know Columbus came to the New World in 1492; it's common knowledge or history. However, few people would know the entire background of his voyage or what happened once he arrived. Information about these would be documented. Once you decide that source material will need documentation, you need to follow the rules:

◆ Put quotation marks around any word, phrase, sentence, or paragraph taken down exactly as it was written in the source. You might want to circle the marks in red to ensure that you KNOW these are directly quoted.

◆ When you quote material, be sure you copy it exactly as it was— even if it contains spelling or punctuation errors.

◆ Document any use of material from a source—whether you put it down as quotation or paraphrase or summary.

◆ A source may be a book, magazine, person, newspaper, or electronic media.

Quotation: a word-for-word "copy" of the original material

Summary: the essential points only, in order they were presented in original text; it is shorter than the original, usually only one-fourth as long

Paraphrase: a restating of the original material, in your own words, in whatever order you choose; it may be shorter or longer than the original material

Most of your material will be paraphrased. Using too many quotations suggests that writers really don't know the material very well or may be confused about their purpose in researching and writing.

Always comment on and interpret what you have taken from sources. What do you make of this information? How does it support your thinking? What is interesting or noteworthy about it?

Maintaining Academic Integrity

Part of the excitement of research is discovering, thinking about, and using ideas from other writers. However, if we use someone else's ideas, and fail to tell our readers that these ideas are not original with us, we are essentially stealing someone else's ideas and hard work. As writers, you know just how much work is involved in developing good ideas and conveying them well. Thus, you can imagine how you would feel if someone took your work and didn't give you credit for it. It just isn't fair or right. In academic research, it is a point of honor to document any work done by others and used by us. Failure to do so is called "plagiarism," and it is considered a very serious offense in academic work at any level. Most students do not plagiarize on purpose, and teachers know that it is usually unintentional; it most often happens because of inexperience in working with source material.

Example

Original text from Hook, J. N. *Family Names: How Our Surnames Came to America.* New York: Macmillan, 1982, page 324.

Sometimes names were changed out of a desire to break completely with an unhappy past. America represented a new life, new hope, new perspective. Why not enter it with a new name, an "American" name that would have no association with the life forever left behind?

Incorrect Use of Hook:

Sometimes, people came to America to get away from an unhappy past, so they changed their names. A new American name would have no association with their past and therefore help them leave their old life behind them forever.

Correct Use of Hook:

According to J. N. Hook, some people came to America to get away from an unhappy past, so they changed their names when they arrived here. A new "American" name would have no reminder of that unhappy past; therefore, it might help them to leave it behind (324).

To avoid problems:

✦ Always note your source (author, title, page number) as the first thing you do when reading and taking notes.

✦ When you have completed reading a segment of information that you want to use, close the book or magazine or look away from the screen. In your own words, write down the ideas you wish to use.

✦ Remember that making changes in the original wording does not change your obligation to document the source. Paraphrasing requires documentation.

✦ Immediately, place quotation marks around everything taken word for word from the source.

Paraphrasing Tips

Remember, when you paraphrase, you are using your own words to restate the ideas found in your source.

1. Skim the material to get the main idea. Read the first and last paragraphs of the piece; then, read the first and final sentences in each paragraph.

2. Read the material again, carefully and slowly, noting key words or phrases.

3. Without looking at the material, write down only the main idea.

4. Review the material once more, checking that you got the main idea right.

5. Write your paraphrase: only essential information, in your own words, in a logical order.

6. Check for accuracy: Can someone get the author's main idea from your notes? Have you cut out too much? Have you left too much in? Is the author's point of view correct?

Quotation Tips

1. Choose quoted material, whether a phrase, sentence, or paragraph, carefully. Use only when you want to preserve a particular wording, a revealing or interesting piece of information, something so important or insightful that only the original author's words will do.

2. Short quotation, fewer than four typed lines: work into the body of your paper. Be sure to put quotation marks around these lines.

3. Long quotation, more than four lines: set off from rest of your text. Indent 10 spaces from left margin. Single-space the quoted lines and use no marks around them. The sentence leading into the quoted material usually ends with a colon.

4. Partial quotation: use the ellipsis (. . .) three periods with a space before/after each.

5. Adding in words not in the quotation, set in brackets [ ]. Use when you have to clarify the meaning or make into a grammatical sentence.

Taking Notes

Most students use note cards when writing from sources. Although some want to use their regular notebook paper, this practice actually makes the process far more difficult. You will have many notes on many different aspects of your topic, and in the end, you will throw out many of these notes. This is a normal part of research: you gather more information than you ultimately will use in the essay or report. If you have taken notes on regular paper, you will have a very difficult time both seeing what you really have and trying to sort out what goes and what stays. The note cards can be grouped and arranged; notebook paper can't, at least not easily.

Bibliography Cards

For the bibliography information (author, title, publisher, date), a small note card, 3 × 5, is fine. You will save time later if you write this information in the exact format needed for your bibliography page, the Works Cited.

Bibliography Card

Smith, Elsdon C. <u>New Dictionary of American Family Names</u>. New York: Harper, 1973.

> Norma, Teresa. <u>A World of Baby Names</u>. New York: Berkeley, 1996.

Note Cards

Note cards should be large enough to write on and not so large that you feel compelled to fill them up. Note means just that—a brief notation of essential information. If you write the general topic at the top of the card, you will ease the later process of sorting through and grouping "like" information. Some students use a highlighter or colored felt-tip pen to color-code their cards. For example, everything pertaining to origin could be blue, whereas everything pertaining to meaning could be green. Or, buy cards in different colors to begin with. You want to make the final process of reviewing, choosing, and arranging information as easy as possible.

One set of cards might be reserved for your "flashes of brilliance." When we read, we often have interesting ideas—if not captured right then, we can lose them. For this reason, keeping a set of cards just for those ideas, insights, that occur while taking notes is a good strategy. Remember, the point of research is not only to learn something but to comment on that learning.

Note Card

> Origin
>
> Jones—from Welsh pronunciation of John
> son of John
>
> Smith <u>New Dictionary</u> 258

```
Meaning

Karim (kareem)—noble or generous
also jewels or precious stones

Norma 374
```

If an author has several books, and you are using more than one, be sure to put key words from title on the note card.

Reporting Your Sources: Citations

When you use information from sources, you must tell your readers just where this information came from. You must note the author and exact page or pages where you found the information. If the author is not known (which happens in many dictionaries or encyclopedias), you use the title of the book or article. You are, remember, using work that someone else produced; you must give the original author credit for his or her work. Reporting the sources of your information is done through a citation, the technical name for reporting information taken from sources. In the MLA format, parenthetical citations are used.

Examples:

According to Sara Jones, family names evolved out of necessity. As the population in western Europe increased, people had to find a way to distinguish among family groups (25).

Family names evolved out of necessity. As the population in western Europe increased, people had to find a way to distinguish among family groups (Jones 25).

Sara Jones reports that an "increasing population in western Europe forced people to develop surnames as a means of distinguishing one family group from another" (25).

- ✦ What information must be reported in parentheses?
- ✦ What is the advantage of introducing material taken from sources with the author's name?
- ✦ What are the rules for placement of the parentheses?
- ✦ What are the rules for using quotation marks? For end marks?

USING MLA DOCUMENTATION

As you have already noticed, MLA uses parentheses to provide the reader with information about the source of researched material. You have also figured out the different ways in which that information can be handled; however, it is helpful to see the guidelines. The material that follows will be your "handbook" for the name research project.

For Citations

Authors:

1. Always identify the author or editor. If there is no author or editor listed, use the title.

   In the <u>Oxford English Dictionary</u>, I discovered that "fleche" means arrow (306).

2. If there is more than one author, list both.

   According to H. Amanda Robb and Andrew Chesler, the name <u>Melendez</u> is Spanish in origin, actually a transformation of the name <u>Menendez</u> (452).

3. You can identify the author as you lead into the researched material or in the parentheses.

   In <u>Name Your Baby,</u> Lareina Rule lists Guinevere as meaning "white-cheeked, white wave, [or] white phantom" (76).

   Jennifer is not an original name. Rather, it is derived from the Old Welsh name Guinevere (Rule 68).

4. If you list the author in the parentheses, use only the last name. Only if you have two authors with the same last name would you list a first name.

5. If you use the author as part of your lead into the researched material, use first and last name the first (or only) time you list it. Subsequent references would list only the last name.

   In <u>The Name Book,</u> Dorothea Austin stated that Sandra is Anglo-Saxon in origin and took on the meaning of "helper" (300). Austin also gave an interesting spiritual connotation, "quickened by the spirit" (300).

Page Numbers

1. Always list the page number in parentheses.
2. Place the parentheses immediately after the borrowed material or where a pause would naturally occur; not every parenthesis will come at the end of a sentence.
3. Place the parentheses before internal punctuation and before the end mark.
4. Place the page number after the author or title.
5. Do not use any punctuation between the author and page number.
6. Do not write "page" or "p" before the number.

Note: You can use the author's name as you lead into the researched information or in the parentheses. The page number is *always* placed in the parentheses.

Person as Resource.   When you interview someone, or informally ask for information that later goes into your essay or report, you must let the reader know that this person supplied the information you are using. Suppose you talked with a grandparent:

> My grandmother, Teresa Sanches, told me that our family name was originally Portuguese, even though everyone associates it with Spanish.

> According to my aunt, my name, Ai, was chosen for its meaning, "beloved" in Vietnamese (Nguyen).

In your Works Cited page, you will have to note whether you received this information in a telephone conversation, letter, e-mail, or a face-to-face meeting; you will also need the date.

Special Cases

◆ An author with more than one book: Use the title either as you lead into the information or in the parentheses.

> In <u>American Surnames</u>, Elsdon C. Smith states that <u>Fleche</u> is French for "archer" and Fletcher is English for "arrow maker" (137). Smith gives more information in his <u>Dictionary of American Surnames</u>, where he says Fletcher is "one who made or sold arrows, and sometimes bows as well" (68).

Or if you prefer, use an abbreviated title in the parentheses:

> Elsdon C. Smith states that <u>Fleche</u> is French for "archer" and Fletcher is English for "arrow maker"

(<u>American</u> 137). Smith also notes that Fletcher is
"one who made or sold arrows, and sometimes bows
as well" (<u>Dictionary</u> 68).

✦ If you use two or more authors reporting essentially the same information, list them in the parentheses. Use a semicolon to separate the names.

Every source I consulted said that Susan means
"lily" (Smith 21; Webb 13).

✦ If you use an indirect source, use the phrase *qtd. in* _____
to indicate where you found the information. In the following example, the student used Dunkling's book for her research—not Lawson.

A study by E. D. Lawson suggested that "men and
women largely agreed about stereotyped images
associated with names" (qtd. in Dunkling 14).

✦ A quotation that is four or more lines: Indent and single-space the quoted lines, do not use quotation marks around them, and place the parentheses outside of the end mark of the final sentence. The indentation indicates that the material is quoted.

J. N. Hook provides information on how Japanese surnames evolved:

> Most Japanese surnames consist of two parts, not necessarily related in meaning, that were combined centuries ago by people who happened to like the sound or the connotations of the combination. The same component may be used in many names. For example, a character transliterated <u>ta</u> or <u>da</u> means "rice field" and appears in these names as well as many others:
>
> Arita "have, rice field"
>
> Fujita "wisteria, rice field"
>
> Morita "forest, rice field"
>
> Honda "base, rice field"
>
> Tanaka "rice field, middle"
>
> As those examples show, a given component, like <u>ta</u>, may appear in either the first or second position. (313–314)

For Works Cited

The Works Cited page is always a separate page. It is the final page, the final number, of your researched essay or report. It has a specific form for listing each type of resource (e.g., book, magazine, person, newspaper, electronic database). It lists only those sources found in the body of your paper.

These are the general rules for preparing your Works Cited page:

1. Alphabetize by the author or editor's last name. If there is no author or editor, alphabetize by the first major word in the title; that is, omit *A, An, The*.

2. Do not use numbers in front of the last name or title.

3. If listing the source takes more than one line, each subsequent line must be indented five spaces. The first line is flush with the left margin.

4. Double-space each entry. Do not "double the double space" between each entry.

5. Use italics or underline the title of the source.

6. If more than one copyright date is given, use the most recent one.

7. If several cities are given as place of publication, use the first one.

8. If the city is not well known or could be confusing, list the state as well.

9. Omit any title (e.g., Dr.) or degree (e.g., Ph.D., M.D.) from author's name.

10. Skip two spaces after each period in the entry.

11. Skip two spaces after the author and the title, one space after other items.

Special Case for Works Cited.   When you use more than one source by the same author, use three hyphens (---) followed by a period after the first listing of the author's name. Use alphabetical order of the titles.

```
Smith, Elsdon C.  American Surnames.  Baltimore:
     Chilton, 1969.

---.  The New Dictionary of American Family
     Names.  New York: Harper, 1973

---.  The Story of Our Names.  Detroit: Gale, 1970.
```

Order of Information in Works Cited Entry.   Before you begin to take notes, always take down the information needed to document your sources. If you photocopy pages, be sure you have this information—or write it down on the copied pages immediately. Don't leave the copy machine without it.

Books

1. Author or editor
2. Title, underlined or italicized

3. Place of publication; if city not well known, add state

4. Publisher

5. Date of publication (copyright)

> Last name, First name. <u>Title</u>. City: Publisher, Date.

Notice both the order of information and the punctuation:

> Smith, Elsdon C. <u>American Surnames</u>. New York:
>   Harper, 1968.
>
> Godfrey, Stephen, and Sean McKay. <u>Irish Surnames</u>.
>   Chicago: Harper/Collins, 1989.
>
> Jones, Jon, William Smith, and Edward Mills.
>   <u>Understanding Names</u>. Baltimore: American
>   Genealogy Society, 1978.

If you have more than three authors, use all names or <u>et al.</u> (meaning "and others") after the first name:

> Christy, Paul, et al. <u>Finding Our History</u>.
>   Minneapolis: Scandinavian Society, 1979.

If you have an editor:

> Smith, Elsdon C., ed. <u>From Many Worlds</u>
>
> Smith, Elsdon C., and Paul Raney, eds. <u>Tracing Names</u>

If the author is unknown or not listed:

> <u>Rand McNally Commercial Atlas</u>. Skokie, IL: Rand, 1994.

Person as Resource

1. Name of person giving information

2. How information was given

3. Date information was given

> Last name, First name. How information was given. Date.

In Person:

> Golub, Mary. Personal interview. 15 Mar. 1997.

By telephone:

> Mentavalo, Mark. Telephone interview. 16 May 1997.

Personal letter:

> Sanches, Teresa. Letter to author. 8 Mar. 1997.

By e-mail:

1. Name of author of e-mail
2. Address of author in angle brackets
3. Subject line of posting in quotation marks
4. Date e-mail was sent to you
5. Type of communication (personal, distribution list)
6. Date you accessed the message

```
Sanches, Teresa. <TASanches@aol.com>. "Research
    Question." 3 Mar. 1997. Personal E-Mail
    (4 Mar. 1997).
```

Articles

1. Author of article, if given
2. Title of article, in quotation marks
3. Name of magazine, newspaper, or journal, underlined or italicized
4. Volume number (if one)
5. Date of publication
6. Complete page numbers of article

Author's last name, First name. "Title." <u>Periodical</u>. Date: inclusive pages.

```
Halloran, Kerry. "Coming to America." Time. 25 Mar.
    1995:3.
"The New Names." Newsweek. 4 Apr. 1996:14-16.
Merriman, Ann. "Clues to Personal Histories." The
    English Journal 23 (1994):24-26.
```

Reference Book (Encyclopedia, Dictionary)

1. Author if one listed
2. Title of section used, in quotation marks
3. Title of reference book, underlined or italicized
4. Number of edition, if listed
5. Year of publication, edition.

Last name, First name. "Title." Reference text. Year edition.

```
"Surnames." Webster's Collegiate Dictionary. 10th ed.
    1996.
"British Surnames." Encyclopedia Britannica. 1995 ed.
Jones, Alan. "Irish Names." World Book. 1995 ed.
```

Electronic Database.   As a general rule, provide all the information that allows someone else to locate the same document. If you use information from a CD-ROM, provide the publisher. If you use information from an on-line database, give the sponsoring organization or publisher of the material. If you use the Internet, give the Uniform Resource Locator (URL): the form of the resource, the transfer protocol (e-mail, http, telnet, etc.) followed by two forward slashes and the exact location (machine, site, directory, and file) of the document. In brief: How did you get to that document? What information must your reader have to access it? Because standards for citing electronic sources are still evolving, your instructor will provide you with up-to-date methods to cite your sources. However, two commonly needed citations are illustrated here.

Internet Citation in Body of Paper.   When you cite information taken from the Internet in the body of your paper, list only the author's name or title of the document if no author is given. Do not use the URL.

To list Internet in Works Cited page.   Generally, list the following items in this order:

1. Author, if one is given
2. Title of document
3. Date of publication, if given
4. URL in < > or path you took to locate the site. Use forward slash marks to separate the menu choices you made to access that site.
5. Date you accessed the material, in parentheses.

Example: World Wide Web Site

> Author. Title. Publication date. World Wide Web [URL]
> Access date.

```
Lee, Elizabeth.  "The Name Game."  History Fun. 20
    July 1996. <http://www.history.com/name/lee>
    (5 Feb. 1997).
```

As with all citations, your task is to provide the reader with information that allows him or her to access the very same information. Although web sites can change, you have done your job correctly if you provide accurate information of your access on a specific date.

Group Activity

Analyzing Student Drafts.   Have one person read through the draft aloud while the rest follow along. Note how the writer uses and documents information from sources. Specific questions follow each draft.

EXAMPLE A

Ryan comes from a variety of terms, primarily Irish. A close derivative is Ryen, meaning "made from Rye" (<u>Oxford English Dictionary</u> 190). It comes from England, which makes me believe that it became the Irish counterpart, "Rian," which also has several meanings. The first meaning was name given to a pre-Christian river or sea deity. It later became "rhine," and European river now holds that name (Cottle 246). Its Irish meaning was "little king" and was given to the grandson of an Irish king (Smith 88). One historian, whose surname is Ryan said "[it] seems so ancient that its meaning was lost before records began" (qtd. in McLysaught 13).

◆ How many different sources did Ryan use?

◆ Which source has no author? Why?

◆ Why did Ryan insert the brackets [ ] in the quotation?

◆ In the final sentence, Ryan used "qtd. in" to indicate that McLysaught had quoted another author. Why must Ryan use this form here?

EXAMPLE B

My last name originated as an English name spelled S-E-W, but later became a Scottish name with the spelling S-H-E-W, which is currently how my last name is spelled. The name means "an attendant at the meal, one who superintends the arrangement of the table, the seating of the guests, and the tasting and serving of the dishes" (<u>Oxford English Dictionary</u> 574-575, 688).

◆ What do the series of page numbers indicate to the reader?

◆ Notice how the citation fits into the sentence. What rule can you devise for the placement of the citation, punctuation, and so on?

EXAMPLE C

Elsdon C. Smith states in the <u>New Dictionary of American Family Names</u> that Christianson means "son of Christian" (85).

+ How does introducing the source material with the author's name help the reader?
+ How does it help the writer stay clear of plagiarism?
+ Why are quotation marks around "son of Christian"?

EXAMPLE D

In <u>English Surnames</u>, Bardsely tells of how the Norman invaders brought the Dutch names into England. He writes that <u>wallrond</u> and <u>wallrand</u> "hailing from Denmark . . . may have come in from the earlier raids on that shore, or later in the more peaceful channels of trade" (30). It is very plausible, therefore, that the name <u>Rand</u> is Dutch in origin.

+ Who is the author of this source material?
+ What does the ellipsis (. . .) signal to the reader?
+ How are foreign spellings handled?
+ Notice the last sentence. What is the student writer doing with his information?

Introducing Source Material

Being able to work researched information into your own words and sentences is a skill. It takes time and practice. However, having a number of ways to introduce source material is a good start:

+ Elsdon C. Smith expresses it this way: "The names of American blacks begins with the arrival in America of the first slaves" (146). Smith goes on to point out that although African people already had tribal names, cultural custom would prevent them from revealing their true names to strangers (146).
+ Smith reports that it was not unusual for slaves to be given classical names, often taken from Shakespeare or eighteenth-century novels (140).
+ "Place names," says Hook, "are rare among Greek surnames" (256).
+ According to Jon Jones, Stella means star (12). Jones also notes that Stella "first came into use in Latin speaking countries" (14).
+ The name <u>Susan</u>, state Paul Smith and Sara Lee, is Hebrew for lily (45).

- ◆ Smith and Lee trace the name's history from the Middle East to Europe and Britain (46).

- ◆ Susan is not a common name in the 1990s. It is found most often in England but enjoys some popularity on the east coast of the United States (Smith and Lee 47).

- ◆ Sean O'Brien provided a surprising fact:
  Although most people assume Jordan is an Irish name, it is actually French. Its origin was Jourdain. The name traveled to Britain with the Norman invaders in the Middle Ages. The French crusaders may have brought the name back to France, recalling their association with the River Jordan in Palestine. When the Normans came to Great Britain, they carried Jourdain with them. It changed both its pronunciation and spelling in the process. (21)

- ◆ Look at the Jones entry for Susan. What is the rule for using the author's first and last name when introducing material taken from his or her text?

- ◆ Look at the three Smith and Lee entries for Susan. What is the rule for using the authors' names?

- ◆ Look at the O'Brien entry. Everything after "fact" is directly quoted, word for word. What is the rule for a quotation four or more lines long? What is different about the placement of the page number?

Special Marks

Ellipsis.   You have already noticed the ellipsis (dots), which signals that some words have been left out of a quoted sentence. It is a useful device because it allows us to eliminate words or even whole sentences that we really don't need. Notice how it works here:

Three dots (. . .) mean words or phrases have been left out in the middle of a quotation:

Sardoff claims "Smith is an occupational name . . . found among most of the world's languages" (87).

Four dots (. . . .) mean the omitted material falls at the end of a sentence:

> Herndon tells us that "Smith is one of the most common names in the world. . . .easily translated into most of the world's languages due to its association with an occupation" (9).
>
> But Jones argues that "Smith is not all that common . . . " (2).

Brackets. Use brackets [ ] for insertions or changes in quoted material:

> The <u>Oxford English Dictionary</u> was clear in its history of Smith: [The name was] "among the earliest of last names recorded" (987).
>
> "It [Smith] has many forms, including Kovac" (<u>Oxford English Dictionary</u> 987).

Special Circumstances

No Author—Use the Title. With some reference works, no author or editor is listed. In this case, just use the title, as shown above. If you have a lengthy title, you may shorten it as long as you use a key word that will link the title to the full listing in the bibliography:

> The family name Johnson was borrowed from the Norse ("Scand" 13).

In this citation, "Scand" refers to a magazine article entitled "Scandinavian Notes."

One Author with Several Books—Use Key Word in Title. You may find that a single author has written several books on your topic. When you wish to use information from more than one in your essay or report, you must show the reader which book you refer to:

> Elsdon C. Smith notes that Fletcher is English for "arrow maker" (<u>Dictionary</u> 137). Smith also tells us that another meaning, "dealer of flesh," had been absorbed by flesher, "the arrow maker" (<u>Surnames</u> 12).

In the Works Cited page, the reader would have the complete reference to each of Smith's books: <u>Dictionary of American Family Names</u> and <u>American Surnames.</u> You could also introduce the title along with

Smith's name as a way of making clear just which text the information was taken from:

> In the <u>Dictionary of American Family Names,</u> Elsdon C. Smith notes . . .

When to Document

1. Whenever you use the author's exact words, a direct quotation from the book, magazine, video, or other source.

2. Whenever you summarize words and ideas from source. A summary gives the main ideas or points, in the order they were presented in the original text. The only exception is the use of material that is generally known. A summary is always shorter than the original and follows the order of the original.

3. Whenever you paraphrase, restate the information in your words and writing style. Even though you have taken the information and put it into your own words, you are still using someone else's information. Therefore, you must give credit to the original writer. A paraphrase may be shorter or longer than the original text; it may also be arranged differently.

Working with Source Material: Interpreting, Analyzing, and Synthesizing

Whenever you use material from a source, always comment on this material. What do you make of it, how do you interpret it, how does it support your main idea? In brief, you need to let your reader know what you make of it. Otherwise, you are simply stringing someone else's ideas together. As noted earlier, we do research because it helps us answer a question that is important to us; if we don't comment on what we found out, there really is no point in doing the research.

Whenever you use multiple sources, always analyze the information for similarities and differences. Where you find similarities, use them as support. In doing name research, for example, you will find many sources that say the same thing, especially about your first name. And that's fine.

As you thought about combining the "Jordan" information, you were beginning the process of synthesis, or blending information. Whenever you work with research, you will take many pieces of information about your topic and form them into a unified whole. At the same time, you will be blending in your thoughts, your analysis, and interpretation of the material. This will be one of the most challenging parts of your research, but also one of the most rewarding.

An example: My maiden name, Jordan, is listed as follows in different sources. As you read, first think of similarities and differences; then, think about how you might combine the pieces of information.

From H. Amanda Robb and Andrew Chesler Encyclopedia of American Family Names HarperCollins, 95 page 353

"Derived from the name of the river called Jordan, which is derived from the Hebrew word 'yarad,' meaning to descend"

From Evelyn Walls What to Name the Baby Doubleday, 46 page 25

"Hebrew 'to descend,' Jarad was the original name of the River Jordan of the Bible."

From Elsdon C. Smith New Dictionary of American Family Names page 258 Harper, 73

"Jordan, Jorden, Jourdain, Jordon (Eng. Fr.) Descendent of Jordan or Jourdain (flowing down), a personal name sometimes given to one who was baptized with holy water from the river Jordan."

From Withycombe EG Oxford Dictionary of English Christian Names 3/e Oxford, 77 page 180

"Jordan(m): Hebrew 'flowing down', the name of the principal river of Palestine. There was an Old German personal name Jordanes, probably from the same root as Old Norse jordh 'land'. Jordan is found as a christian name in England from the end of the 12th C, and the probability is that its ultimate source was the Old German Jordanes, but that its continued use was due to confusion with the name of the river, which would be familiar to returning Crusaders, who were in the habit of bringing back Jordan water to be used in the baptism of their children."

▬Group Activity▬▬▬▬▬▬▬▬▬▬▬▬▬▬▬▬▬▬▬▬

Analyzing and Synthesizing Research Notes

✦   Using the information on my name, Jordan, decide what you would use and in what order you would use it.

   1. Write at least three sentences, with the correct citations.
   2. Introduce the information with the author's name.

◆ Now try the process with York, a name that has far more information.

1. Read through the following pieces of information (A–E).
2. Sort out the different origins of York.
3. Write a brief paragraph with the correct citations. Introduce the
   authors.
4. Write the Works Cited for your paragraph.

A. *A Dictionary of Surnames.* Patrick Hanks and Flavia Hodges. Oxford
University Press New York 1988.

"Eburacum, the Brit. Name of the city York, England" page 589

York is English in origin and a "habitation name from the city of
York in N England, or perhaps in some cases regional name from
the county of Yorkshire" page 589

"The surname is now widespread throughout England." Page 589

B. *American Given Names.* George Stewart. Oxford University Press New
York 1979.

"York as a family name. York is derived from the northern city and
county of England." Page 256

C. *American Surnames.* Elsdon C. Smith. Chilton Book Company Philadelphia 1968

"York, place of yew trees" page 241

D. *Dictionary of American Family Names.* Elsdon C. Smith. Harper Publishers New York 1956

"York (place of yew trees)" page 24

"wild boar habitats"

"was altered . . . into OE [Old English] Eoforowic (from the elements *eofor* wild boar + wic outlying settlement" page 589

E. *An Entymological Dictionary of Family and Christian Names.* William
Arthur. Gale Research New York 1969.

[York] "derives its name from *Eure-ic* or *Eouer-ric* page 270

"*eurere*, a wild boar, and *ryc,* a refuge" page 270

"a retreat from the wild boars which were in the forest of Gautries"
page 270

"York . . . a city in England next in esteem to London" page 270

Group Activity

Evaluating Student Drafts.   Your instructor will tell you which drafts, perhaps a few or perhaps all of them, to evaluate. As you evaluate each draft, keep in mind these basic criteria: (1) the content is informative, adequate, and relevant, (2) the organization is logical, easy to follow, (3) the writer's voice is present, (4) sentences are clear, (5) grammar, mechanics, and spelling are correct. To these criteria, add these important elements: (6) the writer used multiple sources of information, (7) the writer integrated these sources well, (8) the writer used citations correctly.

DRAFT A

Michael, the English name, has been to some extent changed to Mitchell. It is also a synonum of Mulvihil in Connacht (<u>Surnames of Ireland</u> 152). Michael is a very popular name and has several different meanings. The most popular is descendent of Michael (who is like God) (<u>New Dictionary of American Family Names</u> 170). Another definition is "Who is like God" Hebrew; the archangel captain of the heavenly host (<u>Penguin Dictionary of Surnames</u> 148). More popular forms of Michael in Old French are Mitch, Maul, Miel, and Mil. These are much commoner as surnames (<u>Penguin Dictionary of Surnames</u> 148). Another popular form of Michael is "Mihel," making the surname "son of Michael" (<u>Penguin Dictionary of Surnames</u> 148). The name Mike is a less formal way of saying Michael. Mike the normal pet form of Michael was very rare in its own right it was not used until the 1940s and then it was used only occasionally (<u>The Facts on File Dictionary of First Names</u> 132).

DRAFT B

I found Michael to be a popular English first name with many definitions. The ones I found most fitting are "one who is like a god" and "the archangel captain of the heavenly host." (Cottle 224). These two seem to fit me best because of my religious background, and I believe my parents named me Michael for that reason.

> While looking for Michael in the <u>Oxford English
> Dictionary,</u> I came across the slang name of Michael,
> which is Mike. This I found to be most interesting be-
> cause it meant "to 'hang about' doing nothing waiting
> for a job." After looking at this meaning, I wondered
> why my parents didn't name me Mike!

As you examined the two drafts, what did you find to be the strength of each one? The major problem of each one? What errors in documentation did you find? How would you advise these two students if they were part of your peer response team?

DRAFT C

> Elsdon C. Smith notes in The New Dictionary of Fam-
> ily Names that Kealy means "Gransdon of Caolladhe; or
> of Cadhla (beautiful); one who came from Yorkshire"
> (266). Currently, our last name is spelled K-e-a-l-y,
> and pronounced Kay-lee. After some difficulty in re-
> searching, I managed to uncover a few different
> spellings and pronunciations for my last name. In any
> event, Kealy has a primarily Irish background. Reli-
> able family sources and the family tree also led me to
> this conclusion. Smith adds two other forms of Kealy,
> which share similarities in definition but not in ori-
> gin. He notes that Keely means (Ir.) Descendent of the
> slender man; grandson of Caollaidhe" (266). In addi-
> tion, he states Kaley as (MX. Scot., Eng.) Descendent
> of Caoladhe (slender); the slender man; one who came
> from Cailly (forest), in Normandy; dweller by a cab-
> bage field" (261). The three definitions share the
> similarity of being descendants of Caolladhe. Unfortu-
> nately, I have no clue as to who this was. However, if
> we convene the definitions, our result is trim figured
> man named Kealy (or Keely or Kaley), who is related to
> Caolladhe and is quite fond of cabbage.

Two Challenging Student Drafts

◆ Using the following criteria, evaluate essays by Michelle and Jennifer.

Use of Sources: multiple sources; integrated sources well

Use of MLA Format: citations complete and correctly punctuated

Use of MLA Format: Works Cited complete and in order, correctly punctuated

Content: informative, interesting

Organization: information arranged logically, easy to follow

Expression: sentences clear, word choice appropriate, tone appropriate

Writer's Voice: clear sense of the writer, person talking to person

Grammar: forms correct (e.g., subject-verb agreement, pronouns)

Mechanics: correct punctuation, spelling, capitals, titles underlined or italics, foreign words underlined or italics

Like a Fox

I've always known the name Vosberg was German. My parents and grandparents had been telling me so every since I could remember. Having this knowledge, I thought my search for the name's meaning would be simple, but as you will soon see, the task was not as easy as first thought.

By knowing the country of origin, I narrowed my search considerably. Of the 200 books on names in the library, four dealt strictly with German. I found the books and sat down to begin my research. To my horror, each and every book was written in German--not translated into English, that is. After calming myself a bit, I began to page through the books and realized that I could read the names, but not the captions that followed.

I turned to the V's in the first book and didn't find a Vosberg. I tried the second book, no Vosberg. I searched the third and fourth book and came up with nothing. Had my parents and grandparents been lying to me? Did they make up the name, claiming it was German to cover up some heinous crime? Was I really the descendent of some Irishman? If Vosberg was German,

believe me, it would be in these books. Needless to
say, I left the library with a major identity crisis.

On the second day, I thought it might be wise to
start off with a book I could actually read, so I set
the German books aside. While paging through a book by
J. N. Hook, I stumbled across some information that
set my mind at ease. Hook states that many German
patronyms are dithematic, meaning they are a combination of two themes or words (121). I broke my name
into Vos and Berg, and sure enough, I found each
listed in the German books. Now if I could only read
the captions that followed each. This led me to Dr.
Manfred Poitzch, a German professor whom I hoped would
translate the captions and shed some light on my
research.

According to Dr. Poitzch, Berg is very common,
meaning hill or mountain. The prefix <u>Vos</u> is not as
common. If spelled <u>Vos</u>, it is of Dutch origin and
means "fox." "Spelled <u>Foss</u>, it is of Norwegian origin
and means "spring tumbling down from a mountain." Although Vosberg is still very much German, Dr. Poitzch
suggested that the spelling points to a Scandinavian
backround. He thought Vosberg may have originally been
spelling Vossberg, but changed to a single "s" sometime during immigration.

Other sources confirmed all that Dr. Poitzch had
told me. According to Elsdon C. Smith, Vos was German,
meaning "one with foxlike characteristics or dweller
at the sign of the fox" (224); Berg was listed as a
"dweller near the hill or mountain" (15). William D.
Bowman also stated that Berg meant hill (218). There
was no doubt in my mind that Berg meant hill or mountain, and Hook only confirmed this reasoning when he
noted that German surnames are often taken from places
referring to a landscape feature (121). It was the
prefix <u>Vos</u> that troubled me.

Two sources stated <u>Vos</u> meant "foxlike," but this
would mean it was Dutch in origin. I know my ancestors
came from the area of Hamburg, which is located in the
northern part of Germany. This places Hamburg in close

proximity to both Holland and Scandinavia, and due to the short distance between countries, it is possible that Vos is a combination of both Dutch and German meanings, with a Scandinavian influence as well. From the information available, I've drawn the conclusion that Vosberg literally means a person with foxlike characteristics dwelling near a hill or mountain.

Finding the meaning of Michelle was not as difficult as finding the meaning of Vosberg. According to The Oxford Dictionary of English Christian Names, Michelle is the female form of Michel, which is Michael in English (Withycombe 218). This information directed my search to the name Michael. E. G. Withycombe stated that Michael was Hebrew, meaning "Who is like the Lord?"; it is also the name of one of the archangels, the "leader of the heavenly host" (219). This was a blah meaning, so I decided to go to the real source, my parents.

I approached my parents with that age-old question every child asks: Why did you name me _____? My parents' response, because Michelle was a popular name at that time, was disappointing. That's it? I was expecting something profound, like was named after some queen or movie star or heroine, not because the name was popular just then. Ah, to be blessed with such hip and original parents. There have been many times when I wished my parents had given me a name more unique or exotic than Michelle, but when all is said and done, I couldn't picture myself being anything but Michelle.

Works Cited

Bowman, William D. The Story of Surnames. Detroit: Gale Research, 1968.

Gottschald, Max. Deutsche Namenkunde. Berlin: Walter de Gruyter, 1954.

Hook, J. N. Family Names: How Our Surnames Came to America. New York: Macmillan, 1982.

Poitzch, Manfred. Personal interview. 14 February
     1991.

Smith, Elsdon C. <u>Dictionary of Family Names.</u> New
     York: Harpers, 1956.

Withycombe, E. G. <u>The Oxford Dictionary of English
     Christian Names.</u> Oxford, 1977.

Lady of the Lake

As I began to search for the meaning of my name, I
already had some idea of what Vandermeer meant. I took
my curiosity to McIntyre Library, where I picked out
<u>Engles Woordenboek</u>, a Dutch-English dictionary. I pro-
ceeded to look up the word <u>van</u>, which in English means
"of" or "from" (Bruggencate 831). My search for the
word <u>der</u> proved unsuccessful, so I turned back to see
if Vander was one word. Instead of finding it, I found
<u>Vandaar</u>, which means "from there" (Bruggencate 832).
Then I directed my attention to the term meer. I discovered it means "lake" (Bruggencate 475), and not
"sea" as I had anticipated. In an effort to confirm
this slightly different meaning, I turned to Elsdon C.
Smith's <u>Dictionary of American Family Names</u>. Here I
established that Vandermeer means "a dweller at, or
near, the lake" (221).

I wondered why my family name meant that. As I
paged through <u>American Surnames</u>, also by Smith, I came
across a passage that describes how people were liked
to be named according to where they lived or settled
(196). In a phone conversation with my father, Melvin
Vandermeer, I learned that my grandfather's side of
the family came from a region of the Netherlands known
as Groingen. While I looked at a map, my father explained that Groingen is located in the northeastern
part of the country, its Artic shores converging with
the North Sea. My grandmother's family came from
Friesland, the northwestern region of the Netherlands.
This region is bordered to the west by Ijselmeer, a
vast, inland lake (Bartholomew n.p.). Perhaps some of
my ancesters settled here, but I was unable to draw

any concrete conclusions as to which lake was the "meer" in my name.

Works Cited

Bartholomew, John, ed. <u>The Netherlands</u>. Vol. 3 <u>The Times Atlas of the World</u>. Boston: Houghton, 1955.

Bruggencate, Karl. <u>Engles Woordenboek</u>. Groingen, The Netherlands: Wolter-Nordhoff, 1971.

Smith, Elsdon C. <u>American Surnames</u>. Philadelphia: Chilton, 1969.

---. <u>Dictionary of American Family Names</u>. New York: Harper, 1956.

Vandermeer, Melvin H. Telephone interview. 16 Feb 1992.

Writing Activity

The following essay has wonderful information, but very serious problems in presenting it. As you read:

✦ What did this student use to organize the essay?

✦ Why doesn't this organization work?

✦ What two ways could the information be organized?

✦ What information could be shortened and still get the point across?

✦ What is missing in the part on the surname?

✦ What is wrong with the student's citations?

Your group will do some rewriting of this essay. First, decide how you would group the information. Then, decide on an order for the information you have chosen to use. How would you start the essay? Check the information needed for the citations. Also decide where you will introduce source material by author and where you will place the author in the parentheses. Make necessary corrections on the Works Cited.

The Arrow or the Flesh?

My search turned up a new angle on Fletcher. I knew about the arrow maker, but the implied cowardice

and dealing in flesh surprised me. I went to the
<u>Oxford English Dictionary</u> first. I discovered many
spellings for Fletcher: fleccher, flecher, flecchour,
fle(d)ger, flechier, fleche, flinch, flench, flencher,
flenchir, clechie, flecche, flanch, flitch, fletch,
flick, and flecher. On page 306 I discovered that
"fleche" is from 1710 and means arrow and relates to
the craft of arrow making. On page 318 are "fleccher"
is from 1400 and also means arrow maker. Theser are
both from the Old French. On pae 325, "flinch" is
from 1579 and means to give way or draw back in
battle. It also means to shrink under pain or to
wince (1677). In 1727 it meant to strike, or cut
flesh by striking, with the nail of the middle finger.
On page 332, "flitch" means to cut (a log) into
flitches (steaks) or to cut a fish into flitches
(steaks).

My second source was Eldson C. Smith. I took from
two of his books. In <u>American Surnames</u>, Mr. Smith
states that there were 73,170 people named Fletcher in
the U.S.A. in 1969. The name ranks 320th as a most
common name in the U.S.A. (305). He says flesher means
"the dealer of flesh" and had been absorbed by
flesher, "the arrow maker" (12). On page 3 Mr. Smith
states that Fletchers came here on the Mayflower.
Fleche is French for "archer" and fletcher is English
for "arrow maker" (137).

In his <u>Dictionary of American Family Names,</u> Elsdon
C. Smith says Fletcher is "one who made or sold arrows, and sometimes bows as well" (68).

To pursue the "dealer in flesh", I used <u>The Origin
of English Surnames</u> by P. H. Reaney. He states Flesher
meant the real English term for butcher, "flesh
hewer". It was replaced by Flesher and Fletcher (179).

In <u>The Name Book,</u> I found Dorothea Austin's version
of my first name: Lorreen, Loren, Loring, Lorin. It is
Teutonic in origin and means "honourable warrior". The
spiritual meaning is "God's warrior" (218). I doubt
Mom ever gave any of this a thought. She simply named
her first born after her beloved husband.

Works Cited

Austin, Dorothea. <u>The Name Book</u>. Minneapolis: Bethany House, 1982.

Hook, J. N., Ph.D. <u>Family Names: How Our Surnames Came to America</u>. New York: Macmillan, 1982.

<u>Oxford English Dictionary</u>. London: Clarendon, 1933.

Reaney, P. H. <u>The Origin of English Surnames</u>. London: Routledge and Kegan Paul, 1967.

Smith, Elsdon C. <u>American Surnames</u>. Baltimore: Chilton, 1969.

Smith, Elsdon C. <u>Dictionary of American Family Names</u>. New York: Harper, 1956.

Smith, Elsdon C. <u>The Story of Our Names</u>. Detroit: Gale Research, 1970.

GENERAL TIPS FOR YOUR RESEARCH

Gathering Your Sources

✦ Use multiple sources. Research involves finding and using more than one source of information. Think in terms of human resources, people who are likely to have information you need, print and non-print resources, including on-line.

✦ Develop a good working bibliography. This is a list of potential resources. You may not use all of them, but you need a place to start.

✦ Use the Internet but check out the source of information very carefully. Anyone can put just about anything on the Net; for this reason, research taken from it must be verified through other sources.

Recording Information

✦ Take careful notes. You might want to use two different sizes of note cards: on the larger one, put information for the bibliography (author, title, publisher, date); on the smaller card, record the information you need.

✦ Use quotations sparingly. If you decide that you want the information exactly as the author or source has stated it, put quotation marks around it. Be sure to copy everything exactly as it appears on the original source, even if something is misspelled or grammatically wrong. Write the source, author, page number.

✦ Use paraphrase carefully. Most of your material will be paraphrased. That means you have read the material, thought about it for a few moments, and written down in your own language what the material said. Write the source, author, page number. Regardless of "translating" the ideas, you must credit the author.

✦ Use summary when you need only the main points.

Organizing Your Information

✦ Review your notes. Sort your cards into piles (e.g., one for origin, another for meaning). Then review the information and determine what you will use. Place the piles of cards into a tentative order of use.

✦ Prepare a scratch outline. It should be good enough to see what you have and not so good that you are unwilling to change it.

✦ If you have color-coded your cards, color-code your outline so you can easily see where the information fits.

✦ Place the note cards with direct quotations next to the sections where they will be used in the essay.

Writing a Draft

✦ Review your notes once more, set them aside, and write your first draft.

✦ Use your drafting strategies developed throughout this course.

Setting Deadlines

You should work backward in your deadline setting. That is, start with the due date and count out the weeks or days back to the time you received the research assignment. If you have six weeks, for example, your schedule might look like this:

Due Date: March 17   Peer Response: March 12

Week 1 (Feb. 3)   Complete preliminary bibliography
Week 2 (Feb. 10)   Read and take notes

Week 3 (Feb. 17)	Make scratch outline; continue reading
Week 4 (Feb. 24)	Complete reading; refine outline
Week 5 (Mar. 3)	Begin drafting
Week 6 (Mar. 10)	Complete drafting and revising; peer response
Weekend	Complete editing and prepare final copy

Formatting Your Edited Draft

MLA does not require a separate title page. Unless your teacher directs otherwise, your name, course title, and date of submission will be placed in the upper left-hand corner of the first page of your paper. Leave margins of 1 to 1½ inches on all sides of the paper, and double-space the text. The Works Cited page is also double-spaced, but don't "double" the double spacing when adding each new entry. Each page, including Works Cited, will be numbered sequentially; your last name will precede the number.

Example Page 1

Christine Woicz   Woicz 1
English 110
Dr. Mary Meiser
23 September 1997

                        Of Cabbages and Kings

Indent 5 spaces for each new paragraph

Double-space

Example Page 2

                                                              Woicz 2

Example Page 3 (Works Cited Only)

Woicz 3

Works Cited

- -

Double-space each entry, first line flush with left

margin

Indent 5 spaces with each entry line after the first

one

- -

Peer Response

With your partner or group, exchange drafts (including the Works Cited page) and respond to the following:

- ✦ Use of sources: multiple sources; integrated into text well
- ✦ MLA format: citations correct; Works Cited correct
- ✦ Content: informative
- ✦ Organization: information arranged logically; easy to follow
- ✦ Expression: sentences clear; tone appropriate; writer's voice present
- ✦ Mechanics: titles underlined or italicized; quotation marks; foreign words underlined or italicized

Be very specific (and honest) about areas that need work.

Reflection

Discuss the development of this paper:

- ✦ What was the most interesting part of the research?
- ✦ What was the most frustrating part of the research?

✦ What part of the writing was most challenging? Why?

✦ What part of the writing process was most rewarding? Why?

✦ What part of the writing process needs more time and experience?

✦ What was most satisfying about this research/writing task?

✦ How did your peers help with the process?

Turn in your reflection with your final draft; staple it in as the final page, following the Works Cited page.

WHAT IS FIELD RESEARCH AND WHY DO IT?

Field research takes us out of the classroom and library and into the community. We observe people, places, and events; we analyze and draw conclusions about what we see and hear, and come away with a better idea of what people are like or what goes on in that setting. Some academic courses require field research. An education major, for example, will certainly observe and record what happens in an elementary school classroom; a social work major might have to evaluate a group home; and a sociology or business major might investi-gate the inter-action patterns of males and females in a work setting. Regardless of one's profession, being a good observer and listener is an essential skill in the workplace; it is also essential in any of our relationships.

For your field research project, you will observe and record the role language plays in our daily lives: classes, eateries, and stores. Language here extends to nonverbal as well as verbal, and includes spatial behavior. Native speakers of English (or any language) take a great deal of language "know-how" for granted; if you are a native speaker, you may be surprised at what you learn. If English is your second language, you may be surprised at how much you *have* learned, perhaps much of it informally. This project will provide an appreciation of language and the great task of learning not only the "what" of language but the "how" of daily use.

Collecting Data

For this project, you will collect language data; these data include both verbal and nonverbal material. Your instructor will provide you with the parameters of your data collection; that is, whether you will collect it in one day or over several. The general categories of information will be these:

Verbal Encounters.   What did you and/or others say? Ask? Respond to?

Nonverbal Communication.   How did you and/or others convey meaning without speech? What was the gesture, the facial expression, eye contact, body language?

Paralingual Communication.   What tone or pitch was used? What is signaled through it?

Spatial Behavior.   Where did people place themselves during conversations? In a classroom, where did the teacher stand or sit?

Throughout the day, you interact with many people and in many different situations. A critical aspect of this research, then, will be speed: record the communication during or as soon as possible after the encounter or observation. You don't have to record anything "word for word," but the data should be accurate enough for you to make sense of your notes later. If you do record "word for word," be sure you use quotation marks. When you return to your notes, you will analyze them:

A.   What was the purpose of your communication? How successful were you in achieving your purpose? How did you feel if you weren't successful?

B.   How many different kinds of language did you use in one day? When were you formal? Informal? When did you change the level of formality and why? Did you use slang? Jargon? When were you intimate or distant in tone? Angry, sad, or bored in tone? When did you change tone and why?

C.   How many times was your language dependent upon shared knowledge? That is, you and others understand the situation without further explanation or have a personal history that allows you to put the conversation into the right context.

D.   How many times did you depend on cultural knowledge to interpret the language and situation correctly? That is, you knew the right thing to say, the right tone, the right "manners" or approach—all without any thought about it.

E.   Did age, gender, or cultural differences affect the language used?

F.   Were relationships among speakers evident? Any exclusion? Anyone dominating? Any chains of "command"?

In brief, pay attention to the many ways in which we use language—and link that use to language commonly used in American settings. If you have a home language different from English, use that setting to contrast what happens with English in public settings.

FIELD NOTES

Raw Notes

Field notes are a continuous record of situations, events, conversations, nonverbal behavior—a running record of events, of people, of things heard and overheard, things observed. At the most general level, field notes are more or less a chronological log of "what went on." Notes taken at the field site are called "raw notes." They are predominately descriptive, providing a portrait: a physical description of the setting, the people, details of verbal and nonverbal behavior, an account of events. Raw notes reveal characteristics of sheer reporting: Who is there? Who said what to whom? What responses? What body language? What general events took place? Chains of reaction? Raw notes often contain diagrams to show the physical layout of the site, where people were located, and so forth. Raw notes take several forms: mental notes (orienting yourself to the task of observing and recording data), jotted notes (phrases, key words, quotations), and full field notes (all of these things converted to a running log of observations).

Raw Notes versus Cooked Notes

Raw notes are your data, the information collected at your observation site. Cooked notes are your analysis and interpretation of that data. In "cooking" your notes, you are reflecting on the data, and this act is critical, the heart of your report. Each time you leave the site, you will write up your raw field notes, turning them into cooked notes. You will expand observations; you will reflect, analyze, and interpret; you will add details as appropriate.

Taking Notes

Some general guidelines for taking notes:

✦ Be concrete. You want behavioristic information: what you said, heard, and saw.

✦ If taking verbatim (exact words) notes, mark as such with quotation marks.

◆ If you later recall something, make a note of it but also indicate it was something you recalled, not written down while on site.

◆ When you review your raw notes, you will begin to write analytic notes—your ideas, inferences, and so on. Some may seem obvious to you, even trivial; some may seem a bit far-fetched or improbable. Put them all down.

◆ You will have some personal impressions and feelings, a normal response. Be honest about these responses and keep a record of them. You may need to note some bias later.

◆ If you extend beyond one day, you may have some notes to yourself: questions to help you gather more data, directions telling you to watch for something.

How Long, How Full?

There are no set rules about the length or completeness of your field notes. A rule of thumb, however, says you should have notes full enough to summon up a vivid and accurate picture of the situation and what took place. Let the notes flow. These are private documents, and there is no reason to edit yourself. You will find, though, that most notes are largely pretty dull, very mundane. If they were otherwise, people would be publishing them in a national tabloid.

Keeping Track of Data

Most students use a split-page notebook to record data and respond to it. Raw notes, the actual data, are recorded on the left side; cooked notes, the analysis of data are written on the right side.

Raw Notes	Cooked Notes

After you have reviewed your raw notes and turned them into cooked notes, rank-order your material. What are the most significant and/or frequent features that allow you to draw reasonable conclusions?

Doing this will provide you with different ways of organizing or classifying your data. And should you be doing a longer site project, you will have the significant things to look for in future site visits.

When you have a good sense of the patterns, you are also able to develop tally sheets for coding information on future visits, if required. The tally will save you valuable time and give you a sense of concrete purpose as well.

Topics	Work	Classes	Friends/Gossip	Romance	Parties/Going Out
Male	/ / / /	/ /			/ / / / /
Female		/ / /	/ / / / /	/ / /	/ /

Major Categories of Data

Verbal Behavior:	Topics of conversation, what recurs, among whom, how often, for what purpose, gender differences, age differences, cultural differences
Nonverbal Behavior:	Body language, gestures, facial expressions, gender differences, age differences, cultural differences
Spatial Behavior:	How people place themselves, distance from speaker, gender, age, or cultural differences
Participation:	Who's in charge? Any gatekeeping or exclusion?
Relationships:	Chains of command, avoidance behavior, degrees of intimacy

Major Sites for Gathering Data

In Classrooms.   Keep track of the language used by an instructor and students over the course of a class hour. Later ask yourself:

✦   How much of this language was hands-on, experiential?

✦   How much of it was abstract?

✦   How much information was provided in visual or graphic ways?

✦   What, if anything, was conveyed through nonverbal language?

✦   What, if anything, was conveyed through paralingual (e.g., tone)?

✦ How often did understanding of the language/material depend upon prior knowledge (that is, you already knew "things")?

✦ How often did understanding depend upon cultural knowledge?

✦ How often did understanding depend on educational knowledge?

Keep track of questions or discussion:

✦ How do students "get the floor" or the attention of the instructor?

✦ How do students respond to information? What "messages" come through speech, through body language, facial expressions?

✦ In a discussion, who leads and who follows? What are the "rules" for taking part?

✦ How do you know these "rules"?

✦ How do you know any classroom "rules"?

In Restaurants.   Keep track of the language you or others use in any transaction about getting and paying for your food:

✦ What "rituals" take place when you enter, place a food order, and pay?

✦ How much did you rely on written language? On spoken language?

✦ What nonverbal and paralingual communication took place?

✦ What level of language formality occurred?

✦ Did any language "taboos" occur? Why not?

✦ What knowledge is assumed in this environment? Is it cultural?

✦ If you went to different types of restaurants, what changes in language occurred?

Keep track of the conversation while eating:

✦ What topic(s) emerged?

✦ Did anyone dominate? Obvious leader and followers?

✦ Was anyone excluded?

✦ Were there gender differences in how conversation evolved?

✦ Were there cultural differences?

Keep track of spatial behavior while eating:

✦ Were there differences due to gender, age, or culture?

✦ Did anyone "violate" American expectations of personal space?

In Stores.   Keep track of the language used to get what you needed:

✦ How much did you rely on written language? On spoken language?

✦ Did nonverbal communication take place?

◆   What rituals take place when you check out?

◆   What knowledge is assumed in this environment? Is this cultural knowledge?

When you have the data from your site (the raw notes), review the notes, asking the above questions, and record your thoughts (the cooked notes). Your data will only be as good as your analysis: be honest and thoughtful.

Keeping a Perspective

You know what you are doing, but your subjects don't. Although this may feel as though you are eavesdropping, or worse, keep this perspective on your field activity: Observation of this kind is mostly a matter of self-consciously attending to what goes on every day. Think of how often you orient your consciousness to look, listen, and ask "what's going on here?"; think of how often you ask yourself:

◆   What does he or she mean by that?

◆   Why is he or she using that tone?

◆   Why did he or she say that?

◆   Why doesn't that make any sense to me?

◆   What do I do now?

◆   Why do I have to sit there?

◆   Why is _____ ignoring _____ ?

Your ability to be a skillful observer and careful listener will serve you well.

▬Group Activity▬▬▬▬▬▬▬▬▬▬▬▬▬▬▬▬▬▬

In your small group, compare your data. What similarities and differences turned up? What do you think accounts for either? What is the predominant finding? What was the most surprising finding?

WRITING YOUR FIELD RESEARCH ESSAY

Your instructor will give you specific instructions on how much or how little data to include in your essay. You might focus on only one area (e.g., verbal behavior in a class), or you might extend your focus (e.g., verbal and nonverbal behavior in a store). Various combinations are possible, depending upon the amount of data you collected and page limits for this assignment. Your instructor might also ask you to use a specific format. If not, the following format, typical of those used in social science, can be used.

✦ Introduction

The context of your field study: its purpose, its relevance or importance, its setting, and its subjects

✦ Method

The procedure(s) you followed to collect and analyze data

✦ Results

The presentation of what you found out, with little or no commentary or interpretation

✦ Summary and Discussion

A very brief statement of the results, only to serve as the basis for your discussion of their significance: your analysis, interpretation, exploration of the implication of these results

▬ Peer Response ▬▬▬▬▬▬▬▬▬▬▬▬▬▬▬▬▬▬▬▬▬▬▬▬▬▬▬

With your partner or group, exchange drafts and check for the following:

✦ **Introduction.**   Is the purpose of the research clearly stated? Is its relevance or importance clear (that is, why should readers care about it?) Is the context clear (what's going on?), the setting described? Would a diagram help the reader?

✦ **Method.**   Is the data-gathering process clearly described? Is the analysis process clearly described?

✦ **Results.**   Are the results presented in a straightforward fashion—with no commentary or interpretation?

✦ **Summary and Discussion.**   Are the interpretations, speculations, and so forth reasonable given the data and results? Is the significance of the results clearly presented?

A Note on Editing

Your sentences should be straightforward, crisp, and clear. They should be "active." Don't use passive constructions such as "The study was carried out at Racy D'Lene's Coffee House." Rather, say "I conducted my study at Racy D'Lene's."

A Writer's

Handbook

Working with Sentences

SENTENCE BOUNDARIES

One of the major differences between speaking and writing lies in sentence boundaries. When we speak, we don't always have, or need, boundaries between our sentences. In conversations we have our audience with us. As a result, we are able to run sentences together, blurring the distinction between one thought and the next; we can also utter partial sentences. Our audience can tell us to repeat if necessary, or more likely, understands us without well-formed or correct sentences. Although one might argue that awkward or incomplete sentences can be understood in writing too, the needs and expectations of a reader are different. When we write, we are expected to communicate in complete sentences whenever we write formally, as in school or certain workplace settings. What is appropriate in spoken English—loosely formed and partial sentences—is unacceptable in Standard Written American English.

Fragments

Recognizing sentence boundaries in written English is an important skill. Read the following word groups and decide how you would determine whether or not each constitutes a complete, independent sentence:

A. sitting on the table, a huge calico cat

B. the youngest student in the chemistry class was

C.   Mark, who was the oldest student,

D.   we have been

E.   watching the team shoot baskets, the coach

F.   rock stars

G.   Susan's roommate

H.   the road separating the two farms

It probably didn't take you long to figure out that something important was missing. As readers, we are left hanging, wondering what happened or waiting for an action or a description to follow. The word groups are incomplete. Each group has a subject (who or what) but no predicate (what happened). Now examine these word groups:

I.   looked hungrily at the fish bowl

J.   only thirteen years old

K.   was the best speaker

L.   happy in this neighborhood

M.   believed the kids needed more practice

N.   can have some bad habits

O.   left for England today

P.   was unpaved and dangerous

Again, it probably didn't take you long to realize that you had a partial idea—something important was missing. Now we have the "what happened" or "what about" and have no idea who or what we are talking about. If we join the two groups (e.g., A–I, B–J), however, we have complete sentences.

Checking for complete sentences is far easier in an exercise than it is in paragraphs and complete essays, especially those we have written. Our brain is very efficient; it can read right though and over incomplete sentences. We know what we wanted to say, so we "fill in the blanks," mentally putting in words that aren't on the paper at all. For this reason, you may have to work sentence by sentence, covering up the rest of your paragraph as you go, in order to isolate and find incomplete sentences. Incomplete sentences are known as *fragments*. When we come across a fragment, we need to reread the sentences preceding and following it. Chances are, the fragment will attach to one or the other. We also have the option of completing the fragment, adding information to make a new independent sentence.

ESL Writers

Don't omit the verb:

My brother a good worker.   The river dangerous.
This chapter hard to understand.

Even though a reader understands the meaning of the above word groups, they are incomplete in standard English. Omitting the verb creates a fragment.

PRACTICE   Fragments

Practice 1

Read the following sentences slowly. Test each word group: Is it complete all by itself, making sense? If it isn't, check the word group before and after it. You might want to attach it to another word group, or you might want to form a completely different sentence from it. In either case, you will probably have to add or subtract words as you correct the fragments.

TEENAGE GIRLS: DWELLING ON EMOTIONS

1. It's hardly a surprise. Teenage girls focus on feelings. Just like women. Dealing with stress by focusing heavily on their feelings.

2. And just like their moms. Their emotion-centered coping style makes them less skilled than males at shrugging off hassles.

3. Masculine strategies, such as going after diversions to gain a new perspective on problems. These seem to make teenage boys less vulnerable to stress.

4. Sheri Johnson, a psychologist at Brown University, studied over 300 teenagers. She found both sexes face stress. A similar amount of stress in their environment.

5. Johnson found females reported a greater amount of stress. A gender difference since the environment was the same.

6. The perceived difference in personal distress. It can be accounted for entirely by girls' greater tendency to dwell on emotions. And maybe magnify their emotions.

7. Boys, however, tend to take time out. Reframing their problems after a breather.

8. Should girls learn new strategies? Would they be less "female"? Researchers don't have all the answers. An interesting idea to consider, though.

Practice 2

The following student essay has a number of incomplete sentences. In the opening paragraph, the student might have wanted to use one or two fragments for a special effect, but you should decide how you want to handle them. You might need to add or subtract words as you correct the fragments. And you may disagree with this writer's ideas. But for now, just work on the sentence fragments.

```
                Concerts, Concerts

    Entertainment. The American way of living. Enter-
tainment comes in a variety of different forms. As a
movie, a sports event, a party, and of course, a con-
cert. There are many different types of concerts avail-
able to the American public.
```

Folk music concerts are one type. Music played protesting the black slavery movement. Or also protesting equal rights in the sixties. I often associate folk music as a representative of hard times. A message through song a way of expressing many feelings. People at these concerts express feelings through this type of song. Folk concerts are still around today. Drawing most of their listeners from the 1960s era.

Classical music is another form of music heard at a concert. This type of concert won't be found on the street. Rather in a more formal area. A theater or auditorium. The music played may present a mood somewhat similar to a person belonging to the aristocracy. Most of the music was written in the 1800s. When the aristocracy was well in order. That would probably have something to do with classical music's formality. The music itself is played by a concert orchestra. Or a solo pianist or a quartet of violins. The music provides a rich sound. Enjoyable to the listener's ears. Yet still there is another type of music directing its message towards today's youth.

Rock concerts are very popular. The listeners of rock music are mostly young. The location of rock concerts is almost anywhere. In a field, in a bar, an auditorium, or even in someone's back yard. The rock concert scene is very different than that of folk music or classical. Of course, feelings are brought out in the latter two, but emotions are more apt to be revealed in the loud atmosphere of a rock concert. This type of concert produces more hazards than folk music or classical. Hazards such as drug and alcohol abuse, extremely large crowds, and everyone's friend, general admission.

Rock concerts, classical concerts, and folk music concerts; just a few of the types of concerts available

```
to the American public. They provide a variety in
our American entertainment system, and they're well
worth it.
```

Practice 3

Combine the following into a single paragraph. You may drop out, add, or change the form of some words to make complete and effective sentences.

THE CHOCOLATE CHIP COOKIE: CHEWY MYSTERY SOLVED

A. it was a mystery
B. only the likes of Agatha Christie or Arthur Conan Doyle
C. could have dreamed up this puzzle
D. how do you make chewy chocolate chip cookies
E. how do you make chewy cookies at home

F. oh, it may seem easy enough
G. to solve at first
H. trendy specialty cookie shops produce
I. shops produce the chewy chocolate chip variety all the time
J. most home bakers have discovered
K. the recipe is impossible
L. to duplicate the chewy cookies at home

M. but now the mystery has been solved
N. in the winter issue of *Cook's Illustrated* magazine
O. writer Gail Nagele-Hopkins reveals the secret
P. Nagele-Hopkins tested 40 different variations
Q. the variations on the classic chocolate chip recipe
R. after almost giving up
S. she discovered the secret
T. an extra egg yolk that made the difference
U. the cookie crispy and tender on the outside
V. the cookie soft and chewy on the inside

W. hours after emerging from the oven
X. the cookie remained soft and pliable
Y. the key to the mystery solved

Run-on and Comma Splice

Another sentence boundary problem occurs when we fail to use the appropriate punctuation to indicate where one sentence ends and another begins. In Standard Written English, a capital letter on the first word of the word group indicates that we are beginning a sentence. The end of the sentence is indicated by the appropriate end mark, most often a period or question mark; less frequently, an exclamation point.

A. Tonight's math assignment will take me hours to complete.

B. Where should I meet you?

C. I can't stand all this homework!

When we fail to put an end mark on sentences, we create *run-ons*.

D. The math assignment will take me hours I don't want to even start.

E. Let's meet at the student center in the loft is a good place.

F. The homework makes me nervous letting it go will probably make me sick though.

Run-on sentences are just what they sound like: two or more sentences "running together" with no boundary mark or connector between them. A run-on requires work from the reader, namely, to figure out where one idea ends and another starts. Consequently, most readers become irritated and stop reading. To correct run-ons, you have to first identify the independent sentences:

The math assignment will take me hours I don't want to even start.

Where does the first independent sentence end? How do you know? What end mark would be appropriate at that point? Why? Other options include using a semicolon, a mark that indicates a very close relationship between two sentences, or adding a connector or transition word (see "Ways to Correct"). Try out the different options. Which do you prefer? Why?

Sometimes, writers understand that sentences need to be separated but choose the wrong punctuation mark, most often a comma.

G. Let's meet at the student center, the loft is a good place.

H. The homework makes me nervous, letting it go will probably make me sick though.

When a comma separates two independent sentences without any connecting or transition word, the resulting error is called a *comma splice.* We have many options to correct the error, as shown in the following box.

Ways to Correct

Replace the comma with a period:

Let's meet at the student <u>center. The</u> loft is a good place.

Replace the comma with a semicolon:

Let's meet at the student <u>center; the</u> loft is a good place.

Add a coordinator (and, but, or, for, yet) after the comma:

The homework makes me <u>nervous, but</u> letting it go will probably make me sick.

Add a transition word (however, nonetheless, etc.) before the comma—and add a semicolon at the end of the first sentence, before the transition word:

The homework makes me <u>nervous; however,</u> letting it go will probably make me sick.

The only way to become comfortable with sentence boundaries is to continue working with sentences. The more sentences you read, the more familiar you will be with how sentences look and feel. The more sentences you write, the more familiar you become with the options for making your sentences both complete and clear.

PRACTICE   Run-on and Comma Splice

Practice 1 ■ *Run-on Sentences*

Find the spot where one sentence ends and another begins. Add the appropriate end mark (or semicolon). If you use a period, question mark, or exclamation point, be sure to capitalize the first word of the second sentence. If you use a semicolon, do not capitalize.

YO-YO DIETS

1. Yo-yo dieting endangers physical health it is hard on mental health as well.

2. Yo-yo dieting is linked to higher stress worse mental health then occurs.

3. Dr. John Foreyt of Baylor College of Medicine conducted a study of nearly 500 adults he found people who gained or lost no more than 5 pounds in a year to be psychologically sound.

4. Keeping weight stable was important even obese people were better off emotionally.

5. When the scale climbs, it causes distress weight loss is also stressful however.

6. Foreyt says gradual change toward a goal of a healthier diet is desirable a slim body is not necessarily desirable.

7. Exercise and support groups are positive routes to dieting the yo-yo routine is not a positive route, and in fact, is dangerous.

8. Despite so many people doing it, the yo-yo routine is bad for physical and mental health the body never adjusts or stabilizes.

9. Yo-yo dieting got its name from the old child's toy up and down on a scale is similar to the uneven, up and down motion of the toy.

10. Many Americans engage in yo-yo dieting even if they don't recognize what they're doing their physical and emotional well-being is being sacrificed. (You have a couple of options as to where you divide the sentences.)

Practice 2 ■ *Comma Splices*

When you locate the comma splice, reread the sentences and think about the relationship between them. Review your options for correction.

TUMMY FAT: WATCH OUT FOR STRESS!

1. An inability to cope with stress might increase tummy fat, this would put women at higher risk for heart attacks.

2. People with a high waist-to-hip ratio of fat have a higher risk of heart attacks, researchers also found a link between uncontrollable stress and building up abdominal fat.

3. Yale University scientists learned women who have no special strategies for coping with stress are more likely to have higher waist-to-hip fat ratios, they also secrete more stress hormones.

4. The scientists, both women, note that they can't say for sure stress is the cause of tummy fat, the high hormone secretions, however, can raise the risk of heart attacks.

5. The tummy has more receptors for the stress hormones than do other parts of the body, given this fact, researchers speculate that poor coping strategies may promote both tummy fat and coronaries.

6. Should women start worrying even more, well, the researchers note that far more research is needed.

7. Because men have been the primary heart attack candidates, women have not been the subject of many studies, the results of any study thus have to be speculative. (Read carefully. Only one of the commas separates two independent sentences.)

8. Research studies are very expensive, scientists often have to write grants for funding to run them.

9. Writing grants takes time and energy, there's no certainty of receiving any money either.

10. Women's groups, however, are pressing for more studies dealing with women's health, they are making some progress but not nearly fast enough.

Practice 3 ■ *Run-on and Comma Splice*

As you read this student essay, check for sentences that are run together without any punctuation or have a comma (without any connecting or transition word) separating them. Make the necessary corrections, including substituting the appropriate end mark on some sentences.

Why Are They Rated Anyway?

I found it ridiculous that on the opening night of White Men Can't Jump almost the entire audience consisted of young teens. The movie has an R rating, doesn't that require that you be seventeen or accompanied by a parent or adult guardian. There were no parents or adults with these kids. A movie is rated to provide a standard as to what one should see and what one should not see. Then, with the restrictions set, isn't is necessary that an adult be concerned as to what their child or children are seeing.

Do parents not care what their children see. Movies that are rated R have adult situations and language, are teens now considered adult enough to attend, without someone over seventeen with them. The theaters allows these adolescents in a movie, containing things such as sex, as long as someone older buys their tickets. Parents need to understand the impact that these movies have on their child, when a young teen sees things such as sex in a movie are they really understanding the real meaning in some movies there are mind games that people play, can an adolescent comprehend that.

The Motion Picture Association of America has very set standards as to who can attend the movies they put out. In 1984, they added a new rating to their list PG-13 means that some material may be objectionable for viewers under thirteen. This should provide for the needs of those ranging between the R movies intended for adults and the PG movies which to them are dumb, boring, and childish.

Children today are growing up fast enough anyway is it necessary for them to attend an R movie alone too? Parents are busy today, they have plenty to do but do they have to drop their kids off at a theater and return later to pick them up? There are never enough hours in a day to tend to everything but once in awhile take time out to go to the movies with your

```
children see what they find so interesting about these
R rated movies.
```

Practice 4 ■ *Sentence Boundaries*

Correct the following sentences. You'll find run-ons, comma splices, and fragments.

1. I remember my first day of lifting, I did squats with 125 pounds.

2. You learn to compete with your friends. Not only through sports but also in class.

3. I was addicted and continued lifting, my strength and size increased.

4. I used to get tired and spend a lot of extra time sleeping. Valuable time in which I could have been doing schoolwork.

5. The pride a child has when he surprises his parents with something he made in school, or even a gift for them.

6. A friend of mine told me to come to the phys ed center and start lifting weights it sounded like a good idea so I did.

7. My parents had taken care of me for years, it was time to return the favor.

8. I will not stop either I want to be bigger, more muscular.

9. In high school it was always never, hopefully in college it will be now.

10. If it's not enough that it's against the law, or puts lives in danger, maybe the fact that it will cost a person dearly for driving intoxicated.

BEYOND SENTENCE BOUNDARIES

Sometimes sentences, although technically complete or correct, have other major problems. As readers, we trip over them in some way. Since we want readers to understand our ideas clearly and efficiently on first reading, we need to review sentences for more than their boundaries.

Misplaced Modifiers

Read the following sentences carefully. What's out of place or doesn't make sense?

1. Out of the corner of his eye, the horse jumped the gate.
2. Half asleep from a night on the town, the assignments never got done.
3. Flying high on octane, Lee pushed the Fiat into overdrive.
4. Hanging by a toe, Leslie found her sock.
5. While drinking beer, the TV blew up in the middle of the football game.
6. Trimmed in black lace, Ellie found the perfect gown.
7. At 6'11" tall, the school board was skeptical of Elliot's playing on the grade school team.

Although each word group that starts a sentence provides good information, that information is physically misplaced. The person or thing being described is not the next word in the sentence.

Feeling low, Angela slammed her locker and left.

Who's feeling low? Angela is. In this case, the introductory descriptive information is followed by the person described. In English sentences, we want the description next to the person or thing being described. When we fail to use this arrangement, our readers are distracted—and in some cases, annoyed.

Return to the sentences with misplaced introductory material. There are different ways to repair the sentence:

1. As Jon watched out of the corner of his eye, the horse jumped the gate.

   The horse jumped the gate while John watched out of the corner of his eye.

2. Half asleep from a night on the town, Jon never got his assignments done.

3. Lee pushed the Fiat, flying high on octane, into overdrive.

Make the corrections for sentences 4, 5, 6, and 7. Then try the following sentences, which have the same problem of misplaced description. Remember to ask yourself these questions: Who or what is being described? Is that description next to the person or thing being described?

PRACTICE   Beyond Sentence Boundaries

Practice 1

1. That house is being torn down across the street.

2. The audience can hear the singer in the back of the auditorium.

3. I planted those flowers yesterday in the boxes.

4. The boy chased the dog in his Sunday clothes.

5. Hanging by a thread, Lee found his shirt.

6. Feeling sick, the medication was needed.

7. Remembering the penalty, there was a instant stop to the idea forming in my mind.

8. Returning to the huddle, the crowd yelled at the quarterback.

9. As a member of the army reserve, it would be in my best interest to get my officer's commission.

10. After careful consideration of these criteria, my decision has been made.

11. Because it is viewed as a prime indicator of emotional satisfaction, there is a growing emphasis on sex in a marriage.

12. Because of an inability to see a long-term goal, his recent past has been day-to-day survival.

13. Divorced and recently fired from her job, the bank considered her a poor risk.

14. As the first writer to win the prestigious award, his books are now selling well.

15. Finding no fault with the argument, the loan was approved.

16. Priced at $25, some bookstores have sold out the newest John Grishman novel.

17. At seven feet tall, the NBA is wondering if the basket should be raised for today's youngest and tallest players.

18. Suffering from a fear of heights, the tourist attraction nonetheless draws them.

19. Originally known as Archie Leach, the movies changed the name to Cary Grant.

20. Found guilty, the judge sentenced the shoplifting trio to months of marking price tags in the store they cheated.

Practice 2

Some of the modifiers are misplaced and need to be moved. Draw a circle around the misplaced phrases and make the correct placement either through drawing an arrow or rewriting the sentence.

THE TRUTH ABOUT CATS AND DOGS

Wondering about a recent myth, cats and dogs resembling their owners intrigued me. After looking through our library, researchers at the University of California, Berkeley, say cat and dog owners claim their furry little friends' personalities bear a distinct resemblance to their own. Sociable individuals, for example, tend to describe their pets as more extroverted than other pets, while eggheads think their feline or canine companions are smarter than average. Signing their pawprints to Christmas cards and proudly displaying their photos, researchers may be on to something. Projecting their own personalities onto pets, researchers believe is the real situation. Outgoing folks may simply prefer social breeds suggests one Berkeley researcher. Or perhaps pets get rewarded for behaving like their owners?

Adapted from *Psychology Today*

Another Kind of Misplaced Modifier

As you already know, a modifier should be placed where readers can easily determine what it describes. Sometimes, misplaced modifiers are very difficult to spot because they don't create a silly or ungrammatical sentence. The problem, nonetheless, creates a situation where the reader can't be sure about the meaning the writer intended. Even one word can totally change the meaning. Suppose someone said to you: I love *only* you. What do you take this to mean? But what if someone said: *Only* I love you. Now what meaning do you take from it, besides being a bit miffed at that *only I* statement? The placement of one word, *only,* changes the meaning entirely. Placement of modifiers, therefore, is critical to the meaning you intend. Modifiers are usually placed next to or very close to the word or words they describe.

Modifiers with the most potential for misplacement are those showing when and how: today, yesterday, often, only, nearly, hardly, barely, simply, just, almost, generally. When you use these modifiers, and others like them, you must check on their location and make sure that the modifier is describing the right word. Sometimes, all you have to do is move the modifier; other times, you must reword the sentence. For example:

My landlady told me *yesterday* our rent was due.

Did she tell you yesterday or was the rent due yesterday? How many ways could you correct the problem? In the practice that follows, locate the modifier problem and correct it.

Practice 1

1. Our teacher tells us what her expectations are regularly.

2. My math teacher said there are new problems in computers yesterday.

3. She only bought that car for $500.

4. We barely read 30 pages before the lights went out.

5. A person whose brain is damaged generally has language problems.

6. My sister called and said she would go to Africa today.

7. She almost talked for two hours before I had the courage to hang up.

8. I read that hamsters are only pregnant for two weeks.

Practice 2

Circle the misplaced modifier and move it to the appropriate place. Rewrite any sentence that cannot be corrected by a simple movement of a word or phrase.

Charlie the Tuna as Jerk

Some guys pride themselves on doing things other folks consider disgusting regularly. Like almost entering belching contests every year. Appearing on the <u>Ricki Lake Show</u>. Or eating pieces of tough, smoke-flavored beef known as "jerky." Next time those weird urges strike, reach for Ahi Jerky. Instead of hardly any fat, ordinary beef jerky carries four grams of fat nearly, Ahi is a naturally smoked tuna jerky that's fat free. Simply better for you, nutritionists believe Ahi is the jerky of the future. And yes, it's dolphin

safe. It only has a fishy smell when you first open
the package. What's more, barely different, beef jerky
and tuna jerky have similar texture and spices.

ESL Writers

Most English modifiers occur before the word they describe,
not after it:

The bread white has flavor little—The *white* bread has little
flavor.
My cousin favorite left today—My *favorite* cousin left today.

Parallelism

As readers, we can more easily absorb information when it is presented in similar forms. As you read the following sentences, note which
are easier to follow and understand.

A. I like to walk, jog, and riding my bike.
I like to walk, jog, and bike.
I liking walking, jogging, and biking.

B. She could be a nurse, teacher, or practice law.
She could be a nurse, teacher, or lawyer.

You probably concluded quickly that sentences where words were structurally alike were much easier to read: to walk, (to) jog, and (to) bike;
walking, jogging, and biking; nurse, teacher, and lawyer.

When words or phrases are put into the same grammatical forms,
such as the *-ing* on the verbs *walk, jog,* and *bike,* we say they have parallel structure. Examine the following sentences and find words or
phrases that can be put into parallel form. Then make the necessary
changes.

Practice 1

1. He loved playing golf and to go sailing.

2. With the recent Dracula movies, Alex likes to see one and then going out for a bite.

3. Sam knew how to drive teachers crazy: he always cracked gum, was chewing pencils, and would light the wastebasket on fire.

4. Shopping and to eat out were Lyn's favorite activities.

5. As a running back, Jeff had great stamina and could outrun anyone.

6. Terry hoped to play left field and wanted to bat first of players.

7. Leo thinks to be a lawyer is better than practicing medicine.

8. Chris tried teaching and to be a singer as careers.

Practice 2

Make these sentences parallel:

1. A trip to the supermarket can be fun and a good education for young children.

2. Preschool children, for example, can name colors, shapes, and point out alphabet letters on boxes and signs.

3. As the children ride in the cart or walking along, adults can ask them questions about different products or what the produce are.

4. Older children can try out their math skills by weighing produce and to figure out what the different prices will be.

5. They can also compare prices and to determine which product is the bargain.

6. Even at checkout, children can learn how to sort products or packing groceries to avoid damage or leaking.

7. Youngsters can also learn to be patient and practice politeness in checkout lines.

8. To work with small coins and learning the value of money is another benefit.

Practice 3

As you read this article from *USA Today,* notice how the author used parallel structure. Underline those words or word groups that use parallel structure.

HOW TO GET SOME SHUT-EYE

Suffering from insomnia? Counting the cracks on the ceiling? Here's what the experts recommend to help you get a good night's sleep:

Go to bed and get up at the same time each day.

Avoid caffeine after 2 P.M.

Exercise in the late afternoon but no later than three hours before bedtime.

Don't do anything too stimulating before bed.

Don't use alcohol as a sedative. It leaves the brain restless later in the night.

Stanford researcher William Dement's studies show that if you miss sleep one night, your body keeps a record of the "sleep debt." If the debt isn't paid back soon, you'll start nodding off in the day. Sleep debt accrues until it's paid back. Most people pay back on the weekends by sleeping or napping.

Practice 4

Make the phrases parallel. There may be more than one way to correct each sentence.

1. Last month the workers had to attend a program about sex discrimination and sexually harassing people.

2. The speaker first showed a video and she then was leading a discussion about the situations viewed in the video.

3. The company manager learned that most of the workers didn't know what sexual harassment was, where getting information about it was located, or where to go if they needed help or if they were wanting to talk.

4. The workers discussed solutions for discrimination at work, including to admit that it exists, attending additional programs, and to keep an open line of communication.

5. Although many employees were skeptical of the program at first, they discovered to learn about discrimination and finding ways to address it was helpful.

A Special Parallelism Problem

Some sentences require a bit more study and work. Read the following and look for the comparison, of what to what:

A pair of $200 gym shoes won't last any longer than a boy who buys a $75 pair.

Who or what is being compared? Shoes to shoes? Person to person? We need a parallel: shoe to shoe or boy to boy. Since shoes are the comparison (we can assume the boy will last!), we can make the sentence parallel in this way:

A pair of $200 gym shoes won't last any longer than a pair of $75 gym shoes.

Now try this sentence:

I like my math teacher's lectures better than sitting in English class.

Who or what is being compared? How can you restructure the sentence so that like things are compared? Lecture to lecture or teacher to teacher?

Practice 5

Restructure these sentences so that the parallelism is correct:

1. A good student hits the books daily and is better off than cram sessions at the last minute.

2. Los Angeles' problems seem worse than living in New York City.

3. Going shopping with my sister is more fun than my mother.

4. Cross-country skiing is better exercise than if you were to walk.

5. Anyone who takes up smoking has a better chance of lung cancer than not smoking.

6. I like my brother's attitude more than being around my sister.

7. He was happier with his job at McDonald's than to be a clerk at Best Buy.

8. Going to the party with my cousin is more interesting than my usual date.

9. A Big Mac for lunch adds up to about 56 fat grams more than a person having a grilled chicken sandwich.

10. Someone who works on an essay over time is better than to write it at the last minute.

Another Parallelism Challenge

Some pairs of connecting words demand parallel structure:

either-or   neither-nor   both-and   not only–but also

The problem can be solved with *either* a formula *or* creative thinking.

Neither the book *nor* a help-line will solve my computer problem.

Mark enjoys *both* surfing *and* mountain biking.

The work was *not only* dull *but also* endless.

ESL Writers

either-or = singular verb   both-and = plural verb
neither-nor = singular verb   not only–but also
                                     = singular or plural

Practice 6

Circle the pair of connecting words; underline the words they connect. Then rewrite the sentences with parallel forms. Often, you will reduce the number of words needed.

1. Both swimming and to play tennis are favorite hobbies in summer.

2. Neither sport is very expensive nor is it hard to learn.

3. I can not only have fun but also I am getting exercise.

4. My brother enjoys both skiing and to play football.

5. Either he finds the money for skiing or earning it as needed.

6. My sister is either on the phone or she is at the computer.

7. Neither learning to drive nor cooking is much fun with a parent in charge.

8. Not only was the experience frightening but also it could be dangerous.

Practice 7

The late Michael Dorris, an American Indian writer, writes about being American. As you read this paragraph from "Americans All," underline the parallel structures that you find and explain how parallelism provides both clarity and power to his sentences. Note that for effect, Dorris also uses fragments, something professional writers do for emphasis.

The answer is clear: to be Americans means to be not the clone of the people next door. I fly back from any homogenous country, from a place where every person I see is blond, or black or belongs to only one religion, and then disembark at JFK. I revel in the cadence of many accents, catch a ride to the city with a Nigerian-American or Russian-American cab driver. Eat Thai food at a Greek restaurant next to a table of Chinese-American conventioneers from Alabama. Get directions from an Iranian-American cop and drink a cup of Turkish coffee served by a Navajo student at Fordham who's majoring in Japanese literature. Argue with everybody about everything. I'm home.

From *Paper Trail*

CHAPTER 12

Connecting Ideas

COORDINATION

Writing better sentences may require joining ideas from several sentences. Short sentences that share a relationship can often be joined by a word or punctuation mark that makes the relationship clearer and more focused. As you read the following sentences, (1) isolate the two independent sentences, and (2) circle the word connecting the two sentences. What is the relationship between the two sentences? How does the connecting word (called a coordinator) help a reader grasp the relationship quickly? What punctuation mark is used with the connecting word? Why? How does it help a reader?

A. Jon dislikes sociology, but he has to take it for his major.

B. Lynn plans to be a lawyer, so she's majoring in "talk."

C. Susan decided to go to summer school, and she is really busy.

D. Mark left California, for he saw wonderful opportunities in Colorado.

E. We asked the principal not to punish the class, but he ignored us.

F. Anton will either drag hoses around, or he will put in a watering system.

G. Ellen ate two dozen chocolate chip cookies, yet she never gained a pound.

Connector (Coordinator)	Meaning
and	Addition
but	Contrast
yet	Contrast
for	Reason, idea in second sentence explains idea in first sentence
so	Cause and effect
or	Option or alternative

Connecting sentences with one of these connectors is called *coordinating*. It means that we have two sentences, each capable of standing alone, and each conveying equally important ideas. When you began speaking your native language, one of the first sentence combinations you made was with *and* or *but*. And you might have also used these two connectors for your first written sentence combinations as well. The coordinators are endlessly useful. We use *yet* and *for* less often in our speech and writing, but for academic and business writing, you will find them handy alternatives.

Although these coordinators are most commonly used to connect two sentences, we sometimes use *and* and *but* as the first word of the sentence.

> Jonathan is a great guy. And I really mean that.
>
> Krista is a comic. But I can only take so much.

Using the coordinators in this way gives emphasis to the meaning. However, don't overuse this structure, especially in academic or business writing.

One more caution: We use these coordinators not only to connect sentences but also as sentence parts.

> The man is both a doctor and a lawyer.
>
> His weight is okay but not his height.
>
> She'll paint the garage or clean the basement tomorrow.

In the following example, we have one subject and one verb, a single sentence. The word *and* connects sentence parts, not complete sentences. There is *no* comma.

> s   v
> The man is both a doctor and a lawyer.

In the next example, we have two sets of subject and verb, two independent sentences. *And* connects two sentences. We need the comma.

$$\overset{S}{\text{The}} \overset{V}{\text{man is}} \text{ a doctor, and } \overset{S}{\text{he}} \overset{V}{\text{also is}} \text{ a lawyer.}$$

Be sure you have two independent sentences on either side of the coordinator *before* you insert a comma.

PRACTICE   Coordination

Practice 1

Join the two sentences with an appropriate coordinator. Be sure to add the comma before each coordinator. For example:

Leo left the house early. His work wasn't done.
Leo left the house early, but his work wasn't done.

THEIR JUST DESSERTS

1. No amount of cash buys you a seat at the exclusive Barton Bistro.

   Avoiding food fights in the lunchroom might get you in.

2. Good behavior earns a seat at Clara Barton Elementary School's

   most exclusive restaurant. Kids are eager to enter.

3. The restaurant features classical music, a maître d' in tuxedo, real

   silverware, real beef, and ice cream. Kids find it a treat.

4. Principal Leonard Schwartz initiated the elite eatery in the school's

   art room. He believed kids needed rewards for good behavior in the

   lunchroom.

5. A group of 29 second graders found their principal in black tails. He handed them menus and ushered them to their tables. He treated them with the utmost respect.

6. Five waitresses served the children lunch. The children could have beef. They could have pasta casserole.

7. Barton Bistro patrons drink out of cups, not cartons. They use real silverware, not "sporks," a combination fork and spoon made of plastic.

8. The food comes from the regular school cafeteria. There's no special budget.

Practice 2

Examine this student's paragraph for use of coordinators and appropriate punctuation with them. Make any needed corrections.

Week 1

My first week of classes has seemed like an exercise program. Before classes began, I had to buy my books and supplies. Thus I had equipment and I was ready for the first drill. When I started my classes, I needed to find my way around and get used to my teachers. This is what I refer to as my warm-up period. I had to walk up hills so my legs got a workout. I also had to walk for miles between classes. I would run at times for I feared walking in late. And at times, I would end up sitting in front of the teacher or in the worst seat in the class, one behind a pillar. I thus got to stretch out my body or at the very least, I got to stretch my neck a lot. But the final aspect is a continuous process. I must make it a rou-

```
tine to get to my classes on time and never give up
for like an exercise program I will become useless to
myself if I cease the routine.
```

Practice 3

Use the following information from the Center for Substance Abuse Prevention to develop a paragraph. You will need to add information from your own observation and experience. Try to use all the coordinators at least once.

THE ALCOHOL THREAT

College students in the United States spend $5.5 billion a year on alcohol.

One study revealed alcohol is one of the major reasons for absenteeism from class.

The same study showed that 25 percent of student deaths are associated with alcohol.

Alcohol was involved in 90 percent of college rapes.

In the 1991 College Alcohol survey, 70 percent of the college administrators responding believed alcohol contributes significantly to campus violence.

Alcohol is a factor in 40 percent of student academic problems.

More than 7 percent of the 1996 graduating class will drop out of school because of drinking.

Out of 12 million college students, more than 250,000 will eventually die of alcohol-related causes.

COORDINATING WITH A SEMICOLON

Semicolons sometimes seem mysterious. They're not. And they're downright useful, especially in academic writing. However, because students sometimes have half-learned rules for this punctuation mark, you're better off going "blank" and starting new here. First, study these sentences and determine how semicolons are used:

The cartoon character Bart Simpson drives some teachers crazy; he is "hell on wheels" in school.

Homer Simpson lost his job at the nuclear energy plant; he fell asleep at the switch.

Why don't we need a coordinator or other connecting word to make the meaning clear? What other punctuation mark could replace the semicolon?

The semicolon separates two independent sentences; on either side of the semicolon, the word group can stand completely alone and make sense. Because the relationship between the two sentences is so clear, we don't need a connecting word.

PRACTICE   Semicolons

Practice 1

Join these sentences with a semicolon. Remember, you must have two independent sentences, one on either side of the semicolon. You can change the placement of information, as well as add or delete words. You can substitute *he, Thomas, the founder,* and so on. Your goal is two closely related sentences, easily understood by a reader.

BURGERS AND DIPLOMAS

1. Dave Thomas is the founder of a U.S. corporation known to most kids, Wendy's. The corporation has more than $3.6 billion in annual sales.

2. Most people have seen Thomas on television. Thomas does the ads for his restaurant chain.

3. Thomas appears to be a "regular" guy. He's a little overweight, of average height, and white-haired.

4. Thomas, however, is no regular guy. He was a high school dropout who founded a billion-dollar business.

5. Thomas has received six honorary university degrees. Last week Dave Thomas received his high school diploma.

6. He dropped out of school at age 15 to work full-time in a restaurant. Forty-five years later, he passed the GED exam in Florida, his home state.

7. Thomas urges students to stay in high school. He believes good jobs today demand the knowledge and skills learned in high school and beyond.

Practice 2

Join independent sentences with a semicolon where it seems useful to do so. Remember, the relationship between the idea in the first sentence and that in the second sentence must be perfectly clear to the reader. Use other coordinators as needed. You may substitute *he, Page, judge.* Your goal is a clear, easily read paragraph.

HERE COMES THE JUDGE

Pro football Hall of Famer Alan Page has a new uniform.

Page now wears the robes of a Minnesota Supreme Court justice.

Page, 47, is the first black to serve on the state's highest court.

Page won the seat with 47 percent of the vote in the November 1992 election.

He invited 140 fourth graders to Monday's swearing-in.

He told them, "Success comes with hard work."

He told them, "It comes with preparation."

"And when you do prepare, then you can achieve your hopes and dreams," said Page.

Page played for the Minnesota Vikings and the Chicago Bears.

Page earned his law degree in 1978 from the University of Minnesota.

He retired from football two years later.

He worked in private practice and as a prosecutor.

OTHER TRANSITIONS BETWEEN SENTENCES

We have one more way to join two independent sentences—a set of transition words. Among the most useful of these transition words are the following:

for example   nevertheless   therefore
in fact   however   thus
as a matter of fact   on the other hand   consequently
for instance

moreover
additionally
furthermore

Paul is a perfect student; moreover, he's a great athlete.

Julie lost her scholarship; therefore, she's out of school.

Alan wants to join swing choir; however, he has to work.

Dr. Inkwell gives tough assignments; for example, I have ten chapters to read before tomorrow.

Notice the punctuation used with these transition words. Read each sentence slowly and determine how the punctuation works to help the reader.

What information does each of the transition words provide for the reader?

PRACTICE   Transition Words

Practice 1

With your group or writing partner, develop 10 sentences using the transition words listed. Note your reason for using each transition word. How does it help the reader?

Practice 2

Use the following information to construct a paragraph. Use as many transition words as appropriate.

GENTLE GIANTS TAKE TIME TO TUTOR

Jeff Zgonina is gone.

The Purdue defensive lineman is not forgotten.

Zgonina, Big Ten Defensive Player of the Year, graduated in December.

He wanted to leave his college community with something more than football memories.

Last September he organized a tutoring program to help students with special needs.

He called the program Gentle Giants.

"I wanted to leave something behind that I started up," says the 6-2, 270-pound Zgonina.

"Everybody thinks football players just want to play football and not do anything else."

"This is one way to show that we want to help people in the community."

Zgonina and 20 teammates participated in the program, which has been an overwhelming success.

ANOTHER WAY TO USE TRANSITION WORDS

You can also use the transition words this way:

Jon wants to play tennis. However, his left knee is wrecked.

Sara lost the bet. Consequently, she owes Lee $50.

You'll have to read that chapter. Additionally, you have 20 problem sets to solve before tomorrow.

A period marks the end of the first independent sentence. Then, the transition word links that sentence to the one that follows. The period has replaced the semicolon, but the comma following the transition word stays put. As you read, note how you slow down at the comma. The comma acts as an advanced organizer: something important is coming up.

PRACTICE

Add an appropriate transition word to the second sentence, and in some cases, a third or fourth sentence. You want to show the relationship between ideas and help the reader understand them more clearly. Be sure to add a comma after the transition word.

YOUR BRAIN: USE IT OR LOSE IT

1. Certain nerve cells in the brain are short in uneducated people. These cells are longer in people who are educated. People who continue to challenge themselves intellectually have longer brain cells.

2. UCLA researchers examined the brains of 20 people who had died. They learned that dendrites, threadlike portions of nerve cells, were longer in people who remained intellectually active.

3. Researchers analyzed the life histories of the people they studied. They don't know if people with longer dendrites were more likely to attend college, or if going to college made the dendrites grow longer. They believe the latter interpretation is correct.

4. Animal studies provided earlier information on nerve cells. Researchers base their beliefs on these studies. Skeptics can always say, "People aren't rats."

5. Scientists, however, believe in the animal studies. They believe in the link with human studies. They say if you put an animal in an enriched environment, you see an increase in dendritic material and enhanced problem solving. If you move a rat to an impoverished environment, the material decreases.

REVIEW: JOINING INDEPENDENT SENTENCES

When You Want to:	Coordinator	Transition Word
Add an Idea	and	additionally moreover furthermore
Show Contrasting Idea	but yet	on the other hand however nevertheless
Show Cause or Effect	for so	therefore as a result consequently thus
Show Alternative	or	
Show Time Relation		first meanwhile then next last

REVIEW: PUNCTUATION JOINING INDEPENDENT SENTENCES

Comma Before Connecting Word: Coordinators

Semicolon Before and Comma After: Transition Words

Semicolon Alone

PRACTICE   Using Various Methods

Practice 1

Try out different coordinators as you connect the following ideas. You may add or delete words as necessary to make a clear, easily read sentence. There are several ways in which to make the connections.

SLIPS OF THE TONGUE

The slip of tongue could have been disastrous.

Professor Daniel Wegner wrote a note about a change of lunch plans to a colleague he didn't like.

He intended to write, "I hope you can dine without me."

He wrote, "I hope you can die without me."

Wegner caught his error before sending the note.

How often has something rude been said when the offender was trying extra hard to be polite?

How often has one been surprised by such a mistake?

The tendency to say or do exactly the opposite of what we intend is a human frailty.

Ever since Freud, psychoanalysts have believed such slips were by-products of the subconscious mind.

Wegner and his colleagues have laboratory experiments that support Freud's hypothesis.

Other psychologists disagree with the theory.

They contend that under conditions of stress or failure, a lot of ideas pop into the mind at the same time.

In this confusion, errors of thinking result.

It doesn't mean there's a lot of unconscious activity.

Wegner and his colleagues believe people are more sensitive to their suppressed ideas than to things consciously being considered.

People can suppress a thought under normal conditions.

They have trouble controlling their thoughts when they are under pressure or have other things on their mind.

They end up blurting out the very thoughts they want to suppress.

Psychologists say there are ways to keep our thoughts in check while dealing with stress or pressure.

One way is to stop trying to suppress unwanted thoughts.

Practice 2

Remember, there are several ways in which to connect the sentences.

GARTH BROOKS: THE PRICE OF STARDOM

Before fame made it impractical, Garth Brooks hung around the stage after his show.

He would sign autographs.

These weren't ordinary autographs.

Women would ask him to sign their undergarments or parts of their bodies.

Garth says he doesn't understand why women find him attractive.

He wonders if they are blind.

He says there are some superhunks.

He is not one of them.

Garth notes he is "pale as a sheet," has three chins, and is losing his hair.

He says if he were a girl, he'd be looking for someone like George Strait.

Garth says the attention he gets is weird.

The attention is also flattering.

From the time he started performing, he attracted women fans.

Garth admits he likes to flirt.

He likes to make love with his music in front of women.

Garth's wife says he has always been a sexual person.

She believes it was his ego making him want to conquer women.

It didn't mean anything to him.

Garth's wife finally threatened to leave him.

The most controversial song on Garth's first album was "Everytime That It Rains," about a one-night stand.

Garth won't say if it is true or not.

He will say that the woman in that song will know who wrote it.

There were two other writers besides Brooks.

Because of his wife, he no longer autographs women's body parts or underwear.

Garth admits temptation is still a problem for him.

Because his music is sexual, it always pushes those buttons.

CHAPTER 13

Subordination

When you coordinated ideas, you created two independent sentences. When you subordinate an idea, however, you create a single sentence with both an independent and a dependent part:

Even though Josie can be really annoying, I like her.

This sentence resulted from two ideas being joined:

Josie can be really annoying.
I like Josie.

The connector (called a subordinator) provides the reader with the relationship between the two ideas. In this case, the writer chose *even though* to express a contrast. The introductory part, "Even though Josie can be really annoying," cannot stand alone; it is dependent upon the second part, "I like her," to complete its meaning. If you cover "I like her" with your hand, you'll quickly conclude that you're left hanging—waiting for the rest of the idea. Working together, however, the two parts provide a reader with good information, efficiently and clearly.

Read through the following sentences and identify (1) the independent part, (2) the dependent (subordinate) part, and (3) the key word in the dependent part—the word or word group showing the relationship between (1) and (2). Note the punctuation: Where does it consistently come? How does it help the reader?

A. Unless my teacher explains problems clearly, I'm lost.
B. When my teacher explains problems clearly, I understand.

C. If my teacher explains problems clearly, I understand.

D. Although my teacher explains problems clearly, I'm lost.

E. Because my teacher explains problems clearly, I'm doing fine.

F. As long as my teacher explains problems clearly, I'm okay.

G. Once my teacher explains problems clearly, I understand.

You can reverse the order of the dependent and independent parts. Notice the position of the key word, the one showing the relationship between the parts, when you reverse order. Also notice the punctuation. What has happened? Can you think of some reasons for this change?

I'm lost unless my teacher explains problems clearly.

I understand once my teacher explains problems clearly.

Whether you place the dependent part first or second is your choice. But you will want some variety in your sentences, so familiarity with both arrangements is important.

PRACTICE   Subordination

With your group or writing partner, discuss the following sentences. Indicate which part is independent and which is dependent. Note the key word linking the two parts. What is its meaning? How does it help us understand the relationship between the two parts?

BART SIMPSON: HERO OF THE 80s

A. Even though Bart Simpson has been one of the most popular cartoon characters of the 1990s, many people find his antics too obnoxious.

B. Because Bart says and does things that many kids would like to do, he's a popular figure with teens and young adults.

C. Some psychologists believe Bart Simpson is popular because he's the underachiever, the kind of kid most teachers ignore.

D. If a few political analysts are right, "The Simpsons" satirizes the 1980s and the Reagan administration.

E. We're all in trouble if Homer Simpson represents the typical nuclear plant employee—totally inept.

F.   Whenever Bart gets a bright idea, trouble follows.

G.   When the police come to the Simpsons' home, the neighbors can only sigh and say, "About time."

H.   Although Marge Simpson often shows compassion and common sense, most viewers are too absorbed with her massive blue hair to notice.

I.   The baby sucks her pacifier more fiercely while any crisis is under way.

J.   Since Bart is the nontypical child, he calls his father "Homer."

COMMON SUBORDINATORS			
Time	**Place**	**Condition**	**Cause**
when whenever before after during while as soon as	where wherever	although even though if once	because since

Practice 1

Add content to the following subordinators. Think about the meaning of the subordinator before you add material. Remember, you need a subject and verb in both the dependent and independent part.

Example: While _____ , _____ .

While Jon studied, I watched the ball game.

1. After _____ , _____ .

2. Even though _____ , _____ .

3. Since _____ , _____ .

4. Whenever _____ , _____ .

5. If _____, _____.

6. _____ because _____.

7. _____ while _____.

8. _____ before _____.

9. _____ once _____.

10. _____ when _____.

Practice 2

Choose five subordinators and construct a sentence using each one. Remember, you'll have two parts to the sentence: one dependent and one independent. If your sentence starts with the dependent part, be sure to add a comma at the end of the dependent part.

Practice 3

With your group or writing partner, write a brief paragraph or two describing or explaining a favorite television show. Use as many subordinated sentences as appropriate. Underline the subordinator and, if one is needed, the comma.

Practice 4

Combine the following sentences into a paragraph. Review the common subordinators before you begin, and then, as appropriate to your meaning, use some subordinated sentences in your paragraph. You may have to add or delete some words.

FAT CHANCE

The common medical assumption says that women are generally fatter than men.

This assumption may be a slur based upon cultural bias rather than on good science.

An advanced technique for dissecting the human body electronically can measure fat and muscle content slice by slice.

This technique has found no real differences between normal males and females.

Yale University researchers are working on this question.

Women all over America are eager for further results.

MORE SUBORDINATION: EMBEDDING

We can join sentences in many different ways. One of the most useful is called "embedding." What happens in the following pairs of sentences? How does one part "embed" itself into the other? How do the commas around the embedded part help the reader?

A.   Stephen King has a large following among teenage readers.

B.   Stephen King is famous for his horror fiction.

Stephen King, who is famous for his horror fiction, has a large following among teenage readers.

Stephen King, who has a large following among teenage readers, is famous for his horror fiction.

A.   Bart Simpson is irreverent and mouthy.

B.   Bart Simpson is a terrible role model for kids.

Bart Simpson, who is a terrible role model for kids, is irreverent and mouthy.

Bart Simpson, who is irreverent and mouthy, is a terrible role model for kids.

We can get even more variety out of embedded sentences. Note how we can simplify and move the embedded part:

Bart Simpson, who is a terrible role model for kids, is irreverent and mouthy.

Bart Simpson, a terrible role model for kids, is irreverent and mouthy.

A terrible role model for kids, Bart Simpson is irreverent and mouthy.

We'll look at these variations in more detail shortly. First, we'll review ways of embedding one sentence into another.

WAYS OF EMBEDDING

Who, Whom, Whose   Refer to people

That, Which   Refer to objects, ideas, things, places

Stephen King, who lives in Maine, is a prolific writer.

Stephen King, whose best-selling novels have been made into movies, is considered the master of horror.

Stephen King, whom I would like to meet, writes scary stuff.

The book that I liked best was *Cujo*.

Cujo, which I liked best, has left me with a fear of dogs.

Noting Punctuation

Notice what happens when *that* and *which* begin the embedded part. Why are there commas around "which I liked best"? Why can't we set off "that I liked best"? What is its relationship to the rest of the sentence? What rule can you formulate for when we need commas?

I want the book that is on the table.

The book that's on the table is the one I want.

Which book? Any book?

Sometimes, we don't even bother to put *that* or *that is* into the sentence:

I want the book on the table.

However, grammatically, *that* is understood to be there. So, we really have two sentences, one embedded into the other. Native speakers of English don't even think about these things; their long experience with the language helps them form many types of sentences unconsciously and easily. It's only when we write, when we have to add punctuation, that we run into some problems.

I want a girl just like the girl that married dear old Dad.

Which girl? Any girl?

Leinenkugel's, which is a small brewery beer, is pretty good.

Do we need to identify which beer we're talking about? What function does "which is a small brewery beer" serve? Do we have to have it to make complete sense? What's the difference between good information and essential information?

Leinenkugel's, which has an Indian maiden on its label, is known throughout Wisconsin.

Leinenkugel's, whose reputation has spread to Chicago through tourists, is considered a specialty beer.

When to Use Commas

When the idea is added information, good but *not* essential, we use *which* and commas.

When the idea is essential to the sentence, helping us identify the main idea, we use *that* and no commas.

We use commas to set off extra or added information.

PRACTICE   Embedding

Practice 1

With your group or writing partner, embed one sentence into the other. Vary your use of *who, whose, whom, that,* and *which.* Remember to add commas.

A LONG-RUN SHOW: *M*A*S*H*

A. *M*A*S*H* was one of the most popular television shows of the 1970s.

*M*A*S*H* is enjoying reruns in the 1990s.

B. *M*A*S*H* satirized the army and war.
    The army was portrayed as bureaucratic and stupid.

    _____

    _____

C. Hawkeye Pierce was a first-rate surgeon and comic cutup.
    Hawkeye covered his anger and pain with jokes.

    _____

    _____

D. Trapper John McIntyre was Hawkeye's bunk mate.
    Trapper was also a surgeon and cutup.

    _____

    _____

E. Margaret O'Houlihan was in charge of the nurses.
    Margaret was called Hot Lips by Hawkeye and Trapper.

    _____

    _____

F. Radar O'Reilly was one of *M*A*S*H*'s most lovable characters.
    Radar was gentle and childlike.

    _____

    _____

G. Radar kept a teddy bear.
    The teddy bear was ragged and tattered.
    The teddy bear was his best friend.

    _____

    _____

H.   Hawkeye and Trapper kept trying to defy army regulations.
     The army regulations made no sense to them.

     _____

     _____

I.   Henry Blake was the commanding officer.
     Blake's orders made little sense.

     _____

     _____

J.   Hawkeye and Trapper kept tormenting Frank Burns.
     They called Frank "Ferret Face."

     _____

     _____

K.   Max Klinger was another memorable character.
     Klinger's wardrobe consisted of dresses.

     _____

     _____

L.   *M*A*S*H* showed the idiocy of war.
     *M*A*S*H* also showed the excellence of medical care in the field
     hospital.

     _____

     _____

More Ways of Combining and Modifying Sentences

When you were embedding one sentence into another, you might
have noticed that you could delete some words and still convey the
meaning you wanted. For example:

Stephen King, who is a master of horror fiction, lives in Maine.

Stephen King, a master of horror fiction, lives in Maine.

Notice that *Stephen King* and *master* refer to the same person. We often use this writing strategy to provide a bit more information for our reader. However, because this information is "extra," not essential to the meaning of the independent sentence, it is set off by commas. In other words, the same rule operates: Set off nonessential information with commas.

To achieve even more variety in sentences, we sometimes move these "extra info" parts:

A master of horror fiction, Stephen King lives in Maine.

Again note that a comma separates the description from the independent sentence.

Alan, the best point guard on the team, will start.

The best point guard on the team, Alan will start.

Although "the best point guard on the team" is helpful information, it is not needed to complete the main idea of the sentence—Alan will start. For this reason, we need commas. Notice how the commas help us read and absorb ideas more easily.

Practice 2

Examine the following paragraphs for examples of this sentence strategy. Underline them.

HUBBA-HUBBA, BUBBA

We've got a new year, a new president, Bill Clinton—and new words vying for a place in the dictionary. No slouches on research, editors at *Random House Webster's College Dictionary,* the most popular student dictionary, say they are carefully sifting through thousands of possibilities to distinguish between "flashes in the language pan and . . . permanent fixtures in the English firmament." The dictionary staff, a large group of academics, does a massive search of American writing and speech usage to determine the staying power of new words and new meanings given to old words.

Among the front-runners likely for inclusion in the next edition, editors say, is "bubba," a term popularized by the media during Bill Clinton's presidential campaign to characterize the South's good ol' boys. Many promising terms are emerging from the computer world. "Netiquette," the rules of etiquette for using computer bulletin boards, is one such term. Another favorite term is "emoticon," a word formed from "emote" and "icon." This term is used to describe a collection of symbols that can be typed on a keyboard to convey a thought, such as :). When you turn it sideways, you'll see a smiley face—have a good day!

A DOG'S LIFE

Ah, the upscale life of a dog. At Paws Inn, a new storefront-level boarding kennel in Manhattan, the guests can lounge in bed watching TV. On a recent Friday, for example, Chloe and Crystal, two Maltese, were engrossed in an "Oprah" episode about interracial dating. More akin to a spa than a detention center, Paws Inn offers leather couches, enough toys to stock a canine FAO Schwarz, and a VCR. The favorite videos, *101 Dalmatians* and *Benji,* are available 24 hours a day. The cost of this canine pampering, $30 a day, doesn't deter dog lovers.

CLASS-Y DINNER TIME

Kids who have to stay at the table till they clean their plates now have something to do between bites. They can read their place mats. Amy Kaliman Epstein of Brooklyn, the creator of Read a Mat, believes that her invention fits the parents of the 90s. Read a Mat, an educational place mat, perfectly fits the mindset of the modern parent, a mindset that abhors downtime for children. The 61 patterns range from the alphabet, shapes and numbers to the solar system, rain forests, foreign languages, great American women and maps of the world. Epstein's company, Straight Edge, sells more than $2 million in mats annually at stationery shops and toy stores in all 50 states.

ONE MORE STRATEGY: USING *-ing* AND *-ed*

Here is one more way of adding information without adding another sentence:

Crashing into the mailbox, Ellen mailed her letters the hard way.

Signaling to the referee, the quarterback stopped the clock.

Thinking about the exam, Josh got a massive headache.

Worried about the results, the math teacher junked the test.

Convinced that half the class failed, the teacher wept.

How does the *-ing* add to our understanding of the action? How does *-ed* add to our understanding? What is the relationship between the information in the *-ing* or *-ed* part and the independent sentence?

Again note that the punctuation sets off extra information—good information but not essential to the meaning of the independent sentence.

PRACTICE Using *-ing* and *-ed*

Practice 1

Examine the following for examples of this sentence strategy. Circle introductory word groups that modify or describe through use of *-ing* or *-ed*.

ELVIS, SPECIAL DELIVERY

Leaving his stamp on the world of rock 'n' roll, Elvis Presley now has left his stamp on the doors of the U.S. Postal Service. The first official Elvis Presley stamp was sold to his daughter, Lisa Marie, on January 7, 1993. Featuring live cut-in spots from the ceremony, the cable television network celebrated Presley's 58th birthday. Thousands of fans came to Graceland to participate in the King's birthday and the new stamp honoring him. Milling about the grounds, approximately 15,000 people waited in pouring rain to buy the first Elvis stamps. Timed to coincide with Presley's birthday, a five-day *Elvis: Special Delivery* tribute featured back-to-back Elvis movies on TNT.

Practice 2

Using *-ing* or *-ed,* create introductory word groups that modify or describe. If you're not sure about the spelling of an *-ing* or *-ed* verb form, check the dictionary. For example:

_____, Lee left the party.

Losing his date, Lee left the party.

Or:

Torn by indecision, Lee left the party.

1. _____, Sally took the exam.

2. _____, Paul passed the ball to Ken.

3. _____, Kerry thought about the movie.

4. _____, Ellen and Jan went shopping.

5. _____, Sam drove out of the driveway.

6. _____, the mail carrier ran.

7. _____, the barber made some mistakes.

8. _____, the halfback started to run.

9. _____, Abner gave up golf forever.

10. _____, LuAnn charged out of the room.

REVIEWING WAYS TO JOIN IDEAS			
When You Want to:	**Coordinator**	**Subordinator**	**Transition Word**
Add an Idea	and		also additionally furthermore moreover
Show Contrast	but yet	although even though	however nevertheless
Show Cause or Effect	for so	because since	therefore thus consequently as a result
Show Condition		if unless once	
Show Time Relation		before during when after	first meanwhile then last next
Show Alternative	or		
Use Punctuation Only	;		
Embed One Sentence into Another:	who whose whom that which		

PRACTICE   Ways to Join Ideas

Practice 1

Using the following information on sharks, write a paragraph in which you practice the various sentence strategies in this chapter.

KING OF THE SEAS

It took millions of years of evolutionary honing.

The shark became king of the seas.

The shark is the predator at the head of the aquatic food chain.

It's taken only about ten years for the shark to be overmatched.

Man has overmatched the shark.

Man is the most deadly killer on earth.

Each year tens of millions of sharks are killed.

The sharks are killed for food.

Sharks are also killed accidentally.

Sharks are caught in nets intended for shrimp, swordfish, or tuna.

Sharks caught in nets are often clubbed to death aboard ship.

Sharks are then tossed back into the water.

Many sharks are dying.

Some researchers are afraid the species will die out.

Environmentalists and fisheries scientists have been pressing a shark-saving plan on the U.S. Department of Commerce.

They began pressing in 1989.

The Bush administration never acted on the issue.

Enthusiasts may go to court.

Enthusiasts may look to the Clinton-Gore administration.

Selling the shark's cause is not easy.

Sharks are generally portrayed as mindless killing machines.

Sharks are considered more like the Saddam Husseins of the natural world.

Sharks are not the kind of animals that inspire films like *Born Free.*

Sharks are like lions and tigers.

Sharks are important predators and scavengers.

They prune weak and dying animals from their habitat.

Few children fall asleep clutching a stuffed, saber-toothed fish.

Must we kill what we haven't learned to love?

Practice 2

With your group or writing partner, combine the following sentences into several paragraphs. You will delete some words and phrases, add connecting words, and make some structures parallel.

MAN'S BEST—AND OLDEST—FRIEND

In an intriguing reassessment of man's best friend, researchers at the University of California have determined that the partnership between humans and dogs began more than 100,000 years ago.

It began long before the coming of the household cat.

It began long before any other domesticated animal.

It may have begun long before the dawn of civilization itself.

A sophisticated genetic analysis of 67 breeds from around the world shows that all kinds of dogs are essentially domesticated wolves.

All the dogs evolved from one ancient canine forebear.

All the dogs evolved directly.

The dogs have no ancestors among coyotes, jackals, dingos, or other similar species.

Researchers used physical evidence to determine the appearance of domesticated dogs.

Physical evidence of fossilized bones and skulls suggested dogs as we know them today first appeared about 14,000 years ago.

Domestic cats appeared about 7,000 years ago.

Most modern dog breeds are only a few hundred years old.

Most researchers believe that animals were first tamed and domesticated between 10,000 and 14,000 years ago.

Animals were domesticated about the time humans started building cities and planting crops.

The UCLA researchers analyzed the lineage of 162 wolves.

The wolves were taken from 27 places around the world.

They analyzed 140 dogs belonging to 67 breeds.

They analyzed five coyotes and 12 jackals.

To determine how long ago dogs emerged, the researchers looked at the DNA sequences.

The DNA sequences came from a control region of the mitrochondrial genome.

This genome has a very high mutation rate.

This genome is the same molecular clock used by other scientists to trace the descent of human beings.

The descent of humans was traced to early African ancestors.

Researchers were surprised at the enormous diversity of genetic sequences they found.

They found far more than could have evolved in a mere 14,000 years.

Researchers used estimates of how quickly mutations could happen.

The estimates led them to believe dogs could have originated as long as 135,000 years ago.

The estimates also led them to believe dogs could have originated as early as 60,000 years ago.

CHAPTER 14

Revising Sentences

People sometimes use the words *revising* and *editing* interchangeably, as though they mean the same thing. They don't. When we revise a sentence, we are reworking it. We are trying to make it better: clearer, more effective, more vivid or interesting. When we edit a sentence, we are correcting it, making it correspond to Standard Written English. In editing, we are checking that grammar, punctuation, and spelling are correct. However, it's important to note that a correct sentence doesn't necessarily mean a good sentence—one that is easy to read and clearly reflects the intended meaning of the writer. For this reason, we'll concentrate first on revising sentences and second on editing them.

We revise sentences through expanding them, deleting words or phrases from them, or combining them. We also revise by changing single words.

EXPANDING

We can expand sentences by adding descriptive words or phrases. Here are some questions that help us expand:

What detail would help describe more clearly?

Who's this sentence about?

What's this sentence about?

Why?

Where?

When?

Some adults don't like the cartoon character Bart Simpson.

teachers   a mouthy, aggressive fourth grader
parents   disrespectful
                defies authority
                mocks learning

Some parents dislike the cartoon character Bart Simpson, a mouthy, aggressive fourth grader who defies authority.

The revised sentence is more precise and gives the reader some reasons why adults wouldn't like this character.
    Note the differences in the following pairs of examples:

A. My math teacher is hard to follow.
B. Dr. Inkwell, my math teacher, speaks in short, rapid sentences, swallowing words as he goes.

A. He gives too much work.
B. A typical daily assignment from Dr. Inkwell consists of three chapters of problems. Each chapter takes most students at least two hours to complete.

A. I was late for math class once and felt upset.
B. The door was tightly shut when I reached math class. Through it, I could hear Dr. Inkwell's booming bass voice, yelling about lazy students. Trembling, I opened the door and tiptoed to the first empty seat, trying to avoid his steely eyes.

What role is the comma playing in these expanded sentences?

PRACTICE   Expanding Sentences

Practice 1

Give exact names when possible, substitute general words with concrete sensory (sight, sound, taste, touch) words, and replace verbs with more active ones.

1. My cousin is talented.

2. The basketball team is the worst.

_____

3. Her hair is unusual.

_____

4. My boss is too picky.

_____

A Word About Commas

Most punctuation helps us read and understand ideas more clearly and more efficiently. You may have been exposed to punctuation as rows of rules. Here, we'll look at punctuation as part of constructing and revising sentences. Learning how to use commas, for example, helps you express yourself more clearly and at the same time helps your readers understand you. When we speak, we use our voice—intonation, pitch, pauses, and so on—as punctuation. In writing, we have to learn how to give that same life through good punctuation.

When we expand sentences, we often have to set off those additional words and phrases with commas. In fact, most commas are used for this purpose. Notice the following:

Jeff, tired but happy, left the playing field.

Angry at the pay cut, the workers walked out.

Jess sat at her desk, wondering what to start first.

Why are the commas there? Could you eliminate the information enclosed with commas and still have a sensible, stand-alone sentence? What rule can you form about the use of these commas?

Jeff, my best friend, is a great musician.

Jeff, a great musician, is my best friend.

Jeff, whose mother is a rock star, is my friend.

Nashville, the home of country-and-western music, is a great place to visit.

Minneapolis, site of the 1992 Super Bowl, surprised many fans.

Does the comma rule hold for these sentences too? Why? What does the material enclosed by commas do for the reader?

Practice 2

With your group or writing partner, expand the numbered sentences by modifying key words. You will probably need to add commas to set off descriptive words or phrases. For example:

Dame Edna Everidge is in reality a male.

Dame Edna Everidge, a lavender-haired, sequined entertainer, is in reality a male.

Dame Edna Everidge is in reality a male, Australian Barry Humphries.

1. The photographers swarmed around John F. Kennedy, Jr.
2. The crowd loved Michael Jordan.
3. Jerry Seinfeld shocked a few television watchers.
4. Tom Cruise plays squeaky-clean characters.
5. Spike Lee made the film *Malcolm X.*
6. David Letterman entertains night owls.
7. Jay Leno is another late-night entertainer.
8. My mother doesn't miss a single day of *Oprah.*
9. My grandmother hates *Beavis and Butt-head.*
10. Stephen King is a favorite author of many teens.
11. McDonald's is getting competition from Burger King and Wendy's.
12. New York can be a hassle.
13. If you like history, try Boston.
14. My new computer talks to me.
15. *The X Files* has a loyal following.

CHANGING A SINGLE WORD

Sometimes, changing a single word changes the sentence into a far more lively or precise one. When we talk, we often make such changes without even thinking about it. If you tell someone that the concert was "awesome," you don't stop there. You go on to describe and explain, so the general "awesome" is broken down into flesh and blood terms. When we write, we have to be careful to break down a general term, sometimes by expanding but just as often through substituting one word for another. A good vocabulary is a writer's tool. Fortunately, we have reference books to help us enlarge that vocabulary. If you are not familiar with books such as *Roget's Thesaurus,* check them out in the bookstore or library.

The boy looked at the car. →

The fifteen-year-old couldn't keep his eyes off the Mazda RX-7.

The teenager stared at the vintage Mustang.

The old man walked into the store. →

The old man stumbled into the store.

The old man shuffled into the 7-Eleven.

PRACTICE   Changing Words

Practice 1

With your group, make as many substitutions as possible.

1. The student left class.

2. The girl ate the food.

3. Her dress is unusual.

4. My boss is too strict.

Practice 2

Part A

With your group or writing partner, use the information provided below as the base of your sentences. Whenever possible, expand the sentence with words or phrases that give the reader a much better "picture."

FLUFF 'N' STUFF

1. I noticed that Hostess Cup Cakes were no longer being packaged on that cardboard.

2. Instead, the cupcakes were now sitting in a plastic tray.

3. This changed the whole cupcake experience for me.

4. It changed it because the best part of eating Hostess Cup Cakes (or Twinkies) is removing them from the package.

5. Then I can run my finger along the cardboard to get the pastry residue.

6. Eating the residue is the most fun.

7. I called the Hostess consumer-response line.

8. A woman told me that the change had taken place because too many cupcakes had been damaged in their trip from the bakery to the grocery shelf.

9. I asked why Twinkies are still packaged on cardboard.

10. The woman was stumped.

11. But Hostess Cup Cakes will travel in plastic.

12. I have since given up Hostess Cup Cakes in favor of Twinkies.

Part B

Now examine how Paul Lukas, a writer for the *Philadelphia Inquirer,* wrote the Hostess Cup Cake story as part of a larger article on customer service—asking some very strange corporate questions! Underline the words or phrases that make his piece specific and lively. Compare these descriptions to those you came up with.

Company: Continental Baking Co.

Reason for Inquiry: In early 1994, I noticed that Hostess Cup Cakes were no longer being packaged on the familiar little piece of cardboard. Instead, the cupcakes were now sitting in a very unattractive molded plastic tray. This totally ruined the whole cupcake experience for me, because as everyone knows, the best part of eating Hostess Cup Cakes (or Twinkies or Suzy-Qs) is removing the confections from the package and then running your finger along the cardboard, thereby salvaging the pastry residue that inevitably sticks there.

Method of Inquiry: Phone call to the Hostess consumer-response line.

Response: A personable woman told me that the change had taken place because too many cupcakes had gotten squished and squashed by rough handling during their trip from the bakery to the grocery shelf ("Damage control," she called it—a rare use of this term). When I asked why similar steps had not been taken to protect the equally squishy and squashy Twinkies or Suzy Qs, both of which remain packaged on the cardboard, my Hostess contact was stumped.

Epilogue: I've since given up Hostess Cup Cakes in favor of Twinkies.

Appearing in *St. Paul Pioneer Press*

WORKING WITHIN PARAGRAPHS

When we isolate sentences, as in these exercises, we end up working differently than when we work with paragraphs and complete essays. Within paragraphs, and ultimately full essays, we have to deal with what we just said, as well as what we go on to say. Therefore, our changes have to match a great number of thoughts, not just a single one in a single sentence. Moreover, it's always harder to change our own sentences. We know in our heads what we want to say, and we tend to think that we have—the first time! However, that's seldom the case, and reworking sentences is a necessity.

Notice the vocabulary in this excerpt from a *Newsweek* article about moviemaker Spike Lee:

> About a year ago, as Spike Lee tells it, he was setting up a rally scene for *Malcolm X* on a Harlem Street when an empty car suddenly came hurtling toward him and his crew. Although the car crashed before injuring anyone, its interior chilled the blood. "Someone," says Lee, "had tied a brick to the accelerator and gunned it in our direction."

Three words stand out: *hurtling, chilled, gunned.* They provide the reader with a very precise sense of action and feeling. When we read a paragraph, we aren't always aware of the impact of individual words; we simply absorb and benefit from them. As writers, however, we have to be aware.

PRACTICE   Paragraphs

Practice 1

The following "Profile" from *Sports Illustrated* offers some practice with a paragraph. First, underline the words and phrases that give us a specific picture or idea of what Tim Green is like. Then, consider how the paragraph would read without them. Would the reader have the same sense of Tim Green?

> **RENAISSANCE MAN**
>
> Since his days as an All-America defensive end and English major at Syracuse in the mid-1980s, Tim Green of the Falcons has successfully balanced two passions—football and writing. A first round draft pick by

Atlanta in 1986, Green spent his first four years as a pro fighting through injuries and position changes. But in 1990 he was moved back to end, and he has become the most dependable performer on the Falcon defensive front, despite being small (6'2", 245 pounds) for his position.

After attending an emotional retirement dinner for Atlanta defensive end Rick Bryan, who had suffered recurring neck injuries, Green wrote:

Back in the locker room the next day, I checked my protective neck padding and I pumped some extra air into the padding inside my helmet. Like a gypsy gazing into a crystal ball, I looked at my own distorted reflection in the glossy black surface of my Falcons helmet. The smile let me know I was glad to be there. But there was nothing I could see that told me how long I would last. I'm 28, remember. A 28-year-old defensive lineman. I'm old.

As you worked through the paragraph about Green, you no doubt found a physical picture (a defensive end, height, weight) and perhaps a more interesting picture of the man himself—one who thinks about his future. Green's description of himself holding his helmet, "Like a gypsy gazing into a crystal ball," gives us both a physical picture and a comparison that adds meaning to his action. He then notes his "distorted" reflection in the helmet's "glossy black surface." The word *distorted* is important because it helps us envision Green. *Glossy* also provides instant visualization for us as readers. As writers, we want to do just that: provide our readers with visualization. We also want to appeal to the other senses (hearing, touch, taste). In brief, we want our readers to enter into the world we are sharing with them.

Using the following information from "Renaissance Man," write a paragraph about Tim Green that allows the reader to know Green better. Add your own words to liven things up, but keep the portrait of Green as true as possible to these facts.

Green has written a novel. Its title is *Ruffians.* The novel tells what pro football is really like. It's not published yet.

Green comments on pro football for National Public Radio. He writes a weekly column for the *Syracuse Herald-Journal* during the football season. Green uses a laptop computer during flights to road games.

Green writes well and with feeling. He shows a side of football fans rarely see. There is stress and anxiety. There is love and hate. There is human drama. It's not all anguish.

Green has finished two years of law school at Syracuse University. He'd like to be a trial lawyer. He says he loves reading and writing.

Practice 2

David Gelman, a writer for *Newsweek,* wrote about professional football injuries. In the following article, Gelman uses very specific words to describe what happens. Underline those that provide us with a vivid picture, especially of actions.

THE MOST DANGEROUS GAME

David Gelman

It was a good thing for Kansas City Chiefs quarterback Dave Kreig that he moved out of the pocket at the last moment—and as it turned out, a terrible thing for Jet defensive end Dennis Byrd. As Byrd and teammate Scoot Mersereau thundered toward Kreig like two runaway freight trains on a collision course, the quarterback stepped forward ever so slightly—just enough so that Byrd rammed headfirst into Mersereau's formidable sternum. Byrd doesn't remember what happened next, but when he came to moments later, he told worried doctors he could move his arms a little and his legs not at all.

Football players put their bodies on the line, and injuries of all kinds come with the turf they fight for. This season alone several hundred players have been shoved, shouldered or butted out of action.

Practice 3

Choose someone whom you follow, either admire or dislike, from the world of sports or music. Write a brief paragraph about that person. Try to capture this person through striking words and phrases. In your first draft, just get the ideas down. Then go back and revise the sentences for clarity, vividness, and the like. Remember:

Who or what is this sentence about?

What details would help the reader see or understand this person more clearly?

How can sensory details, those appealing to sight, sound, and touch in particular, help convey the image you want?

Brainstorm words on the following lines. Then work with your group or writing partner to refine the list.

_____

_____

_____

_____

DELETING WORDS AND PHRASES

Besides expanding sentences, we sometimes have to do the opposite—cut them down. Taking out the "deadwood" is another important step in revising sentences. Deadwood is any word or phrase that can be removed without any loss in meaning. For example:

In today's society the average teenager will find that there are few jobs available unless some advanced schooling has been taken.

What's the main idea in this sentence? What's essential?

Today's teenagers will need advanced schooling for most jobs.

Now try this one:

In my opinion, there are many reasons why I believe we should attend this upcoming tournament in the next few weeks.

Cross out nonessential words or repetitions. Then rewrite the sentence:

_____

_____

And this:

It is my belief that it is a matter of great importance for a student to plan a schedule for one semester in order to get prepared for all the work and exams.

_____

_____

Another common piece of deadwood occurs in sentences starting with "It is" or "There is." For example:

> There were four problems that caused the flight delay.
> Four problems caused the flight delay.
> It was the chili dog that caused me to get sick.
> The chili dog caused my sickness.
> This chili dog made me sick.

PRACTICE   Deleting

Practice 1

Cut the deadwood out of these sentences:

1. It was early in the morning when the sun was just coming up when I saw the neighbor's dog.

_____

2. There were a couple of kids playing in the yard.

_____

3. It is my opinion that women still don't have the kind of equity in pay that men have.

_____

4. There are too many barriers that keep women who are qualified out of the very top corporate jobs.

_____

5. I am of the belief that the school term is excessively long and lasts too late in the year.

_____

6. He responded that I should spend it on something special that I would never usually spend money on.

_____

7. Seeing that there were no other seats on the bus, Ella was forced to sit next to the young man who seemed odd.

_____

8. In today's society, I myself find too many choices of things I might do.

_____

9. He is more or less a pretty good looking person in regard to his looks.

_____

10. Dr. Salk's extremely significant research led to a highly important discovery.

_____

11. Regarding that memo in relation to personal relationships, it is not the intention of management to object to employees dating if they so choose.

_____

12. The final World Series game was a disappointment to most baseball fans.

_____

More Deadwood

Certain phrases are always deadwood. Recognizing them gives you an immediate start on deletion:

the reason being that	because
due to the fact that	because
for the reason that	because
in spite of the fact that	despite

Jeff lost the scholarship, the reason being that he broke his leg.

Jeff lost the scholarship because he broke his leg.

Jean lost the scholarship in spite of the fact that she had good grades.

Jean lost the scholarship despite her good grades.

Another set of words that usually lead to deadwood are these:

Wordy	Replace with
in today's society	today
at this point in time	now
in the event that	if or when
in order to	
for the purpose of	to
with regard to	regarding
in reference to	about
with concern to the matter of	concerning
due to the fact that	
the reason for	because, why
regardless of the fact that	despite, although
in this paper I intend to	
point I want to make is	eliminate
in conclusion I want to say	
in my opinion	

Forms of the verb *be* (am, is, are, was, were) also lead to a wordy sentence when they are followed by a noun or adjective. Replacing them with strong, active verbs solves the problem:

The test results were shocking to the teacher.

The test results shocked the teacher.

Although descriptors are important, some are "too much" and need to be cut:

Paul's highly important position is extremely costly in terms of time.

Paul's important position costs him time.

Also look for short or single words that convey the same meaning more directly:

Be sure you have a sufficient amount of gas before you try driving Baja.

Buy enough gas before you drive Baja.

A person who is beginning to ski has many expenses.

A novice skier has many expenses.

Practice 2

Eliminate the deadwood in these sentences.

1. Mr. Jones made it a requirement of the course that we write two essays.

_____

2. The manager was filled with feelings of appreciation when she saw the work.

_____

3. If you feel you are not making any progress toward graduation, you should make an attempt to come to a decision to put some changes into action.

_____

4. If you have a sufficient amount of information about that subject, it is not necessary for you to look into any further research.

_____

5. They related to one another in a very meaningful way, but they came to an agreement to not make any hasty decisions.

_____

Occasionally Deadwood: Passive Sentences

Passive and *active* can describe sentences as well as people.

Active   The first baseman threw the ball to the catcher.

Passive   The ball was thrown by the first baseman to the catcher.

If you're thinking that there is action in the passive sentence, you're right. However, the "doer" of that action is set off in a phrase rather than directly acting. The result is a longer, less clear sentence.

Passive sentences can be useful when we don't know who the doer is, or for some reason do not wish to indicate who the doer is.

The law was supported by several important, unnamed jurists.

The car was smashed sometime between midnight and dawn.

Passive sentences, usually, are longer and far less clear than active ones. For that reason, most of our sentences should be active ones.

Practice 3

Turn these passive sentences into active ones. You may add or subtract words.

1. Her hair was braided by her mother.

_____

2. The books were handed over to the new students by the principal.

_____

3. The vandalism was done by three kids who had been suspended.

_____

4. The football was caught by the wide receiver at the last moment.

_____

5. The exam was graded by the substitute teacher.

_____

6. That awful decision was made by the Mayor's Commission.

_____

7. John was run over by the Frito-Lay Potato Chip truck yesterday.

_____

8. The results were announced by the Pentagon's spokesman.

_____

9. I had been seen by my folks at the movies.

_____

10. The art work was taken down by the principal.

_____

Practice 4

The following piece is filled with various types of deadwood. Find it, underline it, and then eliminate it as you rewrite the passage into a crisp piece of information on those kid favorites, broccoli and brussels sprouts.

A BITTER GENE?

Broccoli and brussels sprouts are said to be naturally bitter reported some scientists. These vegetables can be unpleasantly so because of taste genes people inherit. Findings presented by researchers at a meeting of the American Association for the Advancement of Science divided the whole world into three categories: nontasters, tasters, and super-tasters. In terms of which category one falls into depends upon the intensity of the way in which he or she perceives bitterness, sweetness, and other taste sensations.

On the subject of category, people were found to be one of the three depending upon their response to a taste of a thyroid medicine called PROP. About 25 percent of white people cannot taste PROP at all, so they are generally considered to be in the category that is known as "nontasters." Half are considered "tasters" because they find it mildly bitter. Another 25 percent who are the people known as the "super-tasters" find it grossly bitter. As far as women are concerned they are more likely than men to be super-tasters, and Asians and blacks are for the most part more apt than whites to have this trait. It is assumed by researchers that at some point in time somewhere in human evolution, being a super-taster might have improved the chance of survival in parts of the world where there were many poisonous plants since these tend to taste bitter. It is further assumed that being a nontaster may have been an advantage in a safer environment with a more limited supply of food. In regard to kids in today's world not liking brussels sprouts or broccoli, they probably won't like them no matter what anyone does or says. The reasons are genetic.

"Our Tastes Run the Gamut from Bland to Bizarre"

Many sentences require adding words or phrases to make them clearer and more effective. However, many other sentences require fewer words to achieve the same effect. We have to eliminate words that don't contribute to the sentence's meaning or that repeat what we've already said. At this point, you may be wondering why we add words only to face deleting some later. That's a good question, and the best way to understand the use of these two processes is to consider revision as experimentation with words. We want our sentences to say what we mean—and achieving that purpose takes experimenting with words and phrases. By experimenting, trying out different words or phrases, you'll learn when to add and when to delete. Ask yourself if you really need all those words. Ask yourself if there is a better word to express your meaning. Revising sentences requires time and concentration, but the end result is worth it—your intended meaning comes through.

CHAPTER 15

Editing Sentences

When we revise sentences, we are concerned with making them clearer, more easily understood by our readers; we also want to improve their "punch." Readers appreciate active, vivid sentences and a sharp focus on the idea being presented. When we edit, however, we turn our attention to making our sentences correct; we make them conform to Standard Written American English. Despite the fact that every language and dialect is equally useful and important as a communication system, most languages have a standard form that is taught in school and used in the workplace. In those settings, teachers and employers expect the standard form, and when they don't find it, they get annoyed and even stop reading. Thus, in order for our written thoughts to be taken seriously, we have to use Standard Written American English. Editing is the process that allows us to do so. Although we may make some corrections as we draft or revise, editing should be considered the final process in readying our text for a reader. Editing too early in the writing process could be a waste of time, mainly because the edited sentences could be deleted in the revising process.

GENERAL EDITING STRATEGIES

You need to develop your personal approach to editing. However, knowing a few general strategies can help you be systematic about the process. Some students use the following:

1. Reading the essay aloud, slowly and deliberately. There's considerable difference between reading silently and aloud, and many students catch their errors when they switch to an oral reading.

2. Using a ruler or a piece of paper to force a slow and careful reading of each sentence. We can skim right over sentences we have written, and the tendency to do so lessens when only one or two sentences are visible.

3. Reading "backward" from the end to the start of the piece. This action forces us to concentrate on a single sentence.

4. Writing a note on the top of each page of the draft: "Check for _____ ." It's easy to overlook certain errors, so the note serves as a reminder.

5. Using an error log. Data from the log can be applied to the next writing task. We can anticipate places where we are likely to make errors, and then check the piece for those errors. What most students find is a pattern: they tend to make certain kinds of errors. It's usually comforting to see the log: students know they are making fewer errors than they thought; they can zero in on errors giving them the most trouble; and they can refer to something concrete as a guide to editing.

SAMPLE LOGS

Error	Correction	Cause of Error
There is plenty of boys	There are	Starting with there
The boys, they knew	The boys knew	Repeating oral pattern

Type of Error	Examples	Probable Cause	How to Correct
Apostrophe	Idea's value	Not think of ownership unless person	Check for ownership

You'll find that the time and attention given to maintaining logs pays off. Writing becomes easier when we have definite strategies to help us revise and edit, as well as specific areas where we know we tend to make mistakes.

SUBJECTS AND VERBS

Before looking at some of the problems that occur with subjects and verbs, we need to review briefly just what we mean by the terms *subject* and *verb*.

Subject

When we talk about the subject of a sentence, we are taking note of *who* or *what* that sentence is about:

Who Jon (a specific person)

Who neighbor, boxer, athlete (person)

What cat, pencil (concrete things)

What idea, value (abstract things)

Jon left the car running. (Who left it running?)

That athlete is a jerk. (Who's the jerk?)

My cat is a nuisance. (What's the nuisance?)

His idea was the best. (What was the best?)

Their values are really different. (What's different?)

Verb

When we talk about the verb of a sentence, we are taking note of what the subject does, is, or has. We are saying something about the subject: "What about _____ ?"

Does Jon runs marathons. (What does Jon do?)

That athlete competes nationally. (What does that athlete do?)

Is My cat is classy. (What is my cat? What about that cat?)

Their ideas are welcome. (What about their ideas?)

Has Their plans have merit. (What do the plans have? What about the plans?)

Examine these sentences:

The kid in the last desk seems tired.

Who or what are we talking about? What is the key word? What about this kid? What information do we get?

That information is practically useless.

Who or what are we talking about? What about it?

Playing basketball can be fun.

What are we talking about? And what about it?

Mel runs the best marathon in the city.

Who? What does he do?

Verbs that show physical or mental action are usually easy to pick out: *run, talk, hit, think, believe,* and so on. Verbs that act as connectors (that is, have no action) sometimes are a bit more difficult to spot: *is, are, were, seem.* However, if you keep in mind that we need information on both "who or what" and "what happened," you'll keep the sentence sense.

Subject-Verb Agreement

In Standard Written English, the subject and verb must agree in number—singular to singular and plural to plural.

> *s   v*
> The boy sings too loudly.

> *s   v*
> The boys sing too loudly.

> *s   v*
> The idea is really good.

> *s   v*
> The ideas are really good.

One of the obvious problems for many speakers is the way in which English uses -*s*. We use it on nouns to indicate a plural and on verbs to indicate singular! Students who are learning English as a second language usually have to make subject-verb agreement an editing check for themselves.

Some American dialects, notably Black English, don't require subject-verb agreement. Because our home languages are automatic, speakers of other dialects often need to check on this feature of Standard Written

English. Making a shift from automatic to deliberate and conscious takes concentration, so an editing check is usually needed.

Because we write more complex sentences as we mature, anyone can lose agreement between subjects and verbs. By the time we get to the end of the sentence, we may have lost track of the subject. And that's okay. In the editing process, we have a chance to double-check our text and correct any errors in subject-verb agreement.

ESL Writers

In English, an -*s* has two functions:

    1. to make a noun plural: ideas, numbers, boys
    2. to make a verb singular: thinks, cooks, writes

Strategies for Subject-Verb Agreement

1. As a general rule, ignore words separating the subject and verb. Usually, they don't count in terms of subject-verb agreement.

       s   *v*
The man [in the back seat] is my dad.

One [of the roses] looks dead.

The boy [who bit me] left.

2. Ignore word groups beginning with the following:

about	before	in	through
above	below	into	to
across	beside	near	under
after	between	of	upon
among	by	off	with
around	down	on	within
at	from	over	

These words are called *prepositions*. They are very handy for providing us with description and specific information about someone or something. Note how they work:

The box near the sink is pretty heavy. (Which box?)

Jon is playing under the table. (Where?)

The house around the corner is being torn down. (Which house?)

Some member of Congress is under attack. (Of what?)

Dr. Paul's lectures on astrophysics are beyond me. (On what?)

The key word in each of these sentences (the subject), however, comes before the preposition:

box is

Jon is playing

house is

member is

lectures are

Asking "Who or what is this really about?" or "Who or what is doing something?" will keep you on track with finding the subject. Being aware of the preposition will help too. Don't try to memorize them though. You can always refer to the list when you edit.

The other word groups that separate subjects and verbs are these:

who	The boy *who lost his coat* is crying.
which	My coat, *which is too long,* is ugly.
that	The beer *that sits too long* goes flat.

One more special problem involves *-ing* words:

The coat *lying on that chair* is mine.

The box *sitting next to the desk* is yours.

The man *fixing the TV* will charge me $100.

Again, asking "Who or what is this all about?" helps isolate the key word, the subject of the sentence.

3. Remember the only time we have to add *-s* or *-es* to make a verb agree with its subject occurs in the present—not the past or the future. If the subject is singular (one), add *-s* or *-es* to the verb:

The test stinks!

This machine crunches numbers for me.

Allen runs too much.

If the subject is plural (more than one), leave the verb alone:

Tests stink!
These machines crunch numbers for me.
Allen and Paul run too much.

4. We have a parallel to the *-s* rule in some heavily used verbs, such as *to be* and *to have:*

Singular   is   was   has   (all end in *-s*)
Plural   are   were   have

The form for *you* is always plural, no matter what.

You (one person) are right.
You (more than one person) are not telling the truth.
You (one person) have the personality for it.
You (more than one person) have a lot of nerve.

The form for *I* is unique.

I am ready for the test.
I have the right page.

PRACTICE   Subject and Verb

Practice 1

Supply the correct form of the verb:

1. The baby in the crib (scream) _____ every night.

2. Those kids from La Crosse (run) _____ the marathon every year.

3. The guys in the apartment next door (play) _____ the stereo at full blast all night.

4. Those girls near the elevator (seem) _____ approachable.

5. Dr. Lyon's lectures on math continually (bore) _____ me.

6. The house between mine and the corner (shed) _____ paint.

7. The pages within that book (sell) _____ because of photos.

8. Some colleges in the Midwest (draw) _____ students from every part of the United States.

9. Singing in the choir every day (take) _____ time.

10. Working at McDonald's on weekends (give) _____ some financial freedom.

Reversing Order

The usual pattern for subjects and verbs in English sentences is the subject before the verb:

> *s*   *v*
> My neighbor chases his dog every night.

> *s*   *v*
> That idea is pretty weird.

> *s*   *v*
> Sailing is a great sport.

However, we sometimes reverse that order:

> *v*   *s*
> Sitting on the window were ten bottles.

> *v*   *s*
> There were ten bottles on the window.

> *v*   *s*
> Here are the books.

When we start a sentence with *there* or *here,* the subject will follow the verb. When you check for subject and verb agreement, then, you will be searching in reverse order. Keep in mind that *there* and *here* are introductory words, not subjects.

Practice 2

Circle the correct verb.

1. There (is/are) at least 15 students signed up.
2. Here (is/are) the test you asked for.
3. Lying on the davenport (is/are) 20 beer bottles.
4. Across the street (was/were) the fire station and police headquarters.
5. Classes and work (take/takes) all the time I have.
6. The teacher or his assistant (mark/marks) the exams.
7. Jon or Ellen (take/takes) the boxes to the dump.
8. Physics and mathematics (is/are) two areas I avoid.

Compound Subjects

When we have a compound subject, we have to pay attention to the connecting word:

$\qquad\quad$ *s* $\qquad\qquad$ *s* $\quad$ *v*
The old man and his son were hurt in the accident.

$\quad$ *s* $\qquad$ *s* $\quad$ *v*
Rain and sleet made the roads icy.

$\quad$ *s* $\quad$ *s* $\qquad$ *s* $\quad$ *v*
Dogs, cats, and ponies are the featured animals.

And indicates a plural subject. Therefore, we need a plural verb.
Or indicates a singular subject. We are talking about one or the other, not both. Therefore, we need a singular verb.

The teacher *or* the lawyer writes the script.

Snow *or* sleet makes travel impossible.

A party *or* a basketball game consumes Jim's time.

| *and* = both | Use a plural verb |
| *or* = one | Use a singular verb |

Repeating the Subject

When we speak, we sometimes repeat words, including our subject. In the context of conversation, some repeating makes sense and may help the listener. Moreover, in some languages and American dialects, repetition of the subject of a sentence is the normal pattern and expected. However, in Standard Written English, repeating the subject is considered an error.

Jon he left at noon.

That *girl* next door *she* has a hot car.

My *teacher,* who never shuts up, *he's* a real bore.

That *movie,* you know, the one with Madonna, *it's* wild.

ESL Writers

Do not repeat the subject of the sentence:

My brother he likes basketball.	My brother likes basketball.
	or He likes basketball.
Maria and I, we like to shop.	Maria and I like to shop.
	or We like to shop.

If your home language uses the repeating subject pattern, you'll need an edit check for this specific feature.

Checking Verb Tenses

When we write, we have to be consistent about time. Usually, we stick to *present or past* throughout a single piece of writing. We have to have a very good reason to switch from one to another, or we risk losing our reader. *Present* refers to what is happening right now or what usually happens, habitually. *Past* refers to what has already happened.

Too much beer causes trouble.

Too much beer caused trouble.

ENGLISH VERB TENSES		
Tense	Example	When to Use
Present	Alice likes Paul. He eats slowly.	Present time Habitual action
Past	Alice liked Paul.	Action completed/over
Future	Alice will like Paul.	Action after present
Present Perfect	Alice has liked Paul.	Action began in past but continues
Past Perfect	Alice had liked Paul, but she left him.	Action completed before second action in past
Future Perfect	Alice will have dated Alec for two months.	Action from present to future/continuing

Forming Past Tense.   The past tense in English indicates that the action or condition is over. The most common way of indicating past tense is the addition of *-ed* or *-d* to the verb:

She talked for an hour.

They required a written application.

However, we do have English verbs that do not follow this pattern. These verbs, called *irregular,* change their spelling.

I knew the answer.

Ellen rang the doorbell.

I spoke to her yesterday.

If you are not sure whether a verb adds *-ed* or changes form altogether, check the dictionary. Look up the present-tense form of the verb; the dictionary will list forms (present, past, and past participle) of each irregular verb.

The *past participle* is a verb form heavily used in English. It expresses actions or conditions that began in the past but are still in progress. The past participle is used after the helping verb:

Main verb:	I have a book in my locker.
Helping verb + past participle:	I have spoken to him about it.
Main verb:	I had the answer right.
Helping verb + participle:	I had learned the entire lesson.

The past participle of most English verbs is formed by adding *-ed* to the present form, just as we do to get the past verb form:

Past:	I walked the entire course.
Past participle:	I have walked the entire course.

However, many of our irregular verbs have different forms for past and past participle:

Past:	I saw the teacher yesterday.
	Jon tore up the test.
Past participle:	I have seen the teacher.
	Jon has torn up the test.

Note: Check your dictionary for the correct spelling of the past and past participle forms. In written work, you will be expected to use the Standard Written English form.

ESL Writers

The past tenses are the most difficult to learn:

I ate lunch = action completed at particular time in past

I have eaten lunch = action began in past but continues in present or habitual
I have eaten lunch there every day.

I had eaten lunch = action begun and completed in past

I had eaten lunch before I left for school = action completed before a second action

Maintaining Consistency in Verb Tense

When you write paragraphs and essays, you need to maintain consistency in your verb tenses. That is, if you are writing about something that happened in the past, you must use the past-tense verbs throughout the piece. If you are writing about something happening in the present, you must use present-tense verbs, and if something will happen in the future, you use future-tense verbs. A sudden switch from one tense to another can jolt or confuse the reader. For example:

The immigration officer *checks* everyone's passport. However, security guards *lingered* in the area in case of a problem.

The use of present tense in the first sentence, and past in the second, disrupts the reader's sense of time. Changing one of the verbs will correct the problem:

The immigration officer *checked* everyone's passport. *or*
However, security guards *linger* in the area in case of a problem.

Which to use? That depends upon your overall description—present or past? If you were writing about what happened, you would choose the past forms. If you were writing about what happens, in the present or habitually, you would choose present forms. What's important is a check on your timeline, preferably during your prewriting time.

Practice 1

The following sentences form a complete paragraph. Read them through once. Then reread, underline the verbs, and decide on which tense you wish to maintain. Change any verb forms that don't match the tense you have chosen for the paragraph.

1. More students will use financial aid next year.
2. Some politicians think that they needed less support.
3. However, costs rose every year in every area of campus life.
4. Faculty salaries are a large part of rising costs.
5. Maintaining buildings was also a huge expenditure.
6. Students were insisting on more computers.
7. Good computer systems are expensive to purchase and maintain.
8. Therefore, students expected rising costs.
9. Politicians must be realistic about costs.
10. Financial aid and state support need to match reality.

ESL Writers

Even though another word may tell when an action took place, the verb must also show when the action took place:

Yesterday, I see the teacher. → *Yesterday,* I *saw* the teacher.

Tomorrow my dad leave for California. → *Tomorrow* my dad *will leave* for California

---

Practice 2

Read the following paragraph and decide why the writer used these verb tenses. Notice the use of verb forms to complete descriptions (assimilated, devoted). They are not part of the verb phrase, but rather, act as adjectives in this case.

A FACT THAT'S HARD TO SWALLOW

Eating *is* a major source of pleasure for almost all people. Food and drink *account* for 21 percent of all spending in Western countries and more than 50 percent in some Third World nations. Immigrants *seem* to retain their ethnic identity through food long after they *become* assimilated in other ways. And eating *plays* a central role in our development: Nothing *is* more important in early life than learning what *is* edible and what *is* not.

Yet despite its importance to our lives, food *has been* virtually *ignored* by academic psychologists. In the most recent editions of eight leading introductory psychology textbooks, the average number of pages devoted to what humans eat *is* 0.4 out of 668 total pages. In comparison, an average of 12.5 pages *are* devoted to sleep.

Paul Rozen cited in *Psychology Today*

ESL Writers

English verbs can be used in many ways. When they end in *-ing* or *-ed,* they may be used as adjectives, to describe someone or something:

I am *cooking* fish tonight.   *Cooking* oil should have little fat in it.

I *devoted* all my time to math.   Mai is *devoted* to math.

They may also be used as nouns:

Cooking can be fun.   *Walking* is good exercise.   Do you like *singing?*

Problems with -*ed* Endings.   Sometimes we drop off the -*ed* endings when we speak, especially in casual conversations. Our listeners don't mind because the sounds blend together:

I use to visit the library every week. (used)

I was suppose to do the laundry. (supposed)

You might have noticed that the word following the verb started with a consonant. When this combination occurs, we find it hard to distinguish *use* from *used*. Most of us don't even notice the missing -*ed* ending, nor do we have any trouble understanding that the verb refers to past.

In Standard Written English, however, we have no such leeway. We must write the standard form of the past tense and past participle. When you edit, you'll need to check your verbs for -*ed* and -*d* endings.

Using Progressive Tenses

Another form of verbs is called the *progressive*. We form it by adding some form of the verb *to be* (am, is, are, was, were) to the -*ing* form of another verb. For example, adding -*ing* to walk = walking. We can use that -*ing* form in both present and past actions:

I am studying right now.

I am studying all day.

I was studying last night.

Showing ongoing action, whether present or past, is an essential element in much of our writing. We can also use the progressive form to show a future action:

He will be asking for a raise throughout the coming year.

Forecasters believe the storm will be making its way up the Carolina coast in the next 24 hours.

Although you use progressive forms often in speaking, you usually don't have to monitor whether or not you have the correct one. Listeners can follow you or ask for clarification. When you write, however, you must ensure that the progressive forms, just like other verb forms, are consistent throughout the piece.

Forming Progressive Tenses

Basic verb + -ing   (think + ing = thinking)

Form of verb *be* + basic verb + ing   (am + think + ing = am thinking)

Past Progressive	**Present Progressive**	**Future Progressive**
was were	am is are	will be
was thinking	am thinking is thinking	will be thinking
were thinking	are thinking	

ESL Writers

Always use a helping verb (auxiliary) with an *-ing* verb:

I going to library now. ⟶ I *am going* to the library now.

Antonio and Pablo studying ⟶ Antonio and Pablo *were studying*
    last night.   last night.

Tina be traveling tomorrow. ⟶ Tina *will be traveling* tomorrow.

Practice 3

The verbs in this piece are a bit more complicated. How does the writer keep verb tense consistency, despite the different types of forms? Is there any place where you believe the writer used the wrong verb tense? Why?

A LITTLE TASTE OF WINTER

If that Snickers bar *you're eating* seems a bit less than sweet this time of year, you *might be experiencing* a newly discovered symptom of seasonal affect disorder (SAD), the so-called winter depression that *strikes* as many as 15 million people during these sunlight-scarce months. It *turns* out that SAD dampens not only your mood but also your taste buds.

SAD sufferers often *crave* carbohydrates, which *seems* logical because carbo-rich foods *can spark* the production of serotonin, a mood-enhancing element often in short supply in depressed brains. Researcher Paul Arbisi *figured* that the taste buds of such people *might become* more sugar-sensitive, serving as an additional signal to guide them toward those serotonin-boosting carbohydrates. Instead, Arbisi *found* that people with SAD *are* less able to detect sweetness than non-depressed individuals. An explanation for this unexpected discovery, however, *is proving* as elusive as winter sun. It *may be* simply that the disorder *blunts* taste buds indiscriminately: bitter and sour flavors *become* muted as well. Then there*'s* the puzzling finding that while exposing SAD patients to bright light *improves* their mood, their taste buds *stay* out of commission until spring. The bottom line according to Arbisi: "This *is* complicated."

Adapted from *Psychology Today*

Practice 4

Write a brief paragraph in which you describe a television show, movie, or sports event that you recently watched. For your description, use the progressive tense to show ongoing action, as well as your ongoing responses to it. Underline each verb and double-check its tense in the context of your entire paragraph. Exchange your paragraph with your writing partner or bring to your writing group.

PRONOUNS

We use pronouns to vary our writing. Without them, we would be forced to repeat the same word again and again through a piece of writing.

Jon isn't here. Jon is working.
College is different than I expected; college is harder.
I liked the pizza. The pizza didn't have too much sauce.

Jon isn't here. He's working.
College is different than I expected; it's harder.
I liked the pizza. It didn't have too much sauce.

Pronouns, then, are very useful. When we use them, however, we have to make sure they agree with the word they replace and represent—singular to singular and plural to plural.

If students miss class, they'll risk failing.
Valentine's Day has charm all of its own.

Singular	Plural	How Used
I	we	Subjects—actor
you	you	
he, she, it	they	
me	us	Objects—receiver
you	you	
him, her, it	them	
mine	ours	Possessives—owner
yours	yours	
his, hers, its	theirs	

Standard Written English has distinct slots for pronouns:

Subject   I took the bait.
Object   Milo gave me the bait.
Possessive   That bait is mine.

For most people, the problem with getting the right pronoun in the right sentence slot occurs when there is a compound subject:

A. Kyle and him are coming over tonight.

A subject pronoun, *he,* is needed in the sentence. Because speech patterns may suggest that *him* and *me* are correct, we need to double-check. With subject pronouns, mentally erase the other subject:

him are coming

Most native speakers of English would catch the problem at this point. However, speakers with different home languages may need to consult the list of subject pronouns.

B. He runs faster than me.

This sentence is more bothersome. It sounds right to most of us. If we complete the sentence with what is implied, though, we find the problem:

He runs faster than *I do.*
He runs faster than *me do.*

So again some mental deleting and adding will help solve the problem.

PRACTICE   Pronouns

Practice 1

Place an appropriate pronoun in these sentences:

1. Jan and _____ are coming to the party tonight.

2. Please give the pizza to Paul and _____ .

3. I know I can do better than _____ .

4. _____ and I plan to do that work today.

5. If that book is yours, this is _____ .

6. Alex gave Leo and _____ the tickets.

7. The car lost _____ wheel cover.

8. Ellen always runs better than _____ in the 400 relay.

9. Jeff and _____ planned the party last night.

10. You know you can figure that out faster than _____ .

Avoiding Sexist Language

Besides needing agreement in number (singular or plural) with the word they stand for, pronouns must also agree in gender (male, female, neutral). This requirement brings up a special problem: sexist language. Prior to the feminist movement, writers used the male pronoun when referring to someone who could be male or female. Today this practice is considered sexist, implying that women either aren't important or don't exist. Sexism can work in reverse as well. For example, using a female pronoun when referring to a nurse implies that there are no male nurses. Some writers try to use plural forms whenever possible, thus avoiding the he/she distinction. In any case, check your pronouns as part of your editing process. Trace each pronoun back to the word it stands for.

Male:	he, him, his
Female:	she, her, hers
Neutral:	it, its
Male-female:	he or she, his or hers they, them, their, theirs

Practice 2

Use an appropriate pronoun (or two) in these sentences:

1. The police officer looked at _____ records.

2. A football coach has to watch out for _____ team.

3. The committee asked _____ members to do some studying.

4. The flight attendant lost _____ keys in flight.

5. The class gave _____ response in writing.

6. The school board based _____ decision on the facts.

7. Jo and Ellen said the problem is _____ .

8. The basketball team lost _____ first-place ranking.

A Special Set of Pronouns: Indefinites

You're probably unaware of how often you use a special set of pronouns:

everyone	anything	neither
everybody	anyone	every
everything	anybody	nobody
something	each	none
somebody	either	nothing

When you use these pronouns as the subject of a sentence, use a *singular* verb. One of the problems in remembering this rule lies in how we often use them to mean many people; some of these pronouns are *psychologically plural*. Grammatically, however, they are all singular.

Everyone in the room was happy with the outcome.

Everybody contributes to the project.

Anybody is welcome to join.

Neither runs very fast.

Each of the toys has some merit.

Note: When we separate the subject pronoun from its verb, as in the last example, it's easy to get confused. Remember that the words coming between the subject and its verb have no effect on the correct form of verb, singular or plural.

Each (singular) of the toys has (singular) some merit.

Neither (singular) of the boys seems (singular) well suited for the job.

The following pronouns may be either singular or plural; it all depends on the meaning of your sentence:

some   none   any   most

None of the boxes are the right size.

Some of the pages are missing.

Some of the ink is smeared.

A final special rule: When you join two or more subjects with *or* or *nor,* you will use the subject closest to the verb as the determining factor for singular or plural.

Neither my sister nor her friends like the outfits.

Neither her friends nor my sister likes the outfits.

Either that box or those crates are okay.

Either those crates or that box is okay.

Practice 3

Complete the sentence. Remember these pronouns take a singular verb. Stay in the present tense.

1. Anyone _____ welcome to attend the meeting.

2. Someone _____ responsible for the error.

3. Everybody _____ coming to the party tonight.

4. Every kid in school _____ in the school cafeteria.

5. Nothing _____ right when Sara's in charge.

6. None of the students _____ in the room then.

7. Neither _____ good etiquette at the supper table.

8. Something _____ happening tonight.

Practice 4

Choose either a singular or plural verb form to match the subject pronoun.

1. Each of the players (has/have) _____ good ideas for improvement.

2. Neither of the managers (seems/seem) _____ happy here.

3. Some of the players (is/are) _____ ready to quit the team.

4. Some of the owners and one manager (is/are) _____ a bit greedy.

5. Either the manager or the owners (has/have) _____ to give in.

6. Neither the players nor the manager (likes/like) _____ the owners.

7. Either the owners or the manager (needs/need) _____ to meet with the team.

8. Some of the media coverage (is/are) _____ exaggerated.

Common Pronoun Problems

Pronoun Shifts. A common writing problem involves shifting "persons" in a sentence:

> When *one* thinks about super athletes, *you* have to consider Michael Jordan.
>
> Since Japan is an important industrial nation, *people* should know about it. *You* should research its rise to power.

Keep the same "person":
> When *you* think about super athletes, *you* . . .
>
> . . . *people* should know about it. *They* should . . .

Orphans. When a pronoun doesn't refer to a noun, it becomes an "orphan." It has no reference in the sentence:

> In some areas of the world, *they* appreciate the assistance of the United Nations.
>
> (who is they?) →
>
> In some areas of the world, *underdeveloped nations* appreciate the assistance.
>
> My brother admired *people* who devote their lives to medical research, and he decided to become *one.*
>
> (one what?) →
>
> My brother admired people who devote their lives to medical research, and he decided to become a *medical* researcher.

Always check each pronoun that you use; trace it back to a noun either in the same sentence or in the sentence just before it.

Ambiguous Pronouns. Readers must be able to tell just whom the pronoun refers to:

Carrie told her sister that *she* would be better off to quit her job. →
Carrie told her sister to quit her job.

In this sentence, the reader has no idea if *she* refers to Carrie or her sister. The reference is ambiguous, a large word meaning "unclear." Sometimes, you will have to reword the entire sentence to clear up the ambiguity.

Practice 5

Correct the pronoun errors in these sentences. Although you don't need to know the "term" for each type of error, you should be able to explain why the error occurred.

1. When the prize was awarded to the local newspaper, they said it would boost sales.
2. Sally told Lynn that she should attend summer school.
3. Reading about engineering made me think about it as a career, and now I want to become one.
4. When one talks about good manners, you have to mention Sam.

Matching Pronouns with Pronouns

Just as we have to be concerned with pronouns agreeing with their verbs, we also have to check that indefinite pronouns are correctly matched with other pronouns. We use indefinite pronouns when we don't know names or simply want to be more general in our discussion. As noted earlier, the indefinite pronouns are singular; therefore, they require a singular pronoun:

Everyone in the cafeteria was throwing his or her books.

Anyone caught throwing food will have his or her activities taken away for the week.

Matching Pronouns with Collective Nouns

A collective noun—words like *team, family, group, committee, class, army*—requires a singular pronoun whenever the noun refers to a single unit, a group.

The team has lost its tickets.

My family takes its vacations in warm places.

If, however, you are referring to individual members of that unit, you would use a plural pronoun.

Practice 6

Match the subject pronoun with an appropriate form of the verb.

1. Either the blue dress or red suit (is/are) _____ workable.

2. None of those books (is/are) _____ very good.

3. Each of the tests (shows/show) _____ promise.

4. Everyone in the room (has/have) _____ contributed something.

5. Nobody ever (tells/tell) _____ me anything.

6. Either the books or the stereo (has/have) _____ to go first.

7. Neither rain nor snow (stops/stop) _____ the mail.

8. Neither my brother nor my sisters (is/are) _____ here.

9. The team (has/have) _____ lost the game.

10. My class (takes/take) _____ all day for the trip.

Pronoun Antecedent

Pronouns have to agree in number (singular/plural) with the word they stand for:

The boys lost their books on that trip.

The neighbor boy lost his books on that trip.

The cat found its box in the basement.

In short and uncomplicated sentences, we can usually make the connection easily. Many of our sentences, however, are fairly complex. Then, keeping track of pronouns becomes an editing task.

> If *students* insist on missing the 8:00 A.M. class, and then ask for makeup work, *they* will have to see the dean.

> Because of *its* prestige and power, the American Heart *Association* is able to raise millions of dollars for *its* research.

Keep gender problems and collective nouns in mind as you work with pronouns.

Practice 7

Circle the noun that the pronoun must agree with. Then fill in the blank with the appropriate pronoun.

1. For Christians, the Christmas season has (its/their) _____

own rites associated with religion.

2. The record industry did not want government interference; (it/they)

_____ preferred to monitor the issues.

3. Several members of that fraternity volunteer (his/their)

_____ time for community service work.

4. The ski club will hold (its/their) _____ dance next week.

5. Every year violent crimes against women rise; however, (it/they)

_____ may only be a reflection of the increase in reported

crimes.

6. Unlike many colleges, my school still requires English as part of

(its/their) _____ graduation requirement.

7. Watching the duck swim to shore, I began to wonder if something

   was wrong with (its/their) _____ feet.

8. The performers on *Saturday Night Live* had a great time with politi-

   cal candidates, exaggerating (his or her/their) _____ per-

   sonal mannerisms.

Practice 8

Rewrite these sentences, correcting pronoun errors:

1. Even if one does not lose their license, the violation will cost money.

   _____

   _____

2. The youngest child can take advantage of learning from their older
   brothers and sisters.

   _____

   _____

3. When the oldest child gets a D, they want to hide it from parents.

   _____

   _____

4. Not only does it help the relationship but this sharing has also been
   good for us.

   _____

   _____

5. He likes to do this mainly because of the recognition they receive
   in the process.

   _____

   _____

6. Most colleges will not look at an athlete, no matter how good they are, unless they have halfway decent grades.

_____

_____

Demonstrative Pronouns

Demonstrative pronouns point out a specific person or thing, and we use them in different ways and for different reasons:

This is a great book.   _That_ was a terrific dinner.

What do we know about "this" and "that" in this example? First, they are both singular, and second, they refer to something else in the sentence. But there is a difference in their meaning: _this_ refers to something near us in time, place, or thought; by contrast, _that_ refers to something farther away or in the past. The plural forms of these pronouns are _these_ and _those:_

These are wonderful essays.   _Those_ are serious problems.

Just as with any other pronoun and the noun it represents, demonstrative pronouns must agree in number with their nouns, singular and singular, plural and plural:

this book   that dinner   these essays   those problems

Demonstrative Pronouns

Singular: this, that   Plural: these, those

Use for something near in time or place: this, these
Use for something farther away or in the past: that, those

We also use demonstrative pronouns in another way: to describe or to point out which person, place, or thing. In this use, they become adjectives (descriptors):

This coffee is way too strong.
That trip to California last month cost me a month's wages.

These forms have to be filled out correctly.

Those boxes in the corner should be moved.

I need *those* newspapers right away.

What do you think of *this* idea?

He is concerned about *these* bills.

I didn't like *that* reason at all.

When we use the demonstratives in this way, they must agree in number with the noun beside which they are placed.

ESL Writers

Check that the pronoun matches the noun: singular and singular; plural and plural

this book   that box   these books   those boxes

Practice 9

Underline the demonstrative pronouns and adjectives in the following sentences.

1. That lecture on water pollution changed my mind about those new laws.
2. The longer I put off filling out these forms, the harder that job will be.
3. Those aren't very good reasons not to do the work.
4. I enjoy math, but I can't handle these problems.
5. This course is pretty demanding.
6. That was a great idea.
7. These curtains match the kitchen colors better than those do.
8. I should send in my taxes because this is the year I get a refund.

Sometimes, we use the pronoun without a specific noun next to it or in the same sentence:

These will help a lot.   *Those* can be thrown out.

In this case, the pronouns refer to a word or word group in the previous sentence:

I've examined the forms.   *Those* can be thrown out.

When we use pronouns this way, we have to be sure that the pronoun and noun agree in number:

We have two major road *projects* this summer. *These* have caused many problems for residents living on the west side of town.

A better way to write this sentence, however, would place *projects* after *these* in the second sentence: *These projects* have caused many problems . . . .

Practice 10

Underline and correct any error with demonstrative pronouns or adjectives.

1. My brother is eating a low-fat diet and exercising. This activity resulted in better weight control.
2. He learned that those new diet pills can be dangerous.
3. There are good reasons to avoid this easy "get thin" schemes.
4. My brother overate because of boredom, and this was an easy way to get fat.
5. He has my family's support. Those are always helpful.
6. Maintaining his weight is his goal. These are not easy to do.
7. I like the new rules for weight loss. This uses common sense rather than complete deprivation of favorite foods.
8. Those favorite foods are high in fat; however, they can be part of this new rules.

ADJECTIVES AND ADVERBS

Adjectives

What they do: describe or modify a noun or pronoun

the happy children

Where they are placed: usually before the noun but also following certain verbs

The children are happy.   Everyone seems tired.

Adjectives may be created from nouns:

America → American

Some words may be used as either an adjective or a noun:

Both students are here.   Both are here.

ESL Writers

Adjectives may follow these verbs:

am, is, are, was, were, be, been
seem, seems, seemed
appear, appears appeared
remain, remains, remained

Comparing Adjectives

When there is no comparison:

Alan is strong.

When two persons, things, places, or ideas are compared, use either *-er* or *more:*

John is stronger.   That idea is more curious than the last one.

When three or more are compared, use *-est* or *most:*

Elisa is the strongest of all.   This is the most wonderful idea.

> ### ESL Writers
>
> Some adjectives always use *more* or *most* to form comparisons:
>
> careful   helpful   wonderful   caring
>
> Check your dictionary if you are uncertain about the correct form.

Adverbs

What they do: tell how, when, where, how often, and how much

Where they are placed: usually close to the word or words they "describe"

> Chris walked *quietly* into the room. (how?)
> *Yesterday* I lost my purse. (when?)
> I was *in the store* when I saw it. (where?)
> He goes to the movies *every day*. (how often?)
> The book is *entirely* false. (how much?)

But adverbs have flexibility and may be found throughout the sentence.

> *Carefully,* the old man walked toward the house.
> The old man walked *carefully* toward the house.

> ### ESL Writers
>
> Adverbs can be put into four categories.
>
> **Time (when, how often, how long):** today, at noon, by 3 P.M., weekly, daily, every month, briefly, forever, usually
>
> **Place (where, from where):** here, in the box, at the movies, forward, backward
>
> **Manner (how):** slowly, regularly, carefully
>
> **Degree (how much, how little):** too, very, greatly, entirely
>
> Although the *-ly* ending marks many common adverbs, you can also recognize them through the questions that they answer.

Comparing Adverbs

When there is no comparison:

Elena runs quickly.

When two persons, places, things, or ideas are compared, use *-er* or *more:*

Elena runs faster than Kate.   Mrs. Pavlov speaks more clearly than Ms. Smith.

When three or more are compared, use *-est* or *most:*

Sara ran fastest today.   Of all the teachers, Mr. Jones treated us most fairly.

Special Adverbs

well	better	best
badly	worse	worst

Kevin does well in school.   Lee worked better last week. Kate sang best after lunch.

Karen sang badly.   She felt worse after the awards.   Of the four, Kelli looked worst.

ESL Writers

English adjectives and adverbs do not have a plural form:

the black shoe   the black shoes   he runs fast   they run fast

---

REVISING AND EDITING SENTENCES

When we write, we have to look at sentences from two perspectives: Are they correct? Are they effective? Sometimes we write sentences that are complete and technically correct but not very effective.

They are too similar in structure, and whether we are conscious of it or not, as readers, we want and need variety in sentence length and construction. As readers, we also want clarity in our sentences, which comes both through the way we construct sentences and from the storehouse of vocabulary that helps us in that process. Sentence revision, restructuring sentences, is the first step. Checking for mechanical errors, editing, is the second.

__Group Activity__

With your writing partner, rewrite the following with sentences that are both correct and effective, varying sentence length and structure as often as possible. You have to switch from writer to reader for this exercise, putting yourself in the place of someone who will have only your sentences to guide him or her through the information. There is no single or right way in which to write this piece. You and your partner will need to discuss your way through it: How many ways could the sentence be structured? What punctuation is necessary? What punctuation helps the reader? Should this information be presented in one sentence or two? And so forth. Do a final check for correctness: punctuation, capitalization, and spelling.

The following was adapted from W. Hodding Carter, writing for Lands' End, the catalogue people who sponsored his 1997 trip retracing Leif Ericsson's original Viking voyage to North America 1,000 years ago.

IN THE WAKE OF THE VIKINGS, THE PURSUIT OF A DREAM

A.

Nearly a millennium ago in the summer of 1000 Leif Ericsson and his crew of twenty or so sailors left their homes in southern greenland in search of a more wooded and fertile land.

B.

They navigated their knarr (open-decked cargo vessel) using the sun the stars the smell of the air and the shape of the waves. And they set foot where no white man had gone before. Leifs journey is now a matter of history. From the late seven hundreds to 1100 they invaded and sometimes conquered nearly every european kingdom and even made inroads into asia.

C.

The vikings who came to iceland and greenland however were mostly farmers and tradesmen looking for land of their own. They sailed in knarrs loaded down with familiar possessions goats cattle horses and tools. They first settled iceland in the 860s.

D.

Over the next century arable land became scarce and in 985 Eric the Red led a group of settlers to greenland, getting there was no small matter although the vikings were some of the worlds best seamen at that time equaled only by the polynesians.

E.

Many of their ships never reached their destination succumbing to the icebergs and stormy seas of the north atlantic. Of the twenty-five ships that set sail from iceland in 985 only fourteen landed in greenland.

F.

Greenland turned out to be not as green as Eric the Red had promised. They found the entire east coast uninhabitable for grazing animals and within a very short time most of the viable land on the west coast had been claimed.

G.

By the year 1000 it was clear to the norse that self-sufficiency in greenland was out of the question, they did not even have trees to build or repair there boats. That is when leif made his trip to the west.

H.

Leif sailed up to the greenland coast using the prevailing currents made a short crossing to baffin island sailed down the baffin and labrador coasts and then landed somewhere along the southern canadian coast exactly where it is not known.

I.

Our trip this Summer will follow Leifs route as exactly as possible. We will start in southern greenland at eric's old farm, follow leifs trail north west and then south and finish our voyage at L'Anse aux Meadows, Newfoundland—the only confirmed viking settlement in north america.

J.

This is probably the most indirect way to reach Newfoundland imaginable but the route follows the coastline which is what the vikings did due to the fact that they had no radars compasses or even sextants.

K.

I want to make it perfectly clear why leif went adventuring, leif did not try to cross unknown waters to reach unknown land simply because it was there. He performed this heroic journey due to the fact that he and his fellow greenlanders needed him to. It was not a chest-thumping adventure.

▬ Group Activity ▬

The student essay that follows needs both sentence revision and editing. It has plenty of voice—in fact, we can easily hear the writer "talking" to us—but the effectiveness is lost due to wordiness and errors.

Before you meet with your group, read "Life as I Know It." As you read, put a plus (+) next to sentences that really work and a minus (–) next to sentences that don't (too long, too short, unclear in some way). Although there are other problems with the essay, just concentrate on the sentences for now. You will come across some fragmented sentences, but you may find they are used intentionally, to achieve a certain effect. You need to consider the sentences as they work within the paragraph. Do they balance one another (various lengths, different structures, etc.)? You do not have to make any changes or corrections—only determine where they are needed and why. Specific instructions for your group work follow the essay.

Life as I Know It

"Mom Greg saw me in my underwear!" "Daddy Greg hit me really hard." A typical day in the Douglas household. These are just a few of the many drawbacks in being the older brother. Forget what you see on The Cosby Show. Forget about Alex and Jennifers latest squabble on Family Ties. This is the real world and I am a kid dealing with real sibling rivalry.

Over the years I have learned actually more or less been forced to deal with my younger sister Ann. Since as far back as I can remember Ann has always gotten her way while I sat watching in disgust. In matters such as money the "family" car, nightly curfews and the ever so popular teenage drinking I have unavoidably paved the way for her. My parents have already been through all normal teen age problems with me. In their eyes I have done everything wrong so with Ann they now expect it and deal with her teenage life in a more relaxed manner.

The best and most efficient way to illustrate my point is through examples. Although you will never be able to completely understand my situation you will get a feel of the hell I have to go through every day being the older brother.

When I turned fourteen everything changes for me. Mom and dad stopped paying for things such as movies junk food and everything else that wasn't crucial to my survival as they saw it. I lived through this 7th grade only to see my sister three years later never have to deal with it. Every day mom hands Ann a ten dollar bill just in case she might need it. Ann is now sixteen and is still getting money from our parents every time she goes to the show or to the mall. Whenever I question them about this they try to avoid an answer completely or try to justify their actions by saying she doesn't have enough money today or we just want her to be with her friends, which is usually followed by my sister informing me with a huge grin on her face that I have to drive she and her friends to the show.

Ann took finaly driving lessons to which I had to drive her but things sure were different when she got her license then when I got mine. When my friends and

I got our drivers licenses and started going out mom began to worry. The dreaded curfew was hung over my head. Every weekend through High School I could beg her to let me stay out just a little bit longer but she would always say I can't fall asleep until you get home. I don't know how her sleep improved but Ann is able to come home at a "reasonable hour" as mom put it. Also because Ann learned from my mistakes and never argued with mom about when her curfew would be mom began to trust her. Mom no longer has a problem falling asleep. Ann is now able to sneak in at any hour without getting caught. I cannot believe what she gets away with. There was one time when I thought to myself "Ha--now she is going to get it" but as ususal Ann came out on top.

My family and I had planned a trip to Myrtle Beach South Carolina but Ann didn't want to come along because her best friend was moving to Georgia and her boyfriend was leaving for college that week. After a long drawn out argument with our parents she managed to con them into letting her stay home. Before we left mom and dad made sure that Ann understand she was not to have a party. This little talking to meant absolutely nothing to Ann but I wasn't going to tell my parents that. Thus when we returned a week later at ten in the morning we found a line of cars all the way down the street and at least twenty people passed out in our house. My parents were furious needless to say and kicked everyone out of the house. But despite their anger all my sister had to do was clean the bathroom, pick up all the beer cans and cigarette butts and stay in the rest of the day to think about what she had done.

When I was her age I was grounded for a week when I lied to my parents. It was my friends birthday and we

had planned this for a weeks. We told our friends we
were going to sleep over at his house. What we really
did was Tom, Neil, Dave and I had a field party by
ourselves. Our parents didn't know that we got drunk
and passed out. Or that Neil ended up crying because
he thought Dave was dead. Or Tom coughing up Jack
Daniels all night. Or when the bottle blew up in the
fire and caught Neil and Toms sleeping bag on fire
when they were asleep. They didn't even know about
the glass that got shot into Dave's arm. All they knew
was that we weren't at Brents that night because she
called to remind Neil of his dentists appointment. She
called all the other parents and they all decided that
we should be grounded for one week. Of course we were
all the oldest in our familys.

Now in my sisters case it was the first time she
had been caught doing something of this nature and my
parents didn't call any of the other parents to talk
about punishment. She just simply made my sister clean
the house and stay in for a day. Now can you tell me
that this is fair and the oldest don't get the worst
of almost everything?

As a group, take each paragraph in turn and discuss any plus or minus
sentences in it. Talk about why the sentence worked or didn't work for
you as a reader.

1. Sentences that worked: easy to follow; vivid words; ideas clearly related; length appropriate (short or long) to the idea and context of
   the paragraph.

2. Sentences that didn't work: too short or too simple for the idea or
   context of the paragraph; too long, with too many ideas in one
   structure; unclear, confusing, required reading several times.

3. How did the essay "sound": formal, informal, academic, funny, serious, chatty or conversational? How did the sentences contribute
   to the "sound" of the essay? Do you think you might recognize another piece of writing by this same student writer? Why? What dis-
   tinguishes this writer?

4. What's the role of punctuation, specifically commas, in helping readers sort out ideas? Note some places where commas helped, hindered, or were needed.

Writing Partner Activity

We can revise sentences through one of two basic strategies: modify them in some way (add words, delete words, substitute words) or combine them. Together, choose a paragraph from "Life as I Know It" and revise the sentences that are unclear, awkward, or ineffective in some way. Discuss your reason for each revision. What made you decide to delete, add, or substitute words? What made you decide to combine sentences?

Mechanics: Punctuation, Capitalization, Spelling

APOSTROPHES

Quite a few generations of students have hoped that the apostrophe would drop out of use, but it's still with us. We use it for two reasons: to show possession and to make contractions.

Showing Possession

Possession means ownership: someone or something "owns" someone or something else. We can understand this relationship easily enough when "someone or something" is concrete, a person owning an object, for example:

Jon's hat is ten sizes too large.

The girl's dress is torn.

The process is a bit more difficult when something is not concrete, when we can't see it:

Paul's ideas are good ones.

That child's attitude needs adjustment.

The coach's stupidity lost the game.

We have to visualize this relationship as "owns" or "of":

The stupidity of the coach

And we have a bit more trouble when both the "owner" and "what's owned" are less immediately visible and concrete:

> The idea's value was questionable.
>
> The organization's ideals got lost.
>
> Our society's attitudes have changed.

Once we have decided who or what is doing the possessing, we simply add -'s to that word. We could think of the -'s as replacing *of the* and saving us time and space.

The apostrophe shows both ownership and relationship:

Ownership	Relationship
Cristina's paper	Xiong's grandfather
his father's job	in an hour's time
the dog's cage	one dollar's worth of candy

PRACTICE   Apostrophes

Practice 1

Use an apostrophe to show ownership:

1. the rights of the student _____

2. the liberation of the people _____

3. the conclusion of the committee _____

4. the talent of the team _____

5. the usefulness of the idea _____

6. the decision of the teacher _____

7. the merit of his work _____

8. the antics of the star _____

9. the flaws of the contract _____

10. the cell of the plant _____

So far, we have been working with singular words. But what if the word is plural and already has an -*s*? If it does have the -*s* as its last letter, simply add the apostrophe:

The boys' coats were thrown on the floor.

The horses' harnesses were torn.

He listened to the workers' complaints.

The uniforms' logos had to be changed.

Practice 2

Rewrite with the apostrophe:

1. the problems of the workers   —————————————————
2. the voices of the teachers   —————————————————
3. the skins of the rattlesnakes   —————————————————
4. the software of the computers   —————————————————
5. the books of the students   —————————————————
6. the appetites of the wrestlers   —————————————————
7. the beliefs of the Muslims   —————————————————
8. the noise of the agitators   —————————————————
9. the fare wars of the airlines   —————————————————
10. the interdependence of the companies   —————————————————

So far, so good. But some words form their plurals without adding an -*s*:

man   men   child   children   woman   women

And some keep the same form, singular or plural:

sheep   deer

There aren't many of these oddities in English, and in any case, we follow the same rule:

To Show Possession:

If the word showing ownership does not end in -*s*, add '*s*.

If the word showing ownership already ends in -*s*, add the apostrophe only.

If the word showing ownership is a singular proper noun, add '*s*. If it is plural and already ends in -*s*, add the apostrophe only.

The man's hat was stolen.

The men's club meets tonight.

The child's toy is too expensive.

The children's stories are wonderful.

The sheep's coat is ready to cut.

The sheep's coats are ready to cut.

Los Angeles's smog is world famous.

Ray Charles's Pepsi commercials brought a ton of money.

Practice 3

Show ownership with the following words. You'll have to add whatever it is that they "own."

1. Jimmy Conners _____

2. Rolling Stones _____

3. women _____

4. freshman _____

5. Los Cerritos _____

6. lemons _____

7. rug _____

8. CD _____

9. children _____

10. freshmen _____

A note about a different kind of possessive:

The book is *yours.*

His ideas are old-fashioned.

Their car is unreliable.

The pronouns showing possession have *no* apostrophe. The word itself indicates ownership.

Practice 4

List the following: five things that belong only to you; five things that belong to someone in your family or to a friend; five things that are shared by at least two people. Now use an apostrophe or possessive to show ownership. Exchange your list with your writing partner or group to check that each use is correct.

Contractions

Another common use of the apostrophe occurs in contractions. When we use a contraction, we are using a shortcut. We omit a letter or two and push two words together where we have omitted letters:

she is	she's
I will not	I won't
you have	you've
do not	don't

In most college and business writing, however, we usually write out the complete words—no contractions. In personal letters and other informal writing, we can use them.

COLONS

The colon (:) can give versatility to your writing. Examine the following sentences, and note the relationship between the sentence before the colon and the word group that follows it.

My brother has some weird exercises: hanging from trees, wrapping his body around poles, and swinging from lights.

I got the shock of my life: my roommate was reading my mail.

In the 1980s, people had one goal: making money.

World problems are serious: starvation in Somalia, civil war in the former Yugoslavia, and confrontation between the Arab and Western worlds.

Don't forget to check this list: soup, pizza, candy, soda pop, and beer.

What does the colon do? You might have noticed that it takes the place of saying, "I'll tell you what. . . ." For example, "the shock of my life" *is* the roommate snooping in mail; "the goal" *is* making money; and world problems *are* the situations described after the colon. Colons make our writing efficient and easy to follow. We can provide lists, descriptions, and explanations clearly and economically.

> Note the following:
>
> Before the colon, we have a complete sentence.
>
> Do not use a colon right after the verb.
>
> After the colon, we can have any structure—a complete sentence, a single word, or word groups.

PRACTICE   **Colons**

With your group, set up some lists:

1. Jobs you'd like
2. Jobs you'd hate
3. Favorite foods
4. People you admire
5. Places you want to travel
6. Television shows you hate the most
7. Classes you want to avoid
8. Movies everyone should see

Create sentences that use a colon. Be sure to use a complete sentence before the colon.

COMMAS

Separating Items in a Series

In academic or business writing, use a comma to separate three or more words or word groups in a sentence:

Gum, popcorn, and candy bars are high-priced at the movies.

Jon was running, hopping, and skipping.

May, June, July, and August are best for travel.

Note: If you have three items, two commas; if you have four items, three commas; and so on. In brief, use one less comma than the number of items you are separating.

Separating Places and Dates

Within a sentence, separate the city from the state and the state from the rest of the sentence:

I've been visiting San Diego, California, for ten years now.

Also separate the parts of a street address:

Send it to 1500 West Park Place, Chicago, IL 60618.

Note: Do not separate the state from its zip code.

Separate the following parts of a date:

He will return on January 15, 1994, if everything goes as planned.

Note: Do not separate the month from the day.

Using Commas with Modifiers

In the sections on coordination and subordination, we reviewed the use of commas with modifiers. Briefly, here are the rules once more:

Use a comma to separate introductory material from the main sentence:

Listening to Paul, I got a headache.
According to the manual, the plug goes here.

Use a comma to separate words or word groups that provide an extra bit of information. This information may be good, but it is not essential. If we pull it out, the main sentence can stand alone and expresses the same meaning.

My brother, who's a bit of a pest, is only six.
Jon Landen, the best swimmer on the team, dropped out.
I gave the book to Ellen, my best friend.

Contrast the preceding sentences with this one:

The girl who ate the ants got sick.

Who got sick? Any girl? We need "who ate the ants" to provide the identification, to know just which girl we are discussing. Therefore, no commas are needed.

QUOTATION MARKS

Direct Quotations

We use quotation marks to set off someone's exact words:

The coach of the Dallas Cowboys said, "We win because we love each other."

"We win because we love each other," said the coach of the Dallas Cowboys.

Note: The comma sets off the speaker from what is said.

We use quotation marks only when we quote directly, the exact words, of the speaker. Here is an indirect quote:

The coach of the Dallas Cowboys said that they win because they love each other.

No quotation marks are used because it is an indirect quotation.

Punctuation with Quotation Marks

Place periods and commas within the closing quotation mark:

The coach said, "You guys are the greatest."
The players said, "We know we are."
"You're supposed to be more modest," said the coach.

Place colons and semicolons outside of the closing quotation mark:

My math teacher said, "This assignment will take only an hour"; however, he later added, "for most of you."

Place question marks, exclamation points, and dashes inside of the closing quotation mark when they are part of the quoted material:

My math teacher asked, "Will each of you take one problem?"
My English teacher said, "This is the greatest class!"

However, if these marks are part of a larger sentence and not part of the directly quoted material, the marks go outside:

What does the math teacher mean by "one problem"?

Titles

Use quotation marks to set off the following titles:

Short stories	I read "The Frozen Tundra" yesterday.
Poems	He likes Robert Frost's "The Road Not Taken."
Magazine articles	"Too Old, Too Fast?" in *Newsweek* suggests high school kids shouldn't work.
Chapters of books	You should read "The Love Connection" in *Growing Up Male.*
Songs	"You've Got That Loving Feeling" was used in the sound track of the film *Top Gun.*

> **Note:** In academic and business writing, titles of books, magazines, films, and videos are underlined or printed in italic type. One way to remember the rule: the shorter works use quotation marks.

CAPITALIZATION

In standard written English, we are expected to capitalize the following words:

1. The first word of every sentence, including sentences that are direct quotations within a larger sentence:

   The boy screamed, "That is the wrong car!"

2. The names of specific people, places, or groups:

   Patty Lehman visits Miami, Florida, every year.
   Some people are crazy about the Miami Dolphins football team.
   The U.S. Air Force is cutting its recruits.
   The Lakota Sioux were central to the film *Dances with Wolves.*

3. The names of specific events:

   He is a veteran of the Vietnam War, and his dad is a vet of World War II.

4. The names of specific businesses and brand names:

Cray Research builds computers for the world.
I had a Pepsi for lunch.
Hand over the Milky Way bar.
Is that a Sony?

5. The names of specific languages, religions, and organizations:

I wish I knew what these French phrases mean.
He says he is Hindu, but I think he's Catholic.
The Democratic party has its headquarters downtown.

6. The names of specific courses:

Jan is taking Math 203 this semester.
I'm struggling with Chemistry 100.
Take Psych 100, Introduction to Psychology.

7. The titles of books, articles, poems, songs, and artworks:

Rising Sun explores the clash between Japanese and American ways of doing business.
The *Mona Lisa* is one of Leonardo da Vinci's most famous paintings.
I have to read "Ode on a Grecian Urn" for tomorrow.

PRACTICE Capitalization

Correct the capitalization in the following sentences:

1. The reverend jesse jackson is a baptist minister who doesn't limit his congregation to a single church.
2. Reverend jackson has been involved in the civil rights movement for several decades.
3. We've been studying martin luther king, jr., and his leadership of african americans in political science 100.
4. I've been reading malcolm x for my book report in poly sci.
5. The poetry of gwendolyn brooks, such as "we cool," is relevant today,

A Capitalization Problem: Our Relatives

Many writers are uncertain about when to capitalize the names of relatives. Notice the difference in these sentences:

I went to visit *my grandmother.*   I saw *my dad* at the game.

Can you help me, *Grandmother?*   *Dad,* I'm over here.

How old is *Grandma Smith?*   I am going with *Dad.*

When you use a possessive (as *my* in the above), you don't capitalize. But when you use "grandmother" or "dad" as you would a first name, you do capitalize.

I saw *Tom* at the game.   I saw *Dad* at the game.

SPELLING

Why It Matters

English spelling can be frustrating, mainly because we represent sounds by many different combinations of letters. We don't have many useful spelling rules either. Regardless, we are expected to use standard spelling in school and the workplace. For most people, this expectation entails careful editing. Spelling errors, perhaps more than any other aspect of writing, distract and annoy readers. Further, some readers will judge the writer to be unintelligent and uneducated if spelling errors are present—no matter how good or well-developed the ideas in that piece. For this reason, checking for spelling errors is crucial.

Learning a Few, Only a Few, Rules

A few spelling rules can help you with some of the most commonly misspelled words.

I before E except after C.   Use the Rhyme:

Write I before E

Except after C

Or when sounded like ay

As in neighbor and weigh

The following show how the rhyme works for using *ie* and *ei:*

✦ generally, I before E:

  believe   piece   fierce   grieve

✦ except after C:

  receive   conceited   receipt

✦ or when sounded like ay:

  eight   neighbor   weight

✦ But there are exceptions, which you simply have to learn or look up:

  height   weird   neither   leisure   foreign

Check a dictionary or use your computer spelling checker to be sure.

Doubling the Final Consonant

✦ When the consonant is preceded by a vowel and ends a one-syllable word:

  bet–betting   sad–sadder   win–winner   stop–stopped

✦ When the consonant is preceded by a vowel and ends in a stressed syllable (stressed means we put our voice emphasis or accent on that syllable). Say the word aloud to hear the stress (try omit):

  commit–committed   control–controlling   prefer–preferred

✦ An exception, of course. The rule does not apply if you add an ending that doesn't start a vowel, such as *-ment* or *-ness:*

  commit–commitment   sad–sadness   disappoint–disappointment

Dropping the Final, the Silent, E

✦ When you add an ending that begins with a vowel, drop the final *e:*

  age–aging   fame–famous   use–usable   write–writing

◆ When you add an ending that begins with a consonant, keep the final *e:*

lone–lonely   safe–safety   state–statement

◆ Some exceptions: argument, judgment, ninth

Changing Y to I

◆ When you add an ending to a word that ends in *y,* change the *y* to *i:*

happy–happiness   study–studies   family–families

◆ An exception: when the word ends with *-ing,* do not make the change:

study–studying   carry–carrying

◆ Another exception: do not omit the final *y* when a vowel precedes it:

play–playful   buy–buys

Forming Plurals

◆ Most nouns form their plurals by adding *s* to the singular form:

paper–papers   pencil–pencils   house–houses

◆ Nouns ending in *sh, ch, x, s,* and *z* add *es* to the singular form:

dish–dishes   church–churches   box–boxes

◆ Some nouns use the same form for singular and plural:

deer   sheep   fish

◆ A singular noun that ends in *y* (preceded by a consonant) changes the *y* to *i* and adds *es* for the plural form:

fly–flies   baby–babies

◆ A singular noun that ends in *y* (preceded by a vowel) adds *s* for the plural:

monkey–monkeys   valley–valleys

✦ Nouns ending in *o* (preceded by a vowel) add *s:*

radio–radios   studio–studios

✦ Most nouns ending in *o* (preceded by a consonant) add *es:*

tomato–tomatoes   hero–heroes

Note: For musical terms (e.g., piano, solo), add only *s.*

✦ If the noun ends in *f* or *fe,* listen to the sound of the plural:

if the plural ends with the *f* sound, add *s*   (roof–roofs)

if the plural ends with the *v* sound, change *f* to *ve* and add *s* (wife–wives)

if the plural ends with either sound, either spelling is correct   (hoof)

Special Cases

Some English nouns with irregular plurals:

child–children   man–men   goose–geese   mouse–mice

Common foreign words with irregular plurals:

datum–data   crisis–crises   criterion–criteria   radius–radii

---

✦ Plurals of numbers, symbols, letters, and figures are formed with *'s:*

two A's   those %'s   three s's

✦ If there is no confusion, the apostrophe can be omitted:

1990s

✦ If a noun ends in *-ful,* add an *s* to the end of the word:

three spoonfuls of sugar   two tankfuls of gas

✦ Nouns made up of two words (compounds) usually add *s* or *es* to the main or most important word:

sisters-in-law   secretaries-of-state

Writing Out Numbers

+ Numbers from one to nine are usually written as words. All numbers 10 and above are written as numerals:

three   nine   15   360

If you are using numbers to compare or contrast, or to show a range, be sure to keep them in the same form:

8 to 12 year-olds or eight- to twelve-year-olds

+ Use numerals for:

money, decimals, percents, chapter, page, address, telephone, ZIP code, date, statistics, ID numbers

+ Use numerals with abbreviations or symbols: 6 in.   3%
+ Use words to express a number that begins a sentence:

Thirty people attended the lecture.

+ Use a combination or words and numerals for very large numbers:

Research indicated 10 billion people could be affected.
He is reportedly worth 1.6 million dollars.

Confusing Word Pairs

+ **a, an**   Use *a* before a word that begins with a consonant sound; *an* before words that begin with a vowel sound (an honor). Note sound!

+ **accept, except**   *Accept* means "to receive" or "to believe." *Except* means "other than." The teacher *accepted* the boy's excuse. No one *except* the teacher believed it.

+ **affect, effect**   *Affect* means "to influence." *Effect* means "the result." The noise *affected* the audience. The *effect* of the injury was a blood clot.

+ **compare with, compare to**   Things belonging to the same class are *compared with: Compared with* a woman, a man may have no fashion sense. Things in different classes are *compared to:* A woman *compared to* a dog is a sexist insult.

+ **different from, different than**   In formal writing, such as for school or workplace settings, use *different from.*

✦ **farther, further**   Use *farther* to refer to a physical distance; use *further* to refer to additional time, quantity, or degree. Go two blocks *farther.* She is no *further* along in her schooling.

✦ **fewer, less**   *Fewer* refers to something that can be counted in separate units, the number of separate units: I want *fewer* mistakes on the next test. *Less* refers to a bulk quantity, something we can't count in units: He'd like *less* stress. Use *fewer* to answer the question "how many?" and *less* to answer "how much?"

✦ **good, well**   *Good* is an adjective, describing a noun: He is a *good* father. *Well* is usually an adverb, telling how one does something: She swims *well. Well* is an adjective when it describes a state of health: I'm very *well* today.

Note: The opposite of feeling well is feeling bad—not badly.

✦ **it's, its**   *It's* is the short form of *it is* or *it has: It's* around the corner. *It's* been a great vacation. *Its* shows ownership. The dog rolled over on *its* back.

✦ **lay, lie**   *Lay* means " to place" something. *Lie* means to "recline." If you *lay* down that ruler, I will talk with you. If you *lie* down, you might feel better. Knowing (or looking up) the different forms of these verbs is the only way to avoid an error. The oral use is generally incorrect, so always check these forms:

Present Tense	Past Tense	Past Participle	Present Participle
lay	laid	has laid	is laying
lie	lay	has lain	is lying

✦ **lead, led**   *Lead* (sounds like leed) is the present tense of the verb meaning "to guide." *Led* is the past tense of this same verb: He *leads* the group in song every week. He *led* them to the office. When *lead* and *led* are pronounced the same, *lead* refers to the metal: My dad had a *lead* cabinet.

✦ **lose, loose**   *Lose* means to misplace something or not to win: We might *lose* the game. *Loose* means something doesn't fit tightly: This dress is really *loose.*

✦ **quiet, quit, quite**   *Quiet* means an absence of noise. *Quit* means "to stop." *Quite* means "completely."

✦ **real, very, really**   Do not use *real* in place of *very* and *really.* This is *real* ice cream; it is *really* good. Bear Tracks is a *very* tasty flavor.

✦ **than, then**   Use *than* when you make a comparison: Paul is stronger *than* James. Use *then* when you talk about time: *Then* you search the Internet.

◆ **their, there, they're** Use *their* when you want to show ownership: *Their* coats are in the hall. Use *there* when you mean direction: Put the book *there*. *There* is also used to introduce a sentence: *There* is no music here. Use *they're* when you mean *they are*: *They're* my friends.

◆ **through, though** *Through* means finished, or in one side and out the other, or accomplished by: We are *through* here. Go *through* that door. We got that award *through* our hard work. *Though* means although: *Though* he studied hard, he didn't get a good grade on the exam.

◆ **to, too, two** *To* means going toward something or someone: I am going *to* the mall tonight. *To* is also used with a verb: I want *to* leave. *Too* means also or very: Carlos is here *too*. She is *too* quiet. *Two* is the number 2.

Words Often Misspelled

The following words are often misspelled—usually because someone pronounces them in such a way that a sound is left out or changed. The place where the error occurs is in italics.

an*s*wer	dis*app*rove	knowle*dg*e
at*h*lete	do*e*sn't	m*ea*nt
begi*nn*ing	emba*rr*ass	ne*c*essary
beha*vi*or	envir*o*nment	o*cc*asion
ca*l*endar	fam*ili*ar	pos*s*ible
cons*ci*ence	fina*ll*y	*pre*fer
crow*ded*	gover*n*ment	proba*b*ly
de*fi*nite	import*a*nt	sep*a*rate
desp*e*rate	int*e*rest	suc*c*ess
dis*app*oint	jud*g*ment	*sur*prise

Strategies

1. Know your typical errors. Keep a spelling log.

Word	Misspelling	Cause or Type of Problem
definite	*definate*	*Sounding like a*
athlete	*athelete*	*Adding a sound*
site	*sight*	*Confused sound-alike*

2. Understand your own spelling error patterns. Analyze your log for recurring patterns—there'll be some.

The following are common causes of error:

Addition	Adding a letter because of pronouncing an additional sound (like athelete).
Substitution	Substituting a letter for one that sounds similar (like definate).
Deletion	Dropping a letter because it's not pronounced (like goverment instead of government).
Confusion	Mixing up two or more sound-alike words (like there/they're/their).
Demons	Never quite getting the number of double letters right (like necesary instead of necessary).
Reversals	Interchanging letters (like recieve for receive).

3. Use your personal spelling demon list for editing. Careful reading and the use of a computer spelling checker will help you most. One caution, however: The spelling checker cannot distinguish the sound-alike words or errors that result in another acceptable English word.

4. Use a dictionary. If you have trouble with the first letters of the word, ask someone for help.

5. Develop your own methods for remembering problem words.

6. Keep spelling in its correct place: at the end of the drafting and revising processes.

PRACTICE   Sentence Boundaries and Other Punctuation

Read the paragraphs slowly. Try the editing strategies discussed earlier. You may add or delete words.

A

I came home from an average day at school. Except

for my mom was crying and packing her suit case. Great

my parents had an argument and now theyre getting a

divorce. Well at least thats what I thought. What was really wrong was that my grandfather who of course was an alcoholic almost all of his adult life. Was in the hospital after falling off my aunts porch, because he was too drunk to walk up the stairs. He was in a coma and the chance of him coming out of it was very slim so what was my mom upset about. Time passed with our family in ruins but every day we prayed for him to come out of the coma. A month later he finally woke up, and came out with only partial brain damage. He understands everything you say but he can't reply since he doesn't remember how to talk. But boy he has got a great life now he's got people to care for him all day long, he doesn't have to work, he can eat all he wants and each day he can get fatter and fatter until he dies. But there is nothing we can do about it. Because alcohol has already ruined his life.

B

Concerts come in all different types sizes and forms. First for example there is the hard rock concert for the people who like to get rowdy, and party. Another example of a concert would be a jazz concert for the person, who likes to relax and enjoy some mellow music, while eating lunch. I think that this type of concert is the most popular for people who think about and spend time with their boyfriend. This type of concert would be a Lionel Richie concert for example, because he expresses the true feeling of love. In all the songs he sings. One thing that some people do is that they would cut on people for example of a 50 year old man, would attend a hard rock concert people would probably think that he should be attending a jazz concert.

PRACTICE   Mechanics (Punctuation, Capitalization, Spelling)

Edit these paragraphs with special attention to mechanical errors:

A

I was born on february 26th. That gives me some interesting qualities. For example I'm creative and artistic. I've always known that my bad grades in my Music Drawing, and Painting classes were all the teachers fault. They just didnt see what an incredable talent they had in there classes. Linda Goodman had more things to say about me in her book Sun Signs. She could even describe the way I looked. My eyes were simply beautiful my feet a bit small and my hair was light.

B

My astrological sign is gemini as I was born on may 30. Geminis symbol is the twins and mercury is the ruling planet of this sign. In Liz Greenes Star Signs for Lovers people born under this sign are generally talkative charming witty, and extreamly unpredictable. In addition they have the attention spans of house plants. I was very surprize reading this. Although I feel my attention span is a bit longer than that of a Geranium I found Greenes analysis chillingly accurate.

Evaluating Writing

Many students in English or composition classes wonder just how their teachers come up with a grade, especially on an essay. The process appears to be quite subjective, especially when compared with courses like math, where there is one answer, either right or wrong. The grade is calculated from numerical data—so many right, so many wrong. Composition grades, by contrast, emerge from many factors that may not be easily identified by inexperienced writers. As a result, students may get the idea that composition grades are mysterious or even unfair. In most cases, they are neither. Most teachers evaluate the essays on a set of criteria:

Content

    Controlling idea clear

    Relevant and adequate support

    Appropriate organization and transitions

Style

    Writer's voice and individuality

    Wording and phrasing

Form

    Sentence structure

    Grammar

    Punctuation

    Spelling

Additionally, teachers consider the depth of thinking about the topic. Students who present a thoughtful essay will score higher than those who are superficial. Students who show control of the essay—not mastery, but control—will score higher than those who wander off topic or have a fuzzy focus. Students who have not yet gained control of sentences or punctuation will score lower than those who have. Teachers aren't expecting perfection, and most give students a wide berth in which to assimilate and apply new skills. Learning to write takes time and sustained practice. Nonetheless, writing must be evaluated and grades assigned.

If you have not been shown the evaluation process, you no doubt have mixed feelings about it: you understand it must be done, but you don't like it. Many teachers have mixed feelings as well. Nonetheless, evaluating and assigning grades is a responsibility they take seriously. To get a sense of just how teachers and other readers evaluate writing, you will try out the process yourself. The better you understand the criteria used in evaluation, the more easily you can use them as you revise and edit your own work.

EVALUATING STUDENT RESPONSES

Before you read the responses, you need to understand the writing task these students were given. They read a short story entitled "To Kill a King." Then, they were given a single question asking them to respond to the theme of the short story: Explain the boy's action, the "murder." The students wrote their responses within a 50-minute class period.

The main character in "To Kill a King" is a young farm boy who loves wildlife, especially birds. The boy is drawn to a majestic hawk, which becomes the focus of his life and actions. Here are excerpts from the story; they will provide you with enough information to evaluate the students' responses:

TO KILL A KING

Sue Gross

The introductory paragraphs tell of the boy's love of birds of all kinds and of his close relationship with and sensitivity to nature.

But the hawk was different. It was big, aloof, and lonely. The boy thought of how it was always alone when he saw it, far away, remote as the little stars he saw at night. He wondered if the hawk had a mate; if the hawk had a nest to come to at evening, when his side wings ached with weariness and his eyes burned from soaring all day in the sun. He would never know. He could never follow the hawk as he did the redstarts [a bird], could never be intimate with him as with the friendly cardinals. The hawk was a thing apart, unapproachable.

The boy began scanning the sky as he came near the place where he would see the hawk. He stood alert on his hilltop, waiting—watching.

It came floating down out of the east, superb and lazy and lordly. Its movements were all the grace the boy knew, all the art he ever saw. He gazed up at it, letting it be the only thing in all the vast blue sky. Then he raised his glasses, shutting the bird with him in their small circle, getting close to it in the only way he could. His neck began to ache, but while the hawk was there, he was powerless, compelled to watch it. It turned at last and pounded silently away over the far woods. The boy lowered his head, wincing with pain. He stood numbly, rubbing the crick out of his neck with his hand, remembering the hawk: the wide wings, the fanned red tail, the magnificence. He went down the wooded hill. The sparrows bounced along beside him, chattering; he did not hear them. A pewee called and called from a tree somewhere in the forest; he did not care to find it.

The next day the boy takes his rifle and, asked where he's going, says he's going hunting for squirrels, his face burning because of the lie. He climbs to the hilltop and awaits the hawk.

Wheeling, high over the trees, it spread its broad rounded wings and flashed its rust-red tail as it veered away to climb at the sun, and soared down again in long, easy spirals. Through the glasses, the boy followed the hawk's easy flight. He drank in the cruel grace, the mastery, the majesty of the bird, as he had done for days past, and it made him dizzy. He watched the hawk and thought of the gun leaning against the tree trunk! If he could bring that great brute down . . . If he could kill the hawk and tell his friends . . . He knew it wasn't a harmful bird, but it was a king, and to kill a king! He could not take his eyes off the hawk, or his mind from the gun.

He had admired the bird; now he longed to conquer it. He let the glasses drop down on his chest, and moved toward the gun. He held the gun in his hand, still looking at the bird veering over his head. He took a bullet in his fingers, loaded the gun without looking. Then once more he gave himself up to the hawk. It hung in the sky like a golden crumb in an upturned bowl. The boy raised his rifle and aimed carefully, keeping the little black dot of the sight on the hawk's streaked breast as it circled over the forest. Then his brain went white and he fired. The bird fell out of the sky like a plumb cut from the line. Marking where it crashed into the brush, the boy ejected the empty shell and walked down the steep hillside with the smoking gun over his arm.

Twigs lashed his hot face, and long, thorny vines tangled around his feet and tore at his ankles. Cobwebs stretched and broke across his mouth. He stumbled over a root, and then he heard the noise in the underbrush ahead of him. He saw the hawk thrashing in the leaves, dragging one wing on the ground and beating the other in an hysterical effort to rise. He saw the bloody hole where his bullet had torn through the hawk's shoulder. The bird's eyes were dim, its beak opened wide in terror as it clawed deep gashes in the dirt. It would rage that way all night, the boy knew, dragging itself in a pitiful circle, bashing itself to exhausted death.

The boy took another bullet from his pocket, thrust it into place, and slammed down the breech. He cocked the rifle, lowered the muzzle to the hawk's head, squeezed the trigger. The bird jerked and lay still. The boy snapped out the shell, and stood staring at the hawk's crumpled body; the torn wing, the smashed head, the dark blood soaking down through the rotten leaves. His heart hurt suddenly; tears scorched his eyelids. With the butt of his gun, he scraped a little mound of earth and leaves over the body. Then he turned away. With tears running on his dirty face, he walked through the stubbly fields. The rifle weighed a ton in his hands.

The boy's father sees him walking to the farm, quickly understands exactly what has happened, and tells his wife to forget about squirrels and dumplings for supper; in fact, he tells her to throw out the dumplings. The wife protests, and they argue about it. The father finally commands, "There'll be no talk o'squirrels or huntin' tonight," and she responds, "All this fuss over a squirrel or two." The father then says, "It ain't squirrels, Mother . . . You never been a boy . . . or done a murder."

The Writing Task

Explain the boy's action, the "murder," in "To Kill a King." Students were expected to use information from the story to explain why the boy did what he did. If he loved birds, especially the hawk, why did he kill it?

Questions for Evaluating Student Responses

Teachers may not write out questions like these, but they are nonetheless using them "mentally." The questions are a guide to the effectiveness of the response. Keep in mind that such questions evaluate the written response; they are not questions about the short story.

1. What main point does the student writer make? Does the writer explain the boy's action?

2. How does the writer support his or her main point?

3. Does the writer provide enough support? Or does the writer leave the reader with unanswered questions? Does the writer provide good examples or details to support his or her point?

4. Is the support relevant? Or does the writer go off track somewhere, presenting information that is not needed or wrong for the writing task? Does the writer answer the question asked?

5. Does the writer's voice come through? Does the reader get a sense of a human being talking to another human being?

6. Is the response organized well? Can the reader move from idea to idea easily?

7. Is the response difficult to follow because of incomplete or illogical sentences? Is the response difficult to follow because of awkward sentences?

8. Are there errors in Standard Written American English: usage, punctuation, spelling?

9. What would the writer have to do to make his or her response clearer or more convincing?

10. Overall, what are the strengths of the response? The weaknesses?

Rating the Response

Some teachers and students use an evaluation scale to sort out the strengths and weaknesses of a piece of writing. Use the following one to evaluate each of the five responses to "To Kill a King." On this particular scale, the development of the essay is more important than anything else. The multiplication of the score turns the 45-point scale into a 100-point scale.

Scale: 1 = poor   2 = fair   3 = adequate   4 = good   5 = excellent

Content (60%)

Clear controlling idea	1 2 3 4 5	
Relevant and adequate support	1 2 3 4 5	
Organization and transitions	1 2 3 4 5	

_____ × 4 = _____

Style (20%)

Writer's voice/individuality	1 2 3 4 5	
Wording and phrasing	1 2 3 4 5	

_____ × 2 = _____

Form (20%)

Sentence structure	1	2	3	4	5
Grammar	1	2	3	4	5
Punctuation	1	2	3	4	5
Spelling	1	2	3	4	5

_____ × 1 = _____

Total grade = _____%

TRYING OUT THE EVALUATION PROCESS

Most teachers first read through the piece quickly, to get an overall sense of the essay. They then do a second reading, slowly and thoughtfully, applying the evaluation criteria as they read. You can try out the process yourself on the following brief response. Then read the explanation that follows.

> The boy's action for killing the bird was that he wanted to conquer it because he could only admir it from far away and he wanted to tell his friends about killing a king. After the boy killed the hawk, he started crying because he didn't really conquer the bird, he had killed it and the bird was very beautiful. The father's reaction is to leave the boy alone, he leaves the boy alone and doesn't want his wife talking about hunting because he was once a boy and had probably murdered some kind of animal.

Explanation

The student certainly has the right idea initially, but it is not expressed very clearly. The essay is not well developed either. We don't get a good sense of the boy's relationship with the hawk. The part about the father's reaction has nothing to do with the boy's motivation for killing the hawk, so it is irrelevant. The organization isn't bad, but it makes little difference since the writer failed to develop the point.

If we award the student ratings of 2, 1, 3 under "Content," the subtotal is 6 × 4 = 24% on that part.

The student's voice comes through okay, but wording and phrasing are unclear and at times quite awkward.

If we award the student ratings of 3 and 1 under "Style," the subtotal is 4 × 2 = 8% on that part.

Most of us have a combination of strengths and weaknesses in the technical aspect of writing—mainly because it takes a long time to learn how to write. This student is no exception. Quite a few of the sentences are unclear, and a couple are strung together with commas, creating errors. Sentence boundaries require a connecting word with the comma or replacement of the comma with a period or semicolon. The grammar is generally okay, though. There are a couple of punctuation errors. With one exception (the silent *e* on *admire*), the spelling is fine.

If we award ratings of 2, 3, 2, 4 under "Form," the subtotal is 11 × 1 = 11%.

The total for the entire piece is 43% out of 100%. This student would have some significant revising and editing to do before the piece would be acceptable.

What positive remarks would you have for this writer?

What would you suggest for revision? Be specific.

SAMPLE RESPONSES TO "TO KILL A KING"

Even on the preceding short piece, you probably got a good sense of what evaluation is all about. Most teachers I know, including myself, are often unhappy with having to assign a grade. Sometimes it is very evident that a student has shown significant improvement, but nonetheless has not yet achieved a C. At other times, it is evident the student has produced a technically correct paper, but the essay is "empty." It has little sense of the author or of engagement with the topic. It could have been written by a robot. These situations cause real dilemmas in evaluation and the assigning of a grade. The criteria for evaluation become very important; they help teachers determine if an essay meets the standards of acceptability for academic writing.

SAMPLE 1

    If you ever watch birds up close, you'll know that
the beauty and grace they have is a treasure to watch.
The boy was one of the constant, vivid bird watchers.

It seemed he was friends with all birds of every sort, except the hawk. The hawk was a loner, and sang no songs or did any dances for the boy. It preferred to be alone in it's own domain, and was content to stay there.

The boy, on the other hand, felt possessed by it and continued to watch it for days. It didn't fit in with the other birds, and yet it was a bird. When he killed it, he killed it to prove that he was better than the hawk. But afterwards, he saw that it was just a bird like any other bird, and that the act was worthless and had no meaning. I think the father knew this when he saw his son comeing up the drive. He was a boy once and went thru the same thing. He understood the need to be alone, and not to bring up anything that might bring back the memory of the murder.

SAMPLE 2

To explain the boy's action in "To Kill A King" we are going to have to go back and look at how he viewed the hawk he shot. In the boy's eyes, the hawk was an admired bird of beauty, and through days of watching it, became attached to it. The boy regarded the hawk as the king of birds, and to shoot such a king would make the boy feel just as great. After he shot the bird, a great remorse came over him. He had lost an admired friend. When the boy came home, the father could read write through him. The father was quite sympathetic to the boys feelings, for the father had also gone through such a period as a boy. The father figured the boy would want to be left alone, so the father left the boy to do chores by himself.

SAMPLE 3

The boy had an incrediable feeling for birds. He loved them. But what he really wanted was "the king," a hawk.

The hawk was a lonely, big, lordly beast. The boy was powerless when watching the hawks flight. The reason for the boy's urge in killing the hawk was to tell his friends. If he brought the hawk down, he brought down a king. So after viewing the flight of the hawk, he finally shot it down. His heart was in pain. When he reached the hawk, he decided to bury it where it laid rest. On his arrival home, the father saw he didn't have any squirrels. Matter of fact, the father knew what the boy was after when he departed. He knew the boy wanted the ultimate: to kill a king. There feeling was rather mutual. His father knew that killing the hawk was going to make the boy feel power: but what it actually showed was pain in the boy.

SAMPLE 4

The boy liked to go out to the hilltop every morning to watch the hawk hunt the field. His father knew he liked to do that, so he always let the boy go, after the chours were done. One day the boy brought his .22 rifle along and his dad asked why he was bringing it. He was haveing thoughts of shooting the hawk, but he told his dad he might snag a few squirls for supper. That day when the hawk flew over the boy had already through whether he should shoot the hawk or not many times. The hawk kept coming closer and closer until the boy shot. When the hawk was flopping around on the ground the boy felt bad about shooting it, and wished he hadn't have done what he did. Had the hawk stayed far enough away, the boy wouldn't have shot it, but with all the excitment, wonder and unsureness the boy shot it without thinking. Now he was suffering over it, and would think of that hawk every time he went to the hill. On the way home the boy slowly dragged his feet along the dirt. From a distance the father could see the boy had no squirls so he told his wife not to mention any to the boy because he knew the boy had killed the hawk, or done something. The father told the boy to do the milking himself tonight because he wanted the boy to forget the hawk. The father figuered if the boy could fill the rest of the day with work or something it would help the boy forget. This was a learning experiance for the boy, and the father wanted to help him any way he could.

An evaluation of writing, whether by a teacher or peers, provides the writer with specific information for revising and editing. The more specific the information, the easier it is to take a hard look at our own writing.

PRACTICE ESSAY

With your group or writing partner, evaluate the following student essays. The writing task asked students to respond to a question parents or caregivers face: whether or not to tell children the truth about serious family problems (e.g., impending divorce, life-threatening illness, financial trouble).

You will find two views in the essays. Keep in mind that you no doubt have an opinion, and because of it, you have to guard against being biased as you evaluate. You are evaluating the essay, not the view expressed.

Review the evaluation questions. These are your criteria for judging how well the student presented and developed his or her main point. Read the essay through once. Then return to read slowly and carefully as you evaluate.

STUDENT ESSAY 1

How to Tell Kids a Crisis Problem

A child ranks toys, bikes, playtime, and TV time at the top of his or her list of importance. An adult on the other hand ranks job security, income and safety at the top of his or her list of importance. It is obvious that adults and children seen things differently.

Certain things like financial troubles, marital problems, life-threatening illness, and other serious matters should not be discussed with children until certain times.

I believe it is important that children learn about these things, but it is a bad time to discuss them while in the middle of a crisis. The first thing a child will do is to ask questions when told about something new. For adults trying to deal with a stressful problem, like a death in the family or money problems, a child asking questions is just added frustration. In time of a crisis, adults need their full attention on the problem at hand. If they have to take time out to explain to a child what is going on, they get even more stressed out and edgy, and the chances increase that the adult will yell at or strike the child.

I believe the best way to deal with the situation is to not tell the child what is going on during the crisis. I do believe that the child should learn about these situations, but not during the crisis. A parent can take time out before or after a crisis to explain things. This will give the child a better chance to understand the problem. It would also ease any frustration of the parent if the child does not understand.

Although children are bright, some things they will not understand until they experience them. One such example is money. To a child, money is an item that comes out of mothers purse when food, toys, or candy is needed. A child does not understand how hard adults work to earn money. They can be told about crises that deal with money, but to fully understand they must experience the work required to earn the money.

Children do view things differently than adults. They should not be told about crisis problems until the adult has the time and the patience to sit down and really explain things to them.

STUDENT ESSAY 2

Include the Child

Over the past few years parents have been faced with many hard problems, such as financial trouble, marriage problems, life-threatening illness, and differences with inlaws/siblings. The most popular thing for parents to do in these situations is to keep the children in the dark about what the problem is. What parents don't realize is that they may be doing more harm than good.

From the outside a child look weak but on the inside they are strong. When there are problem within the family structure, a child notices it and wants to help. If the parent allows that child to help, he/she may be able to give the parent(s) that push to keep trying, which in turn could possibly solve the problem.

Another problem if parents covering up the truth, is that children feel as though they are the cause of the problem. Children who recive this type of message tend to look elseware for the love and effection they need. Some children choose drugs and alcohol, and other seek love from the wrong people. These coping strategies are harmful to the childs health and may cause major problems, such as addiction or death.

Some people who feel that covering the child ears maybe the answer, are not giving that child a fare chance. Even if protecting the child seem like the thing to do, pleae at least talk with the child and let him/her know that they are not the problem.

When I see a child who is sent away or to his/her room because of family troubles I can only hope that he/she doesn't blame his/her self and cause problems of their own.

SHORT TAKES

SHORT ESSAY A

Did You Ever Notice a Freshman?

Let's face it freshmen stand out, they do everything wrong, nothing ever goes well for them. They
run into all kinds of problems, bad situations, humi-
laties, put downs, and fowl language from upper class.

But did the socalled "Big Shots" on campus every
figure out if they offer help and support in a nice
way. They wouldn't do those fun little mistakes
like, carrying their tray backward in the cafeteria,
walking around the halls aimlessly or for the 3rd,
4th, and 5th time. They just watch and laugh and
holler obsinaties.

All a freshman wants is to fit in, to do well and
have some fun.

SHORT ESSAY B

Traditions

Family traditions is things you do over that your
for fathers before you did. For example making a big
dinner on a day that someone had done something special that was related to you. Another, would be always
saying grace at supper before you eat. One really
weird family tradition is drinking the blood of your
first deer. That you shot while hunting.

SHORT ESSAY C

Concerts

Concerts are fun for all age groups. Teenagers enjoy concernts because the music is loud and everyone their is about the same age. They can act imature and no one will notice. For the middle age group they enjoy sitting around and to relax at concerts. They don't like to stand and get shoved around. Also they enjoy there music softer and more slow. The older people on the other hand like old music like classical, and jazz, but there are older people that rock and country. That goes the same with younger and middle age people. Younger people feel alive and free. Older people feel complete and self assured and middle age feel freedom and way to escape. Concerts are good for every one because a person can be themself.

SHORT ESSAY D

Jobs

Jobs have there disadvantages, but it also has many advantages. A disadvantage of having a job is that it takes up time. By this I mean that sometimes you may have to give up going to a football game because you have to work. Now some advantages are you get money, it's a great experience, you get to meet new people, and you can save your money and have lots of money for college like me. As you can see here many people would rather have a job than go to a football game or something. The job I had was a great experience for me because I met lots of people from the outside. My job also helped my speech very much because I talked to alot of people each day. My job was very hard to quite because it was such an uprising experience for me. There is also jobs that have bad experiences to. The outcome of the job all depends upon the person and the job.

SHORT ESSAY E

Jobs Teach

Jobs are an important part of growing up. I feel jobs are very necessary through out life, In that people can learn important things such as responsibility, and certain business skills. I have had several jobs, anywhere from grocery stores, fast food resteraunts, and carpentry. The fast food industry isn't all its cracked up to be. I worked in a small hamberger stand for 3 weeks before I coulnd't take it anymore. Although I learned how to cook a hamberger it really wasn't that much of a learning experience. The carpentry job helped me learn how to use tools and about taking orders, even if you don't feel there right. Lastly, my job at the grocery store has taught me alot, I've learned all about produce and how to take care of it. I also learned how to figure the percentage of profit we make from sales. I've learned responsibilty because if I don't take care of the produce they will all spoil. Jobs can teach you alot about life, and most importantly yourself.

SHORT ESSAY F

Spiking the Ball

A volleyball spike is when a player is hitting a set ball over the net. Trying to hit the ball hard so the other team cannot return the ball. The spike must be hit at the right time.

The setter sets the ball. The spiker starts his approach. First the spiker gets back to about the 10 foot line. When the ball reaches its peak. The spiker takes two steps toward the net. Then swings his arms back. Now the spiker is ready to hit the ball. He jumps as high as he can. Then hits the ball with an open hand in a downward direction.

The spiker must hit the ball with great force. So the opponent has difficulty trying to return the ball, if the ball was hit correctly. The ball will usually hit the floor or hit a player that cannot return the ball. The ball then goes out of bounds.

PERSONAL EXPERIENCE

PERSONAL-EXPERIENCE ESSAY A

Sunday Hero

As a child, I always had fantasies of being star football player on the Green Bay Packers. Every Sunday after church I'd sit down right in front of the television to watch the Packers. I didn't budge until halftime but I always made it back for the start of the second half. Before I watched the game I made sure that I had my Green Bay Packer shirt on and I put my Packer Football on the television for good luck. As I watched these games I pictured myself being out on the field having everyone cheer for me. After the game ended my brother and me would go put our Packer helmust on and go outside to play football. We would pick a packer player that we wanted to be like and pretend we were them. However my brother who is 3 years old than me always picked the guy I wanted. On the other days of the week I collected football cards. My friends and me would trade cards once a week and of course I traded to get all the packers. I didn't stop collecting and trading until I had the starting offense and starting defense. However by the time I had the starting teams the next season was ready to begin and I would have to start over. In some of these cards I would cross out the name and put mine just hoping that someday a little kid like me would do the same on my football card I still fantasize myself being a football start on the Packers but I've settled down since my earlier days. Its funny watching my little cousin do the same things that I did but it doesn't seem like I would do such a thing.

PERSONAL-EXPERIENCE ESSAY B

The Captain

Driving into New York's Kene Valley was an artistic delight. Even though it was a crisp and cool October morning, Chris Carl and I decided the jeep top should be folded down, as not to obstruct out view of the magnificent fall colors. Mothe Nature had surely outdone herself. Colors ranged from subdued browns and rust, to flaming reds and vivid yellows. We were breathtaken as the valley drew us down to the base of the mountain. It should be an excellent day for a hike.

Upond arriving at the trail head we gather our gear and started our journey. After hiking three miles of steadily rising terrain we entered a clearing. Looking toward the moutnain we saw the "wall" facing us. The smooth pyramid like formation, was made of solid granite approximately 300 yards wide at the base, stretching to about 350 yards up, and angling 30-40 degrees. Chris thought it would be fun to leave the train to climb the face to the top. I agreed and we began our ascent.

Without ropes or other safety gear we climbed about 200 yards only the grip of our hiking boots keeps us on the smooth wall. Suddenly I slipped! Laying flat on my stomach with toes gripping I somewhat regained my composure. At that point I realized "where" I was. A flood of terror cascaded over soaking into every fiber of my soul. Shaking and distressed I clung to the side of the mountain like a kitten to a tree. I felt powerless, helpless. Was ther any escape from doom? Things seemed to get ugly quick. The mountain was no longer beautiful, the colors turned to black and white. A rush of ideas resounded through my brain. One wrong move and I could've been dead--but why would I care?

Coming from a dysfunctional family, being divorced, and feeling betrayed by the service had consumed my thoughts for months leaving me disillusioned. Constantly distracting myself I would do anything and everything to avoid confronting my feelings. Each day dying a bit inside I considered euthanasia as an option. I could just let my feet go from under me and tumble to my death relieving my pain.

Then as if by divine intervention my perspective suddenly changed! No matter how outside "demon" forces tried to defeat me, I was in charge. I had the strength. I was master over my own soul. I wanted to live! I wanted to live now more than ever, but still had to reach the top.

Indulging in new found strength, I gathered myself together, and step by step carefully ascended to the top. I had defeated the "demons" and the mountain.

After reaching the top Chris and I promptly started our decent. I noticed a set of captain's bars pinned to his jacket lapel. Both us being enlisted men, I thought it strange he don the mark of a nemesis, and was compelled to inquire. He said that honory rank was bestowed upon him during a mountain climbing expedition. Against seemingly bad odds his team overcame many obstacles to reach the apex. An officer impressed by Chris's skill gave him the bars as a token of respect.

Chris confided he had sensed my fear on the mountain side. Knowing that I over came it he removed the insignia and give them to me. He felt I had earned them. Little did he know how much I learned that day--not only was I a captain of the mountain, but also the captain of my own heart and soul.

PERSONAL-EXPERIENCE ESSAY C

The Soap

Moments after removing my eight year old sister with incinerating profanity, I mounted the appolusa rocking horse with the triumphant poise of a nine year old with soldierly confidence I appraised my newly won ground, Elated sky blue excitement filled my whole world as I rocked. "It's all mine!" I dreamed an enchanted journey that took me away lightening fast. Off to Florida, California, Denver or Greece. My joy and the July sun made it all very possible.

Exploding my twinkling shell with air hammer corce, Momma's voice rang in my ears for weeks.

"Daniel Lee McMan, you get your filthy mouth over here."

Twice as fast as a barn cat's eye my head and total attention snapped toward my boiling mad mother. A wiffet I sat. The horse, which was reluctant to stop, nagged and pulled at me persuading a timely escape.

"I said move, boy!"

With the speed of interspace transporters, on the U.S.S. Enterprise, I was in front of her. All that filled my consciousness was the tunnel of silence through which mother loomed from higher on the stairs. Fear for my body and soul filled every fissure in my shaking head. I pleaded for quick death from the Allmighty before momma got her chance with me. The steps to the bathroom would be my last. With my left ear and ten or twelve neck haird, Momma hoisted me through the door. The tears this caused cannot be counted by even modern computers. Ill with pain, I heard momma's words.

"Pick up that soap."

Crying like a wounded kitten I cried over and over/"Momma" "Momma" "Momma"

My tears fire hosed.

"Hurry up."

Momma didn't speak twice: ever.

The camay pink bar was mucous like when I picked it up. The executioner's ax was now in my hand.

"Put it in your mouth."

My worst nightmares were never like this. My pleading up turned eyes were met by a lightening fast hand. She shoved the bar all the way to the back. Poison pierced everywhere and stabbed at my throat. Twisting the assulting alien all about, mother said over and over.

"Never again, never again."

"And don't you spit one little bit."

To this day my words are choise not to include the terrible seven.

INFORMATIVE WRITING

INFORMATIVE ESSAY A

On the Road to the NBA

When a boy reaches the age of nine he is usually in the third grade. At this point the kid gets his first chance to play constructive basketball. His coach will teach him the basic fundamentals of the game. His coach will also introduce him to some of the NBA greats by telling the kid to watch the games on television. This is where the fantasy begins. The kid falls head over heals in love with a NBA star. He tries to do all the things the star does to become more like him. The kid figures if he can do the same things as the star he too should be able to play in the NBA. After a few more years of playing basketball the kid enters stage two.

Stage two takes place around the age of twelve. This is where the kid thinks that he is the best one on the team. His skills become more advanced than the rest of the kids at his age. He becomes not only the best player on the team but he thinks that he is the best in the league. Because he is the best in the league he thinks he can go on and become an NBA player. He starts to take basketball more serious than before. He goes out and shoots baskets for two hours everyday. This takes play for about three years. The kid then finally reaches stage three of this fantasy.

Stage three takes place around the age of fifteen. This is where reality sets in and the kid realizes that he isn't quite the grade a ballplayer it takes to be in the NBA. The kid still goes on to play basketball in high school but realizes that high school ball is the end of his basketball career.

This childhood fantasy is common in many young boys. The fantasy is short and sweet but at the time it is something very special to the young boy. The fantasy gives the kid a goal to shoot for even though the fantasy was a little bit farfetched it was an important event that took place in the growing up of a child.

INFORMATIVE ESSAY B

Fantasy Games

Fantasy can be an enjoyable way of excaping the rutine of everyday life. Some people play fantasy games like dungens and dragons. They can image their friends that they're in another world where anything can and will happen. Things that are in the game becomes real in a sense that the person must make the right decisions or die. That sense of danger in a game makes it more fun. People want danger in their life to make it exciting. Since they don't get danger in their real life they can resort to fantasy games. Some people play video games to excape reality momentaraly. People can feel the anxiety when they play a video game. It becomes more real because they know if they don't make the right move they will die or blow up. Of course none of that actually happens to them but it feels like it. People usually play new games that come into an arcade because they want a new challange.

Going to a movie in a theater gives a person a way of excaping into a fantasy world also. They can feel what the character is going through if he is injured or surrounded by vicious monsters. Imaginary things have become more real with special effects so a person can believe in what he/she is seeing. Fantasy is needed by everyone without it life would be too boring.

INFORMATIVE ESSAY C

Where Have You Gone, Joe DiMaggio?

My parents generation grew up in much simpler time. Everybody had a nice little house with a white picket fence. The father went to work, the mother stayed home and baked chocolate chip cookies. The kids went to school and played with their friends. American society was very similar to the television show Leave It to Beaver.

Now our society has changed. The divorce rate has sky rocketed, single parent families have become common place. Crime rates have ballooned. However perhaps nothing has changed more than the way we look at our sports heroes especially baseball players.

In the 1940's and 1950's baseball players were nothing less than "Gods" in this country. They were idolized by millions of children. People like Mickey Mantle, Willie Mays, and Sandy Koufax graced the playing field and rarely did anything to tarnish their image and disappoint their fans. They signed autographs willingly and did not demand truly outrageous salaries for playing the game they so dearly loved. They had respect for their fans and respect for their game. Baseball players gave 100% on the field and also fulfilled their duties off of the field to be role models.

This is not the case today. The salaries of baseball players have risen dramatically. Greed has take over the national pastime. The stars of today can earn as much as six million dollars for one season, while mere average players can easily pull down a cool million.

Players don't sign autographs nearly as much as they used to. When they do sign autographs however it is usually at a baseball card show where kids play money to get an autograph of their favorite player.

Drugs are also something that has changed the game of baseball. Too often we hear of players being suspended for the use of drugs. Young baseball fans see

their "role models" serving jail time for the possession of drugs. This was never the case a generation
ago.

The game of baseball has changed greatly. For today's generation of baseball fans, role models are few
and far between. This is a sharp contrast to my father
as he grew up. He lived during a time when this county
coulf be proud of its baseball heroes, not ashamed.

ARGUMENT

ARGUMENTATIVE ESSAY A

Violent Concerts

Most people don't think of rock concerts as violent
but the fact is they are. Rock concerts are very aggressive and violent. It has been a proven fact that
the loud sound waves coming out of the very large
speakers make people more violent than normal. It has
something to do with the beat of your heart and there
for causes more anxiety and violence than you normally
have. A few years ago there was a large rock concert
in which many people were killed because the crowd
stampled over them rushing up on stage. Criminal violence is also a problem at concerts many people are
stabbed, beaten or even rapped. It cant be said that
all concerts are like that classical, rock or opera
are anything but violant. It could be the crowd that
makes a difference or what people put into themselves
such as alcohol or drugs. But the fact remains rock
concerts are violent.

ARGUMENTATIVE ESSAY B

Just One Credit

What is meant by the term physical education? I
usually think of exercise or an activity that requires
some physical activity, and football clearly falls

under this classification for most people. Relaxation and Ballroom Dancing have to conjure up some doubts about physical exercise/ Clearly going through a full football season--which is year around--is as difficult as these other P.E.courses that I mentioned. This leads me to believe that the university should allow a football payler one credit for every year he is on the team.

Although the P.E. courses that I mentioned earlier are suppose to broaden our horizons; the football team has started a program that lets the players get involved with the public. Football also takes the players to other campuses, teaches then cooperation and teamwork and creates competition just like the classroom.

Once the class room is brought into the case; people will argue that players don't have to pay for football, whereas P.E. classes cost money. Granted the football team is rebuilding, an excellent and exciting team should bring in money to the university.

The university system will have no problem with the grade transcripts because football could be considered a retroactive credit.

Now a problem is that every sport will have to be equal to one credit. So do it. The time required to practice every sport is equal (if not more) to the time spent in P.E. classes.

Although football is totally volunteer there is a choice of P.E. classes. Any class cn be chosen as long as there is no prerequisite. There is no prerequisite for football but I would list it as an advanced course because many people don't have the ability or time (primary education, the reason for no time).

I am all for concentrating on your studies but football will help you become more efficient, and it does look better on your resume than Ballroom dancing.

If the time factor is so important, how dedicated does a player have to be? I speak from experience. The players reported to fall camp on August ninth, studied playbooks and completed tests in running and weightlifting. Once classes started, practices lasted about two hours plus videos once or twice a week. After the season, players lift four times a week (1-2 hours/day), and attend spring practice during april and may.

Regular P.E. classes that are offered as credits don't come close when compared to what football accomplishes. Football is not considered a "blow off" like many P.E. courses, and the time spent on both can't even be compared. As for the physical activity I invite anyone to put forth the effort for just one season of football.

ARGUMENTATIVE ESSAY C

Dogs in the Dorm?

As I walked into my dorm the other day, I caught a glimpse of a four legged animal bounding towards me from down the hall. This four legged creature called Hawkey, lives with my hall director in Towers. Lucky for me, I love animals and was able to catch the dog and play with him for a while. However many people do not feel the same way about dogs or other animals. I have many friends who would shutter at the mere description of a 90 pound black lab, let alone be confronted with one in the lobby. Although residents are not allowed to own pets many hall directors have animals living with them in their apartments.

The resident hall directors live on the first floor of each dorm. They are responsible for enforcing the rules and to keep the dorm problem free. One of the rules they enforce very strictly is the rule that states, no pets allowed in the dorm. I understand this rule is necessary for the good of the residents and the animals but I also believe that the rule should be followed by everyone.

Although the dogs and cats that I have ran into on campus have seemed very well behaved and harmless animals are very unpredictable. Any tame dog could turn on someone especially if evoked. These dogs are family dogs and family dogs will protect their family and their territory if challenged. Hundreds of students walk passed these dogs each day, many of them enjoy yelling at or teasing the dogs as they go by. Although this is not the hall directors fault the dogs could one day react to the teasing by chasing and biting a student.

In most apartment buildings pets are not allowed, the biggest reason is the reason stated above, another reason is that dog make noise. Dogs bark at everything and for the people living directly aboe the dogs area the noise can get very annoying.

Many times the dogs are allowed to run around the lobby. Besides scaring anyone afraid of dogs, there are some obvious health concerns. First when dogs run around they lose hair. This hair settled to the floor but is constantly stirred up by people walking through the lobby. Food including pizza and popcorn is made and served in the same lobby where dog hair is probably floating around. I'm sure you have never heard any complaints about dog hair in the pizza but a few short dog hairs may be easy to miss if you are not paying attention to what you are eating. This hair floating around in the air may also irritate people who are allergic to animal hair and they may feel uncomfortable standing in the lobby.

I understand why hall directors have pets, pets are good companions and add enjoyment to peoples lives. The dogs here have been here all there lives and are somewhat use to the people and the commotion, but like I said previously animals no matter how well trained they are are unpredictable and have minds of there own. So there is always a risk.

Hall directors should not be allowed to have pets in the dorms which serve as a h ome for students for nine months out of the year. This is our home and we spend a substantial amount of money to live here, students should be able to comfortable about what is living in the dorm along with them.

Keeping Track of Writing Skills and Problems

The following logs will help you see both progress and problems—if you consistently use them. Because writing takes time and sustained practice, novice writers sometimes don't feel as if they are making progress, when in fact they are. The logs will help make progress, as well as persistent problems, more visible. Photocopy these logs as you need them. Be honest and thorough when you fill one out.

REVISION LOG

Name _____

Title _____

Date _____

Strengths of this piece:

Problem Area	What I Have to Do
Controlling Idea	
Development	
Organization	
Transitions	
Sentences	

Questions for Instructor:

EDITING LOG

Name _____

Title _____

Date _____

List the errors in sentence boundaries, punctuation, and usage (agreement between subject and verb, agreement with pronouns, plurals, etc.). Try to figure out why the error occurred (just slipped up, don't know the correct form, etc.). Then make the correction, asking for help as needed. Look for patterns. Chances are you are making the same mistake repeatedly rather than many different types of mistakes. Use this list as an editing guide on your next writing task.

Error	Why It Happened	Corrected

SPELLING LOG

Name _____

Title _____

Date _____

List words misspelled. Indicate why the error occurred. Then examine your list for a pattern. What kinds of spelling errors do you tend to make? Use this list as an editing guide on your next writing task.

Correct Spelling	My Spelling	Type/Cause of Error

Index

Sources

Pages 7–8: Michael Rafferty, "The Boxes."

Page 23: Sandra Cisneros, "A House of My Own" from *The House on Mango Street*. Reprinted by permission of Susan Bergholz Literary Services, New York. All rights reserved.

Page 24: Sandra Cisneros, "Beautiful and Cruel" from *The House on Mango Street*. Reprinted by permission of Susan Bergholz Literary Services, New York. All rights reserved.

Pages 31–32: "The Love Revolution and the Rise of Feminism." From Randall Collins and Scott Coltrane, *Sociology of Marriage and the Family: Gender, Love, and Property* (Chicago: Nelson-Hall, 1991), pp. 121–138.

Page 35: Joe Cronick, "The Image of Relationships."

Pages 49–50: Excerpts from *In the Shadow of Man* by Jane Goodall. Copyright © 1971 by Hugo and Jane van Lawick-Goodall. Reprinted by permission of Houghton Mifflin Co. All rights reserved.

Page 91: Ad for Tropic Waters Pet Center, Eau Claire, Wisconsin. Reprinted with permission.

Page 131: Erma Bombeck, "Big Lies Have Small Beginnings," *Eau Claire Leader-Telegram,* January 30, 1992. Reprinted with permission.

Page 132: Joe Schoenmann, "Cheating May Be on the Upswing at UW–Madison," *Capital Times* (Madison, Wisconsin), February 19, 1992. Reprinted with permission.

Pages 136–138: Robert Samuelson, "Teen-agers in Dreamland" from *Newsweek,* April 19, 1989. © 1989, Washington Post Writers Group. Reprinted with permission.

Pages 140–143: Diane Ravitch, "Back to the Basics: Test Scores Don't Lie," *The New Republic,* May 6, 1989. Reprinted with permission.

Pages 157–158: "Self-Centeredness." Reprinted with the permission of Simon & Schuster from *The Closing of the American Mind* by Allan Bloom. Copyright © 1987 by Allan Bloom.

Pages 160–162: Joan Beck, "Why America's Students Are Falling Behind" from *Wisconsin State Journal,* April 26, 1992. Reprinted with permission of Knight-Ridder/Tribune Information Services.

Pages 162–163: Susan Chira, "Renegade Researchers Offer Rebuttal: U.S. Schools Are Better than Many Say" from the *New York Times.* Copyright © 1992 by The New York Times Co. Reprinted by permission.

Pages 167–170: "The Kitten" from *Black Boy* by Richard Wright. Copyright, 1937, 1942, 1944, 1945 by Richard Wright. Copyright renewed 1973 by Ellen Wright. Reprinted by permission of HarperCollins Publishers, Inc.

Pages 171–172: Sandra Cisneros, "Hairs" from *The House on Mango Street*. Reprinted by permission of Susan Bergholz Literary Services, New York. All rights reserved.

Pages 172–173: Susan Kenney, "Mirrors" from *In Another Country*. New York: Viking, 1984.

Pages 174–175: Jennifer Urman, "Passage."

Pages 176–177: Marjorie Harnden, "Christmas Time."

Pages 179–183: "Blue Winds Dancing" by Thomas Whitecloud is reprinted with the permission of Scribner, a division of Simon & Schuster from *Scribner's Magazine*, Vol. CIII, No. 2, February 1938. Copyright 1938 by Charles Scribner's Sons; copyright renewed © 1966.

Pages 184–185: Ruth Aida Cañas, "I Love You, Chava."

Page 186: Catalina Ruge, "Diary."

Pages 188–190: David Schwartz, "Unforgettable Father Rossiter."

Pages 190–192: Tom McDonald, "Shaking Hands with God."

Pages 208–210: Eric Betthauser, "Super Mario: A Member of the Family."

Pages 212–214: Tom McDonald, "Comic Books: Then and Now."

Pages 219–220: Tom McDonald, "In Search of a Good Scare."

Pages 232–236: Lisa Grunwald, "If Women Ran America" from *LIFE* Magazine, June 1992. Lisa Grunwald/Life Magazine. © Time Inc. Reprinted with permission.

Page 240: "Changing Families" from *Eau Claire Leader-Telegram*, October 11, 1992.

Page 241: "America's Family Values" from *Eau Claire Leader-Telegram*, October 11, 1992.

Page 241: "America's Most Important Values" from *Eau Claire Leader-Telegram*, October 11, 1992.

Page 242: Marcy E. Mullins, "Life on the home front" from *USA Today*, March 11, 1997. Copyright 1997, *USA Today*. Reprinted with permission.

Page 243: Marcy E. Mullins, "What hasn't changed much at all" from *USA Today*, March 11, 1997. Copyright 1997, *USA Today*. Reprinted with permission.

Pages 245–246: Angie Bluethman, "Jeremy, 9, Faces Felony Trial" from *The San Diego Union-Tribune*, March 8, 1997, p. A-3.

Pages 246–247: "Cattlemen Sue over Comment on 'Oprah' Show" from *Eau Claire Leader-Telegram*, June 16, 1997.

Pages 252–253: Marjorie Harnden, "A Sign of the Times."

Pages 255–257: Jay Zimmerman, "The Facts about Fur."

Pages 271–272: Judith Christ, "Stop the Labels."

Pages 281–282: Mike Royko, "Legal Marijuana—A Pot of Gold" from *Chicago Tribune*. © Tribune Media Services, Inc. All Rights Reserved. Reprinted with permission.

Pages 287–288, 290–293: Lorie Hilson, "Wanting Winners."

Pages 300–301: Tony Kornheiser, "School Board Gets an 'F' for Coddling Sleepy Students." From the *Milwaukee Journal-Sentinel*, May 29, 1997.

Pages 314–315: Sandra Cisneros, "My Name" from *The House on Mango Street*. Reprinted by permission of Susan Bergholz Literary Services, New York. All rights reserved.

Pages 343–346: Michelle Vosberg, "Like a Fox."

Pages 498–500: Sue Gross, "To Kill a King." From *Literary Cavalcade*, Volume 3, No. 8. Copyright © by Scholastic Inc. Reprinted by permission of Scholastic Inc.